Shakespeare's Global Philosophy

exploring Shakespeare's nature-based philosophy
in his sonnets, plays and Globe

SHAKESPEARE'S GLOBAL PHILOSOPHY

exploring Shakespeare's nature-based philosophy
in his sonnets, plays and Globe

Roger Peters

Quaternary
Imprint

Shakespeare's Global Philosophy
exploring Shakespeare's nature-based philosophy
in his sonnets, plays and Globe

Shakespeare's Global Philosophy
is a companion volume to Volumes 1, 2, 3 and 4
of *William Shakespeare's Sonnet Philosophy*
published as a set by Quaternary Imprint in 2005.

ISBN 978-0-473-38603-0 (pbk)
ISBN 978-0-473-38604-7 (hbk)
ISBN 978-0-473-38641-2 (epub)

Page setup by Maree Horner

QUATERNARY IMPRINT
Published for the Quaternary Institute
www.quaternaryinstitute.com

Maree

Contents

Acknowledgements

Some time ago I wrote on a card: Not every boy gets a girl who is awake to his dreams. Now, it seems even more rewarding to be a man who has a woman who awakes him from his dreams. In my life there is only one person capable of both alerting the recalcitrant mind to the deepest possible intuitions and providing the context and contentedness for those intuitions to be made articulate in some measure. No matter Shakespeare does so in such an extraordinary manner throughout his works, rather I met a person who enabled me to do it in the way I have. Maree Horner in the deepest sense you are extraordinary.

The latest insights into Shakespeare's *Sonnet* philosophy since the publication of *William Shakespeare's Sonnet Philosophy* in 2005 are now available in this volume. The continued progress has only been possible through the unflagging inspiration and support of Maree. She has also prepared the volume for publication by Quaternary Imprint.

Ever present as a vital part of that loving context are my wonderful daughters Talia, Teresa, Katie and Lucy. In your own ways you are exceptional and it is such a pleasure to watch your lives evolve in loving partnerships with Troels, Florian, Neil and Cearne.

Since the year 2000, I have been most fortunate to enjoy the unstinting company of Bryan Vickery. Bryan exemplifies the best in the inquiring mind. As a natural journalist, reporter and facilitator he is generous, fair and assiduous in seeking out and supporting the common good. Our weekly sessions over the last fourteen years have been invaluable for advancing the understanding of Shakespeare's philosophy. Crucially, we are evolving a pedagogy for presenting the ideas at the appropriate level, the Quaternary.

It has also been very enriching to meet a whole family who have already done the ground work for easy receptivity of the *Sonnet* philosophy and its basis for human wellbeing. David Hanna, Bronwen Olds, Luke Hanna, Fran Olds, Kiri Olds and Hana Olds prove that the basic ideas are natural to our global sensibility. Eight intensive weekends at the Quaternary Institute over the last couple of years have immeasurably advanced the pedagogical program. Likewise, individually they are exceptional personalities who demonstrate just how vibrant a Quaternary world will be.

I identify myself as a perpetual investigator – albeit a philosophical one – for which reason everybody I have talked to over the last twenty years has made a contribution to the advancement of the project. I converse not so much to convert but to test the soundness and receptivity of the *Sonnet* philosophy and its ramifications. Hence, I thank anyone I have had contact with, but wish to mention the names of a few who have agreed or disagreed to my greater advantage.

I treasure the continued friendship of Peter Scannell, one of the four present at the reading of the *Sonnets* in Wanganui in 1995. Both he and his close friend Dan Tan have provided many hours of conversation, often fruitfully off the point.

I think of Richard Montgomery, a friend of thirty years who died sadly a couple of years ago. With a sense of quiet outrage, he could never quite get why academia has been and still is so blind to the patent philosophy in the *Sonnets*.

Then there is my peripatetic companion Russell Christensen of many delightful walks on nearby Mount Taranaki. Russell has had the advantage of hearing the philosophy amidst babbling streams and warbling birds.

Chris & Paul Hilford have allowed me the continued use of a ski chalet at Ohakune on the lower slopes of Mount Ruapehu for which I am very grateful. As I spent my formative years in the area, the reconnection with the heart of the volcanic plateau gives an immeasurable boost to the momentum of the project.

If I ever make it to Shanghai, I look forward to a long drink with broadcaster Lawrence Bruce and listening in person to his incomparable reading of the *Sonnets*. While we have never met, Lawrence's frequent emails about matters pertinent to the investigation have added dimensions to the understanding.

In 2001 journalist Juliet Larkin wrote a perceptive article on the findings and continues to provide that wonderful combination of investigation and warmth that can make one's day.

Closer to home, Joachim Schoen follows in the memory of his empathetic mother in expressing a natural assurance about Shakespeare's philosophy while, unlike his mother, bringing an encyclopaedic range into the briefest visit or phone call.

My visits to Wellington are enlivened over coffees with the minds and interests of Matt Plummer, Errol Greaves, Tina Barton, Helen Greatrex & Richard Lomas, Denis Welch, Ben Gray, Martin Patrick, Richard Reddaway & Kate Linzey, Margaret Collins, Bill Lake and John Patterson.

Similarly, my visits to Auckland are made pleasurable talking to Alex van Klink, Michael Gifkins, Russell Withers, Alan Horner, Denis Horner, Richard Poor, Geoff & Miriam Chapple, Stephen Bambury and Michael Hurst. Unfortunately, the early death of the incredibly generous Leigh Davis removed a great protagonist to the ideas.

Elsewhere I have had a number of engaging conversations with Roger Shand, Maureen Leggett, Fridjof Hansen, David Clegg, Peter Wareing & Mercedes Vicente, Martin Campbell-board, Diane Hosler & Peter Nelson, Ross Wilson, Gary Lewis, Andrew Drummond, Joan Morrell, Jim & Pam Allen, Rob & Diana Patience, Ross Gillespie – the first responder to the publication of *WSSP* – and the Duchamp scholar Ecke Bonk – and not to forget Peter Scantlebury who always saw the funny side. I also make particular mention of bookbinder Mary Monckton.

I thank Associate Professor Robert Wicks for ensuring a copy of *WSSP* entered the Auckland University Library after it was blocked by elements in the English Department. Fortunately, then Head of English Peter Simpson saw the injustice and offered to intervene – but a little late.

In August, Professor Michael A. Peters invited me to present a paper at The Creative University Conference at Waikato University. Out of the opportunity arose new insights into the relation between Tertiary and Quaternary pedagogy and deeper insights into Leonardo's *Mona Lisa*. As one of those occasions where the benefits are totally lateral, I am most grateful to his generosity of spirit.

I am beholden to the Rodie Trust for providing funding in the early years of preparing this volume for publication. Special thanks to Ken & Jenny Horner and Mary Bourke.

Preface

Early in 1995, I took part in a reading of Shakespeare's *Sonnets*. A local Shakespeare group decided to read the complete set of 154 sonnets as part of their program of airing all Shakespeare's works. Quite unexpectedly, as we made our way through the set, their philosophic tenor sparked correspondences with my studies of the previous 25 years.

My ambition since the 1970s had been to move past the illogicalities of traditional apologetics to recover a birthright natural philosophy. Extensive researches led to the philosophically astute works of Charles Darwin, Ludwig Wittgenstein, and Marcel Duchamp. The common ground between these disparate thinkers is an ability to eschew extraneous thought and focus on the logical conditions for human life, thought and art within nature.

The biologist Darwin, after his early experiences with the inconsistencies of religious belief, spent fifty years investigating the natural logic of life on earth. The philosopher Wittgenstein, for his part, cut past the excrescences of metaphysical speculation to investigate the logic of everyday language. The artist Duchamp similarly wished to get beyond all mind-based taste to a profound understanding of the natural logic of art at the mythic level.

Since encountering the *Sonnets* in 1995, I have teased out the consistent and comprehensive nature-based philosophy Shakespeare embeds in them. The sonnet philosophy anticipates and encompasses the more specialised contributions of Darwin, Wittgenstein and Duchamp – and by implication all other thinkers and artists.

Shakespeare's decision to articulate his philosophy in a set of sonnets has poetic resonances. He not only presents the natural philosophy of human life, thought and aspirations, he shows his command of natural logic by giving it peerless expression in verse. The precision and evocativeness of his sonnet set bespeaks a period of years he spent writing, rewriting and arranging the 154 sonnets to best articulate his thoughts and emotions in poetry.

It became apparent early on that Shakespeare publishes his 154 sonnets in 1609, twenty years after he starts writing plays, to present the philosophy behind all his plays and poems. I began to appreciate how he uses the argumentative structure of the individual sonnets within the set to lay out, with unmatched integrity and inclusiveness, the natural preconditions by which we all live. He case-studies the implications for religious, political and social expectations in each of his plays and longer poems.

In 2005, after ten years of discovery and writing, I published a four-volume 1760-page slipcase set titled *William Shakespeare's Sonnet Philosophy*. Funded by public grants, the four volumes detail my discoveries since 1995.

Volume 1 examines the way Shakespeare embeds his nature-based philosophy in the 154-sonnet set. It explores in detail the givens of nature, the female/male dynamic, the logic of increase and the dynamic of the mind in terms of incoming sensations (sensory 'beauty'), language ('truth') and sensations peculiar to the mind (intellectual 'beauty') based in those natural givens.

Volume 2 considers each sonnet from the first to the 154th to show they can only be understood when the reader comprehends their inherent philosophy. It also demonstrates why the traditional emendations are unnecessary.

Volume 3 considers Shakespeare's four longer poems and five of his plays in some detail to show that when the sonnet philosophy is applied all the academic quibbles and posturings fall away. The analysis reveals Shakespeare's devastating attack on male-based injustices and, more significantly, details his program for recovering our female/male-based natural philosophy.

The first half of Volume 4 sets out the correspondences between Duchamp and Shakespeare. Then, in the second half, ten essays explain why no one has previously appreciated the sonnet philosophy.

After publishing the four-volume set, I determined to prepare a number of summary volumes to make the ideas available to a wider audience. This first summary volume, *Shakespeare's Global Philosophy*, benefits from a further few years of research in which the relationship between the generic enclave of sonnets, the European continent of plays, and the Globe theatre comes into sharper focus.

The summary also incorporates an insight from 2008 into the nature of mature Shakespearean love. The recent insights allow a more fulsome inter-relationship of the intellectual and emotional aspects of Shakespeare's famous 'love' sonnets and their significance for the intellectual and emotional depths of his plays and poems.

The four volumes of *William Shakespeare's Sonnet Philosophy* and this volume each represent a slice through Shakespeare's profound philosophical, dramatic and poetic achievement. As the philosophy is not appreciated worldwide, the volumes are intermediaries in the process of familiarisation. Ultimately, though, Shakespeare's works best articulate our nature-based philosophy.

(Note on the text: the text incorporates quotes from Shakespeare's works as drop-in images throughout. The modern English typeface in the quotes remains faithful to the 1600's format and spelling from a facsimile of the 1609 Sonnets, Charles Hinman's 1996 Norton facsimile of the 1623 Folio and facsimile editions of the Venus and Adonis and The Rape of Lucrece of 1593 and 1594. The pagination for the plays is also from the Norton facsimile in that the line numbers run unbroken from the first line to the last. The insertion tags remain in the text to help relate the quotes to their point of reference.)

Roger Peters, Kaponga, 2016

Prologue

It is not unusual to suggest nature is Shakespeare's constant recourse throughout his sonnets, plays and poems. What does it mean, though, to say that for Shakespeare nature is the singular given for the human female/male priority with its logic of increase, and that these natural givens provide the basis for the sensory, intellectual and imaginative functions of the human mind?

As Shakespeare frequently evokes the nature/mind continuum in his plays, by way of preliminary we can frame our question from within one of his works. In *As You Like It*, the principal characters forsake the Court for the natural environs of a forest where the consequences of murderous and idealistic inclinations are redressed.

Shakespeare stages a lesson in natural philosophy after Duke Senior and his fellow Lords escape the machinations of his younger brother and seek refuge in the Forest of Arden. As Duke Senior realises, their banishment to the 'woods' provides an unanticipated perspective on their inured courtly prejudices. <ayl_607-11>

Duke Senior Now my Co-mates, and brothers in exile:
Hath not old custom made this life more sweet
Than that of painted pomp? Are not these woods
More free from peril than the envious Court?
Here we feel not the penalty of Adam,
(As You Like It 607-11)

In Act 3, Shakespeare has Touchstone, the witty courtier turned shepherd, define a 'natural philosopher' for Corin, a local shepherd. (Touchstone's parts are under 'Clown' in the 1623 *Folio* but he is called Touchstone in the text – meaning 'criterion or standard' – and, to add to the clownishness, the 'Clown' calls other characters clowns.)

Then, in Act 5, Touchstone defines the logic of the 'lie direct' at the bidding of melancholy Jaques. Through the two exchanges, Shakespeare has Touchstone argue that because a natural philosopher bases his understanding in demonstrable natural facts he is able to distinguish between a fact and a lie.

During the earlier of the two scenes, Corin asks how Touchstone finds 'this shepherd's life'. In response, Touchstone contrasts the values of courtly and country living, and then asks Corin if he has any 'philosophy' in him. When Corin replies phlegmatically to the effect that things are just as they are, Touchstone tells him that 'such a one is a natural Philosopher'. <ayl_1221-30>

Clown Has't any Philosophy in thee shepherd?
Corin No more, but that I know the more one sickens, the worse at ease he is: and that he that wants money, means, and content, is without three good friends. That the property of rain is to wet, and fire to burn: That good pasture makes fat sheep: and that the great cause of the night, is the lack of the Sun: That he that hath learned no wit by Nature, nor Art, may complain of good breeding, or comes from a very dull kindred.
Clown Such a one is a natural Philosopher:
(As You Like It 1221-30)

Later, talking to William, Touchstone likens a 'natural Philosopher' (who tells it as it is) to a 'Heathen Philosopher' who calls a 'grape' a 'grape'. Touchstone combines Corin's common sense with his own 'learned' wit to show how William's 'pretty wit' makes a 'fool' out of a 'wiseman'. <ayl_2372-77>

Then a little later, after melancholy Jaques' formulaic Seven Ages of Man speech, and not long before Shakespeare consigns the witless Jaques and the homi-

> *Clown* Why, thou sayest well. I do now remember a saying: The Fool doth think he is wise, but the wiseman knows himself to be a Fool. The Heathen Philosopher, when he had a desire to eat a Grape, would open his lips when he put it into his mouth, meaning thereby, that Grapes were made to eat and lips to open.
> (As You Like It 2372-77)

cidal younger Duke to monastic isolation, Shakespeare has Touchstone apply natural logic to counter the capacity of language to beguile pretty wits. Touchstone again brings to Corin's guileless evocation of natural philosophy a more sophisticated or courtly understanding of the natural workings of the human mind.

Jaques, whose clichéd diction echoes his dissolute melancholy, is fascinated by the wise foolishness of the circumspect 'shepherd'. When Touchstone mentions the 'seventh cause' or degree of lying, Jaques asks for clarification. To explain, Touchstone recounts a disagreement he had with a Courtier in which they traverse five stages of lying before stopping at the 'sixth', hence avoiding the violent consequences of the 'seventh' – the 'lie direct'. <ayl_2659-76>

> *Clown* I durst go no further than the lie circumstantial: nor he durst not give me the lie direct; and so we measured swords, and parted.
> *Jaques* Can you nominate in order now the degrees of the lie?
> *Clown* O sir, we quarrel in print, by the book: as you have books for good manners: I will name you the degrees. The first, the Retort courteous: the second, the Quip-modest: the third, the reply Churlish; the fourth, the Reproof Valiant: the fifth, the Countercheck quarrelsome; the sixth, the Lie with circumstance: the seventh, the Lie direct: all these you may avoid but the Lie direct: and you may avoid that too, with an If. I knew when seven Justices could not take up a Quarrel, but when the parties were met themselves, one of them thought but of an If; as if you said so, then I said so: and they shook hands and swore brothers. Your If, is the only peacemaker; much virtue in if.
> (As You Like It 2659-76)

Through Touchstone's witty retort, Shakespeare posits that the most effective way to avoid mindless patriarchy-based murder – real or threatened – is to add an 'if' before absolutist imaginary claims. In the context of the play, where homicidal patriarchy exiles incipient common sense to the forest and then is exiled in turn to monastic quarantine, Shakespeare's Touchstone demonstrates the logic of 'if' for reinstating the democracy of naturally occurring facts and thoughts over the dictatorship of enforced religious fantasy.

In the following pages, we will explore how the natural philosophy that runs through *As You Like It* gets its definitive expression in the 1609 *Sonnets* and how Shakespeare applies it within the other plays as if anticipating the nature-orientated global consciousness of the democratic constituencies in the twenty-first century.

Part 1

Mapping the
1609 Sonnets

taking nature to the sonnets

Preliminary to an inquiry into Shakespeare's Sonnets

The experience of reading the 1609 edition of *Shake-speares Sonnets* (original punctuation) for the first time, or any subsequent time, is not unlike encountering tell-tale signs of a long-lost civilisation on the shores of a precipitous landmass.

However, unlike the rediscovered wonders of a civilisation such as Angkor Wat, which lay hidden under tropical verdure and a warp of history until 1861, the interior rationale of the original 154-sonnet set has proved impenetrable and inscrutable for even the most ardent adventurer.

We could compare previous explorations of Q (the commonly used epithet for the 1609 quarto) with Christopher Columbus' hopes when he crosses the Atlantic in 1492 on his first voyage of discovery. When Columbus makes landfall in the islands of the Bahamas, Cuba and Hispaniola, he believes he has pioneered a Western sea route to an Asian continent already mapped from the East during the adventures of his predecessors such as Marco Polo.

However, what we now know as the American continent, interposed between Europe and Asia, is in Columbus' day beyond the celestial calculations of seafarers. The schism in their data should prepare us for the possibility of discovering a deliberate pattern in Shakespeare's *Sonnets* kept from us by our preconceptions.

Because many sense untold organisation within Shakespeare's 154 love sonnets, our investigation will be less a survey of virgin territory than a diligent penetration of the obscuring foliage to find the interior logic of Shakespeare's purpose. Our inquiry, then, into the heart of unmapped territory, will be a search for intelligible structures within the emotional tide-line staked out by the 1609 edition of the *Sonnets*.

Considering the current global fascination with Shakespeare's works, we will keep watch throughout Q for contours of the human mind and love commensurate with the increasingly populated globe he wrote for. If, as many suspect, Shakespeare intellectually and emotionally out-manoeuvres lost-at-sea Christophers, then encountering Shakespeare's thoughts and feelings could inspire modern adventurers to out-Columbus Columbus by mapping for themselves the long-sought philosophy in the global enigma that is Q.

Chapter 1: Penetrating Q

If William Shakespeare intends his complete set of 154 sonnets to be meaningful, what will we discover if we examine them in the original setting of Q? By surveying the 1609 edition, can we locate points of entry for our investigation and hope to map some of the salient features?

1: Rediscovering the sonnets of 1609

We begin our scrutiny of Q aware it contains by reputation the greatest love poems in English literature. Yet when we read the literature, it seems Shakespeare's sonnets are no ordinary love poems. There is division, confusion and outright admission of failure regarding their meaning and purpose. Are they autobiographical or deeply philosophic? Our mission would be successful if we could identify the type of inter-related love and philosophy they embody.

The impenetrability of Shakespeare's *Sonnets* to a barrage of research over the last 400 years leads us to review the status of the 1609 edition. By returning to Q we will see how the original responds to systematic investigation and how previous attempts to understand the 154 sonnets may have been constrained by traditional preconceptions as to Q's meaning and purpose.

We are fortunate on two accounts. There was only ever one edition of Q published in Shakespeare's lifetime and there are still thirteen copies of the original edition of 1609 in existence. Since there are only eight minor variations of spelling, punctuation and typesetting between the thirteen copies, for our purposes it can be assumed they were last-minute corrections made during the original print run.

For the present we can also leave aside issues as to when before 1609 Shakespeare wrote and arranged the sonnets in Q and about the level of his participation during the publishing and printing process. If we find evidence of a substantial structuring in the set and a clear relation between the ideas and emotions embedded in them and the rest of Shakespeare's works, then we could assert he is responsible for the final state of Q and has a controlling hand in its publication.

Because we identify Q as the site for investigation, a facsimile of the 1609 edition is appended so an evaluation can be made as to how faithfully the analysis remains to the evidence and when it slips into preconception or speculation.

Part 1 of the investigation, then, will detail features of the 154 sonnets in Q ready to view. Only after describing the many irregular and regular aspects of the set will we draw conclusions about their relevance and significance.

The method we will use is somewhat analogous to Darwin's approach to the evidence for pre-human evolution in *The Origin of Species*. Darwin's stroke of genius is to look inductively for evolutionary change in the readily available cases of artificial selection and then extrapolate these verifiable facts to the broader tracts of time to deduce consistencies beyond the reach of empirical investigation.

Further, Darwin uses the same method in *The Descent of Man and Selection in Relation to Sex* to reveal that, besides natural selection, 'love' and 'morality' are significant players in human evolution. By searching for recurring evidence of Shakespeare's thoughts and feelings about human nature within nature, it might be possible to grasp how he famously inter-connects the natural world with deep human love and understanding.

By identifying significant patterns in the *Sonnets* in this Part and by exploring similar features in the poems and plays in Part 2, we will be looking for a coherent philosophy that corresponds to the evidence and accounts for the depth of intellectual and emotional maturity readers experience in the 154 sonnets. It would be a bonus if that philosophy is distinctly Shakespeare's.

SHAKE-SPEARES

S O N N E T S

Neuer before Imprinted.

———————————

———————————

AT LONDON
By *G. Eld* for *T. T.* and are
to be folde by *william Afpley.*
1 6 0 9.

Title page

2: Investigating the scope of Q

In Q, the first words appear on the title page. **<snt_titlepage>** It asserts the 'SONNETS' are 'SHAKE-SPEARES', that they are published in '1609', and are 'Never before Imprinted'. 'G. Eld' does the printing for 'T.T', with the copies sold by one of two London booksellers, John Wright or William Aspley (who are named on one or other title page). External evidence identifies the initials 'T. T.' as those of Thomas Thorpe, a well-known publisher of the day.

While the information on the title page can be taken largely at face value, the same cannot be said of the dedication on the following page. **<snt_dedication>**

TO.THE.ONLIE.BEGETTER.OF.
THESE.INSVING.SONNETS.
Mʳ.W.H. ALL.HAPPINESSE.
AND.THAT.ETERNITIE.
PROMISED.

BY.

OVR.EVER-LIVING.POET.

WISHETH.

THE.WELL-WISHING.
ADVENTVRER.IN.
SETTING.
FORTH.

T. T.

Dedication

From first sight, both the overall meaning of the dedication and the significance of some of its elements is mysterious.

They are baffling enough for some to call the dedication in Q the greatest mystery in English literature. We hear words such as 'BEGETTER', 'POET', 'ADVENTURER', we see dots after every word or letter and take particular note of the two sets of initials 'Mʳ. W. H.' and 'T. T.'

The relevance of the unusual wording and letters to the 154-sonnet set is not immediately apparent. For the time being, we will treat the unique configuration of the dedication as an indecipherable key that might reveal its purpose as we examine the 154 sonnets.

At the end of the sonnet set there is a divide in Q between sonnet 154 and the long poem

A Lover's Complaint.
<snt_154tolc> The juncture between the 154 sonnets and the poem is indicated by the blank space under sonnet 154 (containing the word 'FINIS' and the letters 'K A') and by the presence of the title *A Lover's Complaint* at the top of the following page.

The eleven pages of the long poem also differ from the sixty-nine pages of the *Sonnets. A Lover's*

SONNETS.
154
THe little Loue-God lying once a sleepe,
 Laid by his side his heart inflaming brand,
Whilst many Nymphes that vou'd chast life to keep,
Came tripping by,but in her maiden hand,
The fayrest votary tooke vp that fire,
Which many Legions of true hearts had warm'd,
And so the Generall of hot desire,
Was sleeping by a Virgin hand disarm'd.
This brand she quenched in a coole Well by,
Which from loues fire tooke heat perpetuall,
Growing a bath and healthfull remedy,
For men diseasd,but I my Mistrisse thrall,
  Came there for cure and this by that I proue,
  Loues fire heates water,water cooles not loue.

FINIS.

K   A

Sonnet 154 to A Lover's Complaint

A Louers complaint.

BY

WILLIAM SHAKE-SPEARE.

FRom off a hill whose concaue wombe reworded,
 A plaintfull story from a fistring vale
My spirrits t'attend this doble voyce accorded,
And downe I laid to lift the sad tun'd tale,
Ere long espied a fickle maid full pale
Tearing of papers breaking rings a twaine,
Storming her world with sorrowes,wind and raine,

Vpon her head a plattid hiue of straw,
Which fortified her visage from the Sunne,
Whereon the thought might thinke sometime it saw
The carkas of a beauty spent and donne,
Time had not sithed all that youth begun,
Nor youth all quit,but spight of heauens fell rage,
Some beauty peept,through lettice of seat'd age.

Oft did she heaue her Napkin to her eyne,
Which on it had conceited charecters:
Laundring the silken figures in the brine,
That seasoned woe had pelleted in teares,
And often reading what contents it beares:
As often shriking vndistinguisht wo,
In clamours of all sixe both high and low,

Some-times her leueld eyes their carriage ride,
As they did battry to the spheres intend:
Sometime diuerted their poore balls are tide,
To th'orbed earth sometimes they do extend,
Their view right on, anon their gases lend,
                                                To

Complaint* has seven-line stanzas that are half the size of a regular fourteen-line sonnet. Despite the obvious difference in style, *A Lover's Complaint* is published with the 154 sonnets in Q. It may prove useful for assessing our findings in the *Sonnets.* For the time being, though, *A Lover's Complaint* will be set aside as we refocus on the sonnet set.

3: Irregularities in some sonnets

Within the sonnet set, we note three irregularities in the size of individual son-nets – specifically at *99*, *126* and *145* (sonnet numbers italicised here after). This is significant because the other 151 sonnets conform to the usual arrangement of a Shakespearean sonnet.

The regular size of a sonnet in Q is fourteen lines with ten syllables per line (or decasyllabic). Typically, the regular sonnet has an alternate rhyme scheme in which the first twelve line-endings follow the pattern: 'ababcdcdefef', concluded by a couplet: 'gg'. Moreover, individual sonnets are usually arranged internally into three quatrains or groups of four lines, ending with the couplet.

The first of the three irregular sonnets is *99*. With its extra line, it has fifteen lines with the first quatrain rhyming ababa. <snt_99.1-5>

The forward violet thus did I chide,
Sweet thief whence didst thou steal thy sweet that smells
If not from my love's breath, the purple pride,
Which on thy soft cheek for complexion dwells?
In my love's veins thou hast too grossly died,   99.1-5

Then *126* has only twelve lines, with its missing couplet indicated by a pair of brackets. <snt_brackets126>
The dropped couplet draws attention to the odd fact that *126*, unlike all the other sonnets, is composed of six couplets. It does not have alternate rhymes.

126

O Thou my louely Boy who in thy power,
  Doeſt hould times fickle glaſſe,his fickle,hower;
Who haſt by wayning growne,and therein ſhou'ſt,
Thy louers withering,as thy ſweet ſelfe grow'ſt.
If Nature(foueraine miſteres ouer wrack)
As thou goeſt onwards ſtill will plucke thee backe,
She keepes thee to this purpoſe,that her skill.
May time difgrace,and wretched mynuit kill.
Yet feare her O thou minnion of her pleaſure,
She may detaine,but not ſtill keepe her treſure!
Her *Audite*(though delayd)anſwer'd muſt be,
And her *Quietus* is to render thee,
    (   )
    (   )

127

I N the ould age blacke was not counted faire,
  Or if it weare it bore not beauties name:
But now is blacke beauties ſucceſſiue heire,
And Beautie ſlanderd with a baſtard ſhame,
For ſince each hand hath put on Natures power,
Fairing the foule with Arts faulfe borrow'd face,
Sweet beauty hath no name no holy boure,
But is prophan'd,if not liues in diſgrace.
            H 3

Brackets under 126

The other oddity is *145*. It has eight syllables per line rather than the usual ten.

Those lips that Love's own hand did make,
Breathed forth that sound that said I hate,
To me that languished for her sake: 145.1-3

It also has a number of internal and external rhymes on the sound 'eight'. <snt_145.1-3>

The three irregular sonnets may indicate something of the author's intent. Is there some connection, for instance, between the length of *99* and the shortness of *126*?

If we find sound reasons for their irregularity – or for any other variations to the internal organisation of the 151 regular sonnets in the set – then we may be close to a solution of the sonnet logic. We may also be closer to understanding why many resort to Shakespeare's sonnets for their deeply affective expression of love.

4: Extent and division of the sonnet set

Regular or irregular, we know there are neither more nor less than 154 sonnets in Q. They are numbered with Arabic numerals throughout (except for the unnumbered first sonnet). If we are to take Q at its word, and realise the intellectual and emotional potential of the set, then the total number of sonnets could provide a clue to the significance of any internal features we encounter.

Before considering why there are 154 sonnets rather than any other number in the set, we return to the break at *126*. Its twelve lines in couplets and its pair of brackets beneath indicates a division in the 154-sonnet set into sequences of 126 and 28. A look at the two sonnets on either side of the brackets shows *126* is written to a male called 'Boy' and *127* is written to a female called 'Mistress'. <snt_127.9>

Therefore my Mistress' eyes are Raven black,
                127.9

A reading of the first 126 sonnets reveals they are written to a male (who is also called 'Boy' in *108*). In contrast, the 28 sonnets are written to a female (who is called 'Mistress' at either end of the sequence in *127* and *154* and a further three times in *130*). <snt_mistress>

The division of the set into 126 sonnets devoted to a male and 28 to a female seems intentional. There is even a difference in maturity either side of the divide with the 'Boy' sequence appearing decidedly adolescent and the

My Mistress' eyes are nothing like the Sun,
                130.1
Than in the breath that from my Mistress reeks.
                130.8
My Mistress when she walks treads on the ground.
                130.12
But at my mistress' eye love's brand new fired,
                153.9
For men diseased, but I my Mistress' thrall,
                154.12
                Mistress

'Mistress' sequence appearing worldly-wise.

While there is no obvious symbolic significance for the 126 sonnets to the male, or for that matter for the 154 sonnets of the set, the lunar number 28 identifies the Mistress sequence with the number of days in the female menstrual cycle.

5: What does the 154-sonnet set represent

So, is there a reason for the set having 154 sonnets? We note that either side of the gap between the male and female sequences, the word 'Nature' appears in both *126* and *127* and is capitalised. <snt_nature126to127> On inspection, nature occurs a further fourteen times in the male sequence while only the once at the beginning of the female sequence – sixteen times altogether.

The word nature refers predominately to nature at large (thirteen times) but also to human nature (three times). On each of the thirteen occasions Shakespeare refers to nature at large, nature is resolutely singular and encompassing.

There is another correspondence that seems more than fortuitous. The word mistress occurs in both *126* and *127*. <snt_126.5> In *127*, she is the 'Mistress' with a capital 'M', but in *126* she is the 'sovereign mistress' (with lower case 's' and 'm').

126

O Thou my louely Boy who in thy power,
  Doeft hould times fickle glaffe,his fickle,hower;
Who haft by wayning growne,and therein fhou'ft,
Thy louers withering,as thy fweet felfe grow'ft.
If Nature(foueraine mifteres ouer wrack)
As thou goeft onwards ftill will plucke thee backe,
She keepes thee to this purpofe,that her skill.
May time difgrace,and wretched mynuit kill.
Yet feare her O thou minnion of her pleafure,
She may detaine,but not ftill keepe her trefure!
Her *Audite*(though delayd)anfwer'd muft be,
And her *Quietus* is to render thee,

{   }
(   )

127

IN the ould age blacke was not counted faire,
  Or if it weare it bore not beauties name:
But now is blacke beauties fucceffiue heire,
And Beautie flanderd with a baftard fhame,
For fince each hand hath put on Natures power,
Fairing the foule with Arts faulfe borrow'd face,
Sweet beauty hath no name no holy boure,
But is prophan'd,if not liues in difgrace.
                                H3

Brackets under 126

Significantly, Shakespeare calls 'Nature' the sovereign mistress.

If Nature (sovereign mistress over wrack)
126.5

A hierarchy is emerging with 'Nature' (as the sovereign mistress) having priority over the female (as Mistress). The lack of capitals on sovereign mistress suggests 'she' does not represent an entity with a proper name but is a prior condition for the female as Mistress. Nature's status as the sovereign mistress could be a precondition or logical given for the possibility of the Mistress or female.

We also note that 'Nature' commands 'time' in *126*. The word time is mentioned frequently in the set but only in the male sequence. Apparently, the Mistress is not beholden to time as is the Boy. In *126*, 'Nature' dismisses 'time' and brings the Boy to 'Audit'. <snt_126.11-12> Of the entities that might characterise the set, nature is the foremost candidate at the moment.

**Her *Audit* (though delayed) answered must be,
And her *Quietus* is to render thee.**   126.11-12

The only other instance in the male sequence of Mistress or mistress is in *20* where the male is called the 'Master Mistress'. <snt_20.1-2> Sonnet *20*

**A woman's face with nature's own hand painted,
Hast thou the Master Mistress of my passion,**
20.1-2

identifies the Master Mistress as a male with female attributes. Or, in keeping with calling the male 'Boy' and the female 'Mistress', the name Master Mistress could indicate the male derives from the female or is a version of the female with male characteristics.

We now have three entities characterised by the word mistress. Nature is identified as the sovereign mistress, the female is called Mistress and the male is called Master Mistress. We will need further evidence before these characterisations can be considered meaningful for the whole set. Furthermore, if Shakespeare's famous love sonnets represent nature, we will want to know how he connects the female, male and love to nature.

6: What is the status of the three 'God's in the set

To assess nature's status, we can compare Q's treatment of the words nature and God. Traditional religions proclaim the only entity prior to nature is the male God. When we search for uses of the word God throughout the set, we note three occurrences and they seem to refer to different Gods – each with a capital G.

In 58, 'God' is accused of making

That God forbid, that made me first your slave,
I should in thought control your times of pleasure,
58.1-2

the 'I' or author of Q a 'slave' to the Master Mistress. <snt_58.1-2> The sonnet recounts how God's attempts to control the 'pleasures' of the male 'youth' are misguided. The female and male interrelationship in nature makes such proprietorial thought control unnecessary.

Then, 110 talks of a 'God in love' as if the slave-making God of 58 might now be capable of falling in love. <snt_110.12> The third instance in 154 mentions the 'little Love-God'. In order of appearance, there is a transformation from a slave-making 'God' to a

A God in love, to whom I am confined.
110.12

'God in love' to a 'Love-God'. The 'God' who 'forbids' in 58, morphs into a 'God in love' in 110. The 'God in love' then becomes the 'little Love-God' or the 'Cupid' of 153 and 154. <snt_154.1>

The little Love-God lying once asleep,
154.1

Another possibility is that Shakespeare mentions the God of religion intentionally in the male sequence because in the Judeo-Christian tradition the biblical God is characteristically male. Is there is a critique in the male sequence of the excesses of male-based idealism typical of such religions?

Appropriately, between 58 and 110, sonnet 105 seems to warn against the dangers of 'Idolatry'. At first sight 105 appears to be a relic of things past, mislocated in the set. <snt_105.1-2> However, between 58 that calls the male God of religion a slave-maker and 110 where the God falls in love, it dismisses all forms of idolatry. Sonnet 105 celebrates the value of 'fair, kind, and true' that once 'lived alone' but 'which three' are now 'one'. It seems nature transforms the male God into a Love-God more responsive to the vitality of human life.

Let not my love be called Idolatry,
Nor my beloved as an Idol show,
105.1-2

Shakespeare sometimes uses the word heaven

interchangeably with the word God. A search shows nearly half the twenty or so instances refer to the blue or cloudy skies above. When Shakespeare uses the word heaven to refer to the spiritual realm, he does so with irony or with scant regard for religious niceties.

In Q, heaven and hell are interchangeable because one person's heaven can be another person's hell – as 129 and 144 explain. <snt_129.13-14> <snt_144.11-14> When the word heaven first appears within the set at 14, Shakespeare dismisses explicitly the idea of receiving judgment or knowledge from a celestial heaven or stars peopled by goddesses or gods. <snt_14.1-8>

All this the world well knows yet none knows well,
To shun the heaven that leads men to this hell.
129.13-14

But being both from me both to each friend,
I guess one angel in an other's hell.
 Yet this shall I ne'er know but live in doubt,
Till my bad angel fire my good one out.
144.11-14

Not from the stars do I my judgment pluck,
And yet me thinks I have Astronomy,
But not to tell of good, or evil luck,
Of plagues, of dearths, or seasons' quality,
Nor can I fortune to brief minutes tell;
Pointing to each his thunder, rain and wind,
Or say with Princes if it shall go well
By oft predict that I in heaven find.   14.1-8

Also absent from Q are the conventional religious personages such as Christ or Mary or the Trinity or any of the rites and dogmas of the Churches. Nor are there references to other religions of the world. We will want to account for these absences as we explore the implications of nature being the 'sovereign mistress' over the male God and if we want to understand its role in reducing the male-God to the Love-God.

7: A progress report

Our survey began by identifying three odd features in Q, but more significant is the division into male and female sequences. Female and male are not only sexually distinct but also immature and mature. Of the 154 sonnets, 126 sonnets sound adolescently male and 28 resound with female guile. The division of the set into two sexual sequences which, on the evidence so far, accords the female her biological priority over the male, adds further weight to the possibility the whole set represents nature.

In contrast, the one mention of the biblical God indicates the God of traditional faiths hardly gets a look in throughout the 154 sonnets. He is not structured into the main features of the set. He also gets a significant makeover if the trajectory from the heaven-fledged male God to the more earthy Little Love-God holds true.

The previously inscrutable set is revealing not only significant structure – or prior mapping. It is evident Q's author assigns generic names to characterise those structural elements. Unless further evidence surfaces, we identify the whole set with Nature (as the sovereign mistress) and the two sequences with the Mistress and Master Mistress (in order of priority).

As yet there is no explanation for irregularities at 99 and 145. The two changes seem less significant than the differences between the two sequences at the divide following the six couplets of *126*. Sonnet *99* is concerned with a theft and retribution, and *145* with a process of reconciliation from hate to love – with a possible allusion to Shakespeare's wife Anne Hathaway in the 'hate away' of line

I hate, from hate away she threw,
And saved my life saying not you.
                    145.13-14

13 and the 'and' of line 14. <snt_145.13-14> Their relevance to Shakespeare's thoughts and feelings may surface as we continue to investigate.

The salient features of the 154 sonnets suggest Shakespeare arranges them specifically to differentiate between female and male. Moreover, because nature gets more attention than God, we have to presume Shakespeare organises the 154 sonnets to acknowledge nature's priority over mind-based God or gods.

Chapter 2: Further structuring in the set

What is the role of the first fourteen sonnets, which are very literal in their require-ment that the male adhere to the logic of 'increase'? How does the logic of increase relate to the entities identified so far? And why are we seeing logical argument amidst the poetry of Shakespeare's love sonnets?

8: Taking it to the Master Mistress

The name Master Mistress in *20* relates the Boy of *126* directly to the Mistress in her sequence and sovereign mistress in *126*. As the word mistress occurs only twice in the male sequence, what happens in sonnets *1* to *19* to justify naming the male Master Mistress in *20*?

In the first fourteen sonnets, we hear an unrelenting argument about increase, or the logical requirement for sexual reproduction. After the word 'increase' appears in the first line of the first sonnet <snt_1.1> the dedicated increase argument continues until the double appearance of 'truth and beauty' at

> From fairest creatures we desire increase,
> 1.1

the end of *14* (see below). This suggests a divide between *1* to *14* and *15* to *19*.

The definitive argument for the significance of 'increase' appears in *11*. Sonnet *11* presents the immature idealising male with the consequences for love and understanding if he ignores the logic of increase in nature. Without increase the 'world' of humankind would be made 'away' or rendered irredeemably extinct. <snt_11.5-10>

> Herein lives wisdom, beauty, and increase,
> Without this folly, age, and cold decay,
> If all were minded so, the times should cease,
> And threescore year would make the world away:
> Let those whom nature hath not made for store,
> Harsh, featureless, and rude, barrenly perish,
> 11.5-10

The increase argument, after being heralded specifically in the first sonnet and explained in *11*, is evident throughout the group. Sonnet *3*, reminds the 'self' loving male youth he comes from the womb of his 'mother', <snt_3.7-10> and *13* emphasises he had a 'father'. <snt_13.14> The

> Or who is he so fond will be the tomb,
> Of his self love to stop posterity?
> Thou art thy mother's glass and she in thee
> Calls back the lovely April of her prime,
> 3.7-10

> You had a Father, let your Son say so.
> 13.14

increase group draws on an implicit genealogy of generations of female and male forebears who precede the generic Boy.

Then, in the last four lines of *14*, the significance of 'truth and beauty' is emphasised. The young male receives an ultimatum that he should heed the previous arguments about increase (called 'store' in *14*) or else his 'end' (read death of the species) will also be 'Truth's and Beauty's doom and date'. <snt_14.11-14>

Significantly, while the concept beauty occurs a number of times in the previous increase sonnets, the concept truth is absent until the end of *14*.

> As truth and beauty shall together thrive
> If from thy self, to store thou wouldst convert:
> Or else of thee this I prognosticate,
> Thy end is Truth's and Beauty's doom and date.
> 14.11-14

Throughout the 154 sonnets, the word beauty refers to sensations, whether sensory or emotive, whereas the word truth refers to the dynamic of ideas in language. As the act of increase involves a largely sensual activity, we can appreciate why the increase sonnets mention only beauty until the final lines of *14* seemingly in anticipation of the next five sonnets.

What, then, do the five sonnets *15* to *19* have to say about truth and beauty? We first note the word 'increase' occurs in line 5 of *15* as if reiterating the significance of increase from the previous fourteen sonnets.

However, the last lines of *15* also make the first allusion in the set to the process of writing. In the couplet of *15*, in a phrase loaded with double meaning, the sonnet writer offers to 'engraft you new'. The word engraft provides a bridge from the sexual dynamic to the faculty of language. <snt_15.13-14> The double entendre or double-ended meaning of engraft relates the logic of increase to the writing of verse. Writing then remains the topic of the following four sonnets until *19*. <snt_19.9-12>

And all in war with Time for love of you
As he takes from you, I engraft you new.
                                    15.13-14

The introduction of the process of writing or the use of language is the most noteworthy difference between the sonnet groups *1* to *14* and *15* to *19*. After the pithy arguments about increase in the first fourteen sonnets, a number of words in *15* to *19* reflect the development of language out of the logic of increase. Words like 'engraft', 'pencil', 'pen', 'lines', 'verse', 'write', 'papers', 'meter', 'rhyme', appear for the first time in the set.

O carve not with thy hours my love's fair brow,
Nor draw no lines there with thine antique pen,
Him in thy course untainted do allow,
For beauty's pattern to succeeding men.
                                    19.9-12

Following the double introduction of the concepts of truth and beauty in *14*, the group of five provides a transition from the logic of increase to the dynamic of language whether oral or written. The central sonnet of the five, *17*, mentions both 'beauty' and 'truth'. <snt_17.5-10> Its argument is that writing about beauty and truth on paper comes to nothing if the Master Mistress, as the archetypal male youth, does not appreciate the dependence of human understanding and expression on the female/male dynamic and increase in nature.

If I could write the beauty of your eyes,
And in fresh numbers number all your graces,
The age to come would say this Poet lies,
Such heavenly touches ne'er touched earthly faces.
So should my papers (yellowed with their age)
Be scorned, like old men of less truth than tongue,
                                    17.5-10

From *15* to *19* there is a deliberate transition from increase to writing. Sonnet *15* begins by reiterating the logic of increase. Then there is a gradual move toward the possibility of language or verse conditional on the logic of increase in *19*. The five sonnets track the natural evolution from the sensual physicality of the body to the conceptual and emotive functions of the mind.

The increase argument in the first fourteen sonnets follows organically and logically on the givens we have identified provisionally as nature for the whole set and Mistress and Master Mistress for the two internal sequences. Then, at the end of *14*, we hear that both truth and beauty depend logically on the dynamic of increase.

Sonnets *15* to *19* confirm the reading by accounting for the possibility of writing. The implication is that the intellectual and emotive aspects of verse derive from the logic of increase in nature.

9: Evidence of systematic intelligence

The initial survey of Q identifies its generic features as Nature, the Mistress, and the Master Mistress. Then investigation of the first nineteen sonnets reveals purposeful argument in the set. Each sonnet participates in presenting the argument of its particular grouping.

Moreover, each sonnet is a vehicle for argument. Shakespeare structures the majority of sonnets internally into three interconnecting quatrains followed by a couplet. Usually, the first quatrain states a premise, a rejoinder follows in the second quatrain and the third quatrain draws a conclusion. The couplet then sums up the case with poignancy and wit.

The internal sonnet structure does vary somewhat throughout the set. An extreme case is *66* with its ten consecutive lines beginning with 'And'. At a quick glance, the ten lines present a litany of alternative possibilities to counter those occasions where 'simple-Truth' is 'miscalled Simplicity'. <snt_66.3-12>

> And needy Nothing trimmed in jollity,
> And purest faith unhappily forsworn,
> And gilded honor shamefully misplaced,
> And maiden virtue rudely strumpeted,
> And right perfection wrongfully disgraced,
> And strength by limping sway disabled,
> And art made tongue-tied by authority,
> And Folly (Doctor-like) controlling skill,
> And simple-Truth miscalled Simplicity,
> And captive-good attending Captain ill.
> 66.3-12

While examining the argumentative structure of individual sonnets, we note some sonnets are connected logically to others with conjunctions like 'but', 'thus' or 'so'. The conjoined sonnets present one inter-linked argument. There are examples of logical connectives between *5* and *6*, *15* and *16*, *20* and *21*, *50* to *52* and *91* to *93*. <snt_5.13-14&6.1-2> The determined instances of logical argument confirm a significant level of intentionality in Q.

> But flowers distilled though they with winter meet,
> Lease but their show, their substance still lives sweet.
> 5.13-14
> Then let not winter's ragged hand deface,
> In thee thy summer ere thou be distilled: 6.1-2

There are other groupings of sonnets where two, three or four sonnets (plus one group of nine from *78* to *86*) give sustained attention to one topic. They provide further evidence of intent within the set. In addition to the sonnets connected by logical conjunctions, Shakespeare connects others thematically such as *27* and *28* (whose argument seems to continue in *43* and *61*), *32* to *35*, *135* and *136*, and *153* and *154*. Of these, the pairs *135/136* and *153/154* are very distinctive in tone and content.

The largest group from *78* to *86* of nine sonnets concerns an '*Alien* pen' (italicised in *78*). The alien writer – or sometimes writers – is generic as if the group addresses a type of writer and style of writing quite at odds with or even inferior to that of the author of Q. The author anchors the group of nine sonnets at the midpoint of the 154 sonnets immediately after *77*. It draws attention to itself as an alien enclave dedicated to those unable to penetrate the mystery of Q.

10: What we can take as given

Our investigation demonstrates that the whole set as nature, along with its internal female and male sequences, grounds the set in unarguable givens. They form a base for the arguments of the fourteen increase sonnets and the following five sonnets that introduce writing. With the identification of nature with the generic name sovereign mistress and the female and male sequences with Mistress and Master Mistress, individual sonnets seem to participate naturally in the overall structure.

If we examine the thirteen instances in the set where the word 'Nature' refers to nature at large (4 [x2], 11, 18, 20 [x2], 60, 68, 84, 94, 122, 126 and 127) there is no attempt to describe nature as to its origins or ends. <snt_4.3, snt_68.13> Nature is treated as a pre-existing state that needs

Nature's bequest gives nothing but doth lend,
4.3

And him as for a map doth Nature store,
68.13

no explanation. It just is. On the other hand, in the three references to human 'nature' (67, 109 and 111), there is a strong suggestion human nature can be developed willingly for better or worse. <snt_111.6>

And almost thence my nature is subdued
111.6

Similarly, there is no discussion about the origins of sexual differentiation of male from female. Shakespeare treats the existence of the female and male as a precondition, like nature, for the ideas and emotions he discusses and evokes within the set. Shakespeare uses the inarguable status of both nature and the female/male dynamic to provide the structural basis for the overall organisation of the set.

However, the correspondences between nature and female/male dynamic as logical givens differ in an important respect. While the separation of male from female in nature is a logical precondition for being human, the differentiation of female and male in nature is contingent on species survival. Humankind, as the increase sonnets argue, can become extinct. Unlike nature, the continued existence of the female/male relationship is conditional on increase within nature.

When Shakespeare uses nature to refer to human nature, its conditionality relates to conscious human choices. It is as if the two sequences of sonnets dedicated to the female (28) and the male (126) could be subsumed readily back into the 154 sonnets representing nature if humans act contrary to the natural logic of increase and the human mind.

In this natural arrangement of biological fact crossed with imaginative and emotional potential, the first 14 sonnets argue for the logical possibility guaranteed by the givens of nature and the sexual division of male from female. The increase argument at the beginning of the set relates to the natural implications of those givens.

From the first sonnet to the fourteenth, we hear a series of deliberate arguments around the subject of increase. Implied in the separation is the potential for reunification of male with female in nature to produce another, or to increase. However, unlike nature, all females and males could cease to exist. Humankind can decide en masse not to increase (as *11* argues), or worse, do so by default.

The biology lesson of the first fourteen sonnets addresses just such a circumstance. At the same time, the increase group takes account of the degree of intelligence and heightened emotion typical of the human female and male as distinct from other animals that are relatively more instinctual in their increase habits. The first fourteen sonnets not only address the natural separation of male from female within nature. They use the full capacity of human understanding and intuition to argue the natural logic of the situation as it plays out for intelligent beings.

Moreover, Shakespeare's 154 sonnets recognise in *15* to *19* the capacity of language to function conditional on the sexual dynamic in nature. With the natural givens, Shakespeare constructs a bridgehead on which to base his deeply philosophic adventure into the resources of the human mind.

Shakespeare seems to appreciate that the word nature in its generic use is grammatically always singular and never plural. Neither does it accept a definite or indefinite article. We do not say 'a nature' or 'the nature'. The word nature differs in this respect from every other word including universe, world, cosmos and God – all of which are used in ordinary language in the singular and plural.

When Shakespeare connects human nature in all its variability to generic nature, he does so through the agency of increase. It is as if he knows that etymologically the word nature derives from the Latin 'natura' or birth, origin, natural constitution, 'natus' or born and 'nasci' to be born.

The etymology of the word nature is at the heart of natural logic and even at this early stage in unravelling the philosophy from within the *Sonnets* we can see Shakespeare preparing to connect biologically – and hence logically – singular nature with the birth of humans within nature as a way to understand the full potential of their hearts and minds.

If we accept the whole set represents nature, and the female and male sequences locate humankind within nature, then the first nineteen sonnets have a purpose. Certainly, increase is a natural consequence of sexual differentiation in nature. What, then, are the implications of introducing truth and beauty at the end of the increase argument and then writing in sonnets 15 to 19?

Chapter 3: Truth and beauty and the sonnet writer

What is the function of truth and beauty in the male and then the female sequences? How pervasive is the issue of truth and beauty when weighed against other concerns in the set? Moreover, who is the ubiquitous 'I' arguing about increase, love and writing?

11: Finding truth and beauty throughout the sonnets

The injunction at the end of *14* says unequivocally that unless we acknowledge the significance of the previous thirteen sonnets regarding increase then the outcome will be 'Truth's and Beauty's doom and date'. <snt_14.11-14>

> As truth and beauty shall together thrive
> If from thy self, to store thou wouldst convert:
>   Or else of thee this I prognosticate,
>   Thy end is Truth's and Beauty's doom and date.
> 14.11-14

Sonnet *14* presents an ultimatum. Unless the male youth accepts what the increase sonnets say about the dynamic of life, his desire for knowledge and judgment will be void. What, then, is the significance of the double concepts of truth and beauty for understanding Shakespeare's deepest thoughts and feelings?

The words truth and beauty appear in the same sonnet a number of times in the set. After the ultimatum of *14*, they occur together again in *17* where 'beauty' is associated with the 'eyes' and 'truth' associated with the 'tongue'. Then the words truth and beauty appear together in *37*, *41*, *54*, *62*, *69* and *101* in the male sequence but only once in the female sequence in *137*. However, there are frequent mentions of truth and beauty separately in other sonnets to the male. <snt_truthandbeauty>

> Take all my comfort of thy worth and truth....
> For whether beauty, birth, or wealth, or wit,
> 37.4&5
> Where thou art forced to break a two-fold truth:
>   Hers by thy beauty tempting her to thee,
>   Thine by thy beauty being false to me.   41.12-14
>   And so of you, beauteous and lovely youth,
>   When that shall vade, by verse distils your truth.
> 54.13-14
> No shape so true, no truth of such account,...
>   Painting my age with beauty of thy days.
> 62.6&14
> Uttering bare truth, even so as foes Commend....
> They look into the beauty of thy mind,   69.4&9
> For thy neglect of truth in beauty died?
> Both truth and beauty on my love depends: 101.2-3
> Truth and beauty

In the 28 Mistress sonnets, there is a similar focus on truth and beauty but the two words are disposed differently. Remembering truth and beauty are intermixed throughout the male sequence, in the female sequence the word beauty occurs only in the first third (*127* to *137*) and truth only in the second two thirds (*137* to *152*) – with the transitional *137* mentioning both.

There is even a correspondence between the first fourteen increase sonnets that mention only beauty until truth occurs near the end of *14* and the first eleven Mistress sonnets where only beauty occurs until truth appears near the end of *137*. The same disposition of beauty and truth recurs in the first group of sonnets in each sequence.

Sonnet *127*, the first Mistress sonnet, uses the word 'beauty' or 'beauties' six times. <snt_127.1-14> It is replete with information about sensory beauty, which can appear both 'fair' and 'foul'. There are further mentions of the word beauty in *132* and *134* until the final occurrence at the beginning of *137* where it associates 'beauty' with the 'eyes', as does *14*. <snt_137.1-4>

Thou blind fool love, what dost thou to mine eyes,
That they behold and see not what they see:
They know what beauty is, see where it lies,
Yet what the best is, take the worst to be:
137.1-4

In the old age black was not counted fair,
Or if it were it bore not beauty's name:
But now is black beauty's successive heir,
And Beauty slandered with a bastard shame,
For since each hand has put on Nature's power,
Fairing the foul with Art's false borrowed face,
Sweet beauty hath no name no holy bower,
But is profaned, if not lives in disgrace.
Therefore my Mistress' eyes are Raven black,
Her eyes so suited, and they mourners seem,
At such who not born fair no beauty lack,
Slandering Creation with a false esteem,
   Yet so they mourn becoming of their woe,
   That every tongue says beauty should look so.
127.1-14

Then, in the latter part of *137* 'truth' occurs for the first time in the Mistress sequence. Truth appears in association with potential to 'say' or the dynamic of language. <snt_137.11-12>

Or mine eyes seeing this, say this is not
To put fair truth upon so foul a face.
137.11-12

From *138* on, which mentions 'truth' twice, only truth occurs until *152*, which also has 'truth' twice. <snt_truth138_&152> It seems the Mistress sequence is dedicated to the presentation of the dynamic of beauty and then of truth (apart from *153* and *154*, which are quite distinct sonnets in the set).

When my love swears that she is made of truth,
I do believe her though I know she lies,...
Simply I credit her false speaking tongue,
On both sides thus is simple truth suppressed:
138.1-2&7-8
For I have sworn deep oaths of thy deep kindness:
Oaths of thy love, thy truth, thy constancy,...
   For I have sworn thee fair: more perjured eye,
   To swear against the truth so foul a lie.
152.9-10&13-14
Truth

As we investigate the relation of beauty and then truth we may come to understand why Shakespeare uses the word beauty to accommodate both what is conventionally considered fair and what is dismissed derisorily as dark (and labelled 'foul' in *127*). Similarly, we want to understand why he ties the word truth to the tongue or saying and so the use of language, and why saying what is true and what is false are both part of the truth dynamic of language.

12: The Mistress talks for the first time

Although we hear articulate argument throughout the sonnets, we have not identified the voice presenting the argument. There is, though, a pervasive presence named I in most sonnets. This is the I who discusses the Mistress in terms of beauty in *127* to *137* and truth in *137* to *152* and the Master Mistress in terms of truth and beauty in *14* to *126*.

After *137* divides in the Mistress sonnets between beauty and truth, we hear the Mistress speak for the first time in *138*. Her voice joins the singular I as the focus moves from the description of the Mistress' appearance in *127* to *137* to listening to what she says in *138*. As *138* intones, the Mistress 'swears that she is made of truth'. <snt_138.1>

> **When my love swears that she is made of truth,**
> **138.1**

There are different patterns for truth and beauty emerging in the two sequences. In the female sequence, beauty predominates from *127* to *137* after which truth prevails in *138* and *152*. In the male sequence, truth and beauty are not treated separately. There is a composite effect, particularly from *14* and *17* onwards. In some sonnets truth and beauty occur together while in others we hear either truth or beauty. For some reason the male is presented with an argument that co-relates truth and beauty, whereas the female is treated as the source consecutively of beauty and then truth.

13: The basis of love and the introduction of I

We identify a number of entities in Q but none of them is synonymous with the I that permeates the set. The whole set represents nature and the two sequences represent the Mistress as female and the Master Mistress as male. Then, within the female and male sequences, there are groupings to increase (*1* to *14*), to increase and poetry (*15* to *19*), to truth and beauty (*20* to *126*), to beauty and truth (*127* to *152*) plus the two final sonnets (*153* and *154*). A subsidiary group of nine sonnets about the status of alien writers attaches to the middle of the set (*78* to *86*). In addition, there are the three Gods in *58*, *110* and *153/4*.

> **O change thy thought, that I may change my mind,**
> **Shall hate be fairer lodged than gentle love?**
> **Be as thy presence is gracious and kind,**
> **Or to thy self at least kind hearted prove,**
> **Make thee an other self for love of me,**
> **That beauty still may live in thine or thee.**
> **10.9-14**

On closer reading, though, we note I is missing from the first nine sonnets in the increase group, and hence from the first nine sonnets of the set. Why does the voice in the set not refer to itself until *10* where, as if to compensate for its previous absence, we hear 'I', 'me' and 'my'? <snt_10.9-14>

Furthermore, the attitude of I in *10* is quite antagonistic toward the male addressee. There is a similar tone of rebuke back in *9*. At issue seems to be the status of the youth's love.

> **No love towards others in that bosom sits**
> **That on himself such murd'rous shame commits.**
> **9.13-14**

Significantly, *9* is the first sonnet in the set to address interpersonal love. <snt_9.13-14> The word love is used conditionally earlier when *3* criticises the male's 'self love'. <snt_3.7-8> Then, *8* uses lovest when it questions why the Master Mistress 'lovest...not gladly' the 'music' that 'sings' of

> **Or who is he so fond will be the tomb,**
> **Of his self love to stop posterity? 3.7-8**

> **Whose speechless song being many, seeming one,**
> **Sings this to thee thou single wilt prove none.**
> **8.13-14**

natural increase. The 'speechless song' of increase warns against 'single' self-regard. <snt_8.13-14> In contrast, the love introduced in *9* is the love for another.

Not until *9*, then, is the significance of interpersonal love spelt out. The neglect of 'love towards others' is first a 'murdrous shame' in *9* and then a

> **For thou art so possessed with murd'rous hate,**
> **That 'gainst thy self thou stick'st not to conspire,**
> **10.5-6**

'murdrous hate' in *10*. <snt_10.5-6>

A detailed mapping of the set should explain the absence of inter-personal love from the first eight and the personal I from the first nine sonnets respectively. The absence is noteworthy, particularly as love occurs over two hundred times and I three hundred times throughout the remaining sonnets.

The absence of I and the effective absence of love from the first few sonnets in Q are unique in the sonnet sequences of Shakespeare's day. Other sonneteers of the time, who seek to create a utopia or an idealised world in their sonnet romances, invariably mention love and I from the first sonnet to the last in their sequences.

Is it possible Shakespeare's delay in mentioning both love and I provides some clue as to why the mindset of Q appears entrancing to so many, yet still harbours its secrets? What is the nature of the love that draws legions to the *Sonnets* but leaves them feeling confused when they read them?

14: Who is the I in Q

We refer to the author of the set as I, but he remains unnamed. On reflection, the dedication talks of a Poet who wishes the adventurer well in setting forth. We find six mentions of Poet in Q. The name Poet is capitalised in each case.

The first two occurrences are in *17*, the central sonnet of the group of five sonnets that introduce the possibility of writing into the set after the fourteen increase sonnets. <snt_17.1-7 > In *17*, I and the Poet are synonymous.

Who will believe my verse in time to come
If it were filled with your most high deserts?
Though yet heaven knows it is but as a tomb
Which hides your life, and shows not half your parts:
If I could write the beauty of your eyes,
And in fresh numbers number all your graces,
The age to come would say this Poet lies,   17.1-7

Sonnet *17* claims the longevity of the Poet as writer will not depend on his ability to 'write the beauty of your eyes' nor will it rely on an old man's 'tongue' that does not appreciate the logic of 'truth'. Instead, the Poet anticipates the full understanding of his 'verse' will occur in an 'age to come' that values the logic of increase in nature.

Looking back, the dedication identifies the Poet both as the begetter of the sonnets and as ever-living. The meaning of ever-living may not be clear, but some light is cast on it by the argument of the increase group. The whole group, and particularly *14*, suggests there can only be truth and beauty with the potential for mature love if there is human increase in nature. That is, the Poet is ever-living only if there are humans alive in future ages to read his love poetry.

The couplet of *17* confirms the prognosis. If we read the last line using the punctuation of the 1609 edition, the Poet argues that if any children of the Master Mistress were alive at some future time he will live three times over. He will live 'twice' over through increase – he will have his own life validated when he sees his 'child' alive. Plus, he can live once more in the Poet's 'rhyme'. <snt_17.13-14>

The author, who is omnipresent as I

But were some child of yours alive that time,
You should live twice in it, and in my rhyme.
    17.13-14

throughout the set from *10* onwards, refers to himself as Poet when appropriate. He calls himself Poet three times out of the six mentions. On two other occasions, Poet refers to the alien or inferior versifier who writes flattering verse in praise of the youth. In the other instance, the name Poet refers to both himself and the alien Poet.

The Poet of the set accuses the other Poet (in *32* and *79*) of entering Q on false pretences. Why this is the case is not yet clear. The answer may lie in the final reference to Poet in *83* where he suggests it is not possible for either he or the 'others' to capture the 'life' of the Master Mistress in their verse. Neither is it possible for alien Poets to experience mature love if they misrepresent the youth's natural potential for love.

15: So who else is who in Q

We have begun identifying named entities in Q. They all meet one criterion we set for our inquiry. We would consider only sonnet features present in the 1609 original.

So far there is nature or sovereign mistress, God, Mistress, Master Mistress or Boy, the I, Poet, alien Poet, and Cupid. When we compare Shakespeare's sonnet set to other sequences of the period, it does seem odd that the names are generic rather than personal.

Although we encounter no personal names, it is possible that hate away in *145* refers to Anne Hathaway. Two other sonnets in the Mistress sequence have a tone distinct from the rest. In *135* and *136*, 'will' occurs nineteen times in all plus a 'wilt' and a plural 'wills'. Ten of the nineteen wills have a capital 'W' and are italicised. Then, in the last line of *136*, the Poet states his name is *Will*. <**snt_136.13-14**>

It is possible *135* and *136* present an elaborate play on Shakespeare's own name, William, to counterpoint the punning allusion to Anne Hathaway in *145*.

> **Make but my name thy love, and love that still,**
> **And then thou lovest me for my name is *Will*.**
> 136.13-14

Sonnets *135* and *136* are far more effusive about Will than are *57* and *143* with their single mention of the name Will. Does Shakespeare identify his relationship with Anne as the primary source for the intellectual and emotional depths of Q?

16: Further regularities and irregularities in Q

Q is unique in that both love and I do not occur until *9* and *10* respectively. Moreover, *9* and *10* finish and top their respective pages for the first time in the set. <**snt_9to10**> Checking all 154 sonnets, after *10* every twelfth sonnet similarly tops its page.

This distinctive feature in Q means there is a pattern of twelve groups of twelve sonnets between *10* and *153*. The relevance of the groups of twelve sonnets is unclear except we hear a rhyme between the number twelve and the passage of time.

The pattern of twelves unique to Shakespeare's *Sonnets* may have some connection to the presence of the word 'clock' in *12* and the word 'minutes' in *60*.

<snt_time> Though the pattern of twelves extends over both sequences, the word time does not appear in the Mistress sequence.

The realisation every twelfth sonnet after *10* tops a page brings into focus another feature in the layout of *Q*. Throughout the set, individual sonnets intertwine from page to page – except for every twelfth sonnet after *10*. The 154 sonnets straddle pages in a number of combinations all the way from one line at the bottom of a page to thirteen lines on the

Sonnet 10 begins patterns of 12

When I do count the clock that tells the time,
12.1
So do our minutes hasten to their end, 60.2

Time sonnets

next, to twelve lines at the bottom of a page to two lines on the next.

Shakespeare's arrangement of the 154 sonnets, with interconnecting sonnets across the pages plus the twelve sets of twelve, suggests their argument and poetry is continuous yet ordered. The organic pattern enhances the possibility of a nature-based exploration of human understanding and expression.

In keeping with nature-orientated *Q* are the woodblock prints over the title page and the first page. <snt_titlewoodblock> The motifs show a jungle-like profusion of plants, vines, animals and other creatures. <snt_sonnetwoodblock>

At the end of *Q*, after the last stanza of *A Lover's Complaint*, there is a more restrained echo of the earlier panels. <snt_endwoodblock> The simpler pattern suggests *A Lover's Complaint* has nothing of the complexity of the sonnet arrangement.

The 154-sonnet organisation appears as a natural resource with structural elements interspersed. As we investigate the arrangement of *Q* without revision or alteration, our conclusion will have to account for its naturally structured features.

So far, the evidence supports a determining role for nature in the 154 sonnets. Moreover, with love appearing first in *9*, we will want to know how physical love relates to the mature love Shakespeare evokes in the remaining sonnets?

The Mistress sonnets separate into those mentioning beauty and those mentioning truth. To them we can add sonnet 14's unequivocal statement about truth and beauty and the frequent appearance of both truth and beauty throughout the male sequence. It seems the truth and beauty dynamic has a role in determining the status of the other concepts in the set such as time and music – and God.

Chapter 4: Counting sonnets

Do the numbers in the set, such as 154, 28, 126, 14, 9 and 1, have a significance other than structuring the 154 sonnets into male and female sequences, or other groupings and patterns? And, why would Shakespeare bother to give meaning to numbers?

17: Numbers in the sonnet set

In *Q*, we find instances of the word 'number', 'numbers' and 'addition', etc. How does the use of such words relate to numerals that appear in individual sonnets and identifiable groups of sonnets such as the fourteen increase sonnets and nine alien Poet sonnets within the set of 154?

We look first to *135* and *136*, where the words 'number' and 'nothing' appear. The number 'one' and the process of 'addition' also seem interrelated. Together, the two sonnets offer a greater unity if the Poet adds his one will to the Mistress' 'large Will'. The flurry of wills, numbers, nothings, and ones resolves when the Poet invokes the increase argument to avow that 'in thy store's account I one must be'. <snt_136.6-12>

I fill it full with wills, and my will one,
In things of great receipt with ease we prove,
Among a number one is reckon'd none.
Then in the number let me pass untold,
Though in thy store's account I one must be,
For nothing hold me so it please thee hold,
That nothing me, a some-thing sweet to thee.
                                        136.6-12

A clue to the rationale behind the Poet's digital by-play could be in the portioning of the nineteen wills in *135* and *136* into ten that are italicised and nine that are not. The numerical relationship of 1 (10 = 1+0 = 1) and 9 reminds us of *38* where the Poet advocates adding 'one' extra Muse to the 'nine' Muses of old. Then there are the nine sonnets at the beginning of the set and one sonnet at the end that are not included in the pattern of twelves beginning at *10* and ending at *153*.

Shakespeare was not alone in playing with the numbers 1 and 9. We need only look back as far as Phillip Sidney's sonnet-vogue love sequence *Astrophel and Stella*. Sidney wrote his sonnets for the favour of Lady Penelope Rich in the 1580s and they were published in full in 1598.

Sidney's sequence comprises 108 sonnets and eleven songs. The 108 sonnets derive from a game played by the suitors who besiege Penelope in Ithaca while the Greek hero Odysseus undergoes trial by sea for twenty years. The suitors place fifty-four stones to either side and one in the middle to represent Penelope. He who hits the Penelope stone is the winner.

To arrive at a numerological unity, first sum the 108 sonnets to 9, and then add Penelope as 1.

$$108 = 1+0+8 = 9$$
$$9 + 1 = 10 = 1+0 = 1$$

The implication is, when the once victorious but now severely tested Odysseus returns as a matured male, he trounces the suitors and adds his 9 to Penelope's 1, if she will accept him back. [note 1]

Other sonneteers in the period before Q such as Samuel Daniel and Michael Drayton, and other poets in the centuries before, use this type of summary mathematics or numerology to create a unity. Daniel's sequence has fifty-five sonnets and Drayton's sixty-three sonnets plus one sonnet 'To the Reader'.

The most famous sequence of numbered poems is Dante Alighieri's *Divine Comedy* from the early 1300s in which his 100 cantos add to a divine unity.

$$100 = 1+0+0 = 1$$

Just as pertinent is the internal numerological relationship Beatrice has to the God of the 100 cantos. Beatrice was once Dante's unattainable childhood sweetheart who died later in childbirth. She becomes the apotheosised female in Dante's version of Paradise. Beatrice enters the *Divine Comedy* immediately after canto 63 (6 + 3 = 9) and so before the final 36 (3 + 6 = 9) cantos and Dante mentions her name sixty-three times throughout his poem. Her numbering 9 can be added to the divine unity of the whole set allowing her to achieve unity with the Godhead.

$$9 + 1 = 10 = 1+0 = 1$$

It is likely, then, Shakespeare uses these well-known numbered poetry sequences as rudimentary prototypes for his natural groupings in Q. Taking the hint from the 9 and 1 Muses in *38* and the 9 and 1 sonnets around the pattern of twelves, we can add the numbers 154, 28 and 126 that delineate the set.

When we do, nature at 154 adds to a unity.

$$154 = 1+5+4 = 10 = 1+0 = 1$$

The female 28 also adds to a unity.

$$28 = 2+8 = 10 = 1+0 = 1$$

And the male 126 adds to 9.

$$126 = 1+2+6 = 9$$

<diagram_sonnetnumbering>

This suggests the male with the numbering of 9, like the immature Odysseus and the cast-aside suitors to Penelope, needs to recover and mature his natural relationship to the female to regain his unity.

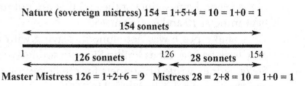

Nature (sovereign mistress) 154 = 1+5+4 = 10 = 1+0 = 1
154 sonnets

1   126 sonnets   126   28 sonnets   154

Master Mistress 126 = 1+2+6 = 9   Mistress 28 = 2+8 = 10 = 1+0 = 1

Numerological relationships in the set

$$9+1 = 10 = 1+0 = 1$$

Shakespeare represents the greater complexity of nature with the number 154 that sums to 1, and the originary status of the female (28 = 1) over the male (126 = 9). These numerical relationships conform to nature as the sovereign mistress, the female as Mistress who derives directly from the sovereign mistress, and the male as Master Mistress who derives in turn from the Mistress. In the natural patterning of Q, the male's lesser status is a consequence of the biological priority of the female.

Q's nature-based structuring conforms to the Poet calling the male Boy in *126*. No wonder the Poet criticises the male God in *58* and transforms the slave-making God into a 'God in love' in *110*. Shakespeare's intent seems clear when we remember Dante wrote the 100 cantos to validate the authority of the biblical God.

Shakespeare's natural numerology overthrows the 1 of the male God and rescues Beatrice by restoring her 9 to a 1 for the Mistress.

The number 28 = 1 recognises the lunar symbolism of the Mistress or female. As the Master Mistress or male at 126 = 9 is one short of unity, there can be no significant power of symbolism devolving on the male until he recovers his intellectual and emotional unity with the female.

Significantly, in Q we encounter no arrangement of ideas or symbols common to traditional sensibilities or beliefs. We will have to explain how *Shake-speares Sonnets* have held the collective imagination and emotions in thrall for so long without connecting back to those dubious certainties.

Significant natural organisation is becoming evident in the 'ensuing sonnets' heralded by the dedication. They also reveal Shakespeare's willingness to exploit numerological calculation.

18: How intertwined sonnets become arithmetic

The numerological findings reveal a second tier of structuring that complements the logical arrangement of the set. Are there other groups of sonnets that reveal logical and numerological patterns?

Knowing the fourteen increase sonnets end at *14*, we note that 14 divides evenly into 154, 28 and 126 with factors of 11, 2 and 9.

<diagram_multiplesof14>

$$154 = 14 \times 11$$
$$28 = 14 \times 2$$
$$126 = 14 \times 9.$$

The 9 (in 126 = 14x9) is familiar from the numerological addition of 126 = 9 for the male sequence.

However, the 11 (in 154 = 14x11) for the whole set and the 2 (in 28 = 14x2) for the female sequence differ from the unities resulting from summing 154 = 1 and 28 = 1 numerologically. If we add the 11 derived from the division of 154 by 14 we have 11 = 1+1 = 2. This means the numbers 1 and 2 represent both nature and the female.

As *14* is the last increase sonnet, the Poet plays on the relation between multiplying biologically and multiplying numerically. The fourteen increase sonnets multiply literally into the whole set and its two internal sequences. The two sexual types of female and male multiply within the unity of nature. We see Shakespeare employing both addition and multiplication.

The capacity for both 1 and 2 to represent nature and the female is explicable if we accept that the whole set as nature is a unity (154 = 1) that divides into two sequences of female and male. Singular nature accommodates the differentiation of the originary female into two sexual types represented by the 28 female sonnets and 126 male sonnets.

Moreover, the female sequence also accommodates two groups. In her sequence, the Poet draws a clear distinction between beauty and truth. In *127* to *137* beauty represents all forms of sensations (as fair and foul) and in *138* to *152* truth represents all forms of language (as true and false).

Just as the Poet distinguishes female and male biologically in Q, he separates beauty and truth logically in the female sequence. If the presumption holds, then the double numbering of 1 and 2 for nature and the female captures both their unity and their separation into two potentialities.

The human male, by contrast, does not differentiate further sexually into two sexual types. In cell biology, the mammalian female is the precurser with the male needing to fulfil a number of genetic and hormonal criteria as he differentiates from the female. While the science of cell biology was not available to Shakespeare, the originary status of the female over the male would have been evident in human sexual, social and cultural interactions.

Shakespeare, not swayed by traditional male-based prejudices evident in Dante's divine unity, restricts the male to the number 9. The male's logical option is to recover his unity of body and mind by acknowledging the generative status of the female. Consequently, the male cannot be the source of the beauty and truth dynamic. He merely plays with its potentialities.

This explains why the male God of religion, who replicates non-biologically, appears only in the male sequence and why the little Love-God appears in the female sequence. Similarly, in the other large group of 9 sonnets in the male sequence, the alien or inferior Poets who do not appreciate natural philosophy are associated with the Master Mistress' number 9.

Sonnet *14* is a pivotal sonnet out of which Shakespeare multiplies the implications of truth and beauty. The simple numbering system he uses allows him to interconnect the natural relationship of thoughts and feelings between female and male and explore its consequences for the human mind.

Considering the numerological context in which Shakespeare wrote, it is quite conceivable he organised Q to give numerical value to his basic ideas. However, because the numbering is only alluded to within the sonnets, we will continue investigating the substantive ideas discovered so far.

Chapter 5: The Mistress explains beauty and truth

Why should Shakespeare divide the female sonnets so decisively between beauty and truth when he does not separate truth and beauty across the male sonnets?

19: The Mistress challenges prejudices about beauty

In Q, the Poet addresses beauty and then truth sequentially in the Mistress sequence. In contrast, he draws the Master Mistress' attention to the dual dynamic of truth and beauty simultaneously.

We will first consider why Shakespeare, under the influence of the female, distinguishes between beauty as incoming sensations and truth as the language dynamic. Then we will consider why he exhorts the male to understand the logic of truth as language or writing, and then beauty (the same word again) as interior sensations or emotions unique to the mind.

From sonnet *127* to the first lines of *137*, the Poet records sensations emanating from the Mistress' external features or perceived appearance. Beginning with *127*, which uses forms of the word beauty six times, he questions the tendency for the word beauty to refer only to the conventionally beautiful. According to his understanding, any sensation, whether black or fair, should be classified under singular beauty. <snt_127.1-14>

In the old age black was not counted fair,
Or if it were it bore not beauty's name:
But now is black beauty's successive heir,
And Beauty slandered with a bastard shame,
For since each hand has put on Nature's power,
Fairing the foul with Art's false borrowed face,
Sweet beauty hath no name no holy bower,
But is profaned, if not lives in disgrace.
Therefore my Mistress' eyes are Raven black,
Her eyes so suited, and they mourners seem,
At such who not born fair no beauty lack,
Slandering Creation with a false esteem,
    Yet so they mourn becoming of their woe,
    That every tongue says beauty should look so.
                                              127.1-14

By way of example, in *128* the Poet relates the beauty of music, or its appeal to the senses, to more basic sensual expectations. The repetition of the word music as 'music music' in the first line heralds the playful sensations from a keyed instrument. <snt_128.1-4> The Poet remarks on the 'boldness' of the wooden keys or 'Jacks' as they rise to the touch of the Mistress' fingertips. Intrigued as he is, he reminds himself the 'saucy Jacks' are no more than musical keys that make sounds.

How oft when thou my music music playst,
Upon that blessed wood whose motion sounds
With thy sweet fingers when thou gently swayst,
The wiry concord that mine ear confounds,
                                              128.1-4

With playful eroticism, the Poet assigns the wooden 'Jacks' to the Mistress' 'fingers' while he accepts her 'lips to kiss'. The Poet accentuates the distinction between 'living lips' with their relationship to articulate language and the 'dancing chips' that are but 'dead wood' until they attract the Mistress' fingers. They, in effect,

To be so tickled they would change their state,
And situation with those dancing chips,
O'er whom their fingers walk with gentle gait,
Making dead wood more blest than living lips,
    Since saucy Jacks so happy are in this,
    Give them their fingers, me thy lips to kiss.
                                              128.9-14

make her fingers 'their' own. <snt_128.9-14> (The two traditional emendations from 'their' to 'thy' in lines 11 and 14 kill the Poet's critique of the difference between indiscriminate sounds and savvy dialogue.)

The Poet increases his focus on incoming sensations in *130*. It lists four of the five primary senses as it accentuates that all sensations, good or bad, are singular effects. <snt_130.1-14> The Poet argues, because all primary sensations both fair and foul precede thought, categories of beauty or ugliness are a matter of taste or convention determined by thought and speech.

My Mistress' eyes are nothing like the Sun,
Coral is far more red, than her lips red,
If snow be white, why then her breasts are dun:
If hairs be wires, black wires grow on her head:
I have seen Roses damasked, red and white,
But no such Roses see I in her cheeks,
And in some perfumes is there more delight,
Than in the breath that from my Mistress reeks.
I love to hear her speak, yet well I know,
That Music hath a far more pleasing sound:
I grant I never saw a goddess go,
My Mistress when she walks treads on the ground.
　And yet by heaven I think my love as rare,
　As any she belied with false compare.   130.1-14

In *131* and *132*, the Poet again views the Mistress as a source of thought-preceding sensations. Only when she becomes aware of her 'black…deeds' does she bring into linguistic focus her sensory beauty's mercurial 'fairest' and 'black'.

Then, in the connected sonnets *133* and *134*, the Master Mistress makes the first of two appearances in the Mistress sequence – the other is at *143/144*. The two sonnets record the spectrum of sensations the Mistress' beauty induces in both the ageing Poet and the youthful male. Their similar reactions underpin their shared susceptibility to her sensory charms. <snt_maleinfemale>

Me from my self thy cruel eye hath taken,
And my next self thou harder hast engrossed,
Of him, my self, and thee I am forsaken,
A torment thrice three-fold thus to be crossed:
　　　　　　　　　　　　　133.5-8
So now I have confessed that he is thine,
And I my self am mortgaged to thy will,
Myself I'll forfeit, so that other mine,
Thou wilt restore to be my comfort still: 134.1-4

The male in the female sequence

For now we leave aside the idiosyncratic sonnets *135* and *136*.

In the first part of *137*, we hear beauty associated with the archetypal sense of seeing. <snt_137.1-4> It is when sensations register on the mind, most typically through the 'eyes', that beauty exhibits indiscriminateness. As the first four lines state, the eyes that supposedly 'know what beauty is' yet 'what the best is' they 'take the worst to be'.

Thou blind fool love, what dost thou to mine eyes,
That they behold and see not what they see:
They know what beauty is, see where it lies,
Yet what the best is, take the worst to be:
　　　　　　　137.1-4

Throughout the eleven sonnets at the beginning of the Mistress sequence, the Poet recounts how the full force of her unprejudiced immediacy teaches him about the natural dynamic of sensory input to the human mind. Only by having a clear understanding of the natural function of sights, sounds, touches, tastes and aromas, can the Poet represent the role of the senses in the logical trajectory from nature to the deep love he shares with the Mistress.

20: The transition from beauty to truth

A shift in understanding occurs between lines 1 to 8 and lines 9 to 14 of *137*. In the first eight lines, the Poet considers the dynamic of incoming sensations he calls 'beauty'. Then, at the end of *137*, he introduces the dynamic of language he calls 'truth'. Shakespeare arranges the transitional sonnet *137* to replicate the pattern of beauty followed by truth evident across the Mistress sequence.

In the first part of *137* the Poet acknowledges the 'eyes' that 'see' where 'beauty...lies' but accepts they cannot discriminate consistently between what is 'best' and what is 'worst'. The change in the second part is from the eyes (and 'heart') that respond to incoming sensations with unthinking 'judgment' (beauty) to the use of language (truth) that allows for conscious discrimination.

The Poet corrects the false expectation that the sensations from the eyes and heart can judge, 'think' or 'know'. Then, he identifies the ability to 'say this is not' (or distinguish 'fair' from 'foul') as critical to assessing 'fair truth' and 'things right true'. Yet he also cautions that the dynamic of saying or truth, while more exacting than sensations or beauty, can cause its own 'false plague'. <snt_137.5-14>

> If eyes corrupt by over-partial looks,
> Be anchored in the bay where all men ride,
> Why of eyes' falsehood hast thou forged hooks,
> Whereto the judgment of my heart is tied?
> Why should my heart think that a several plot,
> Which my heart knows the wide world's common place?
> Or mine eyes seeing this, say this is not
> To put fair truth upon so foul a face.
>   In things right true my heart and eyes have erred,
>   And to this false plague are they now transferred.
>   137.5-14

The shift from beauty to truth in *137* anticipates the Poet's account of the logic of truth in the following sonnets. In *138*, we hear the Mistress and Poet define the limits of language. Although, it requires some philosophic acuity to understand the logic of sensory immediacy (*127* to the beginning of *137*), it is nothing compared to the mental co-ordination needed to understand truth (the end of *137* to *152*).

As we saw on page 20, the first line of *138* affirms we are in the zone of articulate language. When the Mistress 'swears that she is made of truth', we hear her say something to the Poet for the first time in her sequence.

In *138*, the Poet and the Mistress demonstrate through friendly repartee the increased discrimination that saying or language provides. By communicating using the conventions of saying, by swearing to give a word in the context of language meaning, they extend their sensory rootedness from unmediated seeing to the give and take of saying. The lively dialogue between the Poet and the Mistress demonstrates that language provides greater definition and reflectivity than do incoming sensations. <snt_138.5-12>

> Thus vainly thinking that she thinks me young,
> Although she knows my days are past the best,
> Simply I credit her false speaking tongue,
> On both sides thus is simple truth suppressed:
> But wherefore says she not she is unjust?
> And wherefore say not I that I am old?
> O love's best habit is in seeming trust,
> And age in love, loves not t'have years told.
>   138.5-12

The Poet and the Mistress in *138* demonstrate the implications of swearing something is the case for the logic of saying or truth. Throughout the three quatrains they show, because verbal meaning relies on agreed conventions, they can convey the same meaning by knowingly exchanging 'lies'. In this love sonnet, Shakespeare accentuates that understanding the dynamic of language as truth – epitomised by swearing vows and then forswearing them – is a prerequisite for experiencing and expressing mature love.

Behind the interplay of Mistress and Poet is the profound realisation the dynamic of language, while more explicit than inarticulate sounds, is no less or more a repository of certainty than incoming sensations. As the structure of the set indicates, the givens of nature and the sexual dynamic of female and male are the grounds for certainty. In *138*, we hear language thriving on that certainty.

Sonnet *138* affirms that even the most determined form of saying, swearing, is only as meaningful as the swearer's ability to forswear prejudices against nature. For Shakespeare, words are meaningful only if the natural philosophy of life is accepted. Shakespearean deftness depends on a natural rootedness combined with agility in toying with words.

The evidence that natural philosophy is the basis for the interchange between Mistress and Poet in *138* appears in the couplet. There the Poet puns on the relationship between lying to each other through language and lying together in bed. <snt_138.13-14> The steamy setting reminds us that the givens of nature and the sexual dynamic observed earlier in our inquiry

> Therefore I lie with her, and she with me,
> And in our faults by lies we flattered be.
> 138.13-14

provide the earthy certainty upon which beauty and truth anticipate and generate meaning respectively. As *14* argues, it is nature and the sexual dynamic validated through increase that provides the basis for truth and beauty.

In the remaining Mistress sonnets up to *152*, the truth dynamic provides the distinctive focus throughout. The Poet and the Mistress, or the Poet learning from the Mistress, instigate the dynamic of truth or saying.

Sonnet *139* compares the precision of speaking (or 'tongue') to the 'eye's' capacity to entrap the Poet in a net of suggestive glances. <snt_139.3> Then *140* examines the consequences of the Poet being 'tongue tied' so asking the Mistress to rein in her disdainful 'eyes'.

> Wound me not with thine eye but with thy tongue,
> 139.3

<snt_140.1-2&13-14>

Sonnet *141* reaffirms the transition from sensory beauty to tongue-equipped truth. <snt_141.1-10> The litany of sensory impressions received through all five senses – eyes ('with a thousand errors'), ears, feeling, taste

> Be wise as thou art cruel, do not press
> My tongue tied patience with too much disdain: ...
> That I may not be so, nor thou belied,
> Bear thine eyes straight, though thy proud heart go wide.
> 140.1-2&13-14

and smell – recalls *130*. Whereas in *130* the indiscriminateness of beauty is laid bare, in *141* the Poet calls on his 'five wits' (wit is the focus of *140*) as well as his 'five senses' to help comprehend his love for the Mistress. The natural development of Shakespeare's understanding of love from the sensory inputs of *130* to the

> In faith I do not love thee with mine eyes,
> For they in thee a thousand errors note,
> But 'tis my heart that loves what they despise,
> Who in despite of view is pleased to dote.
> Nor are mine ears with thy tongue's tune delighted,
> Nor tender feeling to base touches prone,
> Nor taste, nor smell, desire to be invited
> To any sensual feast with thee alone:
> But my five wits, nor my five senses can
> Dissuade one foolish heart from serving thee, 141.1-10

language dynamic of *141* underscores the relationship between the philosophic content of the 154 sonnets and achieving mature love.

There is even a hint that Q anticipates the distractions preventing others from penetrating its natural philosophy. In *144* and *146* we hear a challenge to age-old prejudices. In *144*, the Poet compares his 'two loves' (the Master Mistress and the Mistress) to 'two spirits' he recalls.

Two loves I have of comfort and despair,
Which like two spirits do suggest me still,
The better angel is a man right fair:
The worser spirit a woman coloured ill.
144.1-4

<snt_144.1-4> He argues that concepts such as 'angels' and 'devils' are entities created entirely using language and hence are isolated irredeemably in the mind. As mind-based entities they are interchangeable, leading to the possibility of 'one angel' being 'in an other's hell'. <snt_144.11-14>

In *146*, somewhat sardonically the earth is called 'sinful' while heaven is panned as a 'costly gay' alternative. Heaven's 'fading mansion' cannot save the 'soul' from the inevitable fate shared by all. <snt_146.9-14> As the last line says, 'death once dead, there is no more dying then'. The mind-based products of language that constitute religious experience have no meaning if their basis or genesis in nature and the sexual dynamic is lobotomised.

But being both from me both to each friend,
I guess one angel in an other's hell.
Yet this shall I ne'er know but live in doubt,
Till my bad angel fire my good one out.
144.11-14

Then soul live thou upon thy servant's loss,
And let that pine to aggravate thy store;
Buy terms divine in selling hours of dross:
Within be fed, without be rich no more,
So shalt thou feed on death, that feeds on men,
And death once dead, there's no more dying then.
146.9-14

Between *144* and *146* lies *145* with its unique eight-syllable stanzas. With a number of internal rhymes on the sound of eight, *145* celebrates its freedom from the doctrines of 'hate'. The Mistress saves the Poet's 'life' by revealing the natural basis of love that predates self-loving religiously induced hate. <snt_145.11-14>

Pointedly, *145* stands between two sonnets in which the Poet predicts why many will fail to understand Q. As we consider the role of the irregular sonnets in the set, we may find a reason for the octosyllables in *145*.

Doth follow night who like a fiend
From heaven to hell is flown away.
I hate, from hate away she threw,
And saved my life saying not you.
145.11-14

With sonnet *145* reconciling Poet and Mistress and *146* revisiting the cost of religious excesses, the Poet begins his approach to the final truth sonnet (*152*) with a realistic depiction of the conflict between emotions and reason in *147* to *150*.

In *147*, the Poet says his 'love is as a fever' with a 'sickly appetite to please'. The Poet's 'reason' (or the ability to argue true and false) has gone, forcing him to 'approve' that unreasoned 'desire' in love is 'death' (*146*). Once 'Reason' is past caring, the Poet's vain 'thoughts and discourse' are, like 'mad men's', at 'random from the truth'. Having 'sworn' her 'fair' he now realises she is 'black as hell'. <snt_147.9-14>

Past cure I am, now Reason is past care,
And frantic mad with ever-more unrest,
My thoughts and my discourse as mad men's are,
At random from the truth vainly expressed.
For I have sworn thee fair, and thought thee bright,
Who art as black as hell, as dark as night. 147.9-14

The illogicality examined in *147* arises when 'mad' faith swears impossible oaths contrary to the logic of truth as saying this or that (*137*). Similarly, in *148*, the Poet accuses 'love' of putting 'eyes' in his 'head' that do not correspond to 'true sight'. His 'judgment' of false and right has 'fled'. <snt_148.1-4> How, the Poet asks, can his 'false eyes dote' on the Mistress as 'fair' when the 'world' considers her 'not so'.

O me! What eyes hath love put in my head,
Which have no correspondence with true sight,
Or if they have, where is my judgment fled,
That censures falsely what they see aright?
148.1-4

If she is not fair, then 'love doth well denote' that 'love's eye' is not 'so true as all men's'. The Poet surmises that 'love's eye', when 'vexed with watching' and 'tears', causes the 'mistake' in his judgment of the Mistress. In the couplet, the Poet says the 'tears' of 'cunning love' keep him 'blind' preventing 'well seeing' eyes from finding her 'foul faults'.

In *149*, the Poet asks the 'cruel' Mistress to 'say' I 'love thee not'. Shakespeare's focus is less on the Mistress' cruelty – as perceived by the over-idealising male of the female in nature. Rather, as in the truth sonnets since *138*, the Poet is asking her to 'say' how she feels towards him. His doubts about her love stem from a pathetic subservience driven not by natural female/male priorities but by the disingenuous consequences of his 'proud' worship of her supposed defects.

The worst of the Poet's or any idealising male's prejudices is to doubt the Mistress' ability to say anything reasonable (or worse, her ability to play with the truth dynamic as she does in *138* and *145*). The susceptible male feels 'commanded' by the female's 'eyes' (*14*) and his blindness to the logic of the eyes out of increase means he cannot separate love from hate ('but love hate on for now') and so lies when he says he knows 'thy mind'.
<snt_149.13-14>

But love hate on for now I know thy mind,
Those that can see thou lov'st, and I am blind.
149.13-14

Sonnet *150* continues the tone of *149* with the Poet admitting that the 'powerful might' of the Mistress' apparent 'insufficiency' made him 'give the lie' to his 'true sight' making him 'swear' there is no 'brightness' gracing the 'day'. Whence, he asks, can she make 'things ill' so 'becoming' that in his 'mind' her 'worst all best exceeds'. How can she make 'love' from 'just cause of hate'?

In the sonnet set, the Mistress is the fully validated female to the male's quibbling love. The Mistress' 'unworthiness' that raises love in the Poet is her completely natural disposition of mind and emotions. But still, the headstrong Poet rates himself 'more worthy' for loving her – despite his querulousness.

Sonnet *151*, the penultimate truth sonnet of the Mistress sequence, reinforces the coherence of the Poet's arguments. It inter-relates 'love' and 'conscience', arguing that love predates conscience or the ability to appreciate the logic of truth. <snt_151.1-2> As the sonnet asks somewhat facetiously, who does not know that 'conscience is born of love'. Mature love, as Shakespeare knows well, is consequent on increase in nature and not on the starry heavens.

Love is too young to know what conscience is,
Yet who knows not conscience is born of love,
151.1-2

The Poet's comment refers back to the increase sonnets *9* and *10* where the possibility of love is conditional on increase. To reinforce his point, the Poet fills the remainder of *151* with sexual innuendo. He highlights the erotic logic of the language that conveys the logic of truth or conscience.

Then, in another concentration of words comparable to *138*, *152* concludes the presentation of the truth dynamic in the Mistress sequence. It is replete with references to swearing, oaths, forswearing and vows and uses the word truth twice. <snt_152.1-14> Again the Poet and the Mistress show that the dynamic of language,

even when oaths are sworn, is subject to natural philosophy because a 'bed-vow' (and so a marriage vow) can be notoriously forsworn. Their mature love is both deeply sensuous and profoundly articulate.

The trajectory from the sensory beauty in *127* to the swearing and forswearing of truth in *152*, leads on to a celebration of erotic love in *153* and *154*. However, why *153* and *154* are so intensely erotic is not yet clear.

> In loving thee thou know'st I am forsworn,
> But thou art twice forsworn to me love swearing,
> In act thy bed-vow broke and new faith torn,
> In vowing new hate after new love bearing:
> But why of two oaths breach do I accuse thee,
> When I break twenty: I am perjured most,
> For all my vows are oaths but to misuse thee:
> And all my honest faith in thee is lost.
> For I have sworn deep oaths of thy deep kindness:
> Oaths of thy love, thy truth, thy constancy,
> And to enlighten thee gave eyes to blindness,
> Or made them swear against the thing they see.
>   For I have sworn thee fair: more perjured eye,
>   To swear against the truth so foul a lie.   152.1-14

Shakespeare's Poet intentionally separates beauty and truth in the female sequence, where he associates beauty with any form of incoming sensation and truth with any form of language characterised by the swearing or forswearing of vows or oaths. We will now turn to the male sequence to see how the Poet's focus on truth and beauty relates to the arrangement of beauty and then truth in the female sequence.

Chapter 6: Truth and beauty mirrors beauty and truth

Why does the Poet introduce the increase argument as well as the relation between increase and poetry or writing at the beginning of the male sequence whereas the female sequence deals with beauty and truth from the start? In what way do the first nineteen sonnets provide an introduction to truth and beauty in the male sequence?

21: The male gets extensive lessons in truth and beauty

As we examine the Master Mistress sequence, we hope to find out why Shakespeare treats truth and beauty concurrently throughout the male sequence, compared to the clear separation of beauty (*127* to *137*) from truth (*137* to *152*) in the Mistress sequence.

Moreover, why does Shakespeare devote 126 sonnets to the male and only 28 to the female? His Poet reports briefly and even quite tersely on his experience of the female as the source of beauty and then truth. In contrast, he instructs the male at some length and with some patience in the logic of truth and beauty.

A clue to the disparity between the number of sonnets dedicated to female and male is in their numerology. If at 28 = 1 the female is already a unity, then the Poet needs to spend more energy on the male who is less than unity at 126 = 9. The Poet seeks to upgrade the male's intellectual and emotional immaturity, afflicted as it is by adolescent idealism. If the male is to attain the level of maturity evident in the repartee between the Poet and the female in her sequence, his excessive idealism needs a feedback loop installed to render it manageable.

The number of increase sonnets at the beginning of the set provides another measure of the Poet's attitude toward the male. The fourteen increase sonnets (out of 126 to the male) are roughly proportional to the two erotic sonnets at the end of the set (out of 28 to the female). The Poet devotes fourteen sonnets to explaining the logic of increase to underpin the male's lengthy sequence, whereas he needs only two sonnets to round out the erotic byplay in the much shorter female sequence.

From the evidence so far, the Poet organises the first nineteen male sonnets into two dedicated groups. Yet beyond those preliminaries, from *20* on, there is an unstructured extent of 107 sonnets. The only prominent feature is the alien Poet group at the centre of the set.

We have seen the same distribution of beauty and truth in the fourteen increase sonnets as in the Mistress sonnets *127* to *137*. The increase sonnets mention only beauty until the last lines of *14* where truth occurs twice. <snt_14.9-14> In *127* to *137*, the Poet only considers beauty until introducing truth in the last lines of

> But from thine eyes my knowledge I derive,
> And constant stars in them I read such art
> As truth and beauty shall together thrive
> If from thy self, to store thou wouldst convert:
>   Or else of thee this I prognosticate,
>   Thy end is Truth's and Beauty's doom and date.
>   14.9-14

137. Moreover, in the transitional increase to poetry sonnets, *17* mentions beauty (in terms of eyes) and then truth (in terms of tongue) in the same order as they appear in *137*, the transitional beauty to truth sonnet. **<snt_17.5-10>**

However, nowhere in her 28 sonnets does the Mistress – or her Poet – dwell on increase or the process of writing. They launch directly into the logic of beauty and then truth. In contrast, the Master Mistress sequence begins with the increase

> **If I could write the beauty of your eyes,**
> **And in fresh numbers number all your graces,**
> **The age to come would say this Poet lies,**
> **Such heavenly touches ne'er touched earthly faces.**
> **So should my papers (yellowed with their age)**
> **Be scorned, like old men of less truth than tongue,**
>
> 17.5-10

argument followed by the introduction of poetry or writing in terms of beauty and truth. In the light of the preconditions, what do the following 107 male sonnets say about truth and beauty?

A survey of beauty in *20* to *126* reveals that, besides references to beauty as incoming sensations, in many cases beauty is associated with poetry, art, painting, images, and ornament. The frequent references to internal sensations evoked by art suggest the beauty they examine is more of the mind and less of the sensate world. The Poet's shift from examining incoming sensory beauty in the female sequence to exploring the potentially exhilarating but also perennially deceptive mind-based sensations explains in part why the male sequence is so long.

When we turn to truth as the dynamic of give and take in language, there are many occasions the Poet uses incisive argument to establish a case against male-based prejudice throughout the male sequence. The word argument appears six times but only in the male sequence and some arguments span a number of sonnets.

The Poet's resort to argument from the first sonnet to *126* differs from his approach in the female sequence. There he learns dutifully that the logic of language or truth is at one with the process of swearing and forswearing something is the case or not. The difference between learning the logic of truth in the female sequence and applying it to make a substantial case for natural philosophy in the male sequence provides a further reason for its length.

It is as if in the male sequence the Poet explores the implications of swearing and forswearing by applying its logic as effective argument. This could explain why the Poet's attitude to the mature female as the source of beauty and truth is both dutiful and bluntly honest. Yet he maintains a critical if concerned attitude toward the idealising male.

In nature, the human female is the basis from which the male differentiates. We can imagine Shakespeare figuring out the biology for himself from the readily observable role of the female in childbearing and rearing. In Q, Shakespeare combines the logical priority of nature for human existence with the biological roles of female and male in the increase dynamic.

The natural relationship Shakespeare gives the female and male in the organisation of Q criticises the usurpation of nature by male-God religions. The only reference to the biblical God appears in the male sequence. His Poet's critique of male-based beliefs directly influences the flip from beauty and truth in the female sequence to truth and beauty in the male sequence. Throughout the male sequence, the Poet discusses writing and art at length because the idealising male misinterprets their correlation to his deepest thoughts and expression.

22: Sonnet 14 as the pivot

With Shakespeare recognising the natural priority of the female over the male in Q, the female provides the logical basis for increase. Although the female gives birth to either female or male, her female progeny reduplicate her priority status whereas the male regains his unity only in concert with the female.

Shakespeare begins the male sequence with the increase argument to remind irredeemably self-loving males of the logic of perpetuation. The Poet confronts the headstrong male with the increase argument in the first fourteen sonnets because increase provides the connectivity across generations that engenders all males – and females – in the first instance. The recalcitrant male regains unity with the female through the biological dynamic.

However, 14 goes further than formulating the logic of perpetuation. It says truth and beauty are logically dependent on the requirement to increase. Without increase, truth and beauty meets its 'doom and date'. The allusion to the mind-crossed doom that the issueless Christ promises in the name of a word-based God may provide a clue to the conversion from beauty and truth in the earthy female sequence to truth and beauty in the idealising male sequence.

Sonnet 14, as the last of the increase sonnets and the one that introduces truth and beauty into the set, emerges as the pivot that launches the poetry of the sonnets from nature's sexual dynamic into the intellectual and emotional gymnastics of the mind. It slots with consummate ease into the numbering of the set and two sequences.

If we listen again to the wording of 14, we hear it separate into two distinct parts. <snt_14.1-8> The first eight lines reject stargazing as the immediate source of judgment or knowledge. Astronomy or astrology suffers from being too remote from the earthy human inter-face where

Not from the stars do I my judgment pluck,
And yet me thinks I have Astronomy,
But not to tell of good, or evil luck,
Of plagues, of dearths, or seasons' quality,
Nor can I fortune to brief minutes tell;
Pointing to each his thunder, rain and wind,
Or say with Princes if it shall go well
By oft predict that I in heaven find.   14.1-8

Shakespeare bases his craft. The goddesses and gods who populate the heavens are no more than imaginative projections of intimations about starry origins from the interior of the human mind.

But from thine eyes my knowledge I derive,
And constant stars in them I read such art
As truth and beauty shall together thrive
If from thy self, to store thou wouldst convert:
  Or else of thee this I prognosticate,
  Thy end is Truth's and Beauty's doom and date.
                                                14.9-14

In the final six lines of 14, the Poet reveals the source of his knowledge or art. It is from the 'eyes' of the Master Mistress he gains his understanding of 'truth and beauty'. He adds the caution that if the youth dismisses the logic of 'store' or increase then truth and beauty will die. <snt_14.9-14>

Throughout the fourteen increase sonnets, the Poet argues that the idealising male too readily tends toward self-love or mental immotility if he neglects his life-giving roots. If the niggard youth, by act of will, cuts his roots – and if all males do likewise – then, as *11* puts it succinctly, humankind will become extinct.

The five sonnets after the fourteen increase sonnets effect the natural transition from the physicality of increase to mind-derived poetry. They begin in *15* and *16* by first reiterating the increase argument. Then, in *17*, they identify beauty with the 'eyes' and truth with the 'tongue'. Here, before *20* to *126* examine the logic of truth and beauty in depth, *17* recalls the significance of the Mistress' lessons about beauty and truth for love and understanding.

We will listen for further reasons in the male sequence why many regard Shakespeare's 154 love sonnets as the pinnacle of literary art yet why they find it so difficult to penetrate their logic. Our account will attempt to reconcile their poetic excellence with their earthy realism.

Once we accept the contentions of *14*, we can examine the presentation of the logic of truth and beauty in the following sonnets.

23: Eye to eye

After *14* brings the eye-to-eye interface into focus, there is frequent use of eye imagery throughout the set. If we imagine the Poet looking into the Master Mistress' eyes, and he into his, we envisage not only their immediate eye-to-eye contact, but also a mutual searching into mind, heart and imaginary soul in a hunt for the interrelationship between ideas and emotions.

The directness of the attack – directly into the face of the youth – is fitting for the immediacy of the increase environment. We are far from the indirectness of appealing to the distant heavens that the first eight lines of *14* dismiss roundly.

Looking ahead from *14*, eye(s) appear in *24*, *25*, *27*, *28*, *46*, *47*, and other sonnets. <snt_ eyes> In every instance, the Poet reinforces the relation of eyes, mind, or heart – and sometimes the imaginary soul. Occasionally

Mine eye hath played the painter and hath steeld,
Thy beauty's form in table of my heart, . . .
Which in my bosom's shop is hanging still,
That hath his windows glazed with thine eyes:
Now see what good-turns eyes for eies have done,
Mine eyes have drawn thy shape, and thine for me. . .
   Yet eyes this cunning want to grace their art
   They draw but what they see, know not the heart.
24.1-2,7-10,13-14

But as the Marigold at the sun's eye, 25.6

And keep my drooping eye-lids open wide,
Looking on darkness which the blind do see.
Save that my soul's imaginary sight
Presents their shadow to my sightless view,
27.7-10

How many a holy and obsequious tear
Hath dear religious love stolen from mine eye,
31.5-6

When I most wink then do mine eyes best see,
For all the day they view things unrespected, . . .
When to un-seeing eyes thy shade shines so?
How would (I say) mine eyes be blessed made, . . .
Through heavy sleep on sightless eyes doth stay?
43.1-2,8-9,12

Mine eye and heart are at a mortal war,
How to divide the conquest of thy sight,
Mine eye, my heart their picture's sight would bar,
My heart, mine eye the freedom of that right, . . .
The clear eye's moiety, and the dear heart's part.
   As thus, mine eye's due is their outward part,
   And my heart's right, their inward love of heart.
46.1-4&12-14

Eyes in the sonnets

we hear a connection from the eyes of the mind to the sexual eye of the body that recognises they are inseparable because both are integrally part of the human body. The Poet knows no reason to divorce the mind's eye from the sexual eye or one form of love from another if the sought after freedom is mature love.

The reiteration of the truth and beauty dynamic from the last lines of *14* and on through the male sequence (with the words truth or beauty mentioned up to *115*) forms the basis for the persistent mention of the eyes, heart and mind. The trajectory through the eyes from sensations to ideas in language and on to the deeper sensations in the mind begins with the sexual dynamic in nature. The organisation of the 154 sonnets suggests Shakespeare appreciates that sensory beauty, truth as language and then artistic beauty are rooted to nature principally through the eyes.

The irreducibility of nature, from which the eyes and thence truth and beauty derive, means mental constructs – such as God – are mind dependent. The natural preconditions in *Q* are the basis for the possibility of conceptual constructs such as regular time intervals, imaginative constructs like the immutable soul and speculative constructs such as intimations of immortality.

Ahead in *104*, the phrase 'your eye I eyed' neatly encapsulates the eye-to-eye interaction that orientates the mind-to-mind connectedness in both sequences of sonnets. It leads directly to heart-to-heart experiences and expressions of mutual love and understanding. The more than sixty appearances of the word heart in the sonnets points to a Shakespeare who opens his heart because his eye/mind/eye is aligned heart-to-heart with the sexual dynamic in nature.

The mind's eye envisions the natural correlate the Poet revitalises continually in the face-off between Poet, Mistress and Master Mistress. At issue is the logic of the interconnection between female and male through eye-to-eye contact in *Q*. Love and understanding derive more from eye-to-eye intercourse and less from starry enlightenment.

Immediately after *14* rejects stars as a source of judgment, *15* reports that 'the Stars in secret influence comment' on the short-lived 'perfection' of youth. <snt_15.1-8> The quip suggests Shakespeare is conscious of the armchair role the stars above (whether the sun or more distant 'candles') have in

> When I consider every thing that grows
> Holds in perfection but a little moment.
> That this huge stage presenteth nought but shows
> Whereon the Stars in secret influence comment.
> When I perceive that men as plants increase,
> Cheered and checked even by the self-same sky:
> Vaunt their youthful sap, at height decrease,
> And wear their brave state out of memory. 15.1-8

human affairs. Their influence is slight compared to the Poet's ability to perform a double role. He can engraft the youth in his verse to remind him of the natural source of eternal youth through increase.

As *14* stipulates, the Poet appreciates that human understanding and emotion connect to the stars through the human life cycle on planet Earth epitomised by the meeting eye-to-eye. Whereas there are some ninety references to the immediacy of the eye(s) throughout the 154 sonnets, the Poet mentions star(s) only eight times. Of those instances, half unambiguously conflate the stars in the heavens with human eyes.

Sonnet *116* captures the dilemma of those who want to hear a whole universe of stars in the sonnets. They are unprepared

It is the star to every wand'ring bark,
Whose worth's unknown, although his height be taken.
Love's not Time's fool, though rosy lips and cheeks
Within his bending sickle's compass come,   116.7-10

to visualise the starlight glistening from Shakespeare's insistence on human intercourse through the eye. <snt_116.7-10> They read *116* as a direct affirmation of their starry hopes. Instead, along with the rest of the set, *116* diverts such hopes through the human eyes. The natural filter of the eyes corrects the errors of those who eye the skies with blind faith.

Our investigation of Q's contents reveals a deeply philosophic set rather than an autobiographic outpouring. The sonnet protagonists are not biographical but archetypal. Biographical readings of Q lead editors for 300 years to emend a number of theirs to thys. Most of the changes occur where the context is patently about looking deep into the two eyes of the other.

Sonnet 14 has a pivotal role at the divide between the physical world of sexual differentiation and the mental world of argument and poetry. Because sonnet 14 also locates the source of truth and beauty in the eyes in terms of judgment and knowledge, Shakespeare derives his philosophy from human nature in nature.

Chapter 7: Looking further into the male sequence

Why does the Poet call the male youth Master Mistress in sonnet 20 and is there a reason why sonnets 20 and 21 are connected argumentatively with a so? By appreciating the logical relationship between the names Mistress and Master Mistress, are we closer to understanding the differing love expectations the Poet has for female and male?

24: The Poet reiterates the ground rules for truth and beauty

Moving past *15* to *19*, which facilitate the transition from increase to poetry, we encounter *20* and *21*. The 'so' connecting *20* with *21* indicates the two sonnets present a continuous argument. Sonnet *20* announces the Master Mistress by name <snt_20.1-2> and reiterates the female/male relationship in nature. Then, sonnet *21* reinforces the logic of truth and beauty at the start of the Poet's lengthy exposition for the benefit of the male youth.

> A woman's face with nature's own hand painted,
> Hast thou the Master Mistress of my passion,
> 20.1-2

After the Poet introduces the Master Mistress by name in the second line of *20*, we hear him describe the male as having the face and manners of a female. The Master Mistress, although a male youth, has the features of a woman because the female engenders him in nature. However, because he lacks a woman's complexity, he appears 'less false' or more ideal to the admiring eyes of men. He even amazes women despite their 'souls' being not so heaven bent toward idealism. <snt_20.3-8>

> A woman's gentle heart but not acquainted
> With shifting change as is false women's fashion,
> An eye more bright than theirs, less false in rolling:
> Gilding the object where-upon it gazeth,
> A man in hue all *Hews* in his controlling,
> Which steals men's eyes and women's souls amazeth.
> 20.3-8

For all that, the Poet cuts through the pretences of male-based beliefs. Contrary to biblical myth, nature made woman first and then derived the male from her because 'for a woman wert thou first created'. <snt_20.9-14> It follows that, because the male derives from the originary female, a male's face is essentially the same as 'a woman's face'.

> And for a woman wert thou first created,
> Till nature as she wrought thee fell a doting,
> And by addition me of thee defeated,
> By adding one thing to my purpose nothing.
> But since she pricked thee out for women's pleasure,
> Mine be thy love and thy love's use their treasure.
> 20.9-14

Significantly, in the couplet, the male youth is no match for women because, if in every other external respect he resembles a woman, he differs in being 'pricked out for women's pleasure'. Consequently, the Poet makes a clear distinction between the 'love' he has for a woman and the 'love' he has toward the male youth.

In the increase sonnets, and particularly *9*, the Poet insists sexual love is the natural source of all other forms of love. Now again, in *20*, the Poet subjects the intellectually and emotionally immature male to the scrutiny of natural logic. Shakespeare's Poet re-asserts the logical relationship of female and male in nature in the first half of the sonnet pair *20/21*.

In the Mistress sequence, we saw the Poet earn the right to be her equal. In contrast, in the Master Mistress sequence the Poet, now the protagonist, encourages the idealistic youth to mature. The youth should accept the originary status of female over male evident in the residual female characteristics in his male physiognomy and psychology.

With *20* restating the arguments of *1* to *14*, *21* can now reintroduce the logic of 'verse' or poetry the Poet outlines in *15* to *19*. In *21* we hear the Poet reiterate the logical distinction between truth and beauty. In line 1, he introduces the Muse – who represents truth in the set. Then, in line 2, he speaks of 'painted beauty'–

So is it not with me as with that Muse,
Stirred by a painted beauty to his verse,
21.1-2

with beauty representing singular sensations generated within the mind and experienced as poetry or art. <snt_21.1-2>

Consistent with our findings, *21* dismisses traditional 'heaven' based 'ornament'. Instead, it favours a 'love' that is 'as fair, as any mother's child' – which recalls the increase argument. <snt_21.9-12> The Poet goes as far as to say he would not write in

O let me true in love but truly write,
And then believe me, my love is as fair,
As any mother's child, though not so bright
As those gold candles fixed in heaven's air:
21.9-12

praise of those whose 'purpose' or aims cannot be sold. It is not possible to 'sell' the airy fantasy of heavenly ideals. <snt_21.13-14>

Let them say more that like of hear-say well,
I will not praise that purpose not to sell.
21.13-14

The Poet is now beginning to examine the implications of truth and beauty heralded in the increase sonnets (*1* to *14*) and the increase to poetry sonnets (*15* to *19*). He signals the transition by references back to the previous sonnets, but *20/21* are devoted primarily to truth and beauty with an affirmation of the significance of truth and beauty for the male, and in the appropriate order of truth and then beauty.

Looking ahead from *20/21* into the male sonnets, we hear the Poet exploring the interrelationship of truth and beauty for the deep feelings of love humankind feels for humankind ('mine be thy love' in *20*). The combination of argument and poetry about language and art leads on to sonnets such as *116* with its 'marriage of true minds'. The Poet's mature examination of truth and beauty seeks to avoid the immature form of love that flips readily into emotions such as hate, fear, anger, jealousy, sympathy and pride.

To weld together the arguments of his nature-based philosophy, we observe Shakespeare continually connecting the potentialities arising from the natural trajectory structuring the set. His Poet forecasts topics ahead, as when he introduces the concept 'truth' in *14*. Equally, he revisits topics from a previous group. He restates the increase argument in *15* and *16* and similarly he reiterates the increase argument in *21* at the beginning of the prolonged consideration of the implications of truth and beauty up to *126*.

The relationship of truth, beauty and increase recurs in inter-connected sonnets such as *95*, *96* and *97*. We saw how interlinking occurs between *126* and

127. Sonnet *127* mentions 'Nature' but nature does not appear again in the female sequence because she is at one with nature. Instead, the single appearance of nature in *127* suggests a connection back to nature in *126* and the frequent mentions of nature in the male sequence.

25: From persons to personae – the dynamic of identity

Sonnets *20/21* relate the female/male dynamic to increase and truth and beauty. However, *20* and *21* also introduce the feminine and masculine characteristics of the mind. The Poet considers both his outward sexual characteristics and his inward gender dispositions as part of a larger unity generated by the female/male sexual dynamic in nature. The interrelationship of persons and personae of Poet, Mistress and Master Mistress should lead to mature love and understanding.

Shakespeare's set recognises that both the Poet and the Master Mistress are males with residual female body parts. As the male forms biologically from the female, it could not be otherwise. Moreover, their feminine and masculine dispositions underpin their mental faculties.

With *20/21* introducing the logic of female and male characteristics and feminine and masculine dispositions, *22* now focuses on the relationship between the mature male persona of the Poet and the immature male persona of the Master Mistress. The sonnet treats the Master Mistress as both an immature youth and as representative of the Poet's own youth. <snt_22.1-8>

My glass shall not persuade me I am old,
So long as youth and thou are of one date,
But when in thee time's furrows I behold,
Then look I death my days should expiate.
For all that beauty that doth cover thee,
Is but the seemly raiment of my heart,
Which in thy breast doth live, as thine in me,
How can I then be elder than thou art? 22.1-8

Because the Poet was himself once a youth, *22* spontaneously and simultaneously accepts the Poet and Master Mistress as separate sexual persons and as gender parts of the same individual. The Poet has within himself residual youthful dispositions and memories. When he looks in the mirror (or 'glass') in *22*, and reflects on his life, he sees himself both as he is at present and as the youthful precursor whose subsequent life experiences, sexual realisations and artistic insights have led him to his present maturity.

In the following sonnets, when the Poet both praises the Master Mistress for his qualities and criticises him for his excesses, he is as much making a self-critique as giving advice to another. The constant switch between love and rebuke across the person/personae interface of the male sequence contrasts with the female sequence where there is a greater sense of two adults interacting maturely and even playfully, particularly in *128*, *135* and *136*, and *138*. Moreover, because the Poet addresses male and female persons as well as feminine and masculine personae in the truth and beauty sonnets to the male, he includes any female whose masculine persona is out of gender balance.

From *20* to *126* there are frequent reminders the Poet and male are one person, and in both sequences there are reminders the Poet, male and female are one within nature and hence at one in their minds. We see instances in *36, 39, 40, 42, 48, 62, 88, 96, 113, 122,* plus *133* and *134.* <snt_personae>

The interrelationship of female and male, feminine and masculine, and their potential for unity within nature, gives the 154 sonnets their simultaneous effect of disunity within unity. The natural poetical symmetry/asymmetry of the set encapsulates both the activities of humankind in the natural world and the internal workings of the human mind.

Amidst the sexual/gender inter-penetrability in Q, there are three occasions where the Poet mentions the female in the male sequence and the male in the female sequence. Sonnets *41/42* mention the female and *133/134* and *143/144* mention the male.

As our account of Shakespeare's philosophy continues, we should be able to explain why he interconnects female and male, and feminine and masculine in each other's sequences. Moreover, we

> But do not so, I love thee in such sort,
> As thou being mine, mine is thy good report.
> 36.13-14
> Oh how thy worth with manners may I sing,
> When thou art all the better part of me?
> What can mine own praise to mine own self bring;
> And what is't but mine own when I praise thee,
> 39.1-4
> No love, my love, that thou mayst true love call,
> All mine was thine, before thou hadst this more:
> 40.3-4
> But here's the joy, my friend and I are one,
> Sweet flattery, then she loves but me alone.
> 42.13-14
> Save where thou art not, though I feel thou art,
> Within the gentle closure of my breast, 48.10-11
> Mine own self love quite contrary I read
> Self, so self loving were iniquity,
> T'is thee (my self) that for my self I praise,
> Painting my age with beauty of thy days.
> 62.11-14
> The injuries that to my self I do,
> Doing thee vantage, double vantage me.
> Such is my love, to thee I so belong,
> That for thy right, my self will bear all wrong.
> 88.11-14
> But do not so, I love thee in such sort,
> As thou being mine, mine is thy good report.
> 96.13-14
> Incapable of more replete, with you,
> My most true mind thus maketh mine untrue.
> 113.13-14
> Thy gift, thy tables, are within my brain
> Full charactered with lasting memory, 122.1-2

Poet and Master Mistress as personae

hope to show why the male appears twice in the shorter female sequence (*133/134* and *143/144*) while the female appears just once in the lengthier male sequence (*41/42*).

26: Beyond style, rhyme and form – Shakespearean love

Throughout the truth and beauty dynamic in the male sequence, Shakespeare also takes account of the emotions we experience as singular effects in the mind. Although not introduced until *9*, the principal or archetypal emotion is love for another. Shakespeare focuses not only on beauty as the singular apprehensions of poetry or art. His Poet discusses the potentiality and effects of the various forms of love including self love.

Significantly, while the word love occurs 164 times throughout the set, it appears in just over half the sonnets. Even counting the various forms of the word love, such as loves, love's, loving, lovest, lover – providing over 200 instances – only 93 out of 154 sonnets mention love or its derivatives.

Frequently anthologised sonnets such as *18, 94, 128, 129,* and *146* do not mention the word (except for *18*'s lovely) and significant sonnets presenting the Poet's arguments such as *1, 11, 14, 17, 38, 68, 84,* and *127* do not either. It seems

Shakespeare's love sonnets, when not encapsulating the deepest possible expression of love, address the logical preconditions for the possibility of love.

The preconditions are evident in the increase sonnets where only selfish love occurs before the Poet introduces interpersonal love conditional on increase in 9. Only then does he explore the depth of love generated as an emotive experience in the human mind and evoked by poetry.

Sonnet 21, soon after 15 to 19 introduce writing, draws a direct relationship between love and poetry. <snt_21.9> Then, in 23, Shakespeare's

> O let me true in love but truly write,
> 21.9

> O learn to read what silent love hath writ,
> 23.13

Poet continues to explore the connection between reading and 'love'. <snt_23.13>

However, it is in 32 that Shakespeare has the Master Mistress reiterate somewhat obligingly the Poet's expectation of mature love. While the Master Mistress acknowledges other Poets will be remembered for their 'style' and 'rhyme', <snt_32.4-7> he asserts the Poet's 'rude lines' will be read 'for his love'. <snt_32.13-14>

> These poor rude lines of thy deceased Lover:
> Compare them with the bett'ring of the time,
> And though they be out-stripped by every pen,
> Reserve them for my love, not for their rhyme,
> 32.4-7

> But since he died and Poets better prove,
> Theirs for their style I'll read, his for his love.
> 32.13-14

There is a similar expression of love unencumbered by style in 80. The Poet positions his 'love' beyond the reach of those 'better' writers who use their talents to merely praise the youth's 'fame' and 'worth'. <snt_80.13-14>

With the Poet reaffirming his ability to sublimate his deepest experience of love into verse beyond its formal and technical

> Then if he thrive and I be cast away,
> The worst was this, my love was my decay.
> 80.13-14

requirements, we are at the heart of his understanding of love. He has every reason to dedicate four times as many sonnets to the male. As a mature Poet at one with nature, he argues patiently for his deep vein of contents and patiently instructs the recalcitrant male in the conditions for mature love.

Shakespeare anticipates why so many consider his love sonnets the greatest in literature but fail to understand them. Starting with the preconditions of nature and the female and male sequences, he moves on to the logic of increase, which introduces the potentiality of love. Then, when he turns to the mind, he examines the dynamic of beauty and truth in the female sequence until he applies the logic of truth and beauty in the male sequence. The natural structuring of Q is what allows the Poet to explore mature love.

In 76, Shakespeare explains why his Poet is capable of evoking deep love in the poetry of the sonnets. In contrast, all other Poets flatter the idealising youth so elbowing aside the mature love that inspires their infatuation in the first place.

Sonnet 76 compares the Poet's 'verse', which keeps 'invention in a noted weed', with that of other Poets who try for 'new found methods' and 'compounds strange'. <snt_76.1-14> Instead of seeking 'variation or quick change', the focus of the Poet's 'argument' is the interrelationship between the youth's youthful immaturity and mature love.

Furthermore, his argument is as old as the 'Sun' because his 'every word' shows its 'birth' from the sexual dynamic in nature. As laid down in the Mistress sonnets, a sound understanding of words or language, and hence argument, is basic to mature love.

Shakespeare bases his sonnet philosophy in both the biological relationship of female to male and

Why is my verse so barren of new pride?
So far from variation or quick change?
Why with the time do I not glance aside
To new found methods, and to compounds strange?
Why write I still all one, ever the same,
And keep invention in a noted weed,
That every word doth almost tell my name,
Showing their birth, and where they did proceed?
O know sweet love I always write of you,
And you and love are still my argument:
So all my best is dressing old words new,
Spending again what is already spent:
  For as the Sun is daily new and old,
  So is my love still telling what is told.   76.1-14

the logical balance of feminine and masculine personae in the human mind. The lengthy sequence to the male recognises that the mind-based dynamic of truth and beauty regulates human potential and contentedness.

In *116*, Shakespeare summarises the logical conditions for mature love arising from the nature-based philosophy he lays out in Q. Sonnet *116*, with its recipe for 'the marriage of true minds', identifies the remedy for male-based intransigence. <snt_116.1-8> Shakespeare's Poet does not base the marriage of true minds on the

Let me not to the marriage of true minds
Admit impediments, love is not love
Which alters when it alteration finds,
Or bends with the remover to remove.
O no, it is an ever fixed mark
That looks on tempests and is never shaken;
It is the star to every wand'ring bark,
Whose worth's unknown, although his height be taken.
116.1-8

shifting sands of ever-changing pantheons of goddesses and gods who reside at the cranial periphery of natural philosophy.

Rather, the Poet symbolises the interrelationship between the sexual eye and the mind's eye with the 'star', as he does in *14*. 'Love'

is not measured by 'Time', or other mind-based conventions, but is intimately associated with the eroticism devolving from the sexual dynamic in nature. <snt_116.9-12>

We hear the connection between the sexual and the erotic when Shakespeare lyricises 'though rosy lips and cheeks within his

Love's not Time's fool, though rosy lips and cheeks
Within his bending sickle's compass come,
Love alters not with his brief hours and weeks,
But bears it out even to the edge of doom: 116.9-12

bending sickle's compass come'. Then, recalling the prognostication of 'doom' in *14*, the Poet asserts that, when there is a clear understanding of truth and beauty, the love engendered by the marriage of true minds 'alters not' even until the end of life. This is because life continues through increase (with a pun in line 12 on 'bears' ~ 'bares').

Shakespeare is so confident of his deep nature-based understanding and expression of love, he vows in the couplet that if it can be proved he is in 'error', he will accept his poetry is as nothing and that 'no man ever loved'. Based in nature

If this be error and upon me proved,
I never writ, nor no man ever loved.
116.13-14

beyond style, rhyme and form, the love Shakespeare celebrates is the basis for all love. Hence no man has loved if the love laid out in the sonnets is in error.

<snt_116.13-14> As his Poet does in 32 and 80, Shakespeare interconnects mature natural love that exists without words with its unprejudiced expression in words.

The crucial role of sonnet 20 and its companion 21 in setting up the logic of truth and beauty as well as introducing the inter-relationship between sexual types and gender dispositions appears basic to appreciating what Shakespeare means by love. Moreover, by basing truth and beauty in nature and the increase dynamic, Shakespeare can characterise the feminine and masculine aspects of the human mind consistently.

Chapter 8: The Master Mistress learns about reason and art

Why does Shakespeare return a number of times to the dynamic of truth as saying or language in the Master Mistress sequence? Why does he insist on the difference between what he calls simple truth and truth called simplicity? And, how does the truth dynamic relate to the form of beauty he frequently associates with art and poetry in the male sequence?

27: The Poet instructs the Master Mistress in the dynamic of truth

Shakespeare, when moving from one logical grouping of sonnets to the next, reiterates lessons learnt in the previous group of sonnets or rehearses topics he discusses in the following sonnets. In *14*, he anticipates the treatment of truth and beauty in the following 112 sonnets. Then in *15/16* and *20/21* he reiterates the increase argument and establishes the criteria for the discussion of poetry or art.

In transitional sonnets such as *1, 14, 15/16, 19, 20/21, 126, 127, 137, 138, 152* and *154* the reiterating/rehearsing is most evident. The patience Shakespeare's Poet shows as he teaches the natural philosophy of love to the Master Mistress imbues his sonnets with their humanising intelligence and deeply realised emotions.

In the philosophy emerging from Q, the Poet establishes a logical connection between nature and the workings of the human mind. From the evidence of the sonnets up to *21*, the Poet instructs the Master Mistress in the logic of beauty and truth, which he learns from the Mistress.

As we look ahead to the mentions of truth in the male sequence, it is worth remembering that *14* associates truth with judgment and knowledge, whereas it associates beauty with art. Then, the Poet reasserts the same dynamic of truth and beauty in the first two lines of *21*.

So what changes on the way from the female to the male sequence to explain the shift from beauty and truth to truth and beauty? On examining the word truth in the male sequence, we find truth continues to refer to any form of language or saying. The emphasis, though, shifts from the Mistress teaching the Poet the logic of swearing and forswearing to the Poet using logical argument to dissuade the recalcitrant idealising Master Mistress from confusing truth and beauty.

The first sonnet to mention truth, after *21*'s reference to the Muse, is *37*. <snt_37.1-8> It reiterates the basis for the youth's 'worth' in 'store' (or the increase dynamic) by recounting a father's delight in his child's 'worth and truth'. For the youth to make his 'father' 'ten times happy' he needs the 'wit' or understanding to accept the natural basis for his burgeoning 'glory' – including his potential to mature in love.

> As a decrepit father takes delight,
> To see his active child do deeds of youth,
> So I, made lame by Fortune's dearest spite
> Take all my comfort of thy worth and truth.
> For whether beauty, birth, or wealth, or wit,
> Or any of these all, or all, or more
> Intitled in their parts, do crowned sit,
> I make my love engrafted to this store: 37.1-8

The Poet interconnects the roots of life and love with an 'abundance' of 'delight'.

Truth next occurs in *41*. The Poet questions whether the male responds

Aye me, but yet thou mightst my seat forbear,
And chide thy beauty, and thy straying youth,
Who lead thee in their riot even there
Where thou art forced to break a two-fold truth:
Hers by thy beauty tempting her to thee,
Thine by thy beauty being false to me. 41.9-14

appropriately or inappropriately to a woman saying no. <snt_41.9-14> The Poet talks first of the youth abusing his 'beauteous' appearance for temptation and assault. The adolescent male's exploitation of 'beauty' for selfish ends shifts the Poet's analysis of beauty as fair and foul in the Mistress' sequence to new levels of sensory manipulation. If mind-based prejudice labels the Mistress in her sequence as foul not fair, the male youth now callously acts out the prejudice.

Then, in 42, the Poet resolves the conflict of persons and personae in 41 by invoking the perpetual inter-relationship between feminine and masculine personae in any person's mind. Because the problem is entirely mind-based, the 'joy' is that all can be 'one' in the mature love the Poet and Mistress experience. <snt_42.13-14>

But here's the joy, my friend and I are one,
Sweet flattery, then she loves but me alone.
42.13-14

And even thence thou wilt be stolen I fear,
For truth proves thievish for a prize so dear.
48.13-14

Sonnet 48 takes another approach. It deflates the idealistic dream of 'truth' as a singular 'prize'. <snt_48.13-14> The aged Poet realises that even if he has matured his own idealism, he cannot always restrain the excessive idealism of the Master Mistress from causing the 'greatest grief'. Despite adolescent idealism being the 'best of dearest' (or the best of the worst, as 31 explains) its headstrong beliefs prove difficult to curtail.

In 54, 'truth' first occurs in the second line where its language dynamic 'doth give' or incite the 'sweet ornament' of 'beauty'. <snt_54.1-2&13-14> Then, in the last line, it re-emerges as a process of distillation after the Poet presents contrasting sensations to the youth's quirky mind.

Oh how much more doth beauty beauteous seem,
By that sweet ornament which truth doth give,...
And so of you, beauteous and lovely youth,
When that shall vade, by verse distils your truth.
54.1-2&13-14

In the previous thirteen lines, beauty and its floral symbol the 'Rose' intertwine to reveal the slippage between 'Canker blooms' that 'die to themselves' and 'sweet Roses' who through 'sweet deaths' perpetuate something of themselves. Only the latter make the 'sweetest odours' or sensations in the mind.

When the youth's beauty fades, it is 'by verse' or the give and take of language (through comparing 'canker and 'sweet' blooms) that the Poet's 'verse' resolves or 'distils' the youth's self-involved understanding, or short-circuiting 'truth'.

Time doth transfix the flourish set on youth,
And delves the parallels in beauty's brow,
Feeds on the rarities of nature's truth,
And nothing stands but for his scythe to mow.
60.9-12

Sonnet 60 confirms we are dealing with 'nature's truth'. <snt_60.9-12> The Poet states that 'beauty's brow' loses its youth and dies in 'time' leaving the Poet's verse as a written record of the youth's youthful 'worth'. 'Nature's truth' addresses the female and male dynamic – premised on increase – which establishes the logic of true and false in the human mind. The nature-based Poet is able to write verse to 'praise' the youth as youth. However, as we saw in *138*, the reliability of the Poet's word is no substitute for increase, so truth is only as rigorous as the youth's confidence in nature.

Next, in *62*, the Poet recalls 'mine own' possessive 'sin of self love' as a youth. He describes not only his memory of iniquitous 'self love', he acknowledges the youth reminds him of the 'beauty' of those 'days'. He struggles with the temptation of 'painting my age' to hide his 'tanned antiquity'. The delusion generated in the Poet's mind of eternal youth and self 'worth'

No shape so true, no truth of such account,
And for my self mine own worth do define,
62.6-7

– where youth 'thinks no face so gracious is as mine' – makes 'no truth of such account'. It voids accountability in the airless heights of fancy. <snt_62.6-7>

Then, after *60* and *62* reiterate the truth dynamic, the most sustained statement about truth occurs in *66*. <snt_66.1-14> As the most determined truth sonnet in the male sequence, it clarifies the confusion surrounding truth when the natural logic of argument is ignored and truth is rendered idealistically singular.

Tir'd with all these for restful death I cry,
As to behold desert a beggar born,
And needy Nothing trimmed in jollity,
And purest faith unhappily forsworn,
And gilded honor shamefully misplaced,
And maiden virtue rudely strumpeted,
And right perfection wrongfully disgraced,
And strength by limping sway disabled,
And art made tongue-tied by authority,
And Folly (Doctor-like) controlling skill,
And simple-Truth miscalled Simplicity,
And captive-good attending Captain ill.
  Tir'd with all these, from these would I be gone,
  Save that to die, I leave my love alone. 66.1-14

In a sonnet of unique form, with consecutive lines beginning with 'And', *66* provides an eleven-line litany of opposed ideas the Poet says are typical of language as truth. It demonstrates the logic of truth by citing eleven examples of the true/false dynamic of propositional language. Moreover, amidst all the 'Ands', the Poet includes the tendency to misrepresent 'simple-Truth' as 'Simplicity' and reiterates the lesson from *152* in the Mistress sequence that even the 'purest faith' can be 'forsworn'.

In the Poet's audit of idealistic expectations, we hear that 'Simple-Truth' is the everyday determination of true and false through language. The Poet insists truth as saying should not be confused with 'Simplicity' or overly idealistic attempts to associate truth with the singular sensations or emotions generated within the mind. Such sensations are a form of beauty. The couplet reflects that the Poet's 'death' would 'leave' the youth 'alone' to face the consequences of being 'alone' without an opportunity to appreciate the logic of increase that drives the oppositional dynamic of language or truth.

We hear Shakespeare's Poet explain what he means by truth and why his understanding of truth conforms to human nature rooted in nature. Along with the 'painted beauty' he heralds in *21* and 'beauty's form' in *24*, which he describes in terms of a 'Painter' and his imagination, he continues to convey to the Master Mistress what he has learnt from the Mistress about sensory beauty and the logic of truth or language. He wants the youth to grasp the implications of confusing beauty as incoming sensations with truth as saying and beauty as art or poetry.

In the next sonnet to mention truth, *69*, the Poet relates truth to beauty as poetry or art. He expands on the suggestion in *54* that the 'sweet ornament' of beauty is available in the Poet's verse. The Poet uses the dynamic of truth or saying to evoke the form of beauty associated with poetry and art. Humankind expresses this beauty in verse or paint or music.

In 69, we hear the Poet claim that giving excessive value to the 'bare truth' of appearance creates a problem. <snt-69.3-4> What is taken for 'truth' by the romantic 'heart' or idealizing 'soul' is simplistic, and 66 dismisses the simplistic view of truth. We hear the Poet insist on the use

> All tongues (the voice of souls) give thee that due,
> Uttering bare truth, even so as foes Commend.
> 69.3-4

of truth as the process of saying that this is or this is not (as in 137). To the youth's 'fair flowers' (or his beauteous appearance) the Poet adds 'the rank smell of weeds' emanating from his denatured idealising mind because it is sundered from grounded logic.

Sonnet 72, which mentions only truth, reasserts the conditional status of verse. <snt.72.5-8> The Poet asks the youth to forget him and his works because in themselves they mean nothing. His love has meaning only in the context of natural logic – and that is the 'niggard truth' or the basis of all that can be said. In keeping with the logic of truth, if the youth devises 'some virtuous lie' then that would be truer to the Poet's worth than the overwrought worth the

> Unless you would devise some virtuous lie,
> To do more for me than mine own desert,
> And hang more praise upon deceased I,
> Than niggard truth would willingly impart.
> 72.5-8

youth and others place on the singular sensations evoked by a 'word'.

Then, 96 lays out the logic of saying true and false when it contrasts those who 'say thy fault is youth' and those who 'say thy grace is youth'. <snt_96.1-4> The youth's idealistic errors of judgment become 'translated' into simplistic 'truths' and are then taken for 'true things'. <snt_96.7-8>

> Some say thy fault is youth, some wantonness,
> Some say thy grace is youth and gentle sport,
> Both grace and faults are loved of more and less:
> Thou mak'st faults graces, that to thee resort:
> 96.1-4

> So are those errors that in thee are seen,
> To truths translated, and for true things deemed.
> 96.7-8

He would not be the first idealistic youth to lead 'gazers' away by disguising his wolfish corruption of truth as a 'Lamb'. We hear Shakespeare invoking the biblical Christ. Again, the Poet acknowledges the youth's error is one the Poet made himself when adolescent, so his argument is full of sympathy for the untutored mind.

The next truth sonnet relates love to the lessons the Poet gives the Master Mistress in truth and beauty. Sonnet 101 distinguishes specifically between 'truth' as a process of discrimination through writing ('pencil') and 'beauty' as an artistic effect based in 'colour'. It criticises those who 'kill' truth by dissociating it from language when they confuse truth with beauty or the imaginary ideals the mind creates within itself.

Better still, in 101 the Poet associates the correct appreciation of truth and beauty with the nature-based love he argues for and gives expression to in his sonnets. <snt_101.1-8> He insists his 'love depends' on the correct understanding of 'truth and

> Oh truant Muse what shall be thy amends,
> For thy neglect of truth in beauty died?
> Both truth and beauty on my love depends:
> So dost thou too, and therein dignified:
> Make answer Muse, wilt thou not haply say
> Truth needs no colour with his colour fixed,
> Beauty no pencil, beauty's truth to lay:
> But best is best, if never intermixed. 101.1-8

beauty'. At this stage in the male sequence, we reach the inner workings of the mind where the deepest love would flourish freely if only the Master Mistress could understand the natural workings of the mind.

Sonnet *110* confirms the benefits of experiencing 'love' in the natural light of 'truth'. If the Poet has 'looked on truth askance and strangely', it enables him to experience 'love' at a depth and greater consistency than that wrongly attributed to the male God. <snt_110.5-8> Instead

> Most true it is, that I have looked on truth
> Askance and strangely: But by all above,
> These blenches gave my heart another youth,
> And worse essays proved thee my best of love,
> 110.5-8

of being a 'slave' to a male God pontificating from the heavens (as *58* recounts) his experience is the natural equivalent to a 'God in love'.

No wonder Shakespeare's readers feel for the depth of love expressed in Q yet cannot understand its genesis and development. Shakespeare shows how to advance beyond the overwrought emotions of youthful idealism to its mature experience and expression under the tutelage of the Master Mistress by the Poet.

We recall how swearing is basic to the truth dynamic in the female sequence. Swearing establishes the interplay between true and false because a sworn oath can be forsworn. In contrast, swearing is not the primary focus of the male sequence. Sonnets that mention the word truth focus deliberately on the dynamic of saying. Swear, swears or swearing are not mentioned although forsworn appears in *66* and *88*, and vow and vows in *89*, *115* and *123* – far fewer times proportionately than in the female sequence.

Instead (as mentioned above) argument, a word not used in the female sonnets, occurs six times (*38*, *76*, *79*, *100*, *103* and *105*). <snt_argument> The Poet argues continually with the male youth throughout the sequence. This is in keeping with the attitude of instruction adopted by the Poet toward the recalcitrant male. The use of truth as argument is evident in the number of logical connectives between pairs or groups of sonnets and the extended arguments of the increase group (*1* to *14*), the increase to poetry group (*15* to *19*) and the alien Poet group (*78* to *86*).

> While thou dost breathe that pour'st into my verse,
> Thine own sweet argument, too excellent,   38.2-3
> O know sweet love I always write of you,
> And you and love are still my argument:
> 76.9-10
> I grant (sweet love) thy lovely argument
> Deserves the travail of a worthier pen,
> 79.5-6
> And gives thy pen both skill and argument.
> 100.8
> The argument all bare is of more worth
> Than when it hath my added praise beside.
> 103.3-4
> Fair, kind, and true, is all my argument,
> Fair, kind and true, varying to other words,
> 105.9-10
>
> Argument

Shakespeare's persistent explanation of the logic of truth as saying in both sequences argues for its structural status in Q. Beauty and truth in the female sequence and truth and beauty in the male sequence relate directly to the givens of nature, the female/male dynamic and increase. The evidence suggests love is free when truth and beauty are grounded in the natural preconditions.

28: Showing the youth the mythic trajectory of art and poetry

We see the Poet learning the truth dynamic of swearing and forswearing from the female in her sequence and then applying it in the male sequence. What happens to the singularity of incoming sensations the Poet calls beauty in the female sonnets, when we examine beauty in the male sonnets from *20* to *126*?

An analysis of the word beauty in *20* to *126* reveals around one-third continue to refer to sensory appearance. The other two-thirds refer to the form of beauty identified as art in *14* <snt_14.9-11> and painted beauty in *21*. <snt_21.1-2>

> But from thine eies my knowledge I derive,
> And constant stars in them I read such art
> As truth and beauty shall together thrive
> 14.9-11

> So is it not with me as with that Muse,
> Stirred by a painted beauty to his verse,
> 21.1-2

As we consider the sonnets that mention beauty, we will need to explain Shakespeare's use of the same word beauty for two activities within the mind that are similar but distinct. Just what is the additional implication of beauty, which in the Mistress sequence means externally generated sensory impressions, when the Poet extends its use to refer to sensations such as intuitions and emotions evoked in the mind by ideas developed through language?

We hear Shakespeare insisting that incoming sensations and enminded sensations are both singular effects unmediated by thought. Because both forms of sensation have the same unbidden repercussion within the mind, he calls them both beauty.

From what we already know about the language dynamic of truth, combining the two forms of sensation under the one word beauty is far more exact than mis-calling beauty truth. The confusion is equivalent to misrepresenting female as male or feminine as masculine.

To gain an insight into the deeper faculties of the mind, we begin with *24*. <snt_24.1-14> There beauty represents sensations in the mind induced by the Poet's reflections on the youth's beauty. No other sonnet in the male sequence focuses so resolutely on the beauty that the mind generates and displays. Sonnet *24* prepares us for instances in the male sonnets of artistic practice where beauty refers to aesthetic effects occurring in the human mind.

> Mine eye hath played the painter and hath steeld,
> Thy beauty's form in table of my heart,
> My body is the frame wherein 'tis held,
> And perspective it is best Painter's art.
> For through the Painter must you see his skill,
> To find where your true Image pictur'd lies,
> Which in my bosom's shop is hanging still,
> That hath his windows glazed with thine eyes:
> Now see what good-turns eyes for eies have done,
> Mine eyes have drawn thy shape, and thine for me
> Are windows to my breast, where-through the Sun
> Delights to peep, to gaze therein on thee.
>   Yet eyes this cunning want to grace their art
>   They draw but what they see, know not the heart.
> 24.1-14

However, along with *24*'s focus on painted beauty, the word 'cunning' in the couplet of *24* reminds us Shakespeare interconnects the eyes of the mind – both sensory and imaginative – with the sexual eye of either sex. Sonnet *24* pictures for the Master Mistress the easy inter-penetrability of body and mind that distinguishes Shakespeare's all-embracing nature-based love from simplistic body-based hedonistic love or mind-based Platonic love.

Then, in 53, the Poet evokes a lost-in-time Platonic world where 'on Helen's cheek all art of beauty set'. <snt_53.7-8> This is

> On Helen's cheek all art of beauty set,
> And you in Grecian tires are painted new:
> 53.7-8

followed in 54 by the 'sweet ornament which truth doth give'. <snt_54.1-2> When we turn to 62, it associates beauty

> Oh how much more doth beauty beauteous seem,
> By that sweet ornament which truth doth give,
> 54.1-2

with art when it says 'painting my age with beauty of thy days'. <snt_62.13-14> Then 63 associates beauty with poetic effects when

> T'is thee (my self) that for my self I praise,
> Painting my age with beauty of thy days.
> 62.13-14

it intones 'his beauty in these black lines be seen'. The colours and forms of art and poetry enliven Shakespeare's sonnets.

> My sweet love's beauty, though my lover's life.
> His beauty shall in these black lines be seen,
> 63.12-13

<snt_63.12-13>

The Poet relates love directly to his poetry in 65. He follows its references to painting and writing by

> Or who his spoil or beauty can forbid?
> O none, unless this miracle have might,
> That in black ink my love may still shine bright.
> 65.12-14

talking of 'beauty' where 'in black ink my love may still shine bright'. <snt_65.12-14> Sonnet 67 retrenches when it characterises as 'false painting' the bankrupt shadows of mind-based imitations of nature's wealth.

> Why should false painting imitate his cheek,
> And steal dead seeing of his living hue?
> Why should poor beauty indirectly seek
> Roses of shadow, since his Rose is true?
> 67.5-8

<snt_67.5-8> This is seconded by 68's dismissal of male-based ideals as 'false Art' contrary to nature-based beauty. <snt_68.13-14>

Sonnet 77 reiterates the intimacy of this mind-based form of beauty and poetry with its 'commit to these waste blacks' because, like

> And him as for a map doth Nature store,
> To show false Art what beauty was of yore.
> 68.13-14

'children nursed', ideas can be 'delivered from thy brain' onto the pages of a 'book'. <snt_77.1-4> In the alien Poet group, 79 laments the robbery that is false art as the Poet accuses the inferior Poet of mimicking the physical appearance of the youth – 'from thy behaviour, beauty doth

> Thy glass will show thee how thy beauties were,
> Thy dial how thy precious minutes waste,
> The vacant leaves thy mind's imprint will bear,
> And of this book, this learning mayst thou taste.
> 77.1-4

he give' – rather than evoking the depths of youth's 'gentle grace'. <snt_79.9-10>

Also within the nine alien Poet

> He lends thee virtue, and he stole that word,
> From thy behaviour, beauty doth he give
> 79.9-10

sonnets, 83 emphasises the relationship between 'speaking' and 'silence' – or saying and not saying. <snt_83.11-14> Again, the Poet rejects the false 'painting' (painting is mentioned twice in the first two lines) that mimics the appearance of the ideal young man in favour of the 'worth' that in you 'doth grow'. The natural extension of the youth's appearance through increase into the emotive operations of the mind is the only way to generate deeply felt beauty,

> For I impair not beauty being mute,
> When others would give life, and bring a tomb.
> There lives more life in one of your fair eyes,
> Than both your Poets can in praise devise.
> 83.11-14

and hence love, which is beyond compare.

Then, 106 makes a connection not seen in the Mistress sequence when it relates beauty unfavourably to 'making beautiful old rhyme'. <snt_106.3-6> The long-lost 'beauty' the Poet seeks in the rude youth predates the 'divining eyes' of the overly civilised mind. To add to the emphasis on beauty as poetry or art, *115* goes further with its dismissive 'tan sacred beauty'. <snt_115.7-8> The Poet discounts imaginary religious love by reminding us of the 'millioned accidents' of increase that 'creep in twixt vows' disrupting celibacy or arranged marriages.

> And beauty making beautiful old rhyme,
> In praise of Ladies dead, and lovely Knights,
> Then in the blazon of sweet beauty's best,
> Of hand, of foot, of lip, of eye, of brow, 106.3-6

> Tan sacred beauty, blunt the sharp'st intents,
> Divert strong minds to th'course of alt'ring things: 115.7-8

There are other sonnets interspersed throughout the Poet's lesson to the male youth that do not mention the word beauty yet, like the beauty sonnets, they refer to sensations that either make themselves apparent only in the mind or when they are transposed into poetry or art. In *31* we see the word 'images', in *47* 'thy picture', in *59* 'your image in some antique book', and in *61* 'thy image'. Sonnet *78* emphasises the importance of inner sensations for all humankind when the Poet says the male youth is 'all my art'. <snt_beautyinimagesetc>

> Their images I loved, I view in thee,
> 31.13
> With my love's picture then my eye doth feast,
> And to the painted banquet bids my heart:
> 47.5-6
> Show me your image in some antique book,
> Since mind at first in character was done.
> 59.7-8
> Is it thy will, thy Image should keep open
> My heavy eielids to the weary night? 61.1-2
> But thou art all my art, and dost advance
> 78.13
> And their gross painting might be better used,
> 82.13
> Which is not mixed with seconds, knows no art,
> But mutual render only me for thee. 125.11-12
>
> Images of beauty as art

In *82* of the alien Poet group, the Poet even talks of 'gross painting' and associates it with the 'strained...Rhetoric' in the 'dedicated words which writers use'. In *125*, we hear the Poet say he 'knows no art but mutual render' that comes from uncompromised love – 'only me for thee'. He contrasts the natural expression of love in his set with the pomp and architecture built by those preening themselves for 'eternity'. Again the Poet rejects the 'form and favour' propping up a supposed 'true soul'. Instead, he argues for the direct line of descent without 'seconds' from nature into the depths of the human mind.

We see Shakespeare considering a variety of singular artistic and poetic effects under beauty throughout the male sequence. This contrasts with the more specific focus on the five senses in the early sonnets of the female sequence. Although the Poet reiterates his findings about sensory beauty from the female in the male sequence for the purpose of instruction, there is now a significant emphasis on beauty as poetry and art.

Shakespeare seems to accept that the most difficult aspect of his philosophy to adapt to is his use of the same word beauty for two apparently different functions of the mind. Once we appreciate the common element between the immediacy of incoming sensory impressions and the immediacy of sensations or emotions that arise unbidden in our minds is their unmediated status, we can see his reasoning is faultless.

Both forms of beauty, as Shakespeare uses them, have an unwilled directness and so are beyond judgment or approbation. Outright beauty is the appropriate word rather than black or foul – as *127* explains. **<snt_127.1-8>** Both forms of sensation are singular effects. Shakespeare's insight is that both can be represented by the same word beauty wherever they appear in his sonnets.

In the old age black was not counted fair,
Or if it were it bore not beauty's name:
But now is black beauty's successive heir,
And Beauty slandered with a bastard shame,
For since each hand has put on Nature's power,
Fairing the foul with Art's false borrowed face,
Sweet beauty hath no name no holy bower,
But is profaned, if not lives in disgrace. 127.1-8

Shakespeare appears to say that deep and abiding love is most constant for those who appreciate the isomorphism between the physical preconditions of nature with its sexual dynamic that give the set of sonnets their external structure and the mind-based possibilities of beauty/truth/beauty in the female and male sequences that provide the internal structure. Only when he bases his understanding in nature and the sexual dynamic as the givens that determine the relationship of incoming sensations to the logic of language and the sensations or emotions of the mind can he give his lively experience and understanding of love its deepest possible expression.

The significance of the concepts of beauty, truth and beauty for Shakespeare's philosophy is asserting its structural logic. We can see that one form of beauty refers to incoming sensations, truth refers to any form of saying and the other form of beauty refers to internal sensations in the mind. Moreover, they have their genesis in the sexual dynamic in nature.

Chapter 9: The swearing and forswearing of mind-based conventions

How does the structural dynamic of beauty/truth/beauty across the two sequences relate to other concepts that appear in the set such as time, immortality, soul, music and even the Rose and the Muse? Why do most commentators miss the significance of the truth and beauty patterns in their rush to prioritise the other concepts?

29: Swearing and arguing

The whole set as nature and the two sequences representing female and male emerge as the unarguable givens structuring the sonnet set. Then follow the increase argument and the five sonnets that introduce writing. In the female sequence, the Poet explores the significance of sensory beauty and language as truth before returning to the male sequence to apply truth as argument and beauty as poetry.

Beauty, truth and beauty emerge from the two sequences as the logical dispositions that structure the human mind. Because the Poet accepts that the preconditions of nature and the female/male dynamic are beyond debate, he is free to deploy the sonnets to beauty and truth in the female sequence and those to truth and beauty in the male sequence as required.

Once the Poet anchors the possibility of swearing/forswearing – and argument – in natural logic, he can discuss the implications of promulgating religious, political or societal conventions or laws. In Q's natural philosophy, the beauty/truth/beauty dynamic provides the logical basis for concepts such as time, God or style. The dynamic also explains why the Muse occurs only in the male sequence in association with verse and argument and why the Poet confines the discussion about writing and art to the male sonnets.

The common denominator amongst the conceits or laws is their mind-based status established through the logic of language or the dynamic of swearing. Crucially, all such conventions are capable of being dis-established through argument or forswearing. For instance, temporal conventions make natural time intervals such as the day, month and year calculable as minutes, hours and weeks. Sonnet *12* talks of time as computation and *60* addresses the illusion of time running out. <snt_time>

When I do count the clock that tells the time,
12.1
So do our minutes hasten to their end, 60.2
Time sonnets

To the conventions that allow an accurate measurement of time, Shakespeare adds those that invert the natural order. The arrangement of the 154 sonnets challenges the first three commandments of Mosaic Law. The three commandments conventionalise the usurpation of natural female priority by a male God culture to embed patriarchal power.

Shakespeare recognises similarly that belief in an immortal soul conventionalises the logic of increase. In each case, the written word cements in place conventions established through language's capacity to generate mind-based constructs.

Shakespeare shows how to recognise and re-evaluate conventions in sonnets like *38*. There he challenges the status of the nine Greek Muses who conventionalise creative capacities. He adds his 'tenth Muse' because she, as the female Muse answerable to nature only, reasserts the natural precursor relationship of female to male. <snt_38.9-12>

> Be thou the tenth Muse, ten times more in worth
> Than those old nine which rhymers invocate,
> And he that calls on thee, let him bring forth
> Eternal numbers to out-live long date. 38.9-12

Shakespeare distinguishes between the conventions of writing that dress 'old words new' and the nonconventional 'argument' of love. <snt_76_9-14>

> O know sweet love I always write of you,
> And you and love are still my argument:
> So all my best is dressing old words new,
> Spending again what is already spent:
> For as the Sun is daily new and old,
> So is my love still telling what is told. '
> 76.9-14

We can reflect on the case of T. S. Eliot. Eliot, an avowed Christian, accuses Shakespeare of having a 'rag-bag philosophy' and no system of morals. [note 2] Eliot much prefers the 'serious philosophy' of Dante's conventionalised Christian morality apparent in the hierarchical *Divine Comedy*. By buying into convention-bound morality supported by self-serving commandments, Eliot is at odds with Shakespeare's nature-based philosophy.

Moreover, the deeply bedded misogyny behind the Ten Commandments makes them 'murdrous', (9) as universal norms for personal, social and political justice. Little wonder Eliot cannot see why Shakespeare refuses to accept the overly mind-based laws of biblical morality.

Amidst the religious mayhem of the Reformation, Shakespeare explains how the short-term benefits of male-based beliefs belie the long-term evil they impose on nature and natural values. He is particularly conscious of their effect on women's rights and the desire to achieve mature love.

30: Keeping time

The sonnet philosophy establishes the logical preconditions for the various functions of the human mind, with the preconditions providing the logical basis for the arguments from *20/21* onwards. Once Shakespeare's Poet sets in place the basic givens, he needs no further ordering within *20* to *126* to delineate the plethora of ideas the mind generates.

Once we move from nature and the female and male and beyond the general characteristics of the mind called truth and beauty, we enter the world of constructs, laws and axioms characteristic of the human mind. These constructs, such as imaginary ideals or goddesses and gods generated in the mind, are products of human language.

Typical constructs are the conventions of time, such as weeks, hours and minutes. Because nature and the female/male priority are not constructs, the word time appears in the Master Mistress sequence but is

```
        10 ◄─────12 sets of 12 = 144─────► 153
sonnets  10 22 34 46 58 70 82 94 106 118 130 142   sonnet
1 to 9  ◄─────────────────────────────────►  154

1       12              60                    154
        Pattern of 12s in the set
```

absent from the Mistress sequence. Similarly, the pattern of 12s in the set do not coincide with the boundaries of the set. They fall short by nine (9) sonnets at the beginning of the set and by one (1) sonnet at the end. <diagram_patternof12s>

Nature and measured intervals of time are logically different entities. The Poet confirms this in 126 where nature disgraces 'time' and kills constructs like the 'minute' on the way to bringing the 'Boy' to a final 'audit'. <snt_126.5-12> When 'Nature' audits the Master Mistress in 126, it harks back to a similar injunction in 4, which mentions both 'Nature' and 'audit'.

If Nature (sovereign mistress over wrack)
As thou goest onwards still will pluck thee back,
She keeps thee to this purpose, that her skill.
May time disgrace, and wretched minute kill.
Yet fear her O thou minion of her pleasure,
She may detain, but not still keep her treasure.
Her *Audit* (though delayed) answered must be,
And her *Quietus* is to render thee.   126.5-12

Attempts to reorganise the 154 sonnets according to conceptual constructs such as time can only fail. Frustrated by their inability to understand the set, commentators decide the error lies with Q rather than with their preconceptions. To compensate, they alter, emend and reorder the sonnets at will.

When Shakespeare bases 44 and 45 on traditional categories of thought, he shows his awareness of the status of constructs. The two sonnets are unique in considering the Aristotelian elements of earth, water, air and fire. Sonnet 44 associates 'earth' and 'water' with the Poet and 45 aligns 'air' and 'fire' with the youth. <snt_aristotleelements> Together the two sonnets argue that the separation of the elements into twos leads to sadness and their reunion ensures gladness.

But that so much of earth and water wrought,
                                    44.11

Yet the conceit has no force because earth, water, air and fire merely
conventionalise mercurial human dispositions. Aristotle ignores the logical
preconditions of female and male in
nature. The four elements are arbitrary
categories that do not have the same

The other two, slight air, and purging fire,...
My life being made of four, with two alone,
Sinks down to death, oppressed with melancholy.
Until lives' composition be recured,
By those swift messengers returned from thee,
Who even but now come back again assured,
Of their fair health, recounting it to me. 45.1&7-12
                    Aristotle's elements

logical rootedness as the givens of nature and the sexual dynamic, which hold the conceptual world of Q together.

As the only two sonnets to consider traditional philosophical categories, they acknowledge Aristotle's nature-based philosophy but parody its elemental constructs. The Aristotelian conventions have no explanatory power for the logic of human understanding and emotions. Shakespeare critiques Aristotle's four arbitrary categories by reasserting the natural female/male dynamic as the logical basis of thought.

There are further sonnets besides 12 and 60 where 'time' interrupts the natural continuity of Shakespeare's verse. The Poet considers the cultural implications of time – and eternity – in 123 to 126. <snt_123.1-4> <snt_124.1-3> <snt_125.1-4> Significantly, after

No! Time, thou shalt not boast that I do change,
Thy pyramids built up with newer might
To me are nothing novel, nothing strange,
They are but dressings of a former sight: 123.1-4

If my dear love were but the child of state,   *126* the word time does not appear in the
It might for fortune's bastard be unfathered, female sequence.
As subject to time's love, or to time's hate,
124.1-3

The time intervals mentioned in the sonnets, such as minutes, hours, and the relation of 12s, are all precise human numerical constructs without natural correlates. The day, month, the cycle of seasons and the annual solar cycle are natural pulses that refuse to comply with the regularity expected of temporal instruments.

Wer't ought to me I bore the canopy,
With my extern the outward honoring,
Or laid great bases for eternity,
Which proves more short than waste or ruining?
125.1-4

31: Natural music

Although the intervals of time such as minutes and hours are numerical constructs, there is in music a natural interval of eight beats to the octave. The two sonnets in *Q* from which this natural beat emanates are *8* and *128*. They are the only two specifically music sonnets in the set. Both mention music twice in their first line and both employ a single instrument throughout to convey their content. Sonnet *8* features a stringed instrument and *128* a keyed instrument.

Music to hear, why hear'st thou music sadly,...
Mark how one string sweet husband to an other,
8.1&10

How oft when thou my music music playst,
Upon that blessed wood whose motion sounds
128.1-2

Music sonnets

<snt_musicsonnets>

Just as *12* and *60* are dedicated time sonnets, *8* and *128* are dedicated music sonnets. The difference is that the time sonnets offer a beat constructed for human computation (a 'clock') while the music sonnets provide a beat predating human machinations (the octave).

Significantly, although the Mistress sequence does not mention the word time, it mentions music three times, with the third mention in *130*. <snt_130.9-10> Sonnet *130*, as the sonnet devoted to incoming sensations, confirms that Shakespeare recognises music as an unmediated sensory effect within nature.

I love to hear her speak, yet well I know,
That Music hath a far more pleasing sound:
130.9-10

Those lips that Love's own hand did make,
Breathed forth that sound that said I hate,
To me that languished for her sake:
But when she saw my woeful state,
Straight in her heart did mercy come,
Chiding that tongue that ever sweet,
Was used in giving gentle doom:
And taught it thus anew to greet:
I hate she altered with an end,
That followed it as gentle day,
Doth follow night who like a fiend
From heaven to hell is flown away.
  I hate, from hate away she threw,
  And saved my life saying not you. 145.1-14

If the time structure in the sonnets is evident in the 12 groups of 12 sonnets from *10* to *153*, is there a similar pattern for music? Of the three irregular sonnets in Q, *145* differs from every other sonnet in having eight syllables per line rather than the regular ten syllables. <snt_145.1-14> Does its litany of eight-syllable lines indicate a pattern based on the octave for a music structure within the set?

Moreover, with the pun on Anne Hathaway in *145*, does Shakespeare give her an aural connection to the logic of music out of the interval of eights? We know *136* names Will as the Poet of the set. If *145* identifies Anne Hathaway, then *136* identifies Shakespeare. When we sum *136* and *145* numerologically, they both form unities – as do the first and last sonnets of the Mistress sequence, *127* and *154*.

$$136 = 1+3+6 = 10 = 1+0 = 1$$
$$145 = 1+4+5 = 10 = 1+0 = 1$$

Between each of the sonnets that add to a unity there are eight sonnets, with *128* being the first of the eight sonnets between the unities of *127* and *136*. **<diagram_ mistressmusic>**

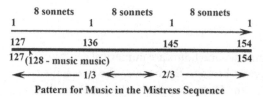

Pattern for Music in the Mistress Sequence

If we extend this pattern across the 154 sonnets, we see the musical pattern extends all the way from the first sonnet to the last with eight sonnets acting as musical intervals to the unitary bars separating them. Appropriately, the first music sonnet *8* falls within the first bar of the musical patterning. **<diagram_mastermistressmusic>**

Are we just imagining a pattern that has arisen out of our desire to make sense of the two music sonnets and *145*? When we realise the pattern coincides with the limits of the set from the first sonnet to *154*, there

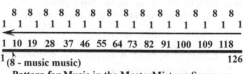

Pattern for Music in the MasterMistress Sequence

may be some justification for asserting the pattern is intentional. Compared to the conceptual construct of time, indicated by the pattern of 12s falling within the bounds of the set from *10* to *153*, the pattern of 8s makes the natural interval of the octave contiguous with the whole set as nature.

If there is an intentional pattern based on the octave in music encompassing the sonnets from the first to the last, it is also fitting that music rings out so clearly from *145*. It appears the octave, as an unmediated natural phenomenon, arises from the roots of the female sequence into the rest of the sonnets. In contrast, the conventions of time arise conditionally within the language capacity of the male sequence and fall short of encompassing the female sequence and nature.

32: The double-sided Rose

Two other convention-bound words stand out because they are always capitalised in Q. The word Rose appears twelve times and across both sequences whereas the word Muse appears seventeen times but only in the male sequence. The Muse does not occur in the female sequence because, while the female sequence examines the derivation of language from sensations, it does not address the logic of writing and poetry.

Shakespeare elevates the two words beyond their traditional symbolic use to give them a function in his exacting natural philosophy – as he does with the words truth and beauty. Amidst the more prosaic names of nature (sovereign mistress), Mistress, Master Mistress and Poet, the Rose symbolises aspects of the logic of beauty and the Muse aspects of the logic of truth.

Throughout *Q*, the word beauty is synonymous with the double-sidedness of the Rose. The Rose, with its associated canker or disease, represents the capacity of beauty to be attractive one moment and repugnant the next. The Muse by contrast is associated throughout the male sequence with the dynamic of saying or language whether it be verse, writing, argument, or articulate thought.

From fairest creatures we desire increase,
That thereby beauty's *Rose* might never die,
1.1-2

The first sonnet of the set associates beauty and *Rose* in its second line.

Roses have thorns, and silver fountains mud,
Clouds and eclipses stain both Moon and Sun,
And loathsome canker lives in sweetest bud.
35.2-4

<snt_1.1-2> In the context of the increase argument, it relates 'Beauty's *Rose*' to the Master Mistress' capacity to choose life through increase rather than death through idealised self-regard. The double-up of beauty and Rose is contrasted with the darkness of an individual's ideal-riven death, as if the flip side of beauty in extremis is unanticipated death.

The next mention of Rose is in 35. There the Poet states clearly its role in presenting the dual dynamic of beauty as shifting sensations that seem one minute sweet and the next 'loathsome'. <snt_35.2-4> Out of those sensations emerges the capacity to discriminate between 'faults' using language.

Oh how much more doth beauty beauteous seem,
By that sweet ornament which truth doth give,
The Rose looks fair, but fairer we it deem
For that sweet odour, which doth in it live:
The Canker blooms have full as deep a dye,
As the perfumed tincture of the Roses,
Hang on such thorns, and play as wantonly,
When summer's breath their masked buds discloses:
But for their virtue only is their show,
They live unwoo'd, and unrespected fade,
Die to themselves. Sweet Roses do not so,
Of their sweet deaths, are sweetest odours made:
  And so of you, beauteous and lovely youth,
  When that shall vade, by verse distils your truth.
54.1-14

Sonnet 54 has three mentions of the Rose, along with 'blooms' and 'buds', each of which refers to either a 'Sweet' or 'Canker' Rose. <snt_54.1-14> As we have seen, the derivation of 'truth' from 'beauty' in 54 is symbolised by the interplay between the two Roses with one dying to itself 'unwooed' and the other living on through its sweet odour. Shakespeare uses the imagery of two types of Rose to invoke the natural logic of the increase argument as the basis for truth and beauty.

Roses of shadow, since his Rose is true?
67.8

I have seen Roses damasked, red and white,
But no such Roses see I in her cheeks, 130.5-6

Then 67 <snt_67.8> and 130 <snt_130.5-6> have two Roses each. In 67 these are the 'Roses of shadow' and a Rose that is 'true', and 130 contrasts the pale cheeks of the Mistress with cheeks the colour of Roses. Significantly, sonnet 68 (which is logically connected to 67

When beauty lived and died as flowers do now, . . .
Ere beauty's dead fleece made another gay: . . .
Robbing no old to dress his beauty new, . . .
  To show false Art what beauty was of yore.
68.2,8,12,14

with a thus) mentions the word beauty four times. <snt_68.2,8,12,14>

With the Poet introducing 'Beauty's *Rose*' in the first increase sonnet, it is no surprise the mention of 'beauty' and 'Rose' in *67* is followed by the theme of increase in *68* with its mentions of 'born' and 'store'. Store – Shakespeare's synonym for increase – occurs in both *67* and *68*. The intimate association of the Rose with increase reminds us of the common use of the Rose as a symbol for the sexual organs of either female or male.

Shakespeare reinforces the connection with the anagram from Rose to Eros, the Greek God of love. He parenthesises the whole set with Rose/(Eros) appearing in the first sonnet and the Roman equivalent of Eros, Cupid the 'little Love-God', reinforcing the erotic logic of language in *153* and *154*. By positioning such traditional symbols and characters within the natural logic of his sonnet philosophy, Shakespeare revitalises them.

33: The missing Muse

When appraising the role of the Muse in the male sequence, we note three sonnets, *38*, *100* and *101*, mention the Muse three times each.

Sonnet *100* addresses the role of the Muse as the advocate for a 'pen' that has both 'skill and argument'. <snt_100.1-14> The Poet encourages the Muse of the Master Mistress to lift her standards from 'worthless song' to, if necessary, the level of 'Satire' (as a fully intentional process of writing). Only then can poetry be a worthy basis of 'fame' in the face of death.

Where art thou Muse that thou forget'st so long,
To speak of that which gives thee all thy might?
Spend'st thou thy fury on some worthless song,
Darkening thy power to lend base subjects light.
Return forgetful Muse, and straight redeem,
In gentle numbers time so idly spent,
Sing to the ear that doth thy lays esteem,
And gives thy pen both skill and argument.
Rise resty Muse, my love's sweet face survey,
If time have any wrinkle graven there,
If any, be a *Satire* to decay,
And make time's spoils despised every where.
  Give my love fame faster than time wastes life,
  So thou prevent'st his scythe, and crooked knife.
                                    100.1-14

Then, *101* addresses the confusion of truth and beauty that occurs when the Master Mistress' Muse neglects the logic of art and language based in increase. We hear that 'truth' is based not in 'colour' but in the language of the 'pencil', and 'beauty' is not based in language but in 'colour'. In *101*, the Poet suggests the traditional confusion of truth for beauty, when idealists treat truth instead of beauty as a singular effect, arises from the neglect of the natural basis of love (as *9* argues) and knowledge (as *14* insists). <snt_101.1-14>

Oh truant Muse what shall be thy amends,
For thy neglect of truth in beauty died?
Both truth and beauty on my love depends:
So dost thou too, and therein dignified:
Make answer Muse, wilt thou not haply say
Truth needs no colour with his colour fixed,
Beauty no pencil, beauty's truth to lay:
But best is best, if never intermixed.
Because he needs no praise, wilt thou be dumb?
Excuse not silence so, for't lies in thee,
To make him much out-live a gilded tomb:
And to be praised of ages yet to be.
  Then do thy office Muse, I teach thee how,
  To make him seem long hence, as he shows now.
                                    101.1-14

The Poet's determination to correct misconceptions about the role of the Muse, and by association misconceptions about the logic of language – and hence art – has its precursor in the other sonnet that mentions the Muse three times. Previous to *100* and *101*, *38* identifies the difference between the Master Mistress' nine errant Muses and the extra Muse the Poet requires for a logical understanding of truth and beauty and hence the pen's potential.

In *38*, the Poet suggests a further Muse supplement the 'nine' Muses of 'old' to make the number of Muses up to 'ten'. <snt_38.1-14>

How can my Muse want subject to invent
While thou dost breathe that pour'st into my verse,
Thine own sweet argument, too excellent,
For every vulgar paper to rehearse:
Oh give thy self the thanks if ought in me,
Worthy perusal stand against thy sight,
For who's so dumb that cannot write to thee,
When thou thy self dost give invention light?
Be thou the tenth Muse, ten times more in worth
Than those old nine which rhymers invocate,
And he that calls on thee, let him bring forth
Eternal numbers to out-live long date.
 If my slight Muse do please these curious days,
 The pain be mine, but thine shall be the praise.
                                                                          38.1-14

The conventional Greek Muses – Calliope (epic poetry), Clio (history), Euterpe (flute playing), Melpomene (tragedy), Terpsichore (dancing), Erato (the lyre), Polyhymnia (sacred song), Urania (astronomy), and Thalia (comedy) – reflect a more idealistic or romantic sensibility. To make them responsive to his heightened sense of understanding and expression the Poet proposes adding a Muse derived from the Mistress sequence of his nature-based sonnets.

He identifies the nine Muses with mere 'rhymers' or inferior Poets. To the nine Muses he adds his Muse who understands the dynamic of truth and beauty based in nature and increase argued for in Q.

The last line of *37* anticipates the arithmetic of *38* by suggesting the Poet would be ten times happier if that were the case. When we add the nine Muses to the one Muse in *38*, we get the anticipated 10:

$$9 + 1 = 10$$

In Q, the numbers 9 and 1 characterise the relationship between the male (9) and the female (1) in nature (1). There is also a 9 and 1 in the pattern of twelve sets of twelve sonnets between *10* and *153*. The 9 and 1 appear in *38* where the male is associated with the nine Muses of old and the female with the one extra Muse required for a mature understanding.

Shakespeare keeps his intellectual and emotional bearings by identifying nature and the sexual dynamic as constitutional of the beauty/truth/beauty dynamic in the human mind. He does not fall prey to misidentifying mind-bound conventions with the natural givens that underwrite the logic of language and art. His works ring true throughout the last 400 years because they are true to nature.

Because Shakespeare connects beauty/truth/beauty to the sexual dynamic in nature, he is able to discuss the concepts of time, soul, etc., against the backdrop of the logical workings of the human mind. He avoids the metaphysical problems that arise when thinkers treat such concepts as self-actuating entities.

Chapter 10: Insults to intelligence

What is Shakespeare's response to headstrong thinkers or poets who ignore the natural dynamic that drives the beauty/truth/beauty potentiality of the mind? What does he have to say about their unwitting entrapment in mind-based conventions? How does this affect the maturity of love such thinkers/poets are able to express in their writings?

34: The mire of poetic incomprehension

Before turning to the alien Poet group from *78* to *86*, we look again at *76*. It amplifies the concerns of *68* by reflecting and anticipating the reasons why *Q* remains impregnable to conventional analysis.

With something of a sexual allusion, the Poet wonders why his verse appears so 'barren' to those who expect 'variation or quick change', 'new found methods', or 'compounds strange'. <snt_76.1-8> He says he knows his verse is 'all one, and ever the same' with its 'invention in a noted weed'. Moreover, he uses the word 'barren' with irony because

> Why is my verse so barren of new pride?
> So far from variation or quick change?
> Why with the time do I not glance aside
> To new found methods, and to compounds strange?
> Why write I still all one, ever the same,
> And keep invention in a noted weed,
> That every word doth almost tell my name,
> Showing their birth, and where they did proceed?
>
> 76.1-8

not only does 'every word doth almost tell my name' the words show 'their birth' through his understanding based in nature and the increase dynamic.

The Poet predicts in *76* why so many fail to understand the contents of *Q*. He suggests prejudices distort the minds of previous commentators making them discount the natural philosophy on which he constructs his – and their – philosophic mapping.

There is irony in that a number of history's worthies perceive Shakespeare's sonnets as 'barren', 'a pother', etc. The Poet anticipates their failure to comprehend his deliberately un-'strange' verse. They refuse to see he bases his thinking in the 'birth' processes of increase in nature and it is from there that his verse proceeds.

The Poet's love for the Master Mistress, then, is the love arising out of *9*, which he develops into a natural regard worthy of mature human beings. He bases his ability to foster sound argument, and thence to love, on the natural philosophy evident in the structuring of the set.

Shakespeare knows his set, with its trajectory from birth to argument, exposes the false art or over-valued expectations of others. Their prejudices prevent them from appreciating the simple but all-encompassing structuring of *Q*.

Shakespeare's Poet addresses the problem in the nine sonnets *78* to *86*. He takes to task the alien or inferior writers who see themselves as his literary superiors. While the Poet praises the natural qualities of the Master Mistress, he criticises his tendency, like inferior Poets, to be distracted by false arts and changing fashions.

The alien Poet group addresses the aspect of the male unwilling to appreciate the Poet's nature-based arguments. The Poet reinforces the connection by dedicating nine sonnets to the alien Poet because there are numerologically 126 = 9 sonnets in the male sequence that contextualises them.

The nine sonnets stand apart from the rest of the set both because of their central location immediately after 77 and because of the Poet's sustained attack on a style of writing alien to the contents of Q. It is as if a vagrant pen infiltrates Q diluting the integrity of the Poet's verse.

There are frequent references to the Muse in the nine alien Poet sonnets. Both the Poet's Muse ('my Muse' who, according to 38, is the Muse that unifies the other nine Muses), and 'all the Muses' are mentioned in 78, 79, 82 and 85.

<snt_muses>

The focus, though, is on the Poet's Muse. The ignorance of her worth characterises the difference between the Poet's verse and that of other Poets. The other Poets exemplify the tendency of the male youth to be beguiled by rhyme and style rather than appreciate the Poet's nature-based contents – which leads to mature love.

Besides the five mentions of Muse and three mentions of Poet in the nine sonnets, they are replete with other references to speech and poetry. Words

So oft have I invoked thee for my Muse,
And found such fair assistance in my verse,
78.1-2
Whilst I alone did call upon thy aid,
My verse alone had all thy gentle grace,
But now my gracious numbers are decayed,
And my sick Muse doth give another place.
79.1-4
I grant thou wert not married to my Muse,
And therefore mayst without attaint o'er-look
The dedicated words which writers use 82.1-3
My tongue-tied Muse in manners holds her still,
While comments of your praise richly compiled,
Reserve their Character with golden quill,
And precious phrase by all the Muses filed.
85.1-4

Muses in Alien Poet group

such as verse, pen, poesy, arts, learning, numbers, argument, word, tongue, say, name, epitaph, read, book, rhetoric, painting, report, quill, tell, story, copy, writ, wit, character, phrase, thoughts, unlettered, clerk, speaking, intelligence, and line, abound.

At issue is the give-and-take of communication and particularly the processes of argument. After establishing the natural givens, the Poet's argument focuses on deriving beauty and truth from the female and the implications of truth and beauty for the male. The Poet encourages the idealising male to develop a consistent understanding of life and art for a deeper poetic achievement. He redirects the youth from idealistic/romantic love/hate to mature love.

Effectively, the 154 sonnets argue that all poets (achieved or inferior) are intimately part of nature with its sexual dynamic of female and male. They are dependent on increase and subject to the logical relation between beauty and truth and truth and beauty.

Although such Poets have no say over their genesis as female or male, they can ignore the logic of increase. If they do, they distort the natural dynamic of beauty as sensory input and truth as language and beauty as poetry or art and remain marooned in immature thought and emotion. Their capacity to discriminate between the natural world based in the sexual dynamic and the imaginary worlds created in the mind diminishes or is lost completely.

The Poet argues for the Master Mistress to take heed of the natural logic of poetry evident in the contents of his more mature verse. If the Master Mistress ignores the advice, his poetry will be as shallow as that of inferior Poets and subject to debilitating love/hate.

No wonder the Poet ring-fences alien Poets at the centre of his set and challenges their prejudices. They wrong the Master Mistress by ignoring his natural propensities. The tendency of inferior Poets to parasitise the external qualities or appearance of the Master Mistress results in poetry based in conceits and conventions, which will be remembered only for its style and rhyme or form (*125*). Shakespeare predicts commentators will likewise write mindless screeds about Q by speculating on a combination of biographical and stylistic trivia.

Amidst his criticism of the stylistic Poet's praise, Shakespeare interlaces reminders of the forces of life and love that should vivify their verse. When we hear the word pen mentioned five times in *78* to *86* we recall the pun on penis from *16* where a distinction is drawn between 'times pencil or my pupil pen'. <snt_16.10> The love the Poet feels for the Master Mistress is natural, while other Poets egotistically conflate their love with their poetic talents.

Which this (Time's pencil or my pupil pen)
16.10

There are also words evoking the increase argument, the increase to poetry group and the erotic allusions that abound from *20* onwards. Words such as store and nature and double entendres like proud, cheek, tongue, saucy bark, pride, boat, short quill, etc., frequent the nine sonnets. In this self-centred group that critiques other Poets who base their poetry on superficial appearances and stylistic touches of 'rhetoric', the words underline the Poet's contents. As the Poet asserts in *83*, he would prefer 'silence' in love to the display of self-loving 'ignorance' written up by such Poets. <snt_83.9-12>

This silence for my sin you did impute,
What shall be most my glory being dumb,
For I impair not beauty being mute,
When others would give life, and bring a tomb.
83.9-12

Sonnet *87*, the first sonnet after the last of the alien Poet sonnets, virtually cuts the self-serving group from its tenuous attachment to the middle of the set. It says 'farewell' to the 'dear' or costly consequences of flattering the Master Mistress (as in *31* 'dear' means costly). The distraction caused by their inflated praise threatens the youth's own sense of 'worth'. If indeed he believes he is a 'King' then he is 'in sleep' and needs a rude 'waking'. <snt_87.13-14>

Thus have I had thee as a dream doth flatter,
In sleep a King, but waking no such matter.
87.13-14

35: Festering flowers

The denial or neglect of the natural logic of increase, typified by the aspect of the Master Mistress mired in the nine alien Poet sonnets, is a constant theme underlying the truth and beauty sonnets to the male youth.

In the sonnets from *20* to *126*, there are occasions when the Poet draws on the admirable qualities of the youth or remembers his own youthful qualities. Frequently, though, the Poet lets loose a howl of indignation at the Master Mistress' intransigence. He recalls his own troubled path to maturity where the Mistress' hate of his excessive idealism in *145* only belatedly turns from 'hate' to 'love' when he accepts the logic of life.

Beyond *87*, in *94*, there is an unpleasant stench of festering lilies, while all around grow lusty smelling weeds. <snt_94.13-14> We previously encounter Roses infected with canker (in *35*, *54*, *67*, *95*, *99* and others) but nothing as rotten as these lilies. In *69*, the Poet encourages the

> For sweetest things turn sourest by their deeds,
> Lilies that fester, smell far worse than weeds.
> 94.13-14

youth to 'add the rank smell of weeds' to 'thy fair flower' because, after all, he 'doest common grow' or is based in nature.

Why in *94* should the Poet accuse the youth of being so fetid? In the first line the Poet encourages the youth to 'hurt' himself physically rather than remain like a 'stone' that cannot respond to the 'temptation' of increase. <snt_94.1-6>

> They that have power to hurt, and will do none,
> That do not do the thing, they most do show,
> Who moving others, are themselves as stone,
> Unmoved, cold, and to temptation slow:
> They rightly do inherit heaven's graces,
> And husband nature's riches from expence,
> 94.1-6

Just previously, in the couplet of *93*, the Poet compares the Master Mistress to 'Eve's apple' because his youthful 'beauty' conceals the 'false heart's history'. In Genesis, eating the beguiling fruit confers the knowledge of both good and evil. <snt_93.13-14> The youthful male falls for the apple scenario as did Adam (heaven's sweet 'creation'). He thinks his 'sweet virtue' is proof against the natural

> How much like *Eve's* apple doth thy beauty grow,
> If thy sweet virtue answer not thy show. 93.13-14

philosophy of life. 'Eve's apple', though, only has its seductive power because the male youth repudiates his inborn natural logic.

So, in *94*, the consequence of refusing the logic of increase and love leads to the Master Mistress inheriting 'heaven's graces' or the imaginary world of false promises. Such adolescent males keep 'nature's riches' to themselves because they overvalue the face-value of their looks while there are 'others' who have learnt how to manage their natural propensities. The joke is that unruly weeds, which revel in the logic of increase, have greater value than beautiful lilies that rot in their own self-love.

36: Truth and beauty with an echo of increase

Because nature generates the sexual dynamic, and consequently the increase argument and the dynamic of beauty, truth and beauty, it is the precondition for those logical entities. Together they provide the only organisation necessary to ensure the coherence of all the other issues addressed in the rest of the set. As the logical precondition, nature is the heartbeat that keeps the intellectual and emotional content of Shakespeare's sonnets coherent.

> Doth spot the beauty of thy budding name?
> 95.3
> To truths translated, and for true things deemed.
> 96.8
> The teeming Autumn big with rich increase,
> 97.6
> Beauty, truth, increase

Reading *94* – one of the

traditionally knottier sonnets – in terms of nature and increase may appear presumptuous. However, as we look ahead we see *95* mentions beauty, *96* mentions truths and *97* mentions increase. <snt_beautytruthincrease> We note also, immediately after *94* considers the 'fester' that can rot a bright lily, *95* continues the floral dichotomy by drawing attention to the double-sided Rose.

In *95*, the Poet addresses the cause of the rotting lilies. He recognises whatever degree the sonnets appear so bright, a 'canker', 'spot' or 'sin' is ever-present. The physical environment is not only dual-natured, the 'tongue that tells the story' is willing to 'praise' what is an 'ill report'. <snt_95.5-8> Effectively, the sensory qualities of beauty and its associated canker have their counterpart in the verbal qualities of the 'tongue' as saying or truth that represents a fact as true or false.

> That tongue that tells the story of thy days,
> (Making lascivious comments on thy sport)
> Cannot dispraise, but in a kind of praise,
> Naming thy name, blesses an ill report.
>
> 95.5-8

It seems the youth's beauty can temporarily blind the Poet's investigative eye to youth's vices and blots by confusing appearances for the sensory eye. The Poet warns the youth to 'take heed' of his privilege of beauty or, like the lily, his beauty will lose its 'edge'.

If *95* considers the logic of beauty for the male's mind, it also refers to his 'budding name' and alludes to the 'tongue that tells the story'. Sonnet *96* picks up on the language cues in *95* by announcing its intention to consider the logic of 'truths translated'. It opens with the dynamic of saying in its first two lines. <snt_96.1-2>

Sonnet *96* investigates the verbal distinction between what the Poet calls faults and graces. Both 'graces' and 'faults' are loved 'more or less' to the extent that 'some say' the Master Mistress' 'fault is youth' and some 'say' his 'grace is youth'.

> Some say thy fault is youth, some wantonness,
> Some say thy grace is youth and gentle sport,
>
> 96.1-2

The first two lines verbalise a distinction for all to see. 'Errors' and 'truths' are both issues for conscious discrimination by those who have the power to 'say'.

In language, words differ from shifting sensations that appear unbidden without conscious control. Whereas there are dictionaries for words, there are no dictionaries for sensations. Words such as 'Lamb' and 'Wolf' create points of discrimination. To confuse beauty (as sensation) with truth (as saying) is to reduce truth to the indiscriminateness of a sensation or to the unfocused experiences of those who *96* refers to as 'gazers'.

The Poet also advises the youth to be wary of relying on the truth dynamic to characterise an experience as irrevocably true – as if it was incapable of being false. It is the Poet's love (based in nature and the sexual dynamic) that provides him with the ability to 'report' on youth's real worth. <snt_96.9-14> With guidance, the youth will be capable of receiving and generating sensations and judging right from wrong with aplomb.

> How many Lambs might the stern Wolf betray,
> If like a Lamb he could his looks translate.
> How many gazers mightst thou lead away,
> If thou wouldst use the strength of all thy state?
> But do not so, I love thee in such sort,
> As thou being mine, mine is thy good report.
>
> 96.9-14

The mention of love in the couplet of *96* and the allusion to the youth as a persona of the Poet ('as thou being mine') leads directly onto *97*. <snt_97.1,6,11,14> There the Poet continues to advocate natural philosophy to the male youth. Sonnet 97 recalls the Winter mentioned in the increase sonnets. The Poet runs the Master Mistress through a gamut of three seasons

> How like a Winter hath my absence been . . .
> The teeming Autumn big with rich increase, . . .
> For Summer and his pleasures wait on thee, . . .
> That leaves look pale, dreading the Winter's near.
>
> 97.1,6,11,14

(Winter, Autumn and Summer) to reinforce youth's dependence on the perennial cycle of nature.

The Poet counters the tendency of the male to deny his logical connection to nature with its sexual dynamic, and imagine instead an ideal world or heaven where he would be free from his natural propensities. The Poet insists that increase or the bounty of nature is an inevitable part of being alive. By refusing the Poet's loving argument, the male youth voids the logic of Q.

Consistent with the sonnet logic, after 94 criticises wayward youth, 95, 96 and 97 provide evidence that the underlying content of Shakespeare's nature-based sonnets requires a coherent understanding of beauty, truth and increase.

Then, in a flourish of flowery rebuke, 98 and 99 open with the Spring that was absent from 97. Lilies, Roses, violets, marjoram, and more flowers proliferate as if to remind the Master Mistress of natural philosophy. Sonnet 99 also interests us because of its fifteen lines. As yet, there is no evidence from within the set to justify its extra line.

Shakespeare's objection to the tendency of lesser thinkers/poets to use flattery through false art to impress the male is equally a criticism of the abuse of the idealising capacity of the mind by male-based beliefs. The misrepresentation of truth and beauty and hence love ignores the natural dynamic and leads to mind-based confusion and conflict and debilitating self-love.

Chapter 11: The utility of the sonnet logic

What does the arrangement of beauty/truth/beauty within the 154 sonnets say of Shakespeare's philosophic insight? How does it accommodate the relationship between sexual types and gender dispositions if truth and beauty characterise so much of the mind's potential? And, what connection does Shakespeare draw between the contents of his set and contentedness?

37: Why should beauty and truth precede truth and beauty

Across the twenty-eight Mistress sonnets, the Poet explains first beauty and then truth. He begins in *127* to *137* by considering the effect the female has on his external senses. Then in *138* to *152*, we hear her in conversation with the Poet using/abusing language conventions with consummate pleasure. The earthy and witty Mistress along with her maturing Poet insist that understanding both the dynamic of incoming senses and the logic of language is crucial for achieving mature nature-based love.

In the male sequence, truth still retains its female sequence relationship to the logic of saying or tongue based on swearing and forswearing through language. There is difference, though, with the Poet now using the truth dynamic to produce frequent passages of focused argument.

The Poet also continues to consider the role of incoming sensations or beauty from the first sonnet to *126*. However, after the increase group, he adds another level of meaning when he uses the word beauty to refer to the evocative potential of poetry or art to generate singular sensations within the mind. The Poet uses words such as art, painting, image, and picture frequently in the male sequence to allude to or evoke the various forms of singular mind-generated internal sensations.

What is the philosophic significance of Shakespeare's clear separation of beauty and truth in *127* to *152* and the intermixing of truth and beauty in *14* to *126*?

From our investigations, the two quite distinct arrangements in the female and male sequences reflect the differences between externally incited sensations and internally generated mind-based language and mind-based sensations and intuitions. Shakespeare draws a clear distinction between sensations originating in the world about and the enlanguaging of those sensations in the mind along with the sensations originating consequently within the mind.

On one side of the logical divide, the five senses register sensory impressions from the world external to the human mind. On the other side, the mind generates both the dynamic of saying or language and the singularity of internal sensations. To reflect the mind's natural separation of incoming sensations from mind-based responses, Shakespeare separates beauty (sensory) and truth in the female sequence but does not separate truth and beauty (poetry) in the male sequence.

To reiterate, in *127* to *137* Shakespeare's Poet assesses objectively, or according to natural criteria, the sensory impression the female has on his organs of sight, hearing, smell, touch and taste. He recognises that the sources of sensory input to the mind are externally observable in nature and singular in effect.

In contrast, in *138* to *152* the Poet recognises that the language-based dynamic of thinking and speaking arises from the language faculty of the mind through sworn and forsworn mind-based conventions. Although language is a response primarily to sounds evoked by incoming sensations, language is not observable objectively throughout nature as are sensory sources.

The truth dynamic the Poet considers in *20* to *126* has the same logical status as the truth dynamic in *138* to *152*. The mind generates language based on swearing and forswearing to create the possibility of argument, which in turn challenges language conventions or constructs.

Similarly mind-based is the beauty dynamic of artistic, poetic and other intuitions the Poet considers in *20* to *126*. The deep sensations language evokes subsequently in the mind are purely psychological in origin so are not directly observable. They can be externalised, though, in the constructs of art, poetry and inventions.

Shakespeare, in his organization of the twenty-eight female sonnets, first accommodates the crucial insight that externally generated sensory impressions experienced as singular sensations in the mind (beauty) differ substantially from the ensuing true/false dynamic of swearing or forswearing ideas (truth). This is because words in language represent the unmediated or unbidden sensations through socially agreed conventions, which his Poet identifies with the swearing and forswearing of oaths, vows, etc.

The Poet separates beauty and truth in the female sequence because logically they represent different faculties of the mind. So, the separation of beauty and truth in the female sequence is a logical reflection of the natural distinction between external sensory impressions and language generated in the mind through human intercourse.

When we turn to truth and beauty in the male sonnets beginning at *20*, Shakespeare is now investigating primarily the internal workings of the mind. The Poet continues to examine the logic of truth he learns from the female in the second part of her sequence with the focus now more specifically on truth as language, argument, writing, etc. To complement the dynamic of truth he adds mind-derived singular effects such as poetry, imagination and intuition, which he also calls beauty.

In the female sequence, the Poet learns and matures the basics of beauty and truth by first observing the Mistress and then listening to her talk until he turns the hate engendered by his corrupt understanding of the human mind into love. Then, in the male sequence, his immediate task is to instruct the Master Mistress in the internal logic of the human mind in terms of truth and beauty so any idealistic youth can avoid mind-based delusions and excesses.

Hence, in the two sequences we face two different modes of address. In the female sequence there is the sensory and verbal give and take between two willing bodies/minds of the mature female and the maturing Poet. Because the female is inherently at one with nature and because the male is an offshoot of the female, it is only in her sequence that the Poet can explain the logic of sensory impressions from the world about.

In contrast, in the male sequence, there is no dialogue between the Poet and the adolescent male youth. Rather the Poet addresses a continuous stand-alone argument to the Master Mistress based on truth and beauty intermixed.

A measure of the difference between the two sequences is the engagement body to mind and mind to mind between the Poet and the Mistress compared to the deliberate engagement mind to mind only between the Poet and the Master Mistress. In *20*, the Poet tells the youth he cannot 'use' him physically and in *116* he offers only a 'marriage of true minds'.

Because the female is grounded naturally, she is the source of beauty and truth. On the contrary, because the male is marooned frequently within his own mind, it takes all the Poet's powers of persuasion to convince the youth he remains terminally at odds with the truth and beauty dynamic unless he recovers his natural relationship to his body and hence his natural connection to the female.

Shakespeare, as the all-embracing dramatist and poet, is well versed to have his Poet explain how language and the imagination develop from their logical basis in nature and the sexual dynamic of female and male. His Poet teaches the male youth that while the internal working of the human mind that produces language and art – with their continual interplay of sensations forming ideas and ideas forming sensations – is the most tantalising of the mind's functions, it can also be the most confounding for any adolescent thinker and/or lover.

Shakespeare's Poet is in no mood to equivocate as he lays down the logic of truth and beauty. By having a clear appreciation of what he calls truth and beauty, Shakespeare achieves an unmatched veracity and maturity of understanding and love in his sonnets and his plays and poems. The quality of love they discuss and evoke is unmatched because he refuses to base his understanding of language and art in conceptual constructs generated purely in the mind.

The incisiveness of Shakespeare's combined treatment of truth and beauty leads to his clarity and depth of poetic and dramatic expression. By basing his understanding in nature and the sexual dynamic of female and male, and by writing the greatest dramas and love sonnets of their kind, Shakespeare shows he understands how to generate and sustain effective poetry and art. Shakespeare's philosophic insights about beauty, truth and beauty set him apart from every other poet and philosopher.

38: Why does the female appear in the male sequence and he in hers

There are instances across the two sequences in *Q* where Shakespeare inter-relates the sexual division of female and male with the gender relationship of feminine and masculine. He infiltrates references to the female/feminine and male/masculine at localised hot spots in each other's sequences. What is the connection between 154-sonnet nature with its sexual division into 28 female sonnets and 126 male sonnets and the anomaly of the female appearing once in the male sequence and the male appearing twice in hers?

We saw the Poet introduce the gender relationship of feminine and masculine into the set in *20* where he calls the male the Master Mistress. Once the Poet establishes the gender characteristics of the mind in *20*, in *21* he can begin to instruct the youth in truth and beauty or the logic of purely mind-based attributes.

When the Poet calls the male Master Mistress in *20*, he identifies both his female/male biology and his feminine/masculine dispositions. <snt_20.1-8> Moreover, because the male is an offshoot of the female, then the name Master Mistress reminds us there are residual male dispositions in the female mind. In *20*, Shakespeare takes account of both the female/male sexual relations and the shared gender dispositions of feminine and masculine personae for both female and male.

A woman's face with nature's own hand painted,
Hast thou the Master Mistress of my passion,
A woman's gentle heart but not acquainted
With shifting change as is false women's fashion,
An eye more bright than theirs, less false in rolling:
Gilding the object where-upon it gazeth,
A man in hue all *Hews* in his controlling,
Which steals men's eyes and women's souls amazeth.
20.1-8

The 'woman' with whom the Poet begins *20* is effectively the default female in nature who creates the Master Mistress as a male with female characteristics. She is the source of the possibility of the female/male dynamic and the gender dispositions of mind.

After *20*, the Poet addresses the combined female/male and feminine/masculine dynamic three more times – in *41/42*, *133/134* and *143/144*. <snt_personaeinsequences> In *41/42*, a 'woman' enters the male sequence to correct male/masculine excesses. In *133/134* and *143/144*, the Poet's male 'friend' appears in the female sequence to pinpoint the issue of male/masculine immaturity. Effectively, the Poet recounts his own progress to maturity from youthful immaturity under the influence of the Mistress.

Hers by thy beauty tempting her to thee,
Thine by thy beauty being false to me.
41.13-14
But here's the joy, my friend and I are one,
Sweet flattery, then she loves but me alone.
42.13-14
Of him, my self, and thee I am forsaken,
A torment thrice three-fold thus to be crossed:
133.7-8
So now I have confessed that he is thine,
And I my self am mortgaged to thy will,
134.1-2
But if thou catch thy hope turn back to me:
And play the mother's part kiss me, be kind.
143.11-12
Two loves I have of comfort and despair,
Which like two spirits do suggest me still,
The better angel is a man right fair:
The worser spirit a woman coloured ill.
144.1-4
Female/male personae

Significantly, in the female sequence the male appears in two sonnets between the beauty sonnets *127* and *137* and in two sonnets between the truth sonnets *138* and *152*. The inclusion of the male in both the beauty and truth groups of the female sequence reinforces the logical division between incoming sensations and language discussed above.

The appearance of the male twice in the female sequence means the Mistress not only teaches the Poet the logic of beauty and truth, but also shows him how to bring his gender relationship of feminine and masculine into balance. The Mistress sustains her own unity and the unity of her offshoot males by maintaining the gender balance between feminine and masculine personae. Only when the Poet understands the sexual/gender relationships is he able to instruct immature males (or overly masculinised females who neglect their feminine persona) in the natural conditions to attain unity.

From the evidence of the four sonnets in the female sequence that mention the male, the Mistress censures the Master Mistress without mercy. If the Poet initially defends the male/masculine intransigence in those sonnets, he does so because both the Master Mistress and he are but personae of the Mistress – albeit one adolescent and the other mature.

We might expect, then, that *41/42* in the male sequence would be critical of the female. We find, though, it is the male youth who is again at odds with the female's nature-based maturity – even to the point of rape as *41* recounts. <snt_41.7-8>

> And when a woman woes, what woman's son,
> Will sourly leave her till he have prevailed.
> 41.7-8

Then, by the end of *42*, the Poet rejoices that the youth and he are effectively one and hence the Mistress loves him 'alone'. <snt_42.13-14> The surprising unity after such interpersonal harm reflects the Poet's insistence the male youth also represents the Poet's memory of his youthful self-indulgence.

> But here's the joy, my friend and I are one,
> Sweet flattery, then she loves but me alone.
> 42.13-14

Despite the apparent disunity of masculine and feminine sensibilities, the masculine and the feminine personae always revert to a one-to-one partnership because of the stability of the biological givens of the female/male dynamic within nature. As the nature-based Mistress encompasses both Poet and Master Mistress, then together they constitute her complete persona. Personae can be suppressed but not eradicated. They are no more reducible than the basic logic of female and male for human life and love.

To correct the imbalance in the feminine and masculine dispositions of the adolescent mind, Shakespeare addresses a sustained argument in the male sequence to counter male-based excesses. In *22*, immediately after *20/21*, the Poet addresses the relationship between the youth's male/masculine predicament and the Poet's own youthful recollections.

In *22*, the crucial issue is the maturation of the masculine persona. Because the Poet has experienced the level of immaturity he depicts in the male youth, he is in a position to instruct him with sympathy away from the debilitating excesses of adolescent male-based idealism toward mature love.

Importantly, in the male sequence Shakespeare's Poet as sonnet writer not only has the role to mature the immature mind of the male who refuses to develop his feminine sensibility (as the generic name Master Mistress suggests). Shakespeare also gives the Poet the role of correcting the overly masculinised mind of females.

Throughout the male sequence, the Poet is continually balancing feminine and masculine dispositions for mature understanding and love. As listed already, *36, 39, 40, 42, 48, 58, 62, 88, 96, 104, 108, 109, 113* and *122* all celebrate the relationship of the Poet and the Master Mistress both as separate sexual individuals and as gender aspects of the Poet's mind – and of the youth's mind or anyone's mind.

We now have a context for *41/42, 133/134* and *143/144*. They extend specifically the female/male sexuality of the Mistress, the Master Mistress and the Poet to include the feminine and masculine personae inherent in the male Poet's mind – or that of a female Poet. Throughout the sonnets, the dynamic of feminine and masculine personae is inherent in the minds of the Mistress and the Master Mistress and Poet.

Significantly, what emerges from the Poet's insights into the dependence of mind-based personae on the female/male dynamic is that nature structures the mind primarily according to gender dispositions and secondarily according to truth and beauty. Shakespeare is pre-eminently aware of the importance of the interrelationship of both for clarity of understanding and for naturally evolving mature love.

39: Predictive mapping

As we investigate Q, layer upon layer of structuring is becoming apparent. The inter-related features evolve from the logical preconditions of the whole set as nature and the two sequences as female and male.

The internal organisation of the set begins with the increase argument and continues through to the introduction of poetry or language and on to the relationship of beauty and truth in the female sequence and then truth and beauty in the male sequence. Secondary structuring is also visible around the octave of music and the concept of time.

The coherent and cross-referenced relationships are beginning to suggest a highly structured philosophy mapped into the 154 sonnets. And, thoughts of mapping recall the double mention of the word 'map' in 68.

In 68, the Poet employs a mapping that relates the logical patterns to the recurrent predicament of the male youth. <snt_68.1-14> Sonnet 68 reflects on a time when the youth's 'cheek' (read face or genitalia) provided a 'map' of a period before 'these bastard signs of fair' 'durst inhabit on a living brow'. The Poet reminds the youth that the logic of increase creates a genealogical map back to the times before 'bastard' ideas inverted the logical patterns of nature in which the female is default for the male.

Thus is his cheek the map of days out-worn,
When beauty lived and died as flowers do now,
Before these bastard signs of fair were born,
Or durst inhabit on a living brow:
Before the golden tresses of the dead,
The right of sepulchers, were shorn away,
To live a second life on second head,
Ere beauty's dead fleece made another gay:
In him those holy antique hours are seen,
Without all ornament, it self and true,
Making no summer of an other's green,
Robbing no old to dress his beauty new,
  And him as for a map doth Nature store,
  To show false Art what beauty was of yore.
68.1-14

Within 68, the Poet further characterises the youth's predicament in language recalling the conceits of religion. We hear references to 'golden tresses of the dead', 'sepulchers', 'second life on second head' and 'holy antique hours'. The Poet continually reiterates his understanding that 'Nature' maps the youth's originary status through 'store' (or increase). Only then can the natural logic of beauty show up the 'false art' of overwrought religious expectations.

The Poet both reminds us in 68 of the logical basis for the patterns already noted and gives reasons why the map of Q's layout has remained indecipherable for so long.

The whole set is founded on natural principles that structure, as if cartographically, the highest levels of cognition. Q remains beyond the understanding of readers because 'false arts' install the 'signs' of death ('sepulchers', etc.,) within the imaginary soul of humankind in place of the logic of life.

Here is a sonnet near the middle of the male sequence that predicts the type of mapping we have been uncovering. More significantly, the Poet relates it directly to the logical givens driving the mapping. He reiterates that nature, the female/male dynamic, store and the logic of beauty and truth and truth and beauty are the prerequisites for mature love and understanding.

40: The contents of the Sonnets

The natural givens identified above provide the logical basis for the range of topics discussed in *20* to *126*, with all their implications for human understanding and emotions. Throughout the commentary to date, the undeniable elements and their implications in Q have been referred to as the content or contents.

As the word content also occurs in all Shakespeare's plays, it comes as no surprise the word content appears in the first sonnet. <snt_1.11> There it combines both contentedness or optimised well-being with the meaningful content contained in the life potential of the female/male dynamic in nature.

> **Within thine own bud buriest thy content,**
> 1.11

The first sonnet accuses the male youth of denying himself life-affirming happiness by burying the life-force of increase under his mind-based idealisations. The Poet argues that only when a male (or overly masculinised female) learns to appreciate the content of his human potential can he be contented.

The first sonnet anticipates the use of the word contents in *55*. From *55*, a clear statement emerges of the subservience of mind-built structures to the organic process of increase in nature.

As *55* explains, although 'sluttish time' erodes the remnants of civilisations, the Poet's 'powerful rhyme' will prevail. Despite the ruins, the youth 'shall shine more bright' in the 'contents' of the Poet's verse. The Poet is adamant that neither 'marble' nor the 'guilded monument' hold the key to the genesis and persistence of the sonnet contents. <snt_55.1-4>

> **Not marble, nor the guilded monument,**
> **Of Princes shall out-live this powerful rhyme,**
> **But you shall shine more bright in these contents**
> **Than unswept stone, besmeared with sluttish time.**
> 55.1-4

However, this does not mean the youth will survive simply because the Poet mentions him in a book of poetry. If the ravages of time or 'war's quick fires' can destroy monuments they are just as likely to waste books.

Further on, the Poet gives the answer. His 'contents' validate the

> **When wasteful war shall *Statues* overturn,**
> **And broils root out the work of masonry,**
> **Nor *Mars* his sword, nor wars quick fire shall burn:**
> **The living record of your memory.**
> **'Gainst death, and all oblivious enmity**
> **Shall you pace forth, your praise shall still find room,**
> **Even in the eyes of all posterity**
> **That wear this world out to the ending doom.**
> **So till the judgment that yourself arise,**
> **You live in this, and dwell in lovers' eies.** 55.5-14

'living record' of the youth's 'memory' and the 'eyes of all posterity'. <snt_55.5-14>
Only because of increase can poetry memorialise the 'living record' of the youth's
natural beauty.

The Poet's assertion that increase in nature is pivotal to human understanding
and wellbeing challenges the traditional presumptions about the thinking behind
Q. The Poet even dissembles expectations that his rhyme or book is more important
than the contents he maps into the set. The surviving evidence of buildings or
words cannot reveal the mystery of Q. Rather, the Poet insists the contents of his
verse, or what his poetry conveys about the generative potential of humankind in
nature, is a prerequisite for human expression on stone or paper.

The 'contents' that do survive the vanquished artefacts of civilisation in 55 are
the 'living record' of the Master Mistress' memory kept alive by his acceptance of
the human need to invest in future generations. Shakespeare's Poet reminds us that
the basis for any civilising activity is the potential for increase in nature, because
everybody born is the beneficiary of increase.

The Poet connects the possibility of human achievement over time to his
'judgment' that the male youth needs to 'arise' beyond myopic self-loving. Only
then can he explore the love evident in the eye-to-eye contact with other bodies
and minds that informs the content of the first fourteen sonnets and leads lovers
to emotional maturity.

If we look ahead to 74, it reiterates the logic of 55 that the poetry of our
'ever-living' Poet 'contains' the basic dynamic of increase out of nature. <snt_74.1-
2&13-14> Echoing the double meaning of the word content from the first sonnet,

But be contented when that fell arrest,
Without all bail shall carry me away,....
The worth of that, is that which it contains,
And that is this, and this with thee remains.
74.1-2&13-14

74 begins 'but be contented...'. It reminds
the youth of the double meaning of the
word line introduced in the increase to
poetry group 15 to 19. The first meaning
is evident in 16 where 'the lines of life that

life repair' refer to the lineage of increase, which   **So should the lines of life that life repair**
is a natural dynamic in the momentum of life.   16.9
<snt_16.9>

Then in 18, in the next reference to line or lines, the word now has the
complementary meanings of both lines of life and lines of poetry. Sonnet 18
glows at the transition from the natural
When in eternal lines to time thou grow'st,   logic of increase to the logic of writing based
18.12   in increase. Its famous phrase, 'in eternal
lines to time thou grow'st', <snt_18.12> captures in a single verse the natural
interrelationship of both meanings of the word lines.

The same double concern appears in 74 where **My life hath in this line some interest,**
the Poet asserts 'my life hath in this line some   74.3
interest'. <snt_74.3> This is borne out when the Poet reflects that once his 'body'
is 'dead' then the 'worth' of his poetry is 'that which it contains'. Only when the
dedication's adventurer plumbs the Poet's contents can the male youth understand
what it is that 'with thee remains'.

The Poet again brings the Master Mistress eye-to-eye with the logic of his set based in nature with its genealogical lines of increase as a precondition for the realisation of the potential of his written lines of poetry for profound understanding and deep love.

The consistency across sensations and language, gender dispositions, body/ mind mapping and the depth of contents in Shakespeare's 154 sonnets suggests an unprecedented level of intentionality. Commentators have long suspected depths of meaning in Q, but have not accounted for its contents.

Chapter 12: Nature's audit

What can we say about those who sense a profound philosophy in Shakespeare's works but fail to discover the consistent patterns evident in his sonnets? Do the sonnets predict why many fail to plumb the relation between the love in Shakespeare's works and love in life?

41: Looking for paradise in Shakespeare

While incidental aspects of Q, such as the identity of 'T. T.', suggest external references, our significant findings derive from an internal analysis of the 154 sonnets. In contrast, most previous attempts to penetrate Q are driven by a missionary zeal to locate features that conform to male-based preconceptions. Such commentators hide their puzzlement about the nature of Shakespeare's philosophy by over-inflating a few sonnets as evidence of male-God belief. They hold up *18, 29, 30, 55, 65, 73, 106, 107, 116, 129 and 146* as promising heavenly returns.

If this be error and upon me proved,
I never writ, nor no man ever loved.
116.13-14

Some commentators narrow their focus onto *116* and *129*. They claim the two sonnets provide the key to the mystery of Q. Because such idealists want to hear a tribute to absolute love in *116* <snt_116.13-14> and a condemnation of absolute lust in *129*, <snt_129.1-2>

Th'expense of Spirit in a waste of shame
Is lust in action, and till action, lust
129.1-2

they claim to have located points of entry for a Christian interpretation of the set.

Yet, from our analysis of the evidence within Q, Shakespeare bases the *154* sonnets in nature with the biblical God barely making an appearance. Shakespeare names him pejoratively in *58*, only to convert him to a 'God in love' in *110* and then reduce him to his roots in the 'little Love-God' of *154*.

Neither does *18's* 'eternal lines' hold a promise of heavenly escape from the liveliness of human understanding and imagination. Rather 18 balances exquisitely between the increase argument and the conditional excitements of verse.

When we examine *116*, as the first of the two sonnets believed to be key, we hear not a hymn to absolute love but a call by the Poet for the Master Mistress to meet him eye-to-eye in a marriage of willing minds. Once the male youth accepts the Poet's logic, then the love they experience should be far less susceptible to pressure or restraint from illogical beliefs usurping the priority of the female in nature to institute male Gods.

The mention of 'star' in *116* recalls insistence that the eyes of the Master Mistress are the 'constant stars'.

It is the star to every wand'ring bark,
Whose worth's unknown, although his height be taken.
Love's not Time's fool, though rosy lips and cheeks
Within his bending sickle's compass come,   116.7-10

<snt_116.7-10> If the imagery of the 'lips' and 'cheeks' in *116* is a sexual metaphor based on facial features, then the word 'star' plays on the double meaning of the eye evident throughout the set. It is both the organ of

sight that 'looks on tempests', as well as the sexual eye through which 'love's' eye is subject to the 'bending sickle' of love's tool.

This means *116* plays its part in presenting the logic of love heralded in the increase sonnets and matured in the truth and beauty sonnets. In redeeming truth and beauty from the doom threatened in *14*, it reinforces the basis for enduring love. The Poet is so sure of his natural philosophy, he vows that if he is in 'error' then 'no man ever loved'.

Turning to *129* from the female sequence, we read it in the context of the emerging pattern of meaning discovered so far. Instead of a rebuke of the Mistress' personal lust, as evangelising commentators claim, we hear a condemnation of the 'Spirit' that takes humankind through extremes of religious cruelty past all reason so their promised 'joy' becomes but a 'dream' and their promised 'heaven' becomes a 'hell' on earth. < snt_129.1-14>

Th'expense of Spirit in a waste of shame
Is lust in action, and till action, lust
Is perjured, murd'rous, bloody full of blame,
Savage, extreme, rude, cruel, not to trust,
Enjoyed no sooner but despised straight,
Past reason hunted, and no sooner had
Past reason hated as a swallowed bait,
On purpose laid to make the taker mad.
Made In pursuit and in possession so,
Had, having, and in quest, to have extreme,
A bliss in proof and proud and very woe,
Before a joy proposed behind a dream,
  All this the world well knows yet none knows well,
  To shun the heaven that leads men to this hell. 129.1-14

The misreading of individual sonnets by commentators both prejudices Shakespeare's intended meaning and provides a melodrama on why previous studies fail to penetrate the depth of Q's intellect and love.

42: The ruins of an ancient architecture

Our task is not so much to fault previous attempts to understand Q. Instead, as from the beginning, we continue to seek evidence from within the set to demonstrate Q has a verifiable level of philosophic meaning and incorporates an expression of mature love. The intimation of significant structuring in Q dependent on nature is borne out by the investigation so far.

If we turn to *64* and *65*, they play with the idea of an ancient architecture amidst the forces of nature. In a group that focuses on time, the two sonnets talk of 'lofty towers' from an 'outworn buried age' plus 'brass' and 'stone' and 'gates of steel'. Then, in the next cluster of sonnets on the theme of 'time', *123* to *125*, there are similar references to structures. We hear of 'pyramids' and 'building', and the 'canopy' that covers 'pomp' and 'fashion'. <snt_architecture>

Significantly, the Poet looks to convince the youth all such architectural achievements come to nothing if there are

When sometime lofty towers I see down razed,
And brass eternal slave to mortal rage. 64.3-4
When rocks impregnable are not so stout,
Nor gates of steel so strong but time decays?
                                              65.7-8
Thy pyramids built up with newer might
To me are nothing novel, nothing strange,
                                              123.2-3
No it was builded far from accident,
It suffers not in smiling pomp, nor falls
Under the blow of thralled discontent,
                                              124.5-7
Wer't ought to me I bore the canopy,
With my extern the outward honoring,
Or laid great bases for eternity, 125.1-3

Sonnet architecture

no humans about to use them. The idealistic 'politics' that misconstrues natural forces belies the politics of the 'heretic' who 'alone stands' against their power. Their power is a 'crime' that should be impeached if it is used to deny the natural philosophy of life.

Shakespeare, while acknowledging the grandeur of achievement represented by evocative architectural sites, cautions that the ruins visible amidst nature tell in favour of enduring humanity. As we have seen, even his 154 sonnets are only vehicles for their contents, and these are the contents our survey of Q reveals.

43: Accountability in sonnet 126

After much investigation we return to 126, the final sonnet to the male before the 28 sonnets to the female. In 126, the Poet identifies nature as the sovereign mistress. Weighing the accumulated evidence and argument from throughout the set, we see why the Poet calls the male a 'Boy'.

As 'Nature' prepares to 'audit' the 'Boy' in 126, it dismisses 'time'. Nature determines whether the youth has matured like the Poet or whether he will remain, like a compromised alien Poet, forever committed to mouthing pious rhetoric and writing fashionable rhyme and style. <snt_126.5-12>

> If Nature (sovereign mistress over wrack)
> As thou goest onwards still will pluck thee back,
> She keeps thee to this purpose, that her skill.
> May time disgrace, and wretched minute kill.
> Yet fear her O thou minion of her pleasure,
> She may detain, but not still keep her treasure.
> Her *Audit* (though delayed) answered must be,
> And her *Quietus* is to render thee.   126.5-12

As nature takes charge of the Master Mistress' fate, we are aware of the consistency of the Poet's contents. His argument has been logical throughout. The Poet does not tell the male youth to increase per se or for that matter to marry. Rather he places before him the logical implications of the excessive idealism or mind-based beauty that leads idealistic males to believe their singleness – as 8 puts it – is preordained.

In 126, nature leaves no doubt about the two options. Either the male recognises the logic of increase and persistence through generations, or he and all like him are subsumed back into nature unincreased. All other options besides increase exist only in the Master Mistress' mind or in the minds of those who might wish to remember him. As a mixed blessing, he could remain forever young in the poetry of those who stylistically record his appearance.

We began our survey of Q at the juncture between 126 and 127. Now, back at 126, the evidence suggests nature and the relationship of sovereign mistress, Mistress and Master Mistress are fundamental to unravelling the depth of Shakespeare's philosophic clarity. While we may not be ready to assert the complete cogency of the discoveries revealed so far, there would have to be telling cross-examination to unseat what we witness with our own minds.

The evidence demonstrates Shakespeare remains clear about the difference between his philosophic achievement and the mind-based desire to avoid the logical implications of the natural world. Instead he predicts those who create conceptual fantasies against nature, whether built, written or thought, engender the seeds of their rapid demise.

Chapter 13: Sexual life – erotic souls

From where does Shakespeare get his insight that allows him to critique the basis of male-based religions with their deeply affective mythologies? How does he write verse critical of excessive belief in mythological creations while continuing to generate works at a mythic level of expression?

44: From the sexual body to the erotic mind

We have yet to account for the last two sonnets in Q, with their different style and tone. The reader (aware of the nature to female/male dynamic bedded in the 154 sonnets) first encounters the fourteen increase sonnets, then moves through the five sonnets to increase and poetry and then into the extensive discussion of truth and beauty and beauty and truth. The journey ends in the intensely erotic sonnet pair *153* and *154*.

Why does Shakespeare have us travel from one end of the set where the verse is deliberately prosaic to the other end where it is intensely florid? What is the relationship between the two ends of the set where one end argues the logic of increase and the other toys with the mythical story of Cupid and Diane?

When we examine the language of the increase group, we find there are no examples of deliberate sexual innuendo. It is as if argument about the biological process of increase needs be unequivocal.

It is not until we consider the five increase to poetry sonnets that we hear in *16* a sexual pun on the word pen playing on the relationship between pencil and pen(is). Because the five sonnets introduce the process of writing, they relate writing to increase metaphorically through its basic instrument, the pen. The Poet's willingness to pun on pen at this point suggests there is a logical

But since she pricked thee out for women's pleasure,
Mine be thy love and thy love's use their treasure.
                                                    20.13-14
Ah but those tears are pearl which thy love sheeds,
And they are rich, and ransom all ill deeds 34.13-14
Beggared of blood to blush through lively veins,
                                                    67.10
Whilst he upon your soundless deep doth ride,
Or (being wracked) I am a worthless boat,
He of tall building, and of goodly pride. 80.10-12
Oh in what sweets dost thou thy sins inclose!
That tongue that tells the story of thy days,
(Making lascivious comments on thy sport)
                                                    95.4-6
Whose worth's unknown, although his height be taken.
Love's not Time's fool, though rosy lips and cheeks
Within his bending sickle's compass come, 116.8-10
    Since saucy Jacks so happy are in this,
    Give them their fingers, me thy lips to kiss.
                                                    128.13-14
    Therefore I lie with her, and she with me,
    And in our faults by lies we flattered be.
                                                    138.13.14
    O cunning love, with tears thou keepst me blind,
    Lest eyes well seeing thy foul faults should find.
                                                    148.13-14
My soul doth tell my body that he may,
Triumph in love, flesh stays no further reason,
But rising at thy name doth point out thee,
As his triumphant prize, proud of this pride,
He is contented thy poor drudge to be
To stand in thy affairs, fall by thy side.
    No want of conscience hold it that I call,
    Her love, for whose dear love I rise and fall.
                                                    151.7-14
                    Erotic passages

difference between the fact of increase and the process of writing.

In the male sequence from 20 onwards we note frequent flourishes of colourful expressions from 'pricked thee out for women's pleasure' (20) to 'beggared of blood to blush through lively veins' (67), to 'he of tall building and goodly pride' (80), to 'though rosy lips and cheeks within his bending sickle's compass come' (116). Then, in the female sequence, we hear 'since saucy Jacks so happy are in this' (128), to 'be anchored in the bay where all men ride' (137), to 'therefore I lie with her, and she with me' (138), to 'stand in thy affairs, fall by thy side' (151). <snt_eroticpassages>

In the final two sonnets (which enlarge on a classical epigram), Cupid, the Roman equivalent of the Greek god Eros, evokes the double role of the eyes. 'My mistress' eye' in the last line of 153 refers to both her mind's eye and her sexual eye. <snt_153.1-14> Sonnet 154 reiterates the erotic dynamic evident in 153. Its 'cure' for the eroticism of imaginary idealisations is the sexual 'love' that heats the 'water' or the female vagina, which in turn excites the male because her 'valley fountain' of enticing water 'cools not love'. <snt_154.1-14>

Cupid laid by his brand and fell asleep,
A maid of Diane's this advantage found,
And his love-kindling fire did quickly steep
In a cold valley-fountain of that ground:
Which borrowed from this holy fire of love,
A dateless lively heat still to endure,
And grew a seething bath which men yet prove,
Against strange maladies a sovereign cure:
But at my mistress' eye love's brand new fired,
The boy for trial needs would touch my breast,
I sick withal the help of bath desired,
And thither hied a sad distempered guest.
  But found no cure, the bath for my help lies,
  Where Cupid got new fire; my mistress' eye.
153.1-14

In a reprise of the first nineteen sonnets, the 'maid' (153) or the 'fairest votary' (154) amongst the 'Nymphs' of the virgin goddess Diane takes it upon herself to override the mythic eroticism of goddesses and gods with a sexual 'cure' for 'diseased' minds who cannot distinguish the eroticism of writing from the physicality of sex.

Sonnets 153 and 154 also repeat the relationship of sovereign mistress and Mistress encountered across the gap between 126 and 127. In 153, the words sovereign and mistress are in lower case, and in 154 Mistress is in upper case.

Many comment on the literalness of the increase sonnets, and we note the literary innuendo on pen in the increase to poetry group. More apparent is the shift up

The little Love-God lying once asleep,
Laid by his side his heart inflaming brand,
Whilst many Nymphs that vowed chaste life to keep,
Came tripping by, but in her maiden hand,
The fairest votary took up that fire,
Which many Legions of true hearts had warmed,
And so the General of hot desire,
Was sleeping by a Virgin hand disarmed.
This brand she quenched in a cool Well by,
Which from love's fire took heat perpetual,
Growing a bath and healthful remedy,
For men diseased, but I my Mistress' thrall,
  Came there for cure and this by that I prove,
  Love's fire heats water, water cools not love.
154.1-14

to the frequent eroticisms in the 107 truth and beauty sonnets in the male sequence and the 26 beauty then truth sonnets in the female sequence.

Yet, the eroticism in 153 and 154 is so marked we have to imagine there is a purpose behind Shakespeare's deliberateness. Concluding the set with two intensely erotic sonnets suggests the deepest human expression using words is logically erotic. Shakespeare's set begins with increase and ends with eroticism. The arrangement emphasises the logical relation between the physical processes of increase and the erotic logic of all myths.

Moreover, looking ahead in Q beyond *154* into *A Lover's Complaint*, we hear it extol with even greater verve the recovery of a maid's natural logic. In a twist on the female led recovery in *153* and *154*, a young man addresses the illogicality of overly venerated female virginity.

In the shift from full-on increase to high-end eroticism, Shakespeare recognises that the mythic notion of a singular God in biblical religions is no more than a highly eroticised mind-based sensation abstracted from the intense eroticism originating from the 'little Love-God' celebrated in *153* and *154*. The natural priority of the increase dynamic in Q leads logically to its erotic correlate in the mind as the basis for profound human love and its expression in consummate verse.

In the final two sonnets, Shakespeare reaffirms the logical conditions for achieving and sublimating the natural unity of Mistress, Poet and Master Mistress. When the Poet (as a male or the masculine persona of a female) applies the logic of the set, the unity of nature and the female/male relationship is secure. Once the Poet appreciates the logical connection between the sexual and the erotic, he can write philosophic love poetry without parallel.

45: The erotic heart of mythological tales

The Poet's deliberate use of eroticism in the 140 sonnets beyond the increase group suggests Shakespeare understands that all language is logically erotic. Couched in words, as *138* explains, the dynamic of language evolves naturally from the sexuality of increase.

What precedent is there in literature for the Poet's logical distinction between the sexual and the erotic? Where in traditional cultural expressions is there a similar logical divide between them?

When we examine myths of origin in the world's religions, which are the deepest form of expression in a culture because they relate human nature to nature at large, they invariably characterise the genesis of humankind in erotic or non-biological terms. In all myths of origin, birth occurs through some other means than biological sex. At the heart of all the world's mythologies is an erotic testament of virgin births, births from the head, rib cage, thigh, or the blood from testicles, through to bodily resurrections, reincarnations and procreation-free eternal life.

All myth, as the deepest form of cultural expression, acknowledges – if unintentionally – that the written word, or any mind-dependent activity, is logically erotic because it is generated from within the mind of a sexual being. With some irony, the erotic logic of myth emerges when prophets evoke otherworldly divinities without realising their goddesses and gods are mind-driven erotic creations founded on the logic of increase in nature.

Myths are stories made of words by sexual beings whose language conforms to the erotic logic of truth and beauty or saying and poetry. Ironically, when the God of the Bible is called the Word (and not, for instance, the Sentence or the

Paragraph), his status as a sensation of the mind is affirmed. The very idea of an absolute God shows the concept of such a God conforms to the erotic logic of singular beauty (or aesthetics) the Poet explores in the male sequence.

Shakespeare's *Sonnets* of 1609 acknowledge the logical relationship between the sexual body and the erotic mind because the human mind is part of nature and the sexual dynamic. Shakespeare resolves the mythological level of expression logically by grounding his appreciation of the sexual/erotic divide in nature.

By doing so, Shakespeare does not compromise the logical priority of the female over the male. This is in contrast to the mythological stories of the last 3000 to 4000 years in which the male usurps the natural priority of the female. If believers accept the inversion as a deeply evocative story, it remains relatively harmless. It they enforce the myth as reality the effects are always disastrous.

We see Shakespeare challenging the illogicality of enforcing the priority of the conventionalised male God. By recovering the natural priority of the female, he counters and supersedes the most basic stylistic convention at the heart of male-based injustices. Failure to break from the traditional convention that inverts natural priorities prevents commentators from understanding the meaning of the *Sonnets*. Without the insights Q provides, they cannot appreciate the thrust of the final two sonnets.

We could ask why Shakespeare resorts to an epigrammatic style just when he has spent 152 sonnets establishing the basis for human love that avoids rhyme and style. He seems to be saying, so long as he recovers the natural originary status of the human female to the male he can use any style of sonnet he wishes and still convey his nature-based contents (as he does in his many plays and poems).

46: The imaginary soul – life and death in nature

In Q, the natural patterning of the basic elements of human life has an air of self-sufficiency. Nature, the sexual dynamic, the logic of increase, the organisation of the mind around truth and beauty, the relationship of personae, the patterns for music and time, the relationships of content and style and now the distinction between the sexual and the erotic all sit conformably within the set. How can the 154 sonnets contain so much information about the human mind and emotions and yet remain beyond the understanding of commentators?

A further question arises. If Shakespeare's set is so full of life, where does the Poet account for the inevitability of death for the individual female or male? When we look for instances of dying and death throughout the set we are drawn back to the increase sonnets where the idea of death is contextualised by the increase dynamic that enables any individual's life to continue into the next generation.

According to the logic of increase, death is part of life because life continues despite the demise of the individual. Nature is the encompassing entity synonymous with enduring life. The demise of the niggardly individual is merely the subsuming of an individual who does not increase into the larger pattern of life that is nature. Sonnet *126* confirms that if the youth does not increase nature audits him to die as part of nature un-increased.

The possibilities of either increasing or returning to nature un-increased are congruent with the world of organic life. However, higher in the achievements of the written word there is another form of immortality available to the male, yet apparently of no concern to the generic female. As the possibility of writing is conditional on the sexual differentiation of male from female, there is a tendency for the male or masculine side of the human mind to seek recognition after death for its mind-based qualities and achievements.

Yet, very few of the billions of human beings living and dying over time are immortalised in print. The chances of being remembered in ages to come are quite remote.

In *15* to *19*, the Poet takes account of the range possibilities from increase to poetry. While increase is the main form of immortality for the Master Mistress, he may also have his beauty recorded in the Poet's verse for future generations to admire or revile – depending on the receptivity of the age. <snt_19.9-14>

> O carve not with thy hours my love's fair brow,
> Nor draw no lines there with thine antique pen,
> Him in thy course untainted do allow,
> For beauty's pattern to succeeding men.
> Yet do thy worst old Time despite thy wrong,
> My love shall in my verse ever live young.
> 19.9-14

The Poet is at pains to point out that such immortality is limited. It can only preserve the youth as he was when caught in the matrix of the Poet's verse. He will 'ever live young' only because the fossil record of poetry buries him when young.

The Poet's philosophic mapping also accounts for the fantasies religions claim are separate from the processes of life in a realm beyond the reach of nature. Q recognises such imaginings as dreams of the imaginary soul that divorce the faculties of the mind from the processes of life with the logical consequence they would 'make the world away' (*11*) if believed in exclusively. <snt_11.7-8>

> If all were minded so, the times should cease,
> And threescore year would make the world away:
> 11.7-8

There are other instances of soulfulness in the sonnets. In *20*, Shakespeare says the youth, who nature creates for women, 'steals men's eyes' and amazes 'women's souls'. <snt_20.8-9> If there is a soul it lies in the nature-based dynamic of which women are the originary entities.

> Which steals men's eyes and women's souls amazeth.
> And for a woman wert thou first created,   20.8-9

Sonnet *26* identifies the soul with 'thought' <snt_26.7-8> and 27 nails it to the imagination. <snt_27.9> In *62*, the 'soul' is possessed of the 'sin of self love'. <snt_62.1-2> In *69*, it is associated with 'all tongues' that are 'the voice of souls' capable of uttering 'bare truth'. <snt_69.3> In *107*, the 'prophetic soul' dreams 'on things to come' unable to control 'my true love' <snt_107.1-2> and *109* houses the soul in the youth's 'breast' rather

> But that I hope some good conceit of thine
> In thy soul's thought (all naked) will bestow it:
> 26.7-8

> Save that my soul's imaginary sight
> 27.9

> Sin of self-love possesseth all mine eie,
> And all my soul, and all my every part;
> 62.1-2

> All tongues (the voice of souls) give thee that due,
> 69.3

Not mine own fears, nor the prophetic soul,
Of the wide world, dreaming on things to come,
107.1-2

than the 'wide universe'. <snt_109.3-4>

It appears Shakespeare has little

time in the male sequence for the heavenly or extraterrestrial soul of religions – and

As easy might I from my self depart,
As from my soul which in thy breast doth lie:
109.3-4

this conforms with his rejection of such astronomy in *14*.

If thy soul check thee that I come so near,
Swear to thy blind soul that I was thy *Will*,
And will thy soul knows is admitted there,
Thus far for love, my love-suit sweet fulfill.
136.1-4

In the Mistress sequence, the word soul appears three times in the first three lines of *136*. <snt_136.1-4> The Poet says that if the Mistress' 'soul' should 'check' the advance of his 'will' or penis as it comes 'so near',

she 'knows' his 'will' is willing to be 'admitted' to the 'blind soul' of her 'treasure' or vagina. Shakespeare is in no doubt the path to the mind's soul is through the woman's 'nothing' that he, on her 'store's account' (or increase), should be at one in.

Poor soul the centre of my sinful earth,
My sinful earth these rebel powers that thee array,
Why dost thou pine within and suffer dearth
Painting thy outward walls so costly gay?
Why so large cost having so short a lease,
Dost thou upon thy fading mansion spend?
Shall worms inheritors of this excess,
Eat up thy charge? is this thy body's end?
Then soul live thou upon thy servant's loss,
And let that pine to aggravate thy store;
Buy terms divine in selling hours of dross:
Within be fed, without be rich no more,
  So shalt thou feed on death, that feeds on men,
  And death once dead, there's no more dying then.
146.1-14

Sonnet *146* holds the heavenly soul not on high but laments it as a 'poor soul' that is the 'centre' of the Poet's 'sinful earth'. It attributes a 'large cost' (the association cost/dear again) to the soul that lives upon death by 'selling hours of dross'. After all, the couplet concludes, once 'death, that feeds on men' is dead there is 'no more dying then'. <snt_146.1-14>

The last sonnet to mention soul is *151*. This time the Poet accuses the 'soul' of deceiving his 'body' by playing off the 'nobler part' against the 'gross body'. However, in the female sequence, the Poet has learnt to recover his 'conscience' by removing the guilt associated with traditional male-based 'love'. He laconically accepts his status as a 'drudge', or as a male derived from the female, as he 'triumphant' regales her with a cascade of erotic verse. <snt_151.5-14>

For thou betraying me, I do betray
My nobler part to my gross body's treason,
My soul doth tell my body that he may,
Triumph in love, flesh stays no further reason,
But rising at thy name doth point out thee,
As his triumphant prize, proud of this pride,
He is contented thy poor drudge to be
To stand in thy affairs, fall by thy side.
  No want of conscience hold it that I call,
  Her love, for whose dear love I rise and fall.
151.5-14

Shakespeare's treatment of the noble soul betrays not a regard for religious verities but an acceptance the soul remains ingrained in the human mind. He avoids the biblical guilt that clouds the human conscience. Instead, the love arising out of nature and spoken of in the increase sonnets is the source of conscience and is the basis for being contented.

Critical to Shakespeare's achievement is willingness to penetrate to the erotic heart of traditional mythologies to extract their faulty logic of life and death. He then creates his own unparalleled poems and dramas by incorporating and reinvigorating mythic expression according to natural prerogatives.

Chapter 14: From the cryptic dedication to logical mapping

What happens if we apply the discoveries made so far to the more incidental aspects of Q? What would a template that maps the 154 sonnets look like, especially after 400 years of misguided commentary?

47: The role of the dedication

When we approached Q through its title page and indecipherable dedication, we tried not to be presumptuous about the depth of contents the Poet 'promised'.

TO.THE.ONLIE.BEGETTER.OF.
THESE.INSVING.SONNETS.
Mʳ.W. H. ALL.HAPPINESSE.
AND.THAT.ETERNITIE.
PROMISED.

BY.

OVR.EVER-LIVING.POET.

WISHETH.

THE.WELL-WISHING.
ADVENTVRER.IN.
SETTING.
FORTH.

T. T.

Dedication

In our examination of the set, we drew overwhelmingly on features evident in the 154 sonnets to reveal meaningful patterns. In the process, we discover mappings that pass all the way from nature as the encompassing given to the presentation of the possibilities for immortality.

Shakespeare even accounts for the impressive edifices of civilisation and their ephemerality. In the previously opaque sonnet layout, life and death proves much more prolific than any imaginary ideal realised ephemerally in concrete. The sonnet logic even offers a rationale as to why previous attempts to understand its mappings fail.

With the structure of Q in hand, can we now tease apart the impenetrability of the dedication? <snt_dedication>

In Q, the dedication consists of a number of words separated by dots followed by the initials 'T. T.'. If we count the dots in the body of the dedication, they number 28. The number 28 suggests the body of the dedication conforms in some way to the 28 Mistress sonnets. It appears the punctuation of the dedication allocates 28 words or letters to represent the Mistress.

If this is so, are there further connections in the arrangement of the dedication to the basic numberings of the set? Can we locate numbers like 154 and 126 or other numerologically interesting numbers such as the 1 and 9 or even the 14 or the 12 and 8?

Accepting that the body of the dedication represents the 28 Mistress sonnets, how might the initials 'T. T.' represent the Master Mistress? Looking for the number 126, we recall *126* is uniquely a 12-line sonnet in rhyming couplets. On closer inspection, the structure of *126* replicates its number. It is '1' sonnet in '12' lines with '6' rhyming couplets.

Taking our cue from what looks like a deliberate ploy to configure *126* to replicate its number, we know the initials 'T. T.' are those of Thomas Thorpe, the publisher of Q. The name Thomas Thorpe is also '1' name with '12' letters and each personal name and family name has '6' letters. Is this the reason Shakespeare makes *126* different from the rest of the set?

By this account, the dedication configures the numbering for both the Mistress and the Master Mistress sequences. When added together, the full dedication embeds in its typography the numbering for nature at 154.

$$28 + 126 = 154$$

With the whole dedication organised numerically, we find the total number of letters in the dedication (including the T.T. and taking 'M'' as one letter) sums to 145. We know *145*, as an irregular sonnet, has particular significance in the set. It is where the Poet relives his reconciliation with the Mistress. At the other end of the set, Shakespeare's introduction of I at *10* means there are 145 sonnets from *10* to the end of the set. The 145 letters suggests the dedication, besides representing nature as 154, also represents the Poet as 145.

To make sense of the possible double meaning of the dedication with its two readings of 154 and 145, we recall the constant refrain in the sonnets about the logical interrelationship of female and male, and feminine and masculine within nature. This could mean Shakespeare arranges the dedication to configure the relationship.

The Poet's philosophy reconciles both the logical priority of the female over the male (28 over 126) and the significance of the feminine/masculine balance in the mind. Effectively, the Poet at 145 = 1 is at one with his dual personae and, as a human being within nature, is reconciled to nature at 154 = 1.

Alert to the nature (154)/Poet (145) isomorphism of the set and dedication, and remembering the author is William Shakespeare, can we make sense of the enigmatic initials 'Mr. W. H'. With Shakespeare in complete control of Q, we note W and H are the first (1) and ninth (9) letters of his name. In Q, the name W̲ILLIAM S̲HAKE-SPEARE in capitals appears below the title of *A Lover's Complaint*.

By combining the 1 (28 = 1) of the female with the 9 (126 = 9) of the male in his dedication, Shakespeare predicts the exact relationship between female/feminine and male/masculine his Poet needs to gain and maintain a mature understanding. Shakespeare's dedication anticipates the logical and numerological structuring needed to create his incomparable set of 154 love sonnets.

No wonder Q has remained impenetrable for so long to readers who have been unable to decipher the mystery of the dedication due largely to their prejudices toward nature.

48: Mapping the 154-sonnet set

We have now uncovered much of the organisation of Shakespeare's 154 sonnets, enough at any rate to unlock the mystery of the dedication. Can we also draw a map of the logical relationships observed during our inquiry?

We first take the relationship between the whole set as nature and the two sequences of female and male. We can create a template of the three givens to relate the priority of nature and the priority of the female over the male. <diagram_

Female/male template

Male/female template

femalemaletemplate>

Then, taking the argument of the increase sonnets, we generate a similar configuration when the male recombines with the female to form a child. **<diagram_ malefemaletemplate>**

We can then combine the two templates to represent the bodily or physical dynamic in nature. The left side of the template is logically prior to the right. **<diagram_bodytemplate>**

In the remaining 140 sonnets, the Poet argues for beauty and truth in the female sequence and for truth and beauty in the male sequence. This means beauty and truth and truth and beauty are the characteristics of the mind immediately consequent on the body dynamic.

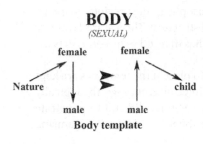

BODY
(SEXUAL)

Body template

We can represent the logical relationship between them by using the word beauty to characterise singular sensations and truth to represent the polarity of language that typically allows the distinction between true and false. From the female sequence we have the beauty/truth template, **<diagram_beautytemplate>** and from the male sequence the truth/beauty template. **<diagram_truthtemplate>**

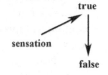

Beauty/truth template

As with the body dynamic, we can represent the dynamic of the mind by combining the two templates. **<diagram_ mindtemplate>**

In turn, the transitional sonnets 15 to 19 facilitate the relationship between the body and mind. They acknowledge the natural givens cannot be argued for. When combining the body and mind templates to form a complete template for the 154 sonnets, a double chevron indicates the role of the transitional sonnets 15 to 19. Consequently, the Body and the Mind templates are isomorphic in that the form of one develops out of the other. **<diagram_naturetemplate>**

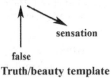

Truth/beauty template

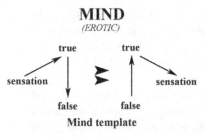

MIND
(EROTIC)

Mind template

By diagramming these logical inter-relationships, we represent the principal features of the set. The Nature Template or map generates all the other possibilities in the set. Love (arising from physical or sensual

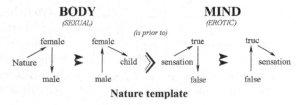

Nature template

beauty as well as from conceptual beauty or intuitions and emotions), music (as an expression of beauty synchronous with nature) and time (as a construct of language), all find their logical home in the Nature Template. <diagram_nature-template_sonnets>

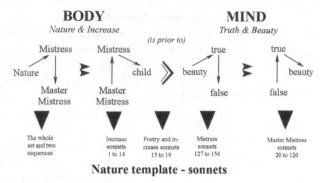

Nature template - sonnets

Following the gradual unravelling of Q's philosophy in the previous chapters, we now derive a set of templates that map its logical structure. The Nature Template gives graphic shape to the philosophy Shakespeare has in mind as he constructs his poems and plays.

The complex of relationships in the set fall into place if the templates are kept in mind while considering the two sequences, the interior groupings, the logically related sonnets and the individual sonnets. What was once difficult to penetrate is made comprehensible by bringing to bear upon the set its own self-organising logic.

However, of the three irregular sonnets in Q, we have explained only two. The octosyllables in *145* can be associated with the octave of music and the six couplets of *126* could map on to the 'T. T.' of the dedication. We have no meaningful explanation for the extra line added to *99*.

For what care I who calls me well or ill,
So you o'er-greene my bad, my good allow?
112.3-4

when a young poet. <snt_112.3-4>

Reading *99* again, we hear its tone of rebuke and accusation. The same tone is also apparent in *112*, where 'o'er-greene' could allude to Robert Greene's insult to Shakespeare

A similar insult to Shakespeare occurs with the publication in 1599 of *The Passionate Pilgrim*. William Jaggard incorrectly attributes a number of sonnets to Shakespeare to capitalise on his growing reputation. It is possible Shakespeare adds an extra line to *99* to acknowledge Jaggard's temerity. The result of adding the 15 lines to the sonnet number 99 gives us the date 1599.

Yet such a prosaic reason for altering a sonnet's length does not accord with the lively contents of the Poet's verse. All this changes, though, if we draw a diagram of the 126 sonnets that takes account of the irregularities of *99* and *126*. If we arrange the 126 sonnets in a row, we get a penile shape with a lip at *99* and a double-dip at *126* to form a glans.

Then, in the 28 female sonnets, the symbolism of the lunar/menstrual cycle brings to mind the circular moon. If we add the brackets between the sequences to the shapes for 126 and 28, we get a suggestive

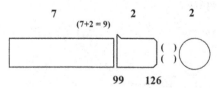

1 14 28 42 56 70 84 98 112 126 ( ) 140 154
1609 Sonnet template

template. <diagram_1609sonnettemplate>

The possibility of the sexual/erotic shape is foreshadowed in *153* and *154* where Cupid lies with his 'brand' steeped in the 'valley fountain' of Diane's maid.

Is it possible Shakespeare took the structuring of his set a step past the logical relationships of the Nature Template to play on the underlying form of sexual/erotic relationships in Q? The evaluation as to whether Shakespeare intends the suggestive shape is best left in the hands of the readers.

49: Changes wrought by previous commentators

If we examine other editions of the sonnets published after 1609 from over the last four centuries, they make many changes to the original. The many alterations and emendations are the consequence of four centuries of misinterpretation of Q by commentators.

While the individual changes may seem innocuous, when we consider the 50 to 100 traditional changes, they blight up to thirty percent of the sonnets in modern editions. Commentators frustrated with not understanding the contents of the sonnets, alter this or that feature of Q to fit their preconceptions.

Moreover, many editions of Q reorder the set. The results skew Q's fidelity to nature. In some cases, sections of the original set of 1609 are missing or are recast tastefully. Because commentators need to rework, dismiss or even denigrate aspects of Q, we have a measure of the divide between their preconceptions and the structuring we reveal.

By flipping end-to-end the Nature Template derived above, we can indicate the commentators' distance from Shakespeare's achievement. With brilliant irony Shakespeare's nature-based philosophy can be used to illustrate how the traditional biblical paradigm based on the convention of a male God inverts the natural body/mind dynamic. We can approximate the inversion by swapping around the Body and Mind components

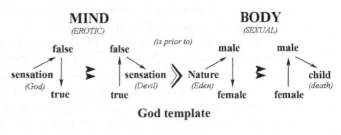

of the Nature Template, effectively making the map read backwards. <diagram_godtemplate>

The resulting God Template, shows how Shakespeare's nature-based template critiques biblical beliefs that prioritise a mind-derived sensation called God over nature.

All the contradictions of apologetics, or the justification of biblical conceits, follow from the illogical move of male usurpation of female priority. True and false lose their evolutionary rootedness in the female/male dynamic. The sensory world is branded evil. Nature becomes idealised as Eden. The male usurps the priority of the female and childbirth becomes a sinful death sentence for disobedience to male-based conventions.

Shakespeare predicts that only when God-believers accept the limitations of the inverted paradigm will they recover their birthright natural philosophy. When they do, they will recognise the apparent obscurities and errors in Q are due to cataracts in their eyes and not to blotches on Shakespeare's page.

50: The Lovers – a textual shift in A Lover's Complaint

We noted the shift in Q from the fourteen-line sonnets to the seven-line stanzas of *A Lover's Complaint*. The change suggests *A Lover's Complaint* is an offshoot of the logic presented in the 154 sonnets.

In the long poem, a young man assails the virtue of a Maid until she relents and allows him his way. The poem finishes with the comment, though, that she would do it again. <lc_323-9>

O that infected moisture of his eye,
O that false fire which in his cheek so glow'd:
O that forc'd thunder from his heart did fly,
O that sad breath his spongy lungs bestowed,
O all that borrowed motion seeming owed,
Would yet again betray the fore-betrayed,
And new pervert a reconciled Maid.
(A Lover's Complaint 323-9)

A Lover's Complaint recapitulates the argument of the sonnets, but with the male now taking the lead to help a female recover her natural philosophy. Remembering the female/male and feminine/masculine interrelationships the Poet develops in the *Sonnets*, we see the masculine persona of the female is being reconciled with her feminine persona by a youth who already has his feminine and masculine personae unified (like the Poet of the *Sonnets*).

Somewhat sardonically, Shakespeare has the Maid 'confess' to a 'reverend man' or 'Father' the plight of her pleasurable encounter. Shakespeare also has her assailant recount how a 'Nun' was more than willing to have her blind devotion to a male God re-addressed by his advances. There is even a possibility the I of the first ten stanzas is the same young man who takes delight in hearing how the maid recovers her natural logic of love in a climate of unnatural religious idealism.

A Lover's Complaint, then, case studies the logic Shakespeare articulates in the 154 sonnets. It shows that Shakespeare's recognition of the priority of the female over the male does not automatically guarantee a logical balance between the feminine and masculine personae in the mind of the female. The Maid, like Isabella in *Measure for Measure* and Katherine in *The Taming of the Shrew*, is a female who learns to overcome the prejudices in male-based culture under the tutelage of a mature male.

As if to increase the connectivity between the two distinct parts of Q, Shakespeare toys with the number of stanzas (47 = 4+7 = 11 or 4x7 = 28) and lines (329 = 3+2+9 = 14). The numbering system, though, is nowhere as meaningful as that in the 154 sonnets. It does accentuate, however, the playfulness of Shakespeare's finishing touches to the sonnets before Q went to press.

When we first surveyed the 154 sonnets, we presumed not to have answers to the many quandaries experienced by commentators over the last four hundred years. The evidence gathered allows us to claim with some confidence that the nature-based philosophy in Q accounts for all the salient aspects of the set and even for its incidental features.

Concluding the inquiry into Shakespeare's Sonnets

We began our investigation of *Shake-speares Sonnets* of 1609 by presuming no knowledge of its organisation or meaning. By returning to the original edition Q our intention was to delve amidst some of the more characteristic features of the love sonnets as well as some of the anomalous aspects to see where our exploration leads.

From the evidence in Q, we reveal a deeply philosophic level of structuring. Moreover, we bring to light a philosophic understanding that overturns the presumptions of traditional philosophy. That many sense a brilliant philosophy in Shakespeare's 154 sonnets does not quite prepare us for the possibility they contain the most meaningful set of biological/logical relationships for deep intellectual and emotional contentedness.

In our section-by-section investigation of the evidence from Q, we discover a logically sound presentation founded on the undeniable givens of nature and the female/male dynamic. As we follow the evidence from the external structure of the set to its inner arguments, we first encounter in *1* to *14* the requirement for increase. Then, in *15* to *19*, we see Shakespeare acknowledge the relationship between the sexual dynamic of female/male and the possibility of writing poetry.

Once we appreciate the significance of the preliminary preconditions, we can consider the remaining sonnets from *20* to *154*. By first examining the Mistress sequence, we see Shakespeare divides it into two groups. The first discusses sensory beauty and the second considers language or saying or what Shakespeare calls truth. When we follow this pattern into the Master Mistress sonnets from *20* to *126* we can see their main argument concerns the relation of truth and beauty as language and art arising within the human mind.

Isomorphic with the basic relation of female to male in nature, Shakespeare also argues for the importance of feminine and masculine gender dispositions of the human mind in understanding and expression. Moreover, he crafts his dedication to prefigure the logic and numbering of the 154 sonnets. We follow Shakespeare as he draws a clear distinction between the sexual dynamic of the body and the erotic dynamic of the mind as basic to any form of expression. The undeniable logic of the relationship is particularly evident in myths of origin.

Shakespeare, though, is not content to articulate just the natural relationships in Q. The exquisite poetry of the sonnets gives us a working model of their philosophy in action. Moreover, through their unique philosophy Shakespeare gives expression to the deepest and maturest form of love of which we are capable.

Consequently, Shakespeare takes apart illogical male-based paradigms and rebuilds them according to the precedent of our lives on the planet under nature. He restores us to the only certainty to which we have recourse – nature.

When we approach the *Sonnets* with an open mind, we meet with the contentedness generated by an understanding that maps the external fact of nature and our lives as sexual beings with the internal workings of our minds. There is no disjunction in Shakespeare's sonnet set (or in its companion poem) between nature and the human mind.

We go further than the wording of the 154 sonnets. We construct templates to show diagrammatically the logical relationships in the set. The templates provide another way to present the natural givens and may help those with a graphic sensibility to appreciate the sonnet logic.

We sought to show how Shakespeare's 154 sonnets work. We have gone some way toward that goal, but what we have uncovered so far is provisional. We need to examine the plays and longer poems to see if they relate to the nature-based sonnet philosophy. The *Sonnets* themselves are anomalous if there is no connection between their philosophy and the logic driving Shakespeare's other works.

We will consider Shakespeare's plays and other poems in Part 2. Then, in Part 3, we will consider the ramifications of the Globe Theatre for Shakespeare's worldwide appeal. Only then might we say Shakespeare bases all his works in the profound philosophy apparent in Q.

Part 2

The European theatre

taking the sonnets to the plays

Preliminary to an examination of the Comedies, Histories and Tragedies

When Christopher Columbus dies in 1506, he still believes the tropical islands he encounters after thirty-five days at sea on his first voyage of discovery are the eastern outliers of Marco Polo's Asian continent. Moreover, he holds faith to the end that the coastline of present day Venezuela and Honduras, where he makes landfall on subsequent voyages, marks the eastern edge of the Asian landmass. Only later did it become evident to others Columbus was exploring the periphery of an intervening continent roughly one-third west from Europe to Asia.

Columbus' undying faith in the whereabouts of his anticipated Asian landfall prevents him from appreciating the significance of his unforeseen American windfall. As we note, his blind faith has echoes in the typical traditional misunderstanding of the 1609 *Sonnets* over the last 400 years. His peremptory mapping of the West Indies as islands off the coast of Asia has its counterpart in the misreading of Shakespeare's *Sonnets* as autobiography, as a disordered miscellany or, worse, as a part of a courtly love tradition or sonnet vogue.

Just as Columbus misreads the longitude of the West Indies and the American continent because of his preconceptions, the conventional *Sonnet* literature is equally at sea about the natural mapping of the philosophy Shakespeare embeds in Q and its relationship to the European expanse of the plays. Columbus' miscalculation of the distance to the Asian continent and his mistaken identification of the West Indies and Central America occur for the same prejudicial reasons scholars misunderstand the logical connection between the generic *Sonnets* and greater Europe as the real life theatre for Shakespeare's plays.

In this Part, we will pursue the double metaphor of conflating Columbus' lost-at-sea journeys from the islands of the West Indies to the isthmus of continental America with a well-founded adventure that advances from the *Sonnets* to the machinations of continental life and politics in the *Folio* of plays (called *F*). Unlike Columbus, Shakespeare does not allow his mythic imagination to countermand the practical reality evident in the European theatre.

Chapter 15: Turning to the 1623 Folio

How might we best approach the plays after our inquiry into the Sonnets? Is there anything in the 1623 Folio to guide us into the thinking behind the thirty-six plays arranged there by Shakespeare's colleagues? And how relevant are the two long poems Shakespeare publishes near the beginning of his career as a playwright?

51: A change in technique

In our survey of the 1609 *Sonnets* in Part 1, we presume no prior knowledge of their underlying structure in the search for intentional patterns that might form a consistent and comprehensive philosophy of life and love. The process of investigation – mimicking induction – has been fruitful. It vindicates the suspicion held by some commentators there is a systematic embodiment of Shakespeare's thought in Q.

We will now argue that if Shakespeare publishes Q to present his philosophy methodically, he does so because of the theatrical constraints on presenting its full philosophic content as a drama on stage. We should not expect, then, that an analysis of each play will reveal an embedded pattern like the *Sonnets*. Our approach to the plays and poems will be less of an investigation and more of a demonstration by the process of deduction that the main features revealed in Q predominate throughout F.

Because even the earliest of Shakespeare's plays reflect the same philosophic awareness as his later ones, we assume he had a clear insight into the natural philosophy of life and love at an early age. This means the logical pattern evident in Q could be the basis for all his poetry and drama.

Part 2, The European theatre, then, will attempt to corroborate the findings from Part 1 to show their role in the plays and longer poems for Shakespeare's representation of our lives and loves. If we do so without misrepresenting Shakespeare or his works, we can move on to examine their global implications in Part 3.

52: Beginning the crossover from the sonnets to the plays

The depth of love and insight across all Shakespeare's poetry and drama points to the possibility he develops his philosophy early in his career. If we are able to connect the recurring themes across Shakespeare's works, then we may be closer to experiencing the basic structure or logic of his thoughts and feelings and hence his unique philosophy.

To begin to appreciate the brilliance of the philosophy, we first explored the 154 sonnets in Q. The uniqueness of the *Sonnets* both in Shakespeare's works and in relation to other sonnet sequences of the period suggests its division into male and female sequences without personal names is purposeful. We find, despite its complexity, the set has a simple foundation.

The Nature Template we derive, representing the basic relationships in the *Sonnets*, is not so much a pattern Shakespeare imposes on the plays and poems. Rather it maps a philosophy in which the logical function of each element is clear and distinct. The freedom Shakespeare experiences as he writes comes from adhering to the natural dynamic of the basic relationships while exploring their capacity to intertwine in human love and discourse.

Foremost in Shakespeare's mind is singular nature. The word nature is always singular when referring to the dynamic of life in general. While nature is composed of a multiplicity of interacting entities, the next level of definitiveness for human beings is the biological division into sexual types. The female and male are separate potentialities whose distinctness is mandatory for increase or the generation of further females and males. Without continual increase, there can be no human life – even if, as Warwick fears, 'that Seed'

> *Warwick* **There is a History in all men's Lives,**
> **Figuring the nature of the Times deceased:**
> **The which observed, and man may prophesy**
> **With a near aim, of the main chance of things,**
> **As yet not come to Life, which in their Seeds**
> **And weak beginnings lie entreasured:**
> **Such things become the Hatch and Brood of Time;**
> **And by the necessary form of this,**
> **King Richard might create a perfect guess,**
> **That great Northumberland, then false to him,**
> **Would of that Seed, grow to a greater falseness,**
> **Which should not find a ground to root upon,**
> **Unless on you.**   **(2 Henry IV 1498-510)**

leads to 'greater falseness'. <2h4_1498-510>

Simultaneously, the logic of increase recognises that not all females and males can increase and, significantly, some are born who have both female and male sexual attributes. We now know this is a natural consequence of the derivation of the mammalian male from the originary female as sexual species arose in the evolutionary process. Shakespeare's prescient clarity about the logical conditions for increase and the multiplicity of sexual dispositions, endows his plays and poems with their uncanny liveliness and their inspirational love.

As we explore Shakespeare's vision for the European theatre, we might expect to find many examples of Q's natural philosophy. We can ask where the plays mention nature, where they consider the relation of female and male and where increase rears its generational inevitability.

If these givens are apparent in the plays, we expect Shakespeare will be equally clear about the demarcation between beauty and truth, and equally as playful in having his characters confound the distinction between truth and beauty. We might be able to explain, then, why he never succumbs to his own mind games as he explores the loves and lives of his stage-struck cast of characters.

53: From the generic to the specific

In keeping with Q's status as the generic site for Shakespeare's nature-based philosophy, the 154 sonnets and their companion *A Lover's Complaint* do not have a specific latitude and longitude. There is not one place name in the sonnets or the adjacent poem. Q is effectively everywhere and nowhere.

The generic set not only lacks geography, it has no biography. Its philosophic purpose transcends personal names. Hard, then, not to think Shakespeare, with some irony, anticipates 400 years of commentators whose desire to identify historic characters ignores the logically exact names in the set: sovereign mistress, Mistress, Master Mistress and Poet.

Nor can we assign a date to the events in the set. Although Q is published in 1609, the sonnets do not answer to BC or AD time zones. Shakespeare sets his natural philosophy in a time-frame free from conventionalised clock calibrations.

As with the decision to return to the 1609 edition of the *Sonnets*, we will investigate the arrangement of the thirty-six plays in the *Folio* of 1623. This is not because *F* contains necessarily the definitive versions of its thirty-six plays. More that it was organised by Shakespeare's colleagues who may have known his intentions for their collected edition. Plus, as Germaine Greer argues, Anne Hathaway, who died in 1623, may have been privy to her husband's preferences. [note 1]

The reading of Q as a generic resource has its corollary in that the plays in *F* embrace a continent of locations in greater Europe. In contrast to Q, *F* is awash with place names. Every play is set in a particular geography from Northern Britain to the Eastern Mediterranean. Named countries and named cities are the staging points for Shakespeare's dramas. He sites each play on the map of greater Europe. Scotland, England, Denmark, France, Greece, Austria, Spain, Albania, Italy, Cyprus, Turkey, and Egypt feature in one or other of the plays.

The fourteen comedies that begin *F* span from Windsor and Arden in England to Illyria in the Balkans and Athens in Greece. Quite differently, all the ten histories in the middle are based in England. The twelve tragedies grouped at the end hold sway from the Scottish Grampians to the Nile Delta.

The group of English histories at the centre of *F* suggests Shakespeare decides to focus on the Kings of England as case studies of the issues he broaches in the comedies and tragedies. We will investigate the possibility the ten histories show how England's male-based Christian monarchy abrogates the natural logic of the 360° world.

There is also a time-frame peculiar to each of the three genres – comedy, history or tragedy. None of the comedies is dated historically or is datable. At best, they evoke a general epoch, most typically sometime in the sixteenth century. In contrast, all the histories have exact dates and are organised chronologically in keeping with their focus on historic events relating to the male-God orientated English Monarchy. While it is possible to date some of the tragedies precisely – as with *Anthony and Cleopatra* to 40 BC, *Julius Caesar* to 33 BC and *Macbeth* between 1040 and 1057 AD – most evoke generalised periods ranging from the legendary events of Homeric Troy to largely fictional events in contemporary Italy, Denmark or Britain.

In addition, because Shakespeare bases each play in the *Sonnet* philosophy, none of the plays suffers from performance out of period costume. His plays have a universal appeal across cultures and time zones. Their universality suggests the reasons how and why are not to be found in Elizabethan or Jacobean incidents or fashions.

Rather the answer lies in the 154 sonnets Shakespeare writes to be answerable only to the givens of nature and the sexual dynamic of female and male. Effectively, he frees his works from stylistic constraints to express their nature-based understanding and love.

54: The precedent of an imaginary island and a European setting

Our first look for evidence in *F* of a generic/European connection need advance no further than its opening play. Written a year or so after Shakespeare publishes *Q* in 1609, *The Tempest's* dramatised mind-games occur west of Italy on an imaginary island off the Tyrrhenian coast.

In *The Tempest*, Prospero creates a conceptual island adjacent to the nepotistic real politic of Milan and Naples. There he practices reconciliatory 'magic' against the backdrop of everyday Italy.

Significantly, when Prospero's daughter Miranda was born, his kneejerk patriarchal rejection of her led him to question his values (*F's* punctuation is crucial in lines 148 to 151). <tmp_148-51> He entered a period of study in which he recovers his female-based natural philosophy – which the Poet presents in *Q*.

Prospero **Thy Mother was a piece of virtue, and She said thou wast my daughter; and thy father Was Duke of Milan, and his only heir, And Princess: no worse Issued.**
(The Tempest 148-51)

Shakespeare effectively maroons Prospero on a generic island to which he draws his culpable brother and other wayward males. The imaginary island acts as a temporary stage for the inculcation of the *Sonnet* logic. At the play's end, after Prospero announces it is time to forgo the imaginary setting, they ship back to the reality of fallible Italy.

The Tempest recalls both the generic status of *Q* and establishes a toe-hold at the beginning of *F* on the European continent. In 1610, Shakespeare makes a direct connection from *Q* into what is the first play in *F*.

55: Forecasting The Tempest scenario in the early 1590s

Is it a coincidence the two long poems Shakespeare publishes in 1593 and 1594 also relate an unnamed location not unlike Prospero's imaginary island with real Italian geography? Around twelve years before *The Tempest*, Shakespeare writes the mythic tale *Venus and Adonis* to reinforce the precursor status of the female and follows it a year later with *The Rape of Lucrece* to critique Italian male-based culture.

Like generic *Q*, the mythic hunting vale in *Venus and Adonis* has no identifiable geography. In contrast, *The Rape of Lucrece* recounts a legendary moment in Roman history that runs the gamut between the towns of Ardea and Colatium south and east of Rome.

When Shakespeare publishes *Venus and Adonis*, which reads as an early essay in the *Sonnet* philosophy, and *The Rape of Lucrece*, which sounds like an example of a philosophical audit in practice, he telegraphs the relationship of *Q* to the fully named continent of plays. For 400 years, commentators who focus on biographical and textual issues miss the philosophic signal Shakespeare implants in the relationship between *Venus and Adonis* and *The Rape of Lucrece*.

We see Shakespeare revisiting the geographical interrelationship of *Venus and Adonis* and *The Rape of Lucrece* near the end of his play-writing career in *The Tempest*. Significantly, *The Tempest* – like *Love's Labour's Lost* of 1595 – is largely of Shakespeare's invention, and both replicate the *Sonnet* logic. At most, when writing *The Tempest*, Shakespeare may have read William Thomas' *History of Italy* of 1549, which mentions a Prospero deposed by his brother, and a contemporary account of a shipwreck and survival on Bermuda in 1610.

In *Venus and Adonis*, Shakespeare returns Ovid's male-based syndrome to a female-based nature/increase dynamic and sites it within Venus' vividly conceptualised hunting ground. Then, in *The Rape of Lucrece*, he examines the cloistered mind-games of male dominance and violence.

Sebastian **Sir you may thank your self for this great loss,**
That would not bless our Europe with your daughter,
But rather loose her to an African,
Where she at least, is banished from your eye,
Who hath cause to wet the grief on't.
(The Tempest 796-800)

Around fifteen years later in *The Tempest*, Shakespeare has Prospero create a conceptual island on which to redraw the mental map of an Italian macho mind-set stretching from Milan to Naples. Moreover, he throws in Tunis on the tip of Africa to emphasise the sexual alienation created when the King of Naples forces his daughter Claribel to marry the King of Carthage. <tmp_796-800>

Hence, only a year or so after he publishes Q Shakespeare reaffirms his natural philosophy in the way he dramatises *The Tempest*. This suggests Shakespeare draws on the two long poems from the early 1590s and the *Sonnets* of 1609 for the natural philosophy of his own play scenario of 1610. The choice to have *The Tempest* head *F* seems deliberate.

56: The prismatic poem of 1601

As early examples of Shakespeare's philosophy outside the plays, *Venus and Adonis* and *The Rape of Lucrece* rehearse the relationship between Q and F. They provide a connection from the generic sonnets to the continent of plays.

On the way to publishing Q in 1609, Shakespeare provides one further aid for the adventurer. Around 1601, he writes the short poem now titled *The Phoenix and the Turtle*. The 1601 poem acts as a prism to focus the light of his natural philosophy so the reader can better penetrate the plays.

Just as seafarers use the telescope to see a distant prospect, Shakespeare crafts a poem that performs the function of the sailor's spyglass. As an intellectual gem, it condenses the *Sonnet* philosophy to throw a spectrum of logical light on the plays.

Shakespeare took the opportunity provided by Robert Chester's poetic tribute on the occasion of Sir John Salisbury's marriage to trigger a moment of pure luminosity. He writes a poem deliberately at odds with Chester's paean to marriage so he can forge a hinge point between the *Sonnets* and the plays. Just as the dedication encrypts the natural philosophy of the *Sonnets*, *The Phoenix and the Turtle* encrypts natural philosophy for the continental dramas in *F*.

57: Comments from Shakespeare's contemporaries

Before we examine the comedies, histories and tragedies, we note *F* is prefaced with commendations from some of those who knew Shakespeare well. If we analyse their eulogies and reminiscences, we find they record Shakespeare's groundedness in nature, the female, increase, and other basic terms from *Q*. Not one of the poems or notes suggests Shakespeare is beholden to the God of religion or other mythological entities. There is no mention of Christ and Mary or Mother Church.

If we extend our research to the other introductory poems written about Shakespeare in the early-to-mid Seventeenth Century we find even Milton, whose *Paradise Lost* and *Paradise Regained* have a religious agenda, makes no mention of the word God in his Epitaph to the 1632 edition of *F*.

Our expectation that the plays might conform to the pattern and wording revealed in the *Sonnets* receives confirmation when we find the thinking of the commendatory prefaces and poems is at one with the wording of *Q*. There are eleven uses of the word nature with a further eight referring to nature as her, she or herself – nineteen in all. Add the references to goddess, mother and Venus and contrast them with the only mention of God as an ejaculation in Leonard Digges' 1640 poem 'On God's name may the Bull or Cockpit have your lame blank verse, to keep you from the grave...'.

Otherwise the plural gods is mentioned twice in one line in relation to temples. The words saints and doomsday are used once each and the one invocation to pray is clothed in wit (Anonymous, in *Troilus and Cressida*, 1609). Yet the muses are mentioned five times and many of the words Shakespeare uses to ground his nature-based philosophy such as increase, got, beget, store, posterity, born and father get a mention, and issue appears twice.

Shakespeare's two friends and acting colleagues John Heminge and Henry Condell, who compiled the thirty-six plays of the *Folio* for publication in 1623, give a succinct witness to his nature-based approach.

In Heminge and Condell's preface 'To the great Variety of Readers', the second paragraph begins by elaborating on their statements made twice elsewhere in the introductory pages that *F* is 'Published according to the True Original Copies'. They aver that Shakespeare ('you') was 'abused with diverse stolen, and surreptitious copies, maimed, and deformed by the frauds and stealthes of injurious imposters'.

They state unequivocally the plays 'are now offered to your view cured, and perfect of their limbs; and all the rest, absolute in their numbers, as he (Shakespeare) conceived them'. Then follows a single sentence that brilliantly summarises Shakespeare's respect for nature and his ability to capture unprejudiced in his writings every aspect of nature – including human nature. Heminge and Condell record that Shakespeare 'Who, as he was a happy imitator of Nature, was a most gentle expresser of it'.

This one sentence, and the preceding condemnation of imposters, also stands as a canny indictment of the next 400 years of bad faith editing of Shakespeare's plays in fear or ignorance of his clearly enunciated nature-based philosophy he articulates so patently in Q as the basis for all the plays.

The dedicatory poems and commendations by Shakespeare's contemporaries record their perception of him and their regard for his works. It seems those who knew him well appreciated his acceptance of the priority of nature and the female, of the significance of increase and of the role of the muses. In contrast, they witness his lack of personal belief in the God of Christianity or other pantheons of goddesses and gods, biblical or otherwise.

We find no evidence in Q of personal names, place names or time periods. However, when we cross into the plays they crowd us with geographic and biographical data. The overall organisation of F with its preliminaries supports an approach based in nature.

Chapter 16: Given nature in the plays

How instructive is it to examine the plays for their treatment of nature and goddesses and gods? What can we expect from those plays, or parts of plays, some commentators believe are exemplary instances of male-God affirmation?

58: Nature is always singular

In Part 1, we explore the role of nature as a logical precondition or given in the structure of Shakespeare's 154 sonnets. When we turn to his plays and longer poems, do we find a similar attitude to nature that would confirm its fundamental role in his philosophy?

In Shakespeare's first long poem *Venus and Adonis*, the mature goddess Venus, who represents nature, addresses the consequences of ignoring the logic of natural increase to the recalcitrant male god Adonis. Then, in *The Rape of Lucrece*, Shakespeare demonstrates in even greater depth the illogicality and calamity of allowing male-based pride to dominate and destroy a female's natural sensibility.

In addition, *The Phoenix and the Turtle* provides a magnifying glass for examining the relationship between *Venus and Adonis*, *The Rape of Lucrece*, the *Sonnets* and the continent of plays. The short poem condenses the nature-based logic of increase and truth and beauty into a precision instrument for penetrating *F*. Further, the prefaces and poems written by Shakespeare's contemporaries mirror the natural philosophy of *Q*.

When we examine *F*, we should hear a constant refrain that predicates all else on nature. A search reveals the word nature appears in all thirty-six plays. While *The Two Gentlemen of Verona* refers only to 'the nature of love' and *The Taming of the Shrew* to 'the nature of our quarrel', in the other thirty-four plays Shakespeare invokes the full resources of nature at large.

> *Lear* ...our largest bounty may extend
> Where Nature doth with merit challenge.
> (King Lear 57-8)

The histories and tragedies all give voice to singular nature. *King Lear*, <lr_57-8> *Hamlet* <ham_639-40> and *Macbeth* <mac_30&45> each have twenty or so references to nature as befits the conceptual alienation of Macbeth, Lear and Hamlet

> *Hamlet* ...we fools of Nature,
> So horridly to shake our disposition,
> (Hamlet 639-40)

from their birthright natural philosophy.

At the other end of the spectrum, *The Two Gentlemen of Verona* and *The Taming of the Shrew* manage without a reference to singular nature. Despite not referring to encompassing nature, both plays address excesses of male-based emotional prejudice that are contrary to naturally avowed love.

> *Captain* The multiplying Villainies of Nature...
> Shipwracking Storms, and dreadful Thunders:
> (Macbeth 30&45)

In *The Two Gentlemen of Verona*, Julia dons a male disguise to rectify overwrought male-

> *Julia* It is the lesser blot modesty finds,
> Women to change their shape, than men their minds.
> (The Two Gentlemen of Verona 2232-3)

based infatuation. <tgv_2232-3> In *The Taming of the Shrew* Petruchio uses his feminine/masculine maturity to save Katherine from the intemperate masculine overdrive she develops in response to her father's patriarchal strictures. As we will see, the dramatic structure of *The Taming of the Shrew* points the way to a natural resolution by over-writing traditional biblical male-based constructs.

In *F*, a few plays open with nature on stage or where natural events determine the outcome of the play. *The Tempest,* <tmp_1> *The Comedy of Errors* <err_79-83> and *Twelfth Night* each begins with a storm at sea that casts the occupants of a shipwreck on shore to initiate the action. In *Macbeth,* three witches enter with the sounds and sights of thunder and lightning. In contrast, *Timon of Athens* ends at the edge of the sea <tim_2587> while *As You Like It, A Mid Summer Night's Dream,* and *King Lear* are set at some point in forests or on heaths.

> A tempestuous noise of Thunder and Lightning heard
> (The Tempest 1)

> Egeon The Sailors sought for safety by our boat,
> And left the ship then sinking ripe to us.
> My wife, more careful for the latter born,
> Had fastened him unto a small spare Mast,
> Such as sea-faring men provide for storms:
> (The Comedy of Errors 79-83)

> Messenger Entomb'd upon the very hem o'th'Sea,
> (Timon of Athens 2587)

Whatever worldview is favoured at any of the continental locations, Shakespeare identifies nature as the common denominator. The singularity of nature shows in his (and our) unvarying use of the word nature as the only generic name for all possible worlds or universes. We never use nature in the plural when referring to all that exists. <1h4_13-15> Shakespeare nails to the cover of *F* the irrefutable singularity of nature.

> Henry IV ...Those opposed eyes,
> Which like the Meteors of a troubled Heaven,
> All of one Nature, of one Substance bred
> (1 Henry IV 13-15)

Nature is one and the same in all the plays that refer to it. None of Shakespeare's characters talks of or invokes natures as they do frequently of gods or worlds. Whether in Homeric Troy or in the forests of Arden or on the Learean heaths, nature is singular and universal. Macbeth, Coriolanus, Orsino, Beatrice, Helena or Portia do not doubt the ground they stand on, or their bodily functions, or the sexual dynamic with its implications for human posterity. <aww_131-3> The incontrovertibility of nature is the recourse when the self-subscribing mind-based laws of God and gods prove murderous.

> Parrolles It is not politic, in the Common-wealth of Nature, to preserve virginity. Loss of Virginity, is rational increase,   (All's Well that Ends Well 131-3)

Only when Shakespeare refers to the variety of human natures, or the many types of human sensibility within nature, does he use the plural to differentiate between the various dispositions evident in the behaviour and attitudes of his characters. <tim_69,84-5> By rooting his logic in nature, in the sexual dynamic and the potential for increase, he is able to create individuals who each epitomise a few of the many psychological dispositions evident across human nature. Consequently, Shakespeare shows how

> Poet You see how all Conditions, how all Minds,
> ...
> Is ranked with all deserts, all kind of Natures,
> That labour on the bosom of this Sphere,
> (Timon of Athens 69, 84-5)

Antonio **But oh, how vild an idol proves this God:**
Thou hast Sebastian done good feature, shame.
In Nature, there's no blemish but the mind:
(Twelfth Night 1885-7)

misunderstanding and prejudice arise when any one of the human dispositions such as belief in a male God usurps the generality of nature. <tn_1885-7>

Shakespeare's *Sonnet* philosophy with its mature understanding of love allows him to create a *Folio* of plays that most nearly in any literature replicates encompassing nature while respecting the intellectual and emotional differences within human nature.

59: Godheads and dogsbodies

When assessing the role of nature in Q, we also evaluated the status of its three Gods. In the male sequence, the Christian slave-making 'God' from *58* morphs into a less judgmental 'God in love' in *110*. However, underpinning them both in the overt mythic eroticism of *153* and *154* at the end of the female sequence, Cupid the 'little Love-God' pre-empts the other two Gods.

How much evidence is there in the plays for similar concerns? What role do the words God or gods play in *F* and to what extent do the plays address the illogicalities of male-based usurpation of female priority?

Shakespeare's single mention of three different male Gods in Q does not prepare us for the multitude of gods – and goddesses – invoked across the plays. As in Q, no one God construct colonises *F*.

Of the fourteen comedies, ten histories and twelve tragedies in *F*, only the ten English histories evoke the same God throughout. The monotheistic Christian God dominates the histories with the plural 'Gods' used once only in *Richard III* and *Henry VIII*. <r3_3427-9> If *F*, like Q, addresses male-based

Richmond **All for our vantage, then in God's name march,**
True Hope is swift, and flies with Swallow's wings,
Kings it makes Gods, and meaner creatures Kings.
(Richard III 3427-9)

inconsistencies in biblical dogma, then we should hear Shakespeare give the God of the English Kings a similar philosophical autopsy. <h8_3058-60>

Unlike the histories, Shakespeare bases only three of the twelve tragedies in

Chancellor **...But we all are men**
In our own natures frail, and capable
Of our flesh, few are Angels;
(Henry VIII 3058-60)

the Christian era. *Romeo and Juliet*, *Hamlet* and *Macbeth* acknowledge the New Testament God. Of the others, only *Othello* is possibly Christian. The remaining eight tragedies are set before the

Christian era. They mention the plural word gods much more often than they mention the singular god.

For Shakespeare, multitudes of gods – and goddesses – from the past populate the human imagination all in a dead-heat with the Christian mono-God. Effectively, unmoderated male-based usurpation of female priority drives all the tragedies whatever pantheon of goddesses and gods the locals believe in.

In the main, the fourteen comedies are also equivocal whether the God, goddesses or gods they mention are Christian, Jewish, Muslim, Greek, Roman, or other religious sects. Shakespeare applies his nature-based philosophy regardless of which male-based religion is prevalent in a culture.

Only *The Merchant of Venice* stages characters whose roles are decidedly biblical. The play dissects the sectarian feuding between Antonio the Christian and Shylock the Jew. <mv_1279-81> To reverse psychologise the feuding sectarian males, Shakespeare has Portia mimic the cross-dressed male God. We will consider the implications of Shakespeare's incisive use of cross-dressing later.

> *Shylock* ...If a Jew wrong a Christian, what is his humility,
> revenge? If a Christian wrong a Jew, what should his suf
> ferance be by Christian example, why revenge?
>   **(The Merchant of Venice 1279-81)**

The Merchant of Venice one of the leading characters calls on the Christian God for succour or thanks. <mv_2104-8> Yet Portia's famous 'mercy' speech is sardonic. God's 'mercy' far from reconciles Shylock and Antonio. Rather, Portia resolves the case by grounding the words 'pound' and 'flesh' in their natural connotations.

> *Portia* But mercy is above this sceptred sway,
> It is enthroned in the hearts of Kings,
> It is an attribute to God himself;
> And earthly power doth then show likest God's
> When mercy seasons Justice.
>   **(The Merchant of Venice 2104-8)**

In *The Two Gentlemen of Verona*, there is only one reference to a god or goddess and that is the love god. <tgv_2014> As one of two comedies that does not refer to singular nature, the Christian God is also missing.

> *Julia* If this fond Love, were not a blinded god.
>   **(The Two Gentlemen of Verona 2014)**

Shakespeare populates his comedies with the motley of religions from across biblical and ancient Europe to correct the mal-consequences of excessive male-based idealism. By subjecting the headstrong perpetrators to the audit of nature with its human female priority, Shakespeare shows how to make the European theatre less a sectarian battleground and more a proto-global democracy.

Of the thirty-six plays in *F*, the one with nearly half again as many references to the Christian God is *Richard III*. The word God plus its derivative God's plus the one plural Gods appear 100 times compared with 65 times in *Henry V* as next best. As the most unrelentingly evil of all of Shakespeare's title characters, Richard Plantagenet not only acts in a play stuffed with wall to wall Christian God evocations, he frequently invokes the same God to assist him implement his reign of terror. <r3_2931>

> *Richard* ...I thank God, my Father, and your self.
>   **(Richard III 2931)**

When we turn to the word Christian, in only four plays do the words Christian or Christians occur more than five times. We find nearly half make no mention and ten make only one mention. By far the most occur in *The Merchant of Venice* where there are twenty-six in the set-to between Christianity and Jewry. <mv_366to508> Next is *Henry VIII* with eight in its expose of

> *Shylock* I hate him for he is a Christian:
> ...
> And spet upon my Jewish gabardine,
> ...
> *Antonio* Hie thee gentle Jew. This Hebrew will turn
> Christian, he grows kind.
>   **(The Merchant of Venice 366, 440, 507-8)**

Henry's murderous misogyny on the way to setting up his Christian sub-sect. In *Hamlet*, four of the seven mentions occur at Ophelia's graveside where her right to a Christian burial is all but necromanced.

Hamlet I think it be thine indeed: for thou liest in't.
Clown You lie out on't, Sir, and therefore it is not yours: for my part, I do not lie in't; and yet it is mine.
Hamlet Thou dost lie in't, to be in't and say 'tis thine: 'tis for the dead, not for the quick, therefore thou / liest.
Clown 'Tis a quick lie Sir, 'twill away again from me / to you.
(Hamlet 3313-20)

<ham_3313-20> Then follows *Richard III*, also with seven mentions, emphasising the tragic irony that Richard III is a Christian King.

In the other eight tragedies Shakespeare brings into play not the Christian pantheon but Greek, Roman, Egyptian goddesses, gods and others. The effect is to reinforce the temporality and peculiarity of any grab-bag portfolio of goddesses and gods. Ironically in *King Lear*, which is often commented upon or produced as a play of Christian transcendence, the pluralised Gods is used throughout with no mention of the singular God. <lr_356>

Bastard Now Gods, stand up for Bastards.
(King Lear 356)

Shakespeare removes all the Christian God references from the earlier anonymous play *King Leir* where the word god or God occurs over forty times. The absence of the biblical mono-God is in keeping with Shakespeare's critique of all religions in which male-based excesses lead to mayhem and murder.

Throughout *F*, Shakespeare draws parallels between the Christian God and other goddesses and gods that populate the European imagination over time. He brings on stage the God of the Infidels, the Turks, the Muslims, the Jews and he scripts in Jupiter, Juno, Jove, Oberon, Titania, Ceres and even throws in witches. And, witches are nothing if not creations of overzealous males conjured to justify their usurpation of female priority (with wicked irony in *Macbeth*).

Neither is Shakespeare intent on replacing gods with goddesses. He uses the words goddess or goddesses in only half the plays and no more than three times in any play. As with his employment of Venus in *Venus and Adonis*, or Iris, Ceres and Juno at the wedding in *The Tempest*, the goddesses (and gods) are not much more than pop-up or drop-down stage devices to facilitate the corrective of the sonnet logic.

In *Cymbeline*, the apparition of Jupiter occurs

Stage Direction Jupiter descends in Thunder and Lightning, sitting upon an Eagle: he throws a Thunder-bolt. The Ghosts fall on their knees.
(Cymbeline 3126-8)

entirely within Posthumus' dream. <cym_3126-8> In *The Tempest*, all such fantasies occur within the context of Prospero's conceptualised island. <tmp_1807-8>

Stage direction ...Prospero starts suddenly and speaks, after which to a strange hollow and confused noise, they heavily vanish.
(The Tempest 1807-8)

Moreover, most God utterances are spontaneous ejaculations rather than religious invocations of God or gods. Many of the evocations of God or Gods in *F* are in the form of involuntary oaths, curses, or interjected pleas and thanks. Appropriately, these unwilled verbalisations of doubt, anguish, pain, and insight give voice to those mind-based sensations for which the name of God lends itself eponymously.

The frequent exclamations, s'oath, marry, etc., also reflexively acknowledge that God, Mary, Christ and others are primarily vocalisations of deeply felt feminine and masculine eroticised eurekas. Shakespeare appreciates the irony that such unbidden and usually forbidden expressions of delight or disgust as fuck and God derive from the erotic roots of language.

The intense mind-based sensation of unity expressed in the exclamation of a word like God is common to many cultures. The deeply affective sensation becomes associated with the name of a deity through enculturalisation. Because the word God is an ejaculation whose only referent is a deeply felt mind-based sensation, those who think otherwise surround the word with blasphemous implications to distract from its erotic origins.

The differing words in use across Europe for the same inward sensation, though, provide a clue to the problem of expecting the deeply felt sensation to function ethically in propositional language. Shakespeare understands that when the singular God is called on to intercede in partisan interests then the God that emerges from deep interior sensations into articulate language magnetises murderous divisions in a way nature never does. The difference is that nature has a reality external to mind-based sensations while the interior sensation vocalised as God is never more than a circumscribed singularity.

When beseechers across Shakespeare's greater Europe seek the assistance of their God to exact revenge, to overcome enemies, to bring riches, to subdue women, etc., the illogicality of maintaining the singularity of the God sensation while beseeching Him in everyday speech to act divisively becomes apparent. As Shakespeare explores in *Richard III*, tragedy arises when both sides of the monarchic/religious conflict seek the same earthly rewards from their personally attentive God in terms of victories or revenge. <r3_1267&2848-9> Not one of them calls on nature for such violent collaboration.

> *Richard* God will revenge it.
> ...
> *Queen Margaret* Cancel his bond of life, dear God I pray,
> That I may live and say, The Dog is dead.
> **(Richard III 1267, 2848-9)**

On those occasions in *F* when Shakespeare employs the word God most religiously he usually scripts it into the mouths of bishops, priests, kings and others who are committed to enforcing subservience to the male-God. <h8_2369-71> The most telling exposé of male-based excesses is in *Henry VIII* where Shakespeare itemises Cardinal Wolsey's cupidity and carnality. So ingrained is the churchman's graft that

> *Wolsey* Had I but served my God, with half the Zeal
> I served my King: he would not in mine Age
> Have left me naked to mine Enemies.
> **(Henry VIII 2369-71)**

when Henry, who is previously blind to Wolsey's abuses, is forced to acknowledge them he strips Wolsey of power. Wolsey reveals his complete corruption later when he bleats sanctimoniously the most disingenuous contrition in all Shakespeare's works. <h8_2294-7>

> *Wolsey* I am able now (me thinks)
> (Out of a Fortitude of Soul, I feel)
> To endure more Miseries, and greater far
> Than my Weak-hearted Enemies, dare offer.
> **(Henry VIII 2294-7)**

Neither are there occasions in a play when the liturgy, prayers or hymns play out within the sanctum of cathedrals or chapels that mark the European landscape. Probably the closest characters come to consecrated space is the sculpture gallery adjacent to the private chapel in Paulina's country house during the last act of *The Winters Tale*.

In Shakespeare's plays, while there are no religious services as such, there are a number of weddings, funerals and coronations. However, most occur offstage with the ceremonial doings relayed to the audience through the mouths of inquisitive dogsbodies. <h8_2504-5>

Third Gentleman **Came to the Altar, where she kneeled, and Saint-like Cast her fair eyes to Heaven, and prayed devoutly.**
(Henry VIII 2504-5)

Although many of the plays open in either domestic, city or country environs, only one play begins in proximity to a church <1h6_3> while another ends around a baptismal font. <h8_3356-7> Where churches or monasteries set the scene, the cast does not perform inside consecrated buildings. Rather characters congregate in rooms such as the Friar's cell part way through *Romeo and Juliet*, in monastery doorways at the beginning of *Measure for Measure* and at the end of *The Comedy of Errors* or the chapel gallery in *The Winter's Tale*. Famously, Hamlet consigns Ophelia to a nunnery but she misreads her cue and ends up in a 'glassy stream'.

Stage direction **Enter the Funeral of King Henry Fifth,**
(1 Henry VI 3)

Stage direction **…two Noblemen, bearing great standing Bowls for Christening Gifts:**
(Henry VIII 3356-7)

A scan shows that Shakespeare uses monastic retreats in Ephesus, Vienna, and Sicily principally as refuges for women rejected, abused or isolated by their experiences in a male dominant world. This is apparently the case with Isabella in *Measure for Measure*, patently the case with Abbess Amelia in *The Comedy of Errors* and wittingly the case with Hermione in *The Winter's Tale*.

Each of the three women emerges from their monastic hideaways when the male world is reconciled with female priority. Abbess Amelia reunites with a male (Egeon) who is under threat of death in the unnatural confusions of a male-male world. Then, near-nun Isabella unites with a male (Vincentio) who has adroitly determined the course of their play. For her part, Hermione withdraws to punish a would-be murderer (Leontes) who reacts to a perceived disloyalty like a vengeful God.

Shakespeare uses the syndrome dramatically to end *The Comedy of Errors* where Egeon is shocked to find his wife Amilia still alive after apparently being lost at sea. Similarly, in *The Winter's Tale* Leontes reunites pseudo-miraculously with his wife Hermione years after arranging to have her murdered. <wt_3207-8> In a brilliant variation in *Measure for Measure*, Vincentio, who has already matured as a male but dons a monkish disguise, stage-manages Isabella's recovery of natural philosophy after her near-monastic experience early in the play. <mm_351-2>

Paulina **To see the Life as lively mocked, as ever Still Sleep mocked Death:**
(The Winter's Tale 3207-8)

In *The Merchant of Venice*, Shakespeare adds a monastic prank when Portia decides to resolve the male-based set-to

Isabella **…I speak not as desiring more, But rather wishing a more strict restraint**
(Measure for Measure 351-2)

Portia I have toward heaven breathed a secret vow,
To live in prayer and contemplation,
...
There is a monastery two miles off,
And there we will abide.
(The Merchant of Venice 1753-8)

between Christianity and Jewry. In a lively mock of the religious intolerance that drives the conflict, she pretends to retire to a monastery near her hilltop town of Belmont. <mv_1753-8>

Portia's 'secret' intention is to cross-dress as a male-cum-God (hence the monastic deceit) to do the work God proves inept at – administering his kingdom. By demonstrating feminine wiles inside her masculine pants, Portia presents Shakespeare's insight that a male God who usurps female priority maroons himself in a merciless moral vacuum.

Furthermore, Shakespeare's critique of religious celibacy is particularly sharp in *Love's Labour's Lost* where the King and three Lords

Berowne What is the end of study, let me know?
Ferdinand Why that to know which else we should not know.
Berowne Things hid and barred (you mean) from common sense.
Ferdinand Ay, that is studies god-like recompence.
(Love's Labour's Lost 59-63)

of Navarre hope to retire for three years of monastic seclusion to achieve 'God-like' recompence. <lll_59-63> But their plans are thwarted initially when Berowne questions the logic of barring women and hence 'common sense' from their plan to achieve extraterrestrial illumination. Then, by the play's end, the four visiting women from France dash the men's monastic hopes. There will be no monastic 'recompense' for the hapless lords. Instead, the savvy females

Queen Your oath I will not trust: but go with speed
To some forlorn and naked Hermitage,
(Love's Labour's Lost 2754-5)

consign them separately to a poor house or hospital to reconsider their excessive idealistic miscalculations. <lll_2754-5>

Not only are there no significant references to Christian Gods, goddesses or the institutional Church in any of the plays, Shakespeare parodies the miraculous claims of those institutions. In *The Merry Wives of Windsor*, Falstaff receives a mock visitation from fairies. <wiv_2529-30> In *Cymbeline*, Jupiter descends on a stage apparatus from the Gods to speak to Posthumus in a dream. In *The Winter's Tale*, Hermione mocks miraculous expectations by returning from semi-monastic seclusion as a white-powdered imitation of a statue that appears to come to life.

The number of times religious commentators refer to these events as miraculous is a wicked irony consequent

Falstaff They are Fairies, he that speaks to them shall die,
I'll wink, and couch: No man their works must eye.
(The Merry Wives of Windsor 2529-30)

on their desperation to convert Shakespeare to their religious affiliations.

The evidence, then, suggests the plays in *F* conform to the priority of nature over God that Shakespeare articulates in *Q*. No amount of speculation about Shakespeare's relationship to Christianity or any other creed can counter the evidence that the continent of the plays in *F* is a natural environment constitutionally free of religious prejudices and written in no small part to counter those prejudices.

The evidence of the plays suggests Shakespeare arrives at the default status of nature after dismissing male-God systems of governance as inherently unstable and murderous. The God-King syndrome prevalent in his day is far worse in practice than any natural disaster.

Chapter 17: How the plays regard the female/male dynamic

What can the organisation of the 1623 Folio tell us about the relation of female to male? And, what happens when we revisit the connection between F and the two long poems published in 1593 and 1594?

60: Sexual differentiation in the Folio

We began Part 2 by exploring the basic relationships between the 1609 *Sonnets* and the 1623 *Folio*. We find considerable support in *F* for an elemental rooting of Shakespeare's works in nature. The plays answer to a natural dynamic when tested against the philosophy laid out in the 154 sonnets.

The *Sonnets*, *Venus and Adonis* and Prospero's island have a generic similarity and there are many other consistencies across Shakespeare's works. For instance, on the model of Q and *F*, it is more than coincidence that *Venus and Adonis* and *The Rape of Lucrece* and the internal dynamic of *The Tempest* each inter-relates the generic with Italian patriarchal prejudice on the coast of continental Europe.

When we turn to the female/male dynamic, both the *Sonnets* and *Venus and Adonis* argue for the priority of the female over the male. As the 154 sonnets imply, the singular status of the human female over the male in nature is a given. Yet, biblical religions for the last 4000 years usurp the natural order by instituting a male God prior to all else. A survey, then, of the plays looking for instances of female priority versus male priority should highlight whether Shakespeare bases his works in nature or in male-based God/s.

The Tempest is an interesting case on two accounts. First, it has a plot largely of Shakespeare's own devising and so not adapted from previous plots or stories. Second, it is the lead play into the 1623 edition. If *The Tempest*'s position at the beginning of *F* is deliberate, we should reflect on *F*'s organisation into three categories of plays: Comedies, Histories and Tragedies.

In *Hamlet*, Shakespeare has Hamlet mock Polonius when he expands *F*'s three genres of plays into pastoral, tragical-historical, etc. – ten altogether. The willingness since of commentators to mimic Polonius' sub-divisions and even provide extra classifications such as problem plays is an admission Shakespeare's plays as a whole are not understood. <ham_1444-8>

> *Polonius* **The best Actors in the world, either for Tragedy, Comedy, History, Pastoral: Pastorical-Comical-Historical-Pastoral: Tragical-Historical: Tragical-Comical-Historical-Pastoral: Scene indivisible, or Poem unlimited.** (Hamlet 1444-8)

If we attend to the thirty-six plays in *F*, in eleven of the fourteen comedies females direct the female/male interplay. Julia in *The Two Gentlemen of Verona*, Beatrice in *Much Ado About Nothing*, Hermia in *A Midsummer Night's Dream*, Rosalind in *As You Like It*, Mrs Page and Mrs Ford in *The Merry Wives of Windsor* determine the outcome of their plays. Helena in *All's Well that Ends Well*, Portia in *The Merchant of Venice*, the Princess of France in *Love's Labour's Lost*, Viola in *Twelfth Night* and Hermione and Paulina in *The Winter's Tale* assume complete control of their plays.

All the females are instrumental in correcting the prejudices of their male counterparts. The predominance of female-led resolution of male-based conflict in Shakespeare's comedies is contrary to religious tenets of the male-God dominated Elizabethan/Jacobean world.

Shakespeare also explores the consequences when female influence is absent. In *The Comedy of Errors*, Amelia the Abbess disappears at the beginning and reappears at the end of her play. The 'errors' in the title arise in her absence when two sets of male twins act out the hilarious equivocation of redoubled masculine personae.

Shakespeare separates Amelia from her husband and twin sons during a storm at sea before the play begins. When at the play's end violence breaks out between the doubly confounded males, it is within the context of a male-based culture that enforces murderous laws for minor offences. Shakespeare ironically has Amelia emerge from a nearby male-based monastery to affect the recovery of female-based natural philosophy.

In *Love's Labour's Lost*, four males resolve to spend three years cloistered from womankind. Instead, four adroit females aided by their astute male colleague Boyet re-engage the hapless four with the natural world. Each male's newfound love then consigns him to a year of social privation to consider his error. As this appears to be a play of Shakespeare's own devising, it argues strongly for his nature-based dynamic that acknowledges female priority.

In the other three comedies, males who demonstrably have their feminine personae at one with their male personae stage-manage the action. They act to correct the female/male imbalance in the minds of their fellow characters. Petruchio restores Katherine's feminine/masculine balance in *The Taming of the Shrew*, Duke Vincentio returns Christian Vienna to sexual and mental sanity in *Measure for Measure* and Prospero rectifies the male-based prejudices of his Italian colleagues in *The Tempest*.

As eleven plays have mature females in control and three have mature males in charge, Shakespeare lets only females or males whose feminine and masculine personae are in balance direct the action. The maturity of Shakespeare's Poet from Q is evident in all fourteen comedies.

Further analysis of the three male-led comedies is instructive. In *The Taming of the Shrew*, Petruchio eases Katherine out of her male-shift misogyny induced by her father's patriarchal strictures. He instils in her a sense of partnership where by the play's end Petruchio's Kate is able to parody female subservience when she gives a tongue-in-cheek avowal of marital duty in the final scene. <shr_2715-22>

> *Kate* And when she is forward, peevish, sullen, sour,
> And not obedient to his honest will,
> What is she but a foul contending Rebel,
> And graceless Traitor to her loving Lord?
> I am ashamed that women are so simple,
> To offer war, where they should kneel for peace:
> Or seek for rule, supremacy, and sway,
> When they are bound to serve, love, and obey.
> (The Taming of the Shrew 2715-22)

In *Measure for Measure*, Isabella forsakes her dive into male God monasticism to recover her female/feminine wiles in a mature relationship with Vincentio.

Meantime, Shakespeare's Duke, disguised as a monk, addresses another excess of male-based idealism in Vienna. The play compares the seclusion in a nunnery, where sex is eroticised in a heady relationship with Jesus or Mary, to life in a whorehouse, where sex is traded as a physical commodity. The Duke requires Lucio, who gets the whore Mistress Overdone pregnant, to marry her. <mm_2908-12>

> *Duke* **If any woman wronged by this lewd fellow**
> **(As I have heard him swear himself there's one**
> **whom he begot with child) let her appear,**
> **And he shall marry her: the nuptial finish'd,**
> **Let him be whipped and hang'd.**
>
> **(Measure for Measure 2908-12)**

Commentators point to the word measure in New Testament Matthew where the evangelist warns that 'judging' or giving 'award' can work both ways. However, Shakespeare's overview of male-God psychology allows him avoid such equivocation.

Shakespeare's proxy, Duke Vincentio, uses a small measure of religious dysfunction by appointing Lord Angelo to rectify the larger measure of male-based iniquity and excesses in Vienna. Meantime, Vincentio adds his own measure for measure. He adapts the role of a monk to oversee the curing of Vienna's malaise and, in keeping with his intent, doffs the robes when the job is done.

Measure for Measure case-studies the use of male-based ill to cure male-based evil by applying the logic Shakespeare lays out in *118* and *119*. Consistent with *Q*, in *Measure for Measure* Shakespeare reworks his source material to apply a controlled dose of distemper to cure a larger evil.

In *The Tempest*, Prospero unburdens himself to Miranda in the first act. He confesses to his male-driven shame that, as his first-born, she was female. <tmp_148-51> Miranda's status as first-born did not fulfil the customary privilege of male primogeniture. When the injustice of rejecting her dawns on him, Prospero abandons his ducal duties and begins 'secret studies'. He discovers that the imaginary basis of male-imposed power can be foiled using imaginary means – hence Shakespeare's metaphorical island.

> *Prospero* **Thy Mother was a piece of virtue, and**
> **She said thou wast my daughter; and thy father**
> **Was Duke of Milan, and his only heir,**
> **And Princess: no worse Issued.**
>
> **(The Tempest 148-51)**

A few lines later in the same scene we discover Prospero's brother Antonio ousts Prospero from Milan in part because Antonio at least produces a son. <tmp_588-9> Prospero's apology to Miranda and his support for her genuine love match with Ferdinand later in the play signals Prospero's willingness – gained through his studies – to make amends for his male-biased offences against nature.

> *Ferdinand* ...**the Duke of Milan**
> **And his brave son,**
>
> **(The Tempest 588-9)**

The nature-based maturity of the three males, who use their feminine/masculine sensitivity to stage manage their own plays, can be shown by comparing Vincentio, Petruchio and Prospero's capacity for oversight to the characters Harold Bloom favours. [note 2] Bloom insists Hamlet and Falstaff are Shakespeare's most intelligently mobile characters because they reinvent themselves during their plays. As fascinating as Hamlet and Falstaff may be as thinking males they are still victims of their own headlines – both die without significant insight into the circumstances of their fate. Shakespeare does not allow them to mastermind their own plays but strands them between half-baked scepticism and self-pity. <ham_1737-9> <wiv_2310-4>

> **Hamlet** Thus Conscience does make Cowards of us all,
> And thus the Native hew of Resolution
> Is sicklied o'er, with the pale cast of Thought,
> (Hamlet 1737-9)

In contrast, Petruchio, Vincentio and Prospero successfully carry out their assignments to realign the feminine/masculine imbalance in their neighbourhoods. They do so without causing the loss of life that blights Hamlet's reputation. Neither are they shamed for cowardice with their parts killed off as was Falstaff in *1 Henry IV* and then reshamed mercilessly on his zombie encore in *The Merry Wives of Windsor*. <wiv_2606-10>

> **Falstaff** ...if it should come to the ear of the Court, how I have been transformed; and how my transformation has been washed, and cudgelled, they would melt me out of my fat drop by drop,   (The Merry Wives of Windsor 2310-4)

> **Falstaff** I was three or four times in the thought they were not Fairies, and yet the guiltiness of my mind, the sudden surprise of my powers, drove the grossness of foppery into a receiv'd belief, in despite of the teeth of all rime and reason, that they were Fairies.
> (The Merry Wives of Windsor 2606-10)

The dumbing down of Shakespeare's empowered women and men is evident in the title of John Dennis' 1702 *The Comical Gallant; or, the Amours of Sir John Falstaff* and Giuseppe Verdi's 1893 *Falstaff*. When such melo-dramatisers name Falstaff in their titles, they destroy the female-based focus of Shakespeare's title *The Merry Wives of Windsor*.

Bloom's enthusiasm for the pathos of psychological end games is accentuated by his even greater failure to account for the extraordinary control Viola, Hermione and the Princess of France (to name just three of Shakespeare's canny and cunning women) have over their plays and the males in them. Bloom is typical of the many commentators who fail to appreciate, and so involuntarily condemn, Shakespeare's brilliant application of natural logic. They are blind to Shakespeare's restoration of female/male priority and the logic of truth and beauty in plays like *The Taming of the Shrew* and *Measure for Measure*.

When we profile Shakespeare's ten English histories, the contrast to the female empowering comedies is striking. All the histories are titled with the names of males – and all of them are named Kings of England – four Henrys, two Richards and a John. Each of the histories examines the illogicality of male dominance, male primogeniture and life or death allegiance to a male God/King.

The point is emphasised in *King John* where Shakespeare inserts the unhistorical character of the Bastard to better show up the prejudices in male-based social/political/religious conventions. (kj_82-5) Commentators have noted the irony in *Henry V* where Shakespeare gives a less than jingoistic account of

> **Philip** But once he slandered me with bastardy:
> But where I be as true begot or no,
> That still I lay upon my mother's head,
> But that I am as well begot as my Liege
> (King John 82-5)

> *Williams* ...for how can they charitably dispose of any thing, when Blood is their argument? Now, if these men do not die well, it will be a black matter for the King, that led them to it; who to disobey, were against all proportion of subjection.　　　　(Henry V 1990-4)

King Henry's victories in France. <h5_1990-4> Then at the end of the play Shakespeare seems to take pleasure in predicting the slide in monarchic fortunes when Henry's son loosens the reins in *1 Henry VI*.

In the scorched world of the tragedies, the contrast is even starker. The male-based injustices in the histories do not all lead inevitably to murder and mayhem or the untimely death of a King. Yet, only with one telling exception, the males named in the titles of their tragedies wreck mortal havoc on themselves, their families or their communities. The exception is Cymbeline whose overly masculinised wife does it for him. <cym_522-4>

> *Queen* Here comes a flattering Rascal, upon him Will I first work: He's for his Master, And enemy to my Son.　　　　(Cymbeline 522-4)

The catharsis of Shakespeare's tragedies lies not only in their fatal outcomes. The inter-layering of comedy and ridicule enhances the catharsis when Shakespeare has secondary characters assert the sonnet logic in the face of the death wish of the main protagonists.

Two of Shakespeare's tragic females demonstrate an awareness of his nature based philosophy. Cordelia in *King Lear* and Desdemona in *Othello* challenge their fathers' male-driven expectation of absolute love early in their plays. Both Cordelia and Desdemona avow that the natural logic of increase determines they give part of their love to their fathers and part to their partners. They argue that persistence through increase has priority over male-driven ideals. (lr_98-110)

> *Cordelia*　　　 ...I love your Majesty
> According to my bond, no more nor less...
> You have begot me, bred me, loved me.
> I return those duties back as are right fit,
> Obey you, Love you, and most Honour you.
> Why have my Sisters Husbands, if they say
> They love you all? Happily when I shall wed,
> That Lord, whose hand must take my plight, shall carry
> Half my love with him, half my Care, and Duty,
> Sure I shall never marry like my Sisters.
> 　　　　(King Lear 98-110)

Conversely, in *Macbeth* Shakespeare illustrates the power-crazed abuse of feminine/masculine interchangeability. Lady Macbeth denies her female/feminine side for the excesses of male-like dominance and violence. (mac_533-38)

Moreover, in those plays in which a leading female dies such as *Hamlet*, *Othello*, *Romeo and Juliet*, *King Lear*, *Anthony and Cleopatra*, and *Macbeth*, the fate of the female (as predicted in *The Rape of Lucrece*) is sealed by male/masculine intransigence and insensitivity to female priority.

> *Lady Macbeth* I have given Suck, and know How tender 'tis to love the Babe that milks me, I would, while it was smiling in my Face, Have plucked my Nipple from his Boneless Gums, And dashed the Brains out, had I so sworn As you have done to this.　　　　(Macbeth 533-38)

There is little doubt *F*'s order of Comedies, Histories and Tragedies distinguishes between the female/feminine driven comedies and male/masculine driven histories and tragedies. The difference is so marked we have to think Shakespeare intended it.

If we draw a logical line through the three genres, it neatly intersects with

Q and the longer poems. The primacy of nature over goddesses and gods and the appreciation of the constitutive value of female/male partnership is a non-negotiable given across Shakespeare's works.

61: Name or no name in the play titles

When we look again at the play titles in each of the three genres as they appear in F, we see Shakespeare adds another level of generality consistent with the trends observed so far. All the comedies in F have generic titles – not one of them bears a name from the cast of characters.

(Pericles, Prince of Tyre was not published in Folio format until 1664. If it had been included in F it might have been called The Prince of Tyre. The Two Noble Gentlemen, the other play not in F but usually accepted into the canon, does have a generic title. It was published in quarto format in 1634 under the combined authorship of Fletcher and Shakespeare.)

The non-specific titling of the fourteen comedies suggests their purpose is independent of the forefront characters. Shakespeare uses their nature and female validating content to defuse the excesses of a God-orientated Europe. Their resolution of male-based inconsistencies and masculine imbalances in both females and males offers a variety of models for the practical realignment of sexual and gender expectations.

The opposite is the case with the ten histories. Their titles name seven English Kings. Shakespeare analyses the malconsequences of allowing delusional males access to power on the presumption of male priority fostered by a male-based religion.

The effect of the double-male usurpation is to marginalise females. Only when the male line of descent is exhausted can a female ascend the throne and then primarily to perpetuate the ruling dynasty. Shakespeare makes the point sardonically when he ends Henry VIII with the birth of Elizabeth Tudor. <h8_2968-73>

> King ...Is the Queen delivered?
> Say Ay, and of a boy.
> Old Lady Ay, Ay my Liege,
> And of a lovely Boy: the God of heaven
> Both now, and ever bless her: 'Tis a Girl
> Promises Boys hereafter.
> (Henry VIII 2968-73)

In his histories, Shakespeare audits the murderous intrigues and senseless wars perpetrated by England's Kings. He has Richard II describe the cut-throat culture succinctly in his play. <r2_1515-20>

> Richard For Heaven's sake let us sit upon the ground,
> And tell sad stories of the death of Kings:
> How some have been deposed, some slain in war,
> Some haunted by the Ghosts they have deposed,
> Some poison'd by their Wives, some sleeping kill'd,
> All murder'd.   (Richard II 1515-20)

Shakespeare shows the dysfunctional syndrome to be largely the upshot of the abrogation of the natural philosophy he articulates in Q. As he has Tarquin argue (albeit disingenuously) in The Rape of Lucrece, while we cannot always avoid the ravages of nature it is well within our capabilities to correct the illogical outcomes of male-driven idealistic excesses. <rl_538-9>

For marks descried in men's nativity,
Are nature's faults, not their own infamy.
(The Rape of Lucrece 538-9)

Like the histories, the twelve tragedies in F carry the name of the male protagonist in their titles. In order of appearance they are Troilus, Coriolanus, Andronicus, Timon, Romeo, Caesar, Macbeth, Hamlet, Lear, Othello, Anthony, and Cymbeline. While most are tragic perpetrators of male-based monarchic/religious, social, political and personal injustices, Romeo by his relative youthfulness seems an unwitting victim of the ruling patriarchy.

The first eleven names identify males directly or indirectly responsible for causing murderous mayhem. In ten of the plays, they also bring about their own demise. In *Troilus and Cressida*, Troilus survives his play and in *Cymbeline* it is his wife and stepson who die. Is there a reason for beginning and ending the tragedies with *Troilus and Cressida* and *Cymbeline* where the title male survives?

In *The Tragedy of Troilus and Cressida*, Troilus survives his double masculinisation. We give full title for the 1623 *Folio* version of *Troilus and Cressida* because it was published previously in a 1609 quarto as a history: *The Famous Historie of Troylus and Cresseid*. However, as we have seen, the only plays F calls histories are Shakespeare's case studies of seven English Kings.

We also need to account for *Troilus and Cressida* appearing as a late addition to F. Not only is *Troilus and Cressida* a history in 1609 and a tragedy in 1623, it is squeezed in with mostly unnumbered pages before *Coriolanus*, which begins the continuous page count from 1 to 399 to the end of the last play, *Cymbeline*. In contrast, *Troilus and Cressida* has only its second leaf strangely numbered 79/80 recto/verso while none of its other 26 pages is numbered.

We first note that *Troilus and Cressida* is the only tragedy to begin with a prologue and 'The Prologue' has a full-page to itself. In 'The Prologue' Shakespeare seems to identify the characteristic feature of all his tragedies – and effectively all his comedies and histories. According to 'The Prologue', the pretext for the 'cruel war' or 'quarrel' between the Greeks and Trojans is the 'ravished Helen, Menelaus' Queen' with whom the 'wanton Paris sleeps'.

While the other Shakespearean tragedies involve the death of the title character or his wife (or both), in *Troilus and Cressida* it is Hector, one of Troilus' brothers, who dies on the 'Dardan Plains' outside 'Priam's six-gated City'. It seems that the first play of the tragedies identifies the underlying injustice behind the tragic outcome of the following eleven plays. Congruent with the *Sonnet* philosophy, the prologue points to a debacle in female/male relationships as the root cause that leads to otherwise avoidable tragedy.

When editors reclassify *Troilus and Cressida* as a tragi-comedy despite the play being included with the other tragedies in F, they ignore the tragic consequence of Hector's about-face after he argues persuasively against Paris' abduction of Helen. <tro_1153-83> Hector first advocates her return

Hector Paris and Troilus...
If Helen then be wife to Sparta's King
(As it is known she is) these Moral Laws
Of Nature, and of Nation, speak aloud
To have her back returned. Thus to persist
In doing wrong, extenuates not wrong,
But makes it much more heavy. Hector's opinion
Is in this way of truth: yet ne'er the less,
My spritely brethren, I propend to you
In resolution to keep Helen still;
For 'tis a cause that hath no mean dependence,
Upon our joint and several dignities.
(Troilus and Cressida 1153-83)

to Greece, but then overrides his own logic in an act of male-brotherly collusion that leads ultimately to his death at the hands of Achilles.

Although Troilus and Cressida survive their play, Troilus recognises that Hector's ignominious death could portend the 'sure destruction' of Troy if the 'gods' do not quickly 'smile at Troy'. Hector, as the one who equivocates over the return of the abducted Helen, symbolises the fatal weakness in the Trojan/Greek rationale for war. His death signals the beginning of Troy's collapse and points to male/female perversion at the cankered heart of Shakespearean tragedy. Shakespeare's play-script argues against the treatment of women as male property and as an excuse for ten years of gratuitous carnage.

Because The Prologue to *Troilus and Cressida* specifically identifies the skewing of the female/male dynamic in nature as the basis for Shakespearean tragedy, and because the same syndrome lies behind all Shakespeare's tragedies, we can now see that the whole play *Troilus and Cressida* with its unnumbered pages acts effectively as a prologue for the following eleven tragedies.

The only other tragedy where a male title character survives his play seems to provide some symmetry in the organisation of the tragedies in *F*. In the last play in *F*, Cymbeline survives despite his patriarchal madness of threatening to kill Posthumus on hearing his daughter Imogen and Posthumus have married secretly.

The tragedy in *Cymbeline* is that his Queen and his stepson Cloten die as a direct consequence of her usurpation of the masculine role of determinator in the biological vacuum created when Cymbeline suffers the consequences of his patriarchal misjudgements. <cym_3288-90> The Queen's death is as much a tragedy as the death of males in the other tragedies as she represents the death of Cymbeline's feminine persona.

Cornelius **With horror, madly dying, like her life,**
Which (being cruel to the world) concluded
Most cruel to her self.   (Cymbeline 3288-90)

Commentators frequently belittle her death – no doubt because she is female – in their determination to reassign the play to tragi-comedy or classify it as a late romance. However, Shakespeare intends Cymbeline to complete the cycle of tragedies if only to show that the overly masculine persona of a female is – Lady Macbeth-like – as potentially murderous as a doubled masculine persona in a male.

Not all the title characters in the tragedies are implicated in their own destruction. Romeo particularly, and to some extent Hamlet, are more or less victims. Romeo and Juliet die as a result of the male-based prejudices festering in the houses of Montagu and Capulet. <rj_23-6> For his part, Hamlet struggles to uncover and comprehend the psycho-logical malaise in the state of Denmark after his uncle murders his father and his mother betrays natural justice.

Gregory **The Quarrel is between our Masters, and us their men.**
Sampson **'Tis all one, I will show myself a tyrant: when I have fought with the men. I will be civil with the Maids, and cut off their heads.   (Romeo and Juliet 23-6)**

Again, traditional ignorance of the 154-sonnet philosophy leaves the commentators scrambling to understand these plays. Their response is to create further categories of plays – the trait mocked so laconically in *Hamlet* – and so dodge their critical obligations. They argue pointlessly over exactly which play goes in which new genre.

Yet, the three categories in *F* are more than adequate to account for Shakespeare's intent to create works that either illustrate in the female/male partnerships of the comedies his philosophy in practice, or show the avoidable consequences when natural philosophy is violated in the religiously male-based histories and tragedies.

The clear influence of Shakespeare's nature-based philosophy in *F*'s organisation is also lost and confused in later editions of the complete plays that present them in order of their first date of writing or performance. Again, commentators waste energy arguing over when the plays were written or produced. The editions that do set the plays out according to their date of writing mix comedies, histories and tragedies. Consequently, the intended division in *F* between the generically titled comedies and the male titled histories and tragedies is lost from view. The recent recourse by many modern commentators to the original presentation in *F* reflects on a history of critical ineptitude.

Jonathan Bate (CBE) demonstrates the confusion amongst editors. Bate adheres to the 1623 *Folio* order of plays in the recent Royal Shakespeare Company edition 2008 of the complete works. Yet, while Bate includes the 154 sonnets, and the longer poems *Venus and Adonis* and *The Rape of Lucrece*, he inexplicably cuts *A Lover's Complaint*.

When questioned, Bate disingenuously claims there was not sufficient space as the volume was limited to 2576 pages. [**note 3**] Yet, not only does Bate find space to include a recently found but very unShakespearean ditty titled *To the Queen*, he finds room enough to add pages of barely relevant genealogical charts of the English Kings and Queens.

The mixed chronology that is a feature of the arrangement of the plays in *F* suggests Shakespeare felt no constraint to write in a particular genre at any time in his playwriting career. Hence, *Henry VIII* (~1613) appears late as a history play just as *Titus Andronicus* (~1592) is an early tragedy and *The Winter's Tale* (~1607) is a late comedy. Over the period 1590 to 1613, Shakespeare felt free to use any of the three genres to articulate both the life-affirming nature-based philosophy structured into Q and critique the illogical practices abounding in the religious and political sects and factions across Europe.

For the commentators to reclassify a tragedy as tragi-comedy completely misses the point of the comedic passages in those plays. Shakespeare interjects comedy into his histories and tragedies to interleave his *Sonnet* logic into the male-based excesses. On stage, the comedies or comedic elements in the histories and tragedies appeal to the natural philosophy inherent in the mind of every member of Shakespeare's audience. Shakespeare's humour circumvents their forebrain dogmatic belief in the convention of a male-based God.

Typically, the audience either appreciates the catharsis of the experience or rejects it as contrary to its beliefs. The latter experience drives most of the alterations and emendations to Shakespeare's works by commentators.

62: Pairing myth and history in the poems of 1593/4

We now return to the mythical geography of *Venus and Adonis* and the Roman history of *The Rape of Lucrece* to explore further their role in forecasting the transition from the *Sonnets* to the plays. We will also subject *The Phoenix and the Turtle* to further analysis.

Venus The tender spring upon thy tempting lip
Shows thee unripe; yet mayst thou well be tasted,
Make use of time, let not advantage slip,
Beauty within it self should not be wasted.
  Fair flowers that are not gathered in their prime,
  Rot, and consume them selves in little time.
    (Venus and Adonis 127-32)

When we look to the mythical hunting ground of *Venus and Adonis*, we see Shakespeare's rearrangement of Ovid's poem dates from 1593. Consequently, similarities with the sonnet logic are evident in its 1194 lines. The most obvious is that Venus, the goddess (or Mistress) next to nature, has priority over the male god Adonis who is cast in the role of the Master Mistress. <va_127-32>

Venus Upon the earth's increase why shouldst thou feed,
Unless the earth with thy increase be fed?
By law of nature thou art bound to breed,
That thine may live, when thou thyself art dead:
  And so in spite of death thou dost survive,
  In that thy likeness still is left alive.
    (Venus and Adonis 169-74)

Early in her poem, Venus impresses the increase argument on Adonis, <va_169-74> but he persists to the end in considering increase 'strange'. The opening stanzas also exhibit the same emphasis on beauty evident in *1* to *14*. However, with Adonis hostile to the logic of increase, Venus is unimpressed as he implodes selfishly. <va_789-92>

Adonis I hate not love, but your device in love,
That lends embracements to every stranger,
You do it for increase, O strange excuse!
When reason is the bawd to lust's abuse.
    (Venus and Adonis 789-92)

In anticipation of the Master Mistress' potential fate in *126*, nature brings Adonis to a final audit when a charging boar gores him in the groin.

At the poem's end, because Adonis refuses pigheadedly to acknowledge the logic of increase in nature, Venus demonstrates that when selfish males die their buried fate is to fertilise flowers. The flower Venus plucks and holds to her bosom is in remembrance of the blindness of Adonis' male-based idealism.

Venus, who represents both nature and archetypal female, is now bereft of a male sexual counterpart so cannot increase (as argued in *11*). Hence, Adonis' inaction voids increase. She returns to Paphos with her generative hopes imprisoned in the truncated flower of male intransigence. Together they are

Thus weary of the world, away she hies,
And yokes her silver doves, by whose swift aid,
Their mistress mounted through the empty skies,
In her light chariot, quickly is conveyed,
  Holding their course to Paphos, where their queen,
  Means to immure her self, and not been seen.
    (Venus and Adonis 1189-94)

immured in their own mythic verse as no poem can substitute for the natural dynamic of increase. <va_1189-94>

Venus and Adonis proves to be a deeply philosophical poem at one with the *Sonnets*. When we turn to Roman Italy, we first note that *The Rape of Lucrece* at 1855 lines is a half-size larger than *Venus and Adonis* and has an extra line per stanza. While the text and typography is similar to *Venus and Adonis*, its extra line per stanza and length seems designed to carry the 'graver labour' Shakespeare promises in the dedication of *Venus and Adonis*.

When we seek reasons for its deeper purpose, we find *Lucrece* lacks the immediate presence of a controlling figure such as Venus as the female who provides a direct connection with nature. Instead, it focuses on three Adonis-like Romans, Colatine, Tarquin and Lucrece, whose fates are a consequence of denying their natural philosophy.

In *Lucrece*, we encounter first the Roman commander Colatine boasting with inflated pride to his friend Tarquin and others of the faithfulness of his wife Lucrece. <rl_8-10> It is as

> *Argument* ...everyone commended the virtues of his own wife: among whom Colatinus extolled the incomparable chastity of his wife Lucretia ...   (The Rape of Lucrece 8-10)

if Adonis' friends in the background of his poem return to create the male-based camaraderie that launches Tarquin's sexual travesty.

However, as we learn later in the poem, Lucrece's faithfulness is maintained by Colatine's possessive control of her activities leaving her unprepared to recognise danger and so defend herself against Tarquin's assault. As in the *Sonnet* philosophy, Shakespeare addresses the illogicality of male priority in *Lucrece* that subjugates the female.

Tarquin acts out the logical consequence of Colatine and Lucrece's unnatural divorce from the logic of life. Colatine's prideful boasting incites Tarquin to seek out Lucrece in her home. He responds so feverishly to her unnatural isolation that despite raping her he fails to ejaculate. <rl 697-700>

> The prey wherein by nature they delight:
> So surfeit-taking Tarquin fares this night:
> His taste delicious, in digestion souring,
> Devours his will that liv'd by foul devouring.
> (The Rape of Lucrece 697-700)

In the last lines of the poem, the culpability of Colatine is evident when he and Lucrece's father fight over her bloodied body. <rl_1800-6> By comparison, Tarquin's more symbolic role is evident in his exile rather than execution. This is despite Colatine's promise to Lucrece that Tarquin would die. Hence, the short title *Lucrece* that appears on the original 1594 title page emphasises that Lucrece's overly male-infected state of mind is the logical centre of the poem, which leads to her rape by Tarquin.

> O, quoth Lucretius, I did give that life
> Which she too early and too late hath spill'd.
> Woe woe, quoth Colatine, she was my wife,
> I owed her, and 'tis mine that she hath kill'd.
> My daughter and my wife with clamours fill'd
>   The dispers'd air, who holding Lucrece's life
> Answer'd their cries, my daughter and my wife.
>   (The Rape of Lucrece 1800-6)

By anticipating the logical structure of the *Sonnets* and the natural balance of its elements, *Venus and Adonis* and *The Rape of Lucrece* serve as a warning to those who engage with the plays. The two poems reprise the natural philosophy of the 154 sonnet set and its adjacent *A Lover's Complaint* by critiquing those who fail to appreciate the priority of nature over mind-based expectations. Both long poems argue for the priority of the female over the male, the logic of increase and the consequent logic of truth and beauty.

In turn, *The Phoenix and the Turtle* at 67 lines is much shorter than the other poems. However, it seems to compensate for its shortness with its richness and intricacy.

Though short, *The Phoenix and the Turtle* reflects the natural patterns in Q. We hear mention of Nature, posterity (increase) and truth and beauty, <pt_59-61> and the familiar dismissal of otherworldly expectations. Married chastity is

Leaving no posterity,
'Twas not their infirmity,
It was married Chastity.
(The Phoenix and the Turtle 59-61)

lampooned as is the traditional Phoenix-like hope of disembodied reincarnation. <pt_65-7>

To this urn let those repair,
That are either true or fair,
For these dead Birds, sigh a prayer.
(The Phoenix and the Turtle 65-67)

Instead, in the last line the Poet asks sardonically that a prayer be sighed over the incinerated bodies of the two birds who have been undone by their headstrong fantasies. Crucial to the correct reading is the comma in the last line removed in modern editions.

We will continue to explore the consistency and frequency with which the plays address these concerns. In what way do nature and the sexual dynamic determine other aspects of Shakespeare's works? If Shakespeare did have the basics of a philosophy already worked out early in his career as a playwright, there should be further evidence it underpins his enterprise for over twenty years.

Shifting more and more into focus is Shakespeare's overview of his project involving the sonnets, plays and poems. The strands of evidence show a consistency between a regard for nature and the natural originary relationship of female and male.

Chapter 18: Increase in the plays and poems

If increase is a natural consequence of the sexual dynamic in nature, how frequently does the potential for increase surface as an issue in the plays? What other aspects of Shakespeare's plays are influenced by the recognition of the logical relation of increase to female and male survival?

63: The frequency of increase in the plays

Taking our lead from Q, we began by evaluating the predominance of nature in F. Nature singular and the same permeates all the plays. It puts in shadow any one of the many goddesses or gods from the regions' religions.

In contrast to nature, the various goddesses and gods receive their cue according to Shakespeare's dramatic requirements in the comedies and tragedies. In the histories, all his leading characters invoke the Christian God. While there is no critique of the status of nature or its effects throughout the plays, in the history plays particularly Shakespeare countermands the frequency of God talk with criticism of God-driven excesses.

We have seen how F separates into female and male orientated genres. Fourteen female-based comedies and twenty-two male-based histories and tragedies echo the division between female and male sequences in Q. As with the lengthier Master Mistress sequence, a greater number of plays deal with the problem of male dominance and its tragic outcomes.

Juno and others Long continuance, and increasing,
(Tempest 1768)
Parrolles Loss of Virginity, is / rational increase,
(All's Well that Ends Well 132-3)
Parrolles ...which is goodly / increase
(All's Well that Ends Well 152-3)
Titania By their increase, ... / We are their parents and original.
(A Midsummer Night's Dream 489-92)
Richard If I have killed the issue of your womb,
To quicken your increase, I will beget
Mine issue of your blood, upon your Daughter:
(Richard III 3081-3)
Cominius My dear Wife's estimate, her womb's increase,
And treasure of my Loins:
(Coriolanus 2400-1)
Titus Like to the earth swallow her increase.
(Titus Andronicus 2480)
Lear Dry up in her the Organs of increase,
(King Lear 793)

Increase in the plays

When we turn to the evidence for the increase argument in the plays, a search reveals that while the word increase occurs in seventeen of the thirty-six plays its natural correlates occur in every play. <list_increasesamples> The word breed or breeds occurs in thirty-two plays as do the words child or children. Shakespeare accentuates these occurrences with many births, begets, issues, posterities, stores and progenies. The proliferation of increase synonyms sustains the theme throughout F.

The reality of increase within nature is the subtext for Shakespeare's own play *Love's Labour's Lost* from the mid-1590s. Jaquenetta is pregnant before the play begins and gives birth after the play concludes. <lll_2628-9> Shakespeare

Costard ...she is gone; she is two months on her way. (Love's Labour's Lost 2628-9)

parenthesises with the universality of increase a play he designs to showcase his nature-based philosophy.

At the other extreme, Lady Macbeth decides at the heart of her play to reject the logic of increase. Her threat to tear a baby from her breast and kill it for her husband's male-based advantage is a dramatic disavowal that leads to premature death by violence for them both. That Macduff was from a 'woman untimely ripped' provides another instance of troubled increase in a play where the very possibility of increase is used as a weapon against life. <mac_2163-4>

Doctor ...unnatural deeds Do breed unnatural troubles: (Macbeth 2163-4)

Like the givens of nature and the female/male dynamic in Shakespeare's plays, the increase of each individual is not subject to doubt or variation as is the idea of God. Every mortal character in the plays is the beneficiary of increase. Yet none of the many goddesses or gods who flit across Shakespeare's European consciousness is the product of increase. As we have seen in Part 1, all goddesses and gods are erotic constructs hanging from the fly-loft of the human mind.

Shakespeare is by no means insistent all his characters should increase even if nature provides. The homely friar in *Romeo and Juliet*, the super-bureaucrat Escalus in *Measure for Measure*, the fool in *King Lear*, cunning Paulina in *The Winter's Tale*, and many others in Shakespeare's cast of human variability are not challenged to increase or questioned about their attitude to increase.

Shakespeare's primary intent is to challenge beliefs illogically indisposed toward increase or even hostile to its natural requirements. The Master Mistress in the *Sonnets* and Adonis in *Venus and Adonis* represent the self-regarding types Shakespeare confronts with arguments against their purely mind-based selfishness.

Bawd ...and which is more, within these three days his head to be chopp'd off. ...and it is for getting Madam Julietta with child. (Measure for Measure 159-64)

All Shakespeare's female and male characters are born of increase and all are surrounded to some degree by mind-generated erotic beliefs that are contrary to increase. The plays in *F* examine a number of ways to address the idealism that dismisses the logic of increase or show the fateful outcome of not recognising the simple logic of life. <mm_159-64> Shakespeare places purpose-made characters in the plays whose function is to challenge the prejudices surrounding the conventions of arranged or forced marriage, stoic virginity and celibacy, whoredom, primogeniture, bastardy and Platonic love.

Typically, Shakespeare argues against arranged marriages in plays such as *Romeo and Juliet*, *The Tempest*, *The Taming of the Shrew*, *As You Like It*, *All's Well that Ends Well*, *A Mid Summer Night's Dream*, *King Lear*, *Troilus and Cressida*, and *The Merchant of Venice*. He combats parental strictures in which the potential for increase is not the natural consequence of freely avowed love. Frequently, the father presumes the right to decide the matrimonial fate of a daughter. The imposition of male-based prejudice curtails the daughter's natural right to manage her own affairs. <list_arrangedmarriages>

Considering Shakespeare's anathema to forced marriage without love, a freely

Egeus As she is mine, I may dispose of her;
Which shall be either to this Gentleman,
Or to her death, according to our Law,
　　　(A Midsummer Night's Dream 50-2)
Portia ...so is the will of a living daughter curb'd by the will of a dead father:
Jessica To be ashamed to be my Father's child,
But though I am a daughter to his blood,
I am not to his manners:
　　　(The Merchant of Venice 218-9 & 788-90)
Duke If you out-stay the time, upon mine honour,
And in the greatness of my word you die.
　　　　　(As You Like It 549-50)
Baptista ...not to bestow my youngest daughter,
Before I have a husband for the elder:
　　　　(The Taming of the Shrew 352-3)
King Why then young Bertram take her she's thy / wife.
　　　　(All's Well that Ends Well 1003-4)
Cressida Words, vows, gifts, tears, & loves full sacrifice,
He offers in another's enterprise:
　　　　(Troilus and Cressida 440-1)
Capulet　　...Paris, get her heart,
My will to her consent, is but a part,
And she agree, within her scope of choice,
Lies my consent,
...
Capulet Hang thee young baggage, disobedient wretch,
I tell thee what, get thee to Church a Thursday,
Or never after look me in the face.
　　　(Romeo and Juliet 263-6 & 2202-4)
Lear Here I disclaim all my Paternal care,
　　　　(King Lear 120)

Arranged marriages

Furthermore, in *Twelfth Night* Olivia and Sebastian (Viola's twin brother) do undergo a Christian marriage. From beginning to end, the play identifies them as psychologically sensitive individuals given to tearful outbursts. <tn_35-7&2404-6> They lack the philosophic robustness of Viola and her matured Orsino. Shakespeare marries Olivia and Sebastian off a few scenes before

Bertram If she my Liege can make me know this clearly,
I'll love her dearly, ever, ever dearly.
　　　(All's Well that Ends Well 3053-4)

the play's end in front of a priest.

Shakespeare spotlights those like Viola who appreciate the natural philosophy of life. Imbued with the *Sonnet* logic, Viola intuits

made agreement to form a loving bond trumps any formal contract or ceremony of marriage. Isabella and Vincentio in *Measure for Measure* and Viola and Orsino in *Twelfth Night* leave the stage united in mature love without the sanction of Church or State. <mm_2933-6>　　<tn_2490-2&2557-8>

Yet Shakespeare was not beyond arranging a marriage for a male or female character who transgresses the natural philosophy of love. Angelo and Lucio in *Measure for Measure* and Bertram in *All's Well That Ends Well* are obliged – or have matured sufficiently – to marry women to whom they had earlier forsworn betrothal, had compromising sexual relations with, or got with child. <aww_3053-4>

Duke　　　　Dear Isabel,
I have a motion much imports your good,
Whereto if you'll a willing ear incline;
What's mine is yours, and what is yours is mine.
　　　(Measure for Measure 2933-6)

Orsino And since you called me Master, for so long:
Here is my hand, you shall from this time be your Master's Mistress.
...
Orsino But when in other habits you are seen,
Orsino's Mistress, and his fancy's Queen.
　　　(Twelfth Night 2490-2 & 2557-8)

Valentine And water once a day her Chamber round
With eye-offending brine: all this to season
A brother's dead love, *(Of Olivia)*
Sebastian ...Which from the womb I did participate.
Were you a woman, as the rest goes even,
I should my tears let fall upon your cheek,
　　　(Twelfth Night 35-7 & 2404-6)

Olivia **Now go with me, and with this holy man**
Into the Chantry by: there before him,
And underneath that consecrated roof,
Plight me the full assurance of your faith,
                    (Twelfth Night 2138-41)

that by cross-dressing she can redress the male-based Christian usurpation of female priority. In contrast, Shakespeare identifies those like Olivia who, at least within the time-frame of the play, seem unable to appreciate natural logic so are suited to the psychology of a Christian marriage. <tn_2138-41>

In his validation of the natural dynamic of increase, Shakespeare shows his disdain for religious celibacy, virginity, and male supremacy. He puns on the sacred notion of incarnation and calls Christ an incony Jew. <lll_901-2&911-2> <h5_852-5&tn_2344>

Clown **My sweet ounce of man's flesh, my in-cony**
Jew:
Clown **...How much Carnation Ribbon**
may a man buy for a remuneration?
                    (Love's Labour's Lost 901-2 & 911-2)

Boy **Yes that a did, and said they were Devils incar**
nate.
Woman **A could never abide Carnation, 'twas a Colour**
he never liked.   (Henry V 852-5)
Andrew **... but he's the very devil incardinate.**
                    (Twelfth Night 2344)

Although the word God appears in the mouths of characters 800 times in *F*, Christ and Jesus enter the fray only twelve times. The word Mary appears only twice while Jesu is more expletive than prayer.

According to the logic of Q, it is only through increase that the female/male dynamic persists from generation to generation. Any system of belief that gives ascendency to virginity and celibacy as a state above the inheritance of those born and yet to be born acts against the natural interests of humankind.

Shakespeare takes delight in scripting passages such as the exchange between Helena and Parrolles in *All's Well that Ends Well*. Parrolles regales Helena with the full in and out

Parrolles **There's little can be said in't, 'tis against the**
rule of Nature. To speak on the part of virginity, is
to accuse your Mothers; which is most infallible
disobedience. He that hangs himself is a Virgin:
Virginity murders itself, and should be buried in highways
out of all sanctified limit, as a desperate Offendress
against Nature. Virginity breeds mites, much like a
Cheese, consumes it self to the very paring, and so
dies with feeding his own stomach. Besides, Virginity
is peevish, proud, idle, made of self-love, which
is the most inhibited sin in the Canon.
                    (All's Well that Ends Well 140-50)

of the increase argument and does so with humour and verve. <aww_140-50>

In *Measure for Measure*, Shakespeare saves an overly enthusiastic novice nun from impending celibacy. He alters the original story to recast Isabella as a nun to underline his argument against the imposition of life-long celibacy over natural increase. *Measure for Measure* sardonically compares celibacy with whoredom because both undervalue the logic of increase for humankind, if humankind wishes to persist beyond the present generation.

A true-to-life scenario occurs in a history play written a decade or more after the 1590s. In *Henry VIII*, the logic of increase prevails over the murderous consequences of male priority and religious misogyny. After the future Queen Elizabeth I is born to Anne Boleyn (Henry's second wife), the play ends with Archbishop Cranmer's witty prediction of Elizabeth's golden reign.

In *Henry VIII*, Shakespeare shows that, despite the machinations of Church and Monarchy, nature, female priority and the democracy of increase prevail. He underscores the illogicality of male-primogeniture. A female inherits the throne eventually and rules successfully despite Henry's God-driven wife-murdering reign.

Closely allied to the injustice of prioritising the male first-born is the social stigma that clings to bastards. Six plays have bastards as significant characters while twenty-five mention the word at least once. <kj_191>

Stage direction **Exeunt all but bastard.**
(King John 191)

In *1 Henry VI*, the Bastard of Orleans assumes responsibility in the stead of his captured brother. In *Much Ado About Nothing* the Bastard Don John is the malcontent brother of the Prince of Aragon. In *Troilus and Cressida* Thersites the sharp-witted commentator discusses his bastardy with Priam's bastard Margarelon.

Bastard A Bastard Son of Priam's.
Thersites I am a Bastard too, I love Bastards, I am a Bastard begot, Bastard instructed, Bastard in mind, Bastard in valour, in every thing illegitimate: one Bear will not bite another, and wherefore should one Bastard? Take heed, the quarrel's most ominous to us: if the Son of a whore fight for a whore, he tempts judgment: farewell Bastard.   (Troilus and Cressida 3487-94)

<tro_3487-94> Shakespeare interposes the fictional commentator Philip Faulconbridge as the Bastard in the history of *King John*. Then, with a twist, Leontes in *The Winter's Tale* labels his own baby Perdita a bastard when he suspects she is not his own child and then attempts to murder her and her mother Hermione. <wt_1068-9>

Leontes The Bastard-brains with these my proper hands
Shall I dash out.   (The Winter's Tale 1068-9)

The most unprepossessing bastard in Shakespeare's Europe, though, is Edmund in *King Lear*. That is, until we realise Edmund exacts filial justice on his father Gloucester and Lear to compensate for the prejudicial treatment he receives through being born out of wedlock. <lr_340-4>

Bastard ...Why Bastard? Wherefore base?
When my Dimensions are as well compact,
My mind as generous, and my shape as true
As honest Madam's issue? Why brand they us
With Base? With baseness Bastardy? Base? Base?
(King Lear 340-4)

Edmund's response to the secondary status of bastards is complementary to Cordelia's response to her father's alienating demands. She avoids conflict by fleeing to France after Lear proves immune to the natural logic of her increase argument.

Edmund is mortified by his father's unwillingness to acknowledge his natural parity with his brother Kent. However, in contrast to Cordelia, Edmund seeks justice in a deadly mock of the blind paternal injustice Lear and his father impose on Cordelia and himself. In summary retribution, he puts out Gloucester's blinkered eyes. <lr_3127-34>

Edgar Let's exchange charity:
I am no less in blood than thou art Edmund,
If more, the more th'hast wrong'd me.
My name is Edgar and thy Father's Son,
The Gods are just, and of our pleasant vices
Make instruments to plague us:
The dark and vicious place where thee he got,
Cost him his eyes.   (King Lear 3127-34)

We have moved logically and so naturally in our investigation of the prevalence of nature and the priority of the female over the male to instances of increase. Shakespeare has females such as Portia, Viola, Desdemona and Cordelia base their actions on the logic of Q. Quite specifically, he has Desdemona echo Cordelia from *King Lear* when she reminds her father early in the play of the increase argument. <oth_526-36>

> *Brabantio* Where most you owe obedience?
> ...
> *Desdemona* I do perceive here a divided duty.
> To you I am bound for life, and education:
> My life and education both do learn me,
> How to respect you. You are the Lord of duty,
> I am hitherto your Daughter. But here's my Husband;
> And so much duty, as my Mother showed
> To you, preferring you before her Father:
> So much I challenge, that I may profess
> Due to the Moor my Lord.   (Othello 526-36)

Shakespeare also allows a handful of his male characters to recognise the imbalance caused by illogical male priority. Berowne in *Love's Labour's Lost* is the one most aware of the increase dynamic. Shakespeare has him paraphrase the final sonnet of the increase argument, *14*. Berowne

> *Berowne* From women's eyes this doctrine I derive.
> ...
> Then fools you were these women to forswear:
>   (Love's Labour's Lost 1701&6)

warns the other three males that truth and beauty derive from the eye of the female (in this case) – both her mind's eye and her sexual eye. <lll_1701&6>

In *The Tempest*, Prospero comments on breeding when eavesdropping on Miranda and Sebastian. <tmp_1325> In *Much Ado*

> *Prospero* On that which breeds between 'em.
>   (Tempest 1325)

> *Benedick*   ...Shall quips
> and sentences, and these paper bullets of the brain awe
> a man from the career of his humour? No, the world
> must be peopled.   (Much Ado About Nothing 1061-4)

About Nothing, Benedick comes to appreciate that the 'world must be peopled'. <ado_1061-4> In *Timon of Athens*, Apemantus notes the relationship of apes to humans. <tim_298-9>

The fourteen increase sonnets are no incidental addition to Shakespeare's program. The universality of increase for humans (and

> *Apemantus*.....The strain of
> man's bred out into Baboon and Monkey.
>   (Timon 298-9)

monkeys) is evident in the arguments of Q, in Venus' argument to Adonis and in the mention of posterity in *The Phoenix and the Turtle*. Then there are the unscripted acknowledgements in the commendatory poems and prefaces and the frequent mentions throughout the plays. The universality of increase points to Shakespeare's profound philosophic appreciation of the significance of human generation with its implications for human cognition, emotion and imagination.

64: Arranged marriages

Shakespeare's attitude to arranged marriages deserves further scrutiny. Over half the plays in the Shakespeare canon feature an arranged marriage. In every case, Shakespeare argues against the imposition of parental, societal or religious conventions that limit the freedom of individuals to choose their own partners based on love and compatibility.

Hermia in *A Midsummer Night's Dream*, Clarabel in *The Tempest*, Portia and

Jessica in *The Merchant of Venice* and Juliet and Romeo in their play are subject to the iniquity of enforced wedlock on pain of banishment or even death. In the comedies, Shakespeare frees women from the strictures of religious and societal inflexibility. However, in the histories and tragedies, he focuses his powerful dramatic talent to highlight the disastrous consequences of enforced nuptials.

Arranged marriage is taken to its farcical extreme when Richard III uses his male guile and seniority to coerce Lady Anne to marry him only a few days after he has murdered her husband King Henry VI. <r3_424-8> As previously, Shakespeare's Richard III stands for the worst excesses of male-based Christianity.

Richard III **Was ever woman in this humour woo'd?**
Was ever woman in this humour won?
I'll have her, but I will not keep her long.
What? I that kill'd her Husband, and his Father,
To take her in her heart's extremest hate,
(Richard III 424-8)

Shakespeare argues that under duress the sacrament of marriage imposes a proscriptive formula on a natural celebration of human love. He examines the consequences for families and communities whenever a religious sect enforces marriage.

The flipside of arranged marriages is the wedding of choice at the play's end, or no wedding depending on the disposition of the committed couple. In only five comedies and one history (*Henry V*) and no tragedies is marriage celebrated in the final scene. <h5_3350-7>

Queen Isabel **God, the best maker of all Marriages,**
Combine your hearts in one, your Realms in one:
As Man and Wife being two, are one in love,
So be there 'twixt your Kingdoms such a Spousal,
That never may ill Office, or fell Jealousy,
Which troubles oft the Bed of blessed Marriage,
Thrust in between the Paction of these Kingdoms,
To make divorce of their incorporate League:
(Henry V 3350-7)

Even then, in *Henry V*, before the on-stage kisses are dry, Shakespeare undermines the God-blessed marriage of 'hearts' and 'Realms'. In the Chorus he anticipates Henry VI's failure to uphold his parents' marriage bond between France and England. <h5_3376-81>

Chorus **Henry the Sixth, in Infant Bands crowned King**
Of France and England, did this King succeed:
Whose State so many had the managing,
That they lost France, and made his England bleed:
Which oft our Stage hath shown; and for their sake,
In your fair minds let this acceptance take.
(Henry V 3376-81)

As we have seen, though, in *Twelfth Night* and *Measure for Measure* mature couples unite in their appreciation of natural philosophy. They walk off the stage secure in the knowledge of each other as natural respondents. Their appreciation of nature, increase and the dynamic of truth and beauty, as the basis for a mature understanding of love, is robust.

Shakespeare treats social and religious practices with judicious irony when Duke Vincentio insists Angelo marry Mariana near the end of

Angelo **And five years since there was some speech of marriage**
Betwixt my self, and her: which was broke off,
Partly for that her promised proportions
Came short of Composition: But in chief
For that her reputation was dis-valued
In levity: **(Measure for Measure 2591-6)**

Measure for Measure. He does the same for the profligate Lucio. In each case, he enforces the logical implications of the character's previous actions.

Angelo   ...Can it be,
That Modesty may more betray our Sense
Than woman's lightness? having waste ground enough,
Shall we desire to raze the Sanctuary
And pitch our evils there?   (Measure for Measure 931-5)

For Angelo the sanctimoniousness and status seeking that led him to reject Mariana's 'levity' and dowry <mm_2591-6> finally trap him when it magnifies his lust for the psychological ice in Isabella. <mm_931-5> Shakespeare quenches Angelo's extreme idealism in the commitment he has previously forged with Mariana. Lucio's transgression is the opposite of Angelo's. Shakespeare makes him face up to the logical consequence of sex – increase – by requiring him to marry a whore whom he gets pregnant.

Measure for Measure encapsulates the two worst offences against natural logic. Both excessive religious idealism and excessive sexual licentiousness are contrary to the natural dynamic of human life set out in Q. In *Measure for Measure*, the Duke and Isabella find true love and true regard by maturing before our eyes beyond the two poles of selfishness – costly religious love and carnal lust. They make a simple avowal of love and respect based in natural philosophy. <mm_2933-6>

Duke   ...Dear Isabel,
I have a motion much imports your good,
Whereto if you'll a willing ear incline;
What's mine is yours, and what is yours is mine.
(Measure for Measure 2933-6)

65: Cross-dressing females challenge prejudice

In Q, we see the Poet naturally interrelating sex and gender. He co-relates the sexual characteristics of female and male with their gender dispositions. Not only are the Mistress and Master Mistress the generic representatives of the female and male as sexual beings, they simultaneously represent the feminine and masculine dispositions in the human mind.

Since nature and the sexual dynamic of female/male establish the givens for all that follows in Shakespeare's Europe-based plays, they are the preconditions for the gender dynamic of the human mind. Shakespeare connects one possibility with the other with evolutionary insight allowing him unprecedented imaginative licence to create a cosmopolitan portmanteau of believable characters.

We watch as Shakespeare organises his plays according to the natural dynamic he articulates in Q. If he looks over the European continent, he sees nothing but nature upon nature extensive and uninterrupted from the North Sea to the Red Sea, from the Iberian Peninsula to Asia Minor and from Mount Blanc to the Dead Sea.

On this geographical stage, he brings into focus the sporadic human presence. It is the sexual/social interrelationship of female and male that drives the nodes of urbanity and networks of communication. In Shakespeare's lifetime, if viewed from above, the lifelines would have been barely discernible during the day and all but invisible at night except for intermittent fire and torch light.

Moreover, along the continental networks of the sixteenth century the most obvious expression of feminine/masculine intensity would have been the skyward gesturing architecture of gothic cathedrals. The churches of Europe and their many subsidiary monasteries, chapels and wayside icons clamour for male/masculine ascendancy. However, theirs is always an over-pitched investment against nature and the natural priority of the female. That all their indulgences obey the laws of nature in the final audit (as *126* explains), seems not to forestall ever more ambitious monuments to masculine pride.

When compared to the grandeur of nature with its mountainous elevations, deep-valleyed rivers and planar extents, such masculine conceits are indeed puny. Yet, as monuments to their imaginary puniverse, they are surprisingly achieved. The devotion to their permanence, though, is misplaced – as highlighted in *64* and *65*. Their true poetry resides in their hapless ruins and the highly eroticised mythical agenda that inspires their gender inversion.

At the deepest level, for a Europe largely Christianised after 1500 years of the violent suppression of competing beliefs, Shakespeare's plays challenge the conceit of enforcing the ascendancy of a male God over nature. For Shakespeare the absolute male God is but a purely masculine or skew-genderised phenomenon. There are no male-alone counterparts in nature to back the mind-based masculine entity called God.

With unintended irony, church dogma recognises the illogicality of the one-sided masculine persona whenever it steps in to enforce its imaginary precepts against the interdependence of gender relationships in nature. The Christ constructed by New Testament evangelists out of the activities of the man Jesus requires continual doctrinal intervention to sustain his imaginary persona across greater Europe and its colonial outposts. In the years up to 1600 and beyond, the threat of death by torture and the prospect of hellfire kept bums on pews.

No wonder, then, that a clear thinker/moralist like Shakespeare uses his thirty-six plays in *F* to argue against the unilateral imposition of Christian theology. In the histories, he exposes the inequities wrought by seven Kings of England who enforce and abuse church monopoly. In the tragedies, Shakespeare makes palpable the inhuman consequences of the merciless imposition of theistic dictatorships. In the comedies, he shows how to remedy male-driven excesses.

Because male-based dogma usurps the biological status of the female in nature, in Shakespeare's plays only female characters cross-dress with impunity to redress the illogicalities of gender inversion. In five of the comedies, Shakespeare's canny females counter female-to-male inversion by cross-dressing as males to parody with double innuendo the male-God usurpation of the originary female.

Shakespeare's use of cross-dressing also addresses the religious misogyny behind the ban on female actors in his day. On the Elizabethan or Jacobean stage, males have no option but to cross-dress to play female parts. Shakespeare takes the opportunity to parody the male dominated world that forbids females a role on stage.

Shakespeare choreographs each act of female cross-dressing to redress the malconsequences of male usurpation on female personal, social and political equality. Then, at play's end, the cross-dressed females perfunctorily doff the staged conceits to remind us of the limited utility of male presumptuousness.

The divesting occurs when Viola retires as Cesario in *Twelfth Night*, Portia as Balthazar in *The Merchant of Venice*, Rosalind as Ganymede in *As You Like It*, Julia as Sebastian in *The Two Gentlemen of Verona*, and Imogen as Fidele in *Cymbeline*. <list_crossdressing>

Shakespeare uses cross-dressing by unwitting males to the same end as cross-dressing by savvy females. He mimics or mocks male-based prejudices. In the two plays in which males cross-dress as females, *The Merry Wives of Windsor* and *The Taming of the Shrew*, the cross-dressed male is more the butt of a joke than an advocate for natural justice.

Lucetta You must needs have them with a codpiece (Madam).
Julia Out, out, (Lucetta) that will be illfavoured.
(The Two Gentlemen of Verona 1028-9)
Portia A thousand raw tricks of these bragging Jacks, Which I will practice.
(The Merchant of Venice 1804-5)
Rosalind That I did suit me all points like a man,
(As You Like It 581)
Viola Thou shalt present me as an Eunuch to him,
(Twelfth Night 108)
Imogen I see a man's life is a tedious one,
(Cymbeline 2082)
Cross-dressing

In *The Merry Wives of Windsor*, Mrs. Ford and Page hoodwink Falstaff into wearing the clothing of a witch. Shakespeare has the two set-upon wives cross-dress plump Falstaff in the 'fat woman of Brainford's' gown. The ploy is a fitting rebuff to Falstaff for subjecting the two women to his male-erotic fancies. Because witches are but creations of the male/masculine brain (Brainford), the two women trick Falstaff into wearing the outward semblance of his mind-based prejudice.

Later, in *The Merry Wives of Windsor*, Slender and Caius are all-but duped into marrying boys

Slender I took a Boy for a Girl: If I had been married to him, (for all he was in woman's apparel) I would not have / had him.
Caius   ...by gar I am cozened, I ha married oon Garsoon, a boy;
(The Merry Wives of Windsor 2676-8 & 2689-90)

dressed as girls. <wiv_2676-8&2689-90> Shakespeare intensifies his parody of male make-believe by cross-dressing his males to spotlight male over-acting.

Shakespeare also uses the prohibition on female actors to sardonic advantage in *The Taming of the Shrew*. In the so-called 'Induction' scene, the Page, most likely played by a boy actor, cross-dresses as Christopher Sly's wife. A prankster Lord and his huntsman friends cross-dress a Page as a 'Lady' after they upgrade the drunken Sly from a 'beggar' to a 'Lord'.

As there are no obvious sources for the Induction characters, and with the *Sonnet* philosophy in mind, it appears Shakespeare simulates elements of New Testament mythology in an opening gambit of his own devising. He seems to parody the transformation of the carpenter's son Jesus into Christ the Lord. Shakespeare coins Christ in Christ-opher Sly's name and has Sly inject other New Testament currency into our hearing. Not only does Shakespeare slyly render Sly a Lord, Sly backhandedly recognises the sleight of hand when he identifies himself as Christendom's most convincing liar. <shr_176-7> Sly then talks of being a 'Lord' with a Lady. As he prattles on in a dream-like state, we hear the words 'our Lady'. <shr_220-6>

Beggar ...score me up for the lyingst knave in Christendom.
(The Taming of the Shrew 176-7)

Beggar Am I a Lord, and have I such a Lady?
Or do I dream? Or have I dream'd till now?
I do not sleep: I see, I hear, I speak:
I smell sweet savours, and I feel soft things:
Upon my life I am a Lord indeed,
And not a Tinker, nor Christopher Sly.
Well, bring our Lady hither to our sight,
(The Taming of the Shrew 220-6)

The 'Induction' scene-sets the dream moment when a common man Jesus becomes the mythical Lord. Moreover, by cross-dressing the Page as a Lady cum 'our Lady', Shakespeare turns the stage ban on women into a pointed comment on the God-head as a trinity of cross-dressed females – plus Mary as a cross-dressed male.

Shakespeare's strategy behind the Induction becomes clearer when from out of its mock proscenium there emerge a troupe of players. They will play out the implications of its biblical subtext to show the audience how to recover their natural philosophy. Then Shakespeare has the Lady describe their forthcoming play, *The Taming of the Shrew*, as 'a kind of history'. <shr_293-5> We hear Shakespeare preparing to give us a history lesson in which he supplants the male-based paradigm of biblical religions with his nature-based philosophy.

Lady No my good Lord, it is more pleasing stuff.
Beggar What, household stuff.
Lady It is a kind of history.
(The Taming of the Shrew 293-5)

Once Shakespeare's intent is clear, we can understand why the characters of the Induction do not reappear at the play's end – literally they are history. In *The Taming of the Shrew*, Shakespeare shows how to graduate from biblical prejudices, which deflect the meaning of language and art into mind-generated cul-de-sacs. He shows how to gain a healthy appreciation of the natural function of words and symbols. No wonder so many see *The Taming of the Shrew* as a so-called problem play.

If in the early 1590s, Shakespeare merely tacks a scene onto *The Taming of the Shrew* to set up his critique of biblical illogicalities, by the early 1600s he is able to write a play in which the transition from male-based excesses to natural contentedness is seamless.

In *Twelfth Night, or, What you will*, to give the play its full title, Shakespeare examines specifically the status of the cross-dressed male God of the Bible. *Twelfth Night* contrasts the divine provenance of Christ-the-Lord's Epiphany twelve nights after the birth of Jesus with living naturally as in doing 'what you will'. Like the earlier play, and essentially like every one of Shakespeare's comedies, he takes us from a world of mind-based confusion and frequent violence to an acceptance of natural philosophy.

During the second scene of the play, Shakespeare shipwrecks identical twins of opposing sexes, separates them at sea and then casts them on shore at different locations. In the sundering of male from female, Shakespeare mimics the sexual division into female and male from a common progenitor. He heightens the drama by allowing the male to come ashore unaware of his sister's preservation.

Viola signals the philosophical distance between herself and her brother when she lands in all-too-real Illyria and imagines Sebastian in Elysium or a goddess/god-bound heaven. <tn_53-4> Shakespeare has Viola cross-dress as a male to mock the cross-dressed male-God of religious myth who

Viola And what should I do in Illyria?
My brother he is in Elysium,
(Twelfth Night 53-4)

usurps the originary female status in nature.

Twelfth Night, then, is a lesson in the short-term utility of inventing a male-God within a culture and the limited durability of the conceit. As the play unfolds, Viola as the mock male God (alias Cesario for the god-emperor Caesar) corrects Orsino's immature infatuation for the eye-watering Olivia. Then, with symbiotic economy, she creates the opportunity for her twin brother Sebastian to marry Olivia in a Christian wedding.

When Viola doffs her male-God disguise as the play concludes, she and Orsino enter a relationship unfettered by the constraints of male-God marriage. Viola has progressively taught Orsino to do 'what you will' using the ploy of male-God psychology to restore his natural philosophy.

Another play that confuses the commentators because it seems to equivocate over the worth of Jewry or Christianity is *The Merchant of Venice*. However, once we realise Portia exploits the role of the cross-dressing God of biblical faiths, then the play makes complete sense. Early in the play Shakespeare has a minor charac-

> *Solanio*   ...Now by two-headed Janus,
> Nature hath fram'd strange fellows in her time:
>   (The Merchant of Venice 55-6)

ter, Solanio, state that the 'two-headed Janus' of the Jew versus Christian face-off is framed by 'Nature'. <**mv_55-6**> The announcement prepares the way for the play to set one God-fearing religion against the other without either emerging honourably.

Later, after Portia guides Bassanio to choose the correct casket, she mocks

> *Portia* I would be trebled twenty times my self,
> A thousand times more fair, ten thousand times
> More rich, that only to stand high in your account,
> I might in virtues, beauties, livings, friends,
> Exceed account: but the full sum of me
> Is sum of nothing: which to term in gross,
> Is an unlessoned girl. unschooled, unpractis'd,
>   (The Merchant of Venice 1500-6)

him in the manner of Katherine at the end of *The Taming of the Shrew* by excessively avowing servitude to her Lord. <**mv_1500-6**> She reveals the extent of the mock by later securing from him the ring he swore never to part with.

Lorenzo then heralds Portia's part in recovering feminine priority when he recognises in her a 'god-like amity' or innate cordiality – again with a pun on Lord. <**mv_1727-30**> Portia increases the female/male tension when she pretends Nerrissa and herself will resort to a 'monastery two miles off'. As pre-viously in the plays, Shakespeare treats monasteries as temporary refuges from male-based excesses – even if in this case only as a ruse.

> *Lorenzo* Madam, although I speak it in your presence,
> You have a noble and a true conceit
> Of god-like amity, which appears most strongly
> In bearing thus the absence of your Lord.
>   (The Merchant of Venice 1727-30)

So when Portia appears in court to make her famous speech about mercy she adopts fully the guise of the usurping male God. When she intones about 'the gentle rain from heaven' and talks of an 'earthly power' that shows 'likest God's', her charade is complete. <**mv_2106-8**> By recovering the female logic of the usurping God who drives the shady morals of both Jews and Christians, Portia is able to dispense natural justice with finesse and fairness. Once the natural basis of

> *Portia* It is an attribute to God himself;
> And earthly power doth then show likest God's
> When mercy seasons Justice.
>   (The Merchant of Venice 2106-8)

language or truth is respected, then the resolution is a matter of words.

We feel empathy for the characters in Shakespeare's plays because he gets inside our genderised heads by recreating the correct relation between sex and gender in nature. The potential to be excessively tearful, idealistic – or otherwise distracted by intense emotions – is universal. Shakespeare's plays show how to break the pattern of a mindset deployed to prevent the recovery of natural contentedness.

The evidence suggests Shakespeare accepts only natural prerogatives as givens and regards all mind-generated conventions as provisional. He argues that increase trumps all commandments and laws especially if they enforce male-based religious and political injustices.

Chapter 19: The cunning pen

How conscious is Shakespeare that his plays align the basic givens of nature and the female/male dynamic with his facility for presenting logical argument and evoking deep sensations? What characters and parts of plays provide instances of his unique reflexivity?

66: Mock plays to mock myths

When examining the overall layout of *Q* we saw the 154 sonnets re-establish the priority of nature over the idealism that invents mind-based Gods. The internal division of the set asserts the precursor status of female to male and the first fourteen sonnets argue for the logic of increase. Then we find *15* to *19* devoted to the transition from increase to poetry.

What, then, is the counterpart in the plays to the five increase to poetry sonnets that are transitional between life and art? If poetry is distinguished from increase in that no amount of poetry will result in the birth of a child, how and where does Shakespeare remind us a play is a play and the content of the plays in *F* amounts to nothing if there are no live readers to read it? We have seen *17* insisting this is the case with the book known as *Q*.

Shakespeare uses a number of dramatic ploys to signal his awareness of the relationship between life and art. He corrects the plots of existing plays by others to render them more consistent with natural philosophy. He introduces a play within a play. He gives select characters a proto-playwright role in their plays. He maintains a clear distinction between the sexual as biological and the erotic as desire. Moreover, he critiques the literal belief in myths that perpetrate male God priority.

In four of his plays, Shakespeare introduces a play within a play to illustrate that even his sophisticated nature-based dramas are never more than plays. *Hamlet, A Midsummer Night's Dream,* and *Love's Labour's Lost* make dramatic use of interior plays. In addition, *The Taming of the Shrew* begins with an apparent false start in which a Lord plays a joke for 300 lines before the title play emerges from the by-play. <list_playwithinplay>

Hamlet   ...we'll hear a play to mor-
row. Dost thou hear me old Friend, can you play the
murder of Gonzago?   (Hamlet 1576-8)
Theseus What Revels are in hand? Is there no play,
To ease the anguish of a torturing hour?
          (A Midsummer Night's Dream 1831-2)
Queen That sport best pleases, that doth least know how.
Where Zeal strives to content, and the contents
Dies in the Zeal of that which it presents:
          (Love's Labour's Lost 2460-2)
Messenger Your Honours Players hearing your amendment,
Are come to play a pleasant Comedy,
          (The Taming of the Shrew 283-4)
Plays within plays

Famously, Hamlet exploits the opportunity provided by a visiting troupe of actors to stage an investigation into Claudius' involvement in King Hamlet's death. <ham_1629-32> Just as

Claudius' murderous act is the pretext for Hamlet staging a trial by theatre, so too does the play *Hamlet* presume on the logic of natural givens for which it is a tragic subtext. More than anything, Shakespeare's *Hamlet* investigates the abrogation of natural logic.

Hamlet **I have heard, that guilty Creatures sitting at a Play,**
Have by the very cunning of the Scene,
Been strook so to the soul, that presently
They have proclaim'd their Malefactions. (Hamlet 1629-32)

Shakespeare not only incorporates a play within a play, he also borrows plots from other authors in preference to writing his own scripts. In all but two or three of the thirty-six plays in *F*, Shakespeare reworks the plays or writings of earlier authors or chroniclers to render them more self-referentially theatrical and truer to natural philosophy. It is as if the philosophy Shakespeare uses to rectify the writings of others is more important than producing entirely new scripts. His habitual borrowing of plots suggests he is a better philosopher than playwright.

The relationship between the two possibilities is crucial for understanding Shakespeare's works. When he writes his own play scripts as in *Love's Labour's Lost* and *The Tempest*, the play is a direct expression of his philosophy. When he uses scripts by other writers, he parodies their philosophical inadequacies by recasting critical roles and most of the language in the mode of *Q*. His nature-based philosophy forestalls any tendency to consider his – or their – plays as anything more than subservient to nature.

The *Folio* is replete with examples of Shakespeare's peremptory attitude to other scripts. For instance, he coins the name 'Othello' for a character previously called 'the Moor' in the short story titled 'A Moorish Captain' in Cinthio's *Gli Hecatommithi* in which there is already a Desdemona. By adding Ot-*hell*-o's 'hell' to Des-*demon*-a's 'demon' he foreshadows the trouble brewing when the patriarchal party ships from mainland Venice to the island of Malta. By renaming them, Shakespeare signals that even the most idealistic characters have potential for evil within them.

A few years later, Shakespeare adapts Robert Greene's play *Pandosto* to create *The Winter's Tale* and in so doing makes it a dramatic lesson in natural philosophy. Whereas in Greene's play Hermione commits suicide, Shakespeare's Hermione triumphs at the play's end by appearing to come back to life <wt_3207-8> after feigning death to escape Leontes' murderous wrath. The dramatic change

Paulina **To see the Life as lively mocked, as ever**
Still Sleep mocked Death:
(The Winter's Tale 3207-8)

enables Shakespeare to lengthen by years Leontes' psychological punishment for his decision to falsely accuse and murderously threaten his wife and worse to banish his infant daughter Mariana with instructions to leave her to die at 'some remote and desert place'.

Stage direction...**Hermione (like a Statue:)**
(The Winter's Tale 3185)

Not only does *The Winter's Tale* critique male-based attitudes to the logic of increase, Hermione's semi-monastic seclusion allows Shakespeare to doubly mock the idea of a miraculous return from the dead when she appears as a powder-puff statue that comes to life. <wt_3185> In his play, Shakespeare substitutes earthly common sense for Greene's suicidal Divine Providence – a scenario trialled earlier in *The Phoenix and the Turtle*.

In *Measure for Measure*, Shakespeare alters the source material from earlier versions of the story in Cinthio's *Hecatommithi* (1565) and George Whetstone's *Promos and Cassandra* (1578). In Shakespeare's rendition, Isabella (Cassandra) keeps her role as a virgin but Shakespeare adds the psychological density of her impending committal to a nunnery. Besides, the original Claudio (Andrugio) is no longer accused and condemned to death for violating a virgin but iniquitously faces the death penalty for the completely natural act of getting his betrothed Juliet pregnant. <mm_159-64> In keeping with the *Sonnet* philosophy, Shakespeare redresses the excesses of puritanical idealism and its consequences for the logic of increase.

> Bawd ...and which is more, within these three days his head to be chopp'd off.
> ...and it is for getting Madam Julietta with child.
> (Measure for Measure 159-64)

Besides featuring a play within a play, Shakespeare also empowers characters to conduct the plot as if they were proto-playwrights. In *Measure for Measure*, Shakespeare has Duke Vincentio state early on that to remedy the problems besetting Vienna he will stage-manage events. Shakespeare has the Duke directing the action to achieve the desired recovery of natural philosophy. <mm_46-7&76-7>

> Duke   ...but I do bend my speech to one that can my part in him advertise; ...I love the people, But do not like to stage me to their eyes.
> (Measure for Measure 46-7 & 76-7)

In *The Tempest*, Prospero acts as a virtual director to stage a play that mimics the fascinations of the troubled human mind. At the play's end, he discards his props <tmp_2001-8> and sends the motley crew of Italians back across the waves to Naples and Milan.

> Prospero ...But this rough Magic I here abjure:
> ...I'll break my staff,
> ...I'll drown my book. (Tempest 2001-8)

Early in her play, *Twelfth Night*, Viola comes ashore from the shipwreck in which she is separated from her twin brother. Shakespeare has her devise a strategy to deal with the dysfunctional males and mournful female who inhabit the aptly named '*Ill*-yrian' setting. In her virtual theatre, she enacts mock-idealistic scenarios to ensure an outcome even Aristotle might applaud. By tiring herself in male garb, she cross-dresses as a theatric ploy by effectively mimicking the short-term utility of the cross-dressed biblical God whose Epiphany *Twelfth Night* critiques.

When Petruchio in *The Taming of the Shrew* comes to the rescue of the stalemated suitors to Bianca by rectifying Katherine's shrewish response to her father's male-driven ultimatums, he demonstrates a no-nonsense approach that dramatically short-circuits an apparent no-win endgame. <shr_2312-9> Katherine's irony-laden speech at the play's end shows she now understands the logic or grammar of language, which

> Petruchio I say it is the Moon.
> Kate I know it is the Moon.
> Petruchio Nay then you lie: it is the blessed Sun.
> Kate Then God be blest, it is the blessed sun,
> But sun it is not, when you say it is not.
> And the Moon changes even as your mind:
> What you will have it named, even that it is,
> And so it shall be so for Katherine.
> (The Taming of the Shrew 2312-9)

was deeply corrupted during her reactionary response to her dad's complicity in patriarchal exploitation.

In *Love's Labour's Lost*, Berowne's lengthy speech at Act 4, scene 3 seems to include a revision of a number of earlier lines that leads some editors to cut them. However, when we examine the two passages in question, we see that in the first he states the increase/ poetry argument in general terms as the natural 'ground' for his male colleagues. He then repeats the argument in terms of

> *Berowne* For when would you my Lord, or you, or you,
> Have found the ground of study's excellence,
> Without the beauty of a woman's face;
> From women's eyes this doctrine I derive,
> ...
> Never durst Poet touch a pen to write,
> Until his Ink were temp'red with Love's sighs:
> O then his lines would ravish savage ears,
> And plant in Tyrant's mild humility
> From women's eyes this doctrine I derive.
> (Love's Labour's Lost 1649-52 & 1697-701)

a 'Poet' who is aware of natural logic. <lll_1649-52&1697-701> Shakespeare has Berowne state and reiterate both cases as if to anticipate the many readings of his work that will fail to account for the extraordinary reflexivity of his art.

The editors' presumptuousness is apparent in the 1998 Oxford *Complete Works* where they remove the first passage from the play and place it under 'additional passages'. The interference continues the lamentable tradition of blaming Shakespeare for their misreading of his works.

Another measure of Shakespeare's awareness of the criteria distinguishing life and art he presents in *15* to *19* is his appreciation of the logical distinction between the sexual and the erotic. If his plays are mythical, as Ted Hughes suggests, then it is not because Shakespeare wants to return to the old mythologies as Hughes thinks, but because he knows all mythologies are literarily erotic as distinct from biologically sexual.

In our examination of Q, we saw Shakespeare begin to draw a line between the sexual and the erotic at *14*. Before *14*, the sexual pertains to the bodily or biological and after 14, the erotic characterises the mind or desire. Shakespeare argues that all human expression through language and art (truth and beauty) is logically erotic because it derives ultimately from the biology of increase or the sexual.

Shakespeare is aware the givens of nature and the sexual dynamic are the basis for the erotic. He need only have his female and male characters make knowing erotic allusions to activate the groundedness of the sexual dynamic as the base chord throughout his dramas. Hence, pervading the plays we hear frequent erotic exchanges and innuendoes issuing from the mouths of many of Shakespeare's more canny characters. There is a flurry of such language from

> *Helena* Bless our poor Virginity from underminers
> and blowers-up. Is there no Military policy how Virgins
> might blow up men?
> *Parrolles* Virginity being blown down, Man will
> quicklier be blown up: marry in blowing him down
> again, with the breach yourselves made, you lose your
> City. It is not politic, in the Common-wealth of
> Nature, to preserve virginity. Loss of Virginity, is
> rational increase,
> (All's Well that Ends Well 125-33)

Parrolles in *All's Well that Ends Well*, <aww_125-33> Juliet in *Romeo and Juliet*

Juliet Played for a pair of stainless Maidenhoods,
Hood my unmanned blood baiting in my Cheeks,
With thy Black mantle, till strange Love grow bold,
Think true Love acted simple modesty:
(Romeo and Juliet 1657-60)

<rj_1657-60> and Hamlet in his play.
<ham_1970-4>

Shakespeare uses erotic banter or repartee throughout his works. The frequent instances in the mouths of female and male characters underpins his appreciation of language's inherent eroticism. The use of such language cannot be dismissed apologetically as ribaldry or bawdy.
<list_eroticexchanges>

Hamlet Do you think I meant Country matters?
Ophelia I think nothing, my Lord.
Hamlet That's a fair thought to lie between Maid's legs.
Ophelia What is my Lord.
Hamlet Nothing.   (Hamlet 1970-4)

Because a play as a play is erotic, rarely are there biological moments in Shakespeare's dramas. In only three plays does the birth of a child occur at some point during the five acts. In each of the plays, the birth is crucial to establishing the prejudice against increase that drives the dramatic outcome.

King I am content, so the Maiden Cities you
talk of, may wait on her: so the Maid that stood in
the way for my Wish, shall show me the way to my
Will.   (Henry V 3316-9)
Mercutio   ...now art
thou what thou art, by Art as well as by Nature, for this
drivelling Love is like a great Natural, that runs lolling
up and down to hide his bable in a hole.
(Romeo and Juliet 1190-3)
Nurse For Juliet's sake, for her sake rise and stand:
Why should you fall into so deep an O.
(Romeo and Juliet 1905-6)
Old Lady   ...the capacity
Of your soft Cheveril Conscience, would receive,
If you might please to stretch it.
(Henry VIII 1239-41)
Ulysses Fie, Fie, upon her:
There's a language in her eye, her cheek, her lip:
Nay, her foot speaks, her wanton spirits look out
At every joint, and motive of her body:
Oh these encounters so glib of tongue,
(Troilus and Cressida 2611-5)
Cressida Troilus farewell; one eye yet looks on thee;
But with my heart, the other eye, doth see.
Ah poor our sex; this fault in us I find:
The error of our eye, directs our mind.
What error leads must err: O then conclude,
Minds swayed by eyes, are full of turpitude.
(Troilus and Cressida 3099-104)
Othello Lie with her? lie on her? We say lie on her,
when they be-lie-her. Lie with her: that's fulsome:
(Othello 2412-3)
Erotic exchanges

In *Titus Andronicus*, a black baby is born of the union of Aaron the Moor and Tamora the Queen of the Goths to dramatise the prejudice around colour over such a natural event as childbirth. <tit_1750-55&1805-10> In *The Winter's Tale*, Leontes brands his newborn child a bastard <wt_978-83> because he suspects Hermione has consorted with his friend Polixenes, with dramatic reverberations throughout the rest of the play. In *Henry VIII*, Elizabeth's birth near the end of the play challenges the male God driven monarchical custom of male primogeniture to which Henry VIII lends his bloody arm. <h8_2968-73) For Shakespeare, the irony is that Elizabeth assumes the throne for over forty years and reigns more judiciously and regally than her father.

There are also occasions where Shakespeare toys with the eroticism basic to mythologies. For instance, when he calls Jesus an 'incony Jew' he highlights the divide between the man Jesus and the mythological construct Christ who, unlike the proverbial rabbit (cony),

Nurse A joyless, dismal, black and, sorrowful issue,
Here is the babe as loathsome as a toad,
Amongst the fairest breeders of our clime,
The Empress sends it thee, thy stamp, thy seal,
And bids thee christen it with thy dagger's point.
Aaron ...is black so base a hue?
...

Aaron He is your brother Lords, sensibly fed,
Of that self blood that first gave life to you,
And from that womb where you imprisoned were
He is infranchised and come to light:
Nay he is your brother by the surer side,
Although my seal be stamped in his face.
(Titus Andronicus 1750-55 & 1805-10)

has no offspring and definitely no biological parents. He accentuates the universality of eroticised births and deaths of goddesses and gods in all myths, which speaks to their mind-based status.

Shakespeare is unrelentingly critical of the idealistic male-based biblical myths. He is particularly concerned about the disastrous consequences when believers enforce such myths literally as political and cultural norms against the biology of human originary female in nature. His nature-based philosophy corrects the usurpation of female priority to create a mythic level of writing free of the illogicalities and prejudices resulting from male-based myths.

It follows naturally, then, that the originary relationship of female over male Shakespeare presents in the *Sonnets* forms the basis for all his mythic dramas. Is it any wonder that Harold Bloom misreads plays such as *Hamlet*? Bloom does not take account of the natural logic of the female/male dynamic in nature the *Sonnets* argue for, and so ignores the role of female and male as argument places in Shakespeare's plays.

Paulina   ...The good Queen
(For she is good) hath brought you forth a daughter,
...
Leontes A mankind Witch? Hence with her, out o'door:
A most intelligencing bawd. (The Winter's Tale 978-83)

Bloom's personal favourites amongst Shakespeare's characters, Hamlet and Falstaff, are blunderers not leaders in their plays. Instead of appreciating Shakespeare's critique of Hamlet and Falstaff, Bloom dismisses Petruchio for exhibiting 'paranoid mania' and calls Vincentio peculiar, anarchistic, sanctimonious, equivocal, lustful, half-crazed, wayward, a savage reductionist, manipulative and blandly idiotic. [note 4]

Bloom belches out his hateful invective on his way to completely misunder-

King   ...Is the Queen delivered?
Say Ay, and of a boy.
Old Lady Ay, Ay my Liege,
And of a lovely Boy: the God of heaven
Both now, and ever bless her: 'Tis a Girl
Promises Boys hereafter.   (Henry VIII 2968-73)

standing two characters who do have Shakespeare's confidence to run their own plays. Because Bloom misses the determining role of Shakespeare's cunning females, how much are Hamlet and Falstaff merely projections of

Bloom's overactive masculine persona.

Vincentio, Petruchio, Prospero, and Viola are far more inventive in countering traditional illogicalities than Hamlet and Falstaff who instead reflect Bloom's inadequate understanding of human invention. Neither Hamlet, nor Falstaff, nor Bloom would get a job fronting the comedies.

67: Mock characters and mock arguments

To contextualise his dramas within his nature-based philosophy – in keeping with the role of the increase to poetry group – we see Shakespeare writing plays within plays. He also creates characters as proto-playwrights to dictate the action and outcome. He makes explicit the distinction between the sexual and the erotic to critique traditional myths within his nature-based mythic dynamic.

Also within his nature-based plays that respect the logic of life and art, Shakespeare parodies apologetic or ungrounded argument with witty repartee while contextualising the exchanges within the overall argument of each play. Moreover, within his dramas, Shakespeare frequently adds a coterie of minor characters whose speech and demeanour accentuate the pretensions and prejudices of the major protagonists.

To set the scene for the minor characters, Shakespeare has all his leading characters act out positively or negatively the implications of the generic argument places corresponding to the *Sonnet* roles of female, male and Poet. To heighten the dramatic effect, Shakespeare's minor characters in many instances argue for common sense or represent its absence where their superiors or betters have lost or want the 'natural touch' – as Lady Macduff says of Macduff in *Macbeth*. <mac_1721-2>

> *Macduff's Wife* ...He loves us not,
> He wants the natural touch.
>   (Macbeth 1721-2)

Because Shakespeare scripts the thirty-six plays in *F* as one continuous argument for his nature-based logic, then each female or male character within the plays acts as an argument place for the female/male-based philosophy laid out in the 154 sonnets. Only when we appreciate the natural philosophy of the sonnet set as the determining criteria for the various characters can we understand the role of the minor characters who engage in mock debate.

Shakespeare's critique of the apologetic practice of arguing from unsound premises to create a sense of validity is evident when he mocks Aristotelian syllogistic debate. Whereas Shakespeare's own arguments proceed from verifiable premises (nature, female, male, increase, incoming sensations and language) and so his conclusions have credibility, the arguments of the apologists proceed from the imaginary premise of the existence of an extra-terrestrial God or other idealised entities.

> *Feste* Two faults Madonna, that drink and good counsel will amend: for give the dry fool drink, then is the fool not dry: bid the dishonest man mend himself, if he mend, he is no longer dishonest; if he cannot, let the Botcher mend him: any thing that's mended, is but patched: virtue that transgresses is but patched with sin, and sin that amends is but patched with virtue. If that this simple Syllogism will serve, so: if it will not, what remedy? As there is no true Cuckold but calamity, so beauty's a flower. The Lady bade take away the fool; therefore, I say again, take her away.   (Twelfth Night 335-45)

In *Twelfth Night*, for instance, Shakespeare gives the fool Feste the job of dissembling the pretences of the love-confused Olivia. Feste takes wicked delight in running proverbial rings around Olivia's attempts to dismiss a fool she cannot abide. <tn_335-45> Yet she continues to argue with the fool because he represents the sanity she has forgone in the pursuit of forlorn love.

The fool in *King Lear* serves a similar function of dissembling the pretensions of the paternalistic Lear, who treats the world as a one-man stage on which to indulge his delusions unchallenged. <lr_681-3>

Fool **For wisemen are grown foppish,**
And know not how their wits to wear,
Their manners are so apish.
(King Lear 681-3)

In the mock arguments between Speed and Proteus and Speed and Launce in *The Two Gentlemen of Verona*, Shakespeare provides two instances that parody the illogicality of religious imagery. Speed and Proteus play with the shepherd and sheep metaphor that the New Testament uses to characterise Christ. <tgv_76-97>

Speed **Twenty to one then, he is ship'd already,**
And I have played the Sheep in losing him.
Proteus **Indeed a Sheep doth very often stray,**
And if the Shepherd be awhile away.
Speed **You conclude that my Master is a Shepherd then,**
and I Sheep?
Proteus **I do.**
Speed **Why then my horns are his horns, whether I**
wake or sleep.
Proteus **A silly answer, and fitting well a Sheep.**
Speed **This proves me still a Sheep.**
Proteus **True: and thy Master a Shepherd.**
Speed **Nay, that I can deny by a circumstance.**
Proteus **It shall go hard but I'll prove it by another.**
Speed **The Shepherd seeks the Sheep, and not the**
Sheep the Shepherd; but I seek my Master, and my
Master seeks not me: therefore I am no Sheep.
Proteus **The Sheep for fodder follow the Shepherd,**
the Shepherd for food follows not the Sheep: thou
for wages followest thy Master, thy Master for wages
follows not thee: therefore thou art a Sheep.
Speed **Such another proof will make me cry baa.**
(The Two Gentlemen of Verona 76-97)

Then in Speed's later interchange with Launce, Launce first identifies the issue as a 'Christian' one and, by arguing the toss over Launce's love for a Milk-maid, criticises the male-based illogicalities of the Churches. <tgv_1330-1345> The hilarious exchange between Speed and Launce continues to the end of the scene – in all for 113 lines.

Shakespeare recognises that even children see through the charades their parents erect to conceal their indulgences. In *Macbeth*, after Macduff has fled Scotland for England, his child tells Lady Macduff he doubts his father's ability to tell the truth. If his father is a traitor who tells lies to protect the truth and might hang because of it, then there may be not enough honest men about to hang everyone. <mac_1766to1777> The son

Launce **I am but a fool, look you, and yet I have**
the wit to think my Master is a kind of a knave: but
that's all one, if he be but one knave: He lives not now
that knows me to be in love, yet I am in love, but a
Team of horse shall not pluck that from me: nor who
'tis I love: and yet 'tis a woman; but what woman, I
will not tell my self: and yet 'tis a Milk-maid: yet 'tis
not a maid: for she hath had Gossips: yet 'tis a maid,
for she is her Master's maid, and serves for wages. She
hath more qualities than a Water-Spaniel; which is
much in a bare Christian: Here is the Cate-log of her
Condition. *Imprimis.* **She can fetch and carry: why**
a horse can do no more; nay, a horse cannot fetch, but
only carry, therefore is she better than a Jade. *Item.*
She can milk, look you, a sweet virtue in a maid with
clean hands.
(The Two Gentlemen of Verona 1330-1345)

Son **What is a Traitor?**
Wife **Why one that swears, and lies.**
...
Son **Then the Liars and Swearers are Fools: for there**
are Liars and Swearers enow, to beat the honest men,
and hang up them. (Macbeth 1766 to 1777)

suggests he could just as easily have another father if his natural one is so corrupt.

Alongside minor characters who present mock arguments there

are purpose-made characters whose mere presence mocks the gullibility of their superiors. They exaggerate the illogicalities and superfluities of leading characters, especially those responsible for male-based excesses.

The Curate, the Pedant and the gallant Armado in *Love's Labour's Lost*, Malvolio in *Twelfth Night*, Falstaff in *1 & 2 Henry IV* and *The Merry Wives of Windsor*, all pre-occupy their own highways to self-proclaimed glory and dominion. In so doing they become crash-test dummies for their socially superior counterparts.

Armado ...Comfort me Boy, What great men have been in love?
...
Holofernes ...you have done this in the fear of God very religiously: and as a certain Father faith.
...
Pedant He draweth out the thread of his verbosity, finer than the staple of his argument.
(Love's Labour's Lost 370-1 & 1312-3 & 1757-8)

The language-mangling Curate and Pedant in *Love's Labour's Lost* mock the pretensions and prejudices of the Church and Academia. <lll_370-1&1312-3&1757-8> The Latinate wordiness of the Pedant Holofernes and the literary worthlessness of the Curate Nathaniel duplicate the disconnectedness from the natural philosophy of life of the four leading males.

In *The Merry Wives of Windsor*, the Welshman Doctor Caius overrates his chances of marrying Anne Page. <wiv_503-7> He mimics the inability of her parents to accommodate themselves to Fenton, her natural love choice. Furthermore, in Shakespeare's shaming of England's benighted Sir John Falstaff, he takes wicked delight in trouncing a character his audience then and still (Bloom)

Caius   ...do not you tell-a-me dat I shall have Anne Page for my self? by gar, I vill kill de Jack-Priest:...by gar, I will my self have Anne Page. (The Merry Wives of Windsor 503-7)

have incorrectly elevated to the role of a garrulous knight errant when he was never meant to be other than a preposterous lecher who deserves to be mocked. <wiv_2465-9>

Mistress Page If he be not amaz'd he will be mocked: If he be amaz'd, he will every way be mock'd.
Mistress Ford We'll betray him finely.
Mistress Page Against such Lewdsters, and their lechery, Those that betray them, do no treachery.
(The Merry Wives of Windsor 2465-9)

Shakespeare lays out in his 154 sonnets the logical conditions for human life within nature. From the givens of nature and the sexual dynamic he forges a philosophy of unprecedented consistency and comprehensiveness. In what sense, then, is Shakespeare aware of traditional philosophical issues.

When we scan the thirty-six plays for signs of noted philosophers, they name Aristotle twice. We hear the first mention in *The Taming of the Shrew* and the other in *Troilus and Cressida*. They remind us of the comings and goings of the four Aristotelian elements in 44 and 45. Does Shakespeare give Aristotle a similar run-around in the plays?

We ask, first, why there are no references to Aristotle's teacher, Plato. Although Shakespeare does not mention Plato by name, throughout his sonnets and poems and plays he maintains a relentless dismissal of Platonic idealism. Platonism is contrary to the logic of truth as saying and beauty as sensations and intuitions that

Shakespeare expounds in his sonnets – particularly in 66 and 101.

Plato turns the natural relation of truth and beauty on its head. He gives sensations or intuitions generated by the mind, which he calls universals, primacy over the natural world. Aristotle challenges Plato's conceit by insisting universals are objects of experience.

However, even though Aristotle corrects Platonic metaphysics, he does not see, as Shakespeare does, that such universals represent but sensations of the mind. Both Plato and Aristotle's confusion arises because they do not appreciate that the sexual dynamic of female and male is the basis for both language and sensations. As we consider a few plays, we will see Shakespeare dismissing the four elements as the basis for morality and aesthetics.

When Lucentio, in *The Taming of the Shrew*, broaches the topic of 'Philosophy', his man Tranio responds with what sounds like a paraphrase of Shakespeare's sonnet-based understanding. Tranio specifically criticises Aristotle's 'checks' or his moral philosophy. We also hear Shakespeare – through Tranio – accuse Ovid of being too devoted to Aristotelian logic. <shr_316-39> We remember how in *Venus and Adonis* Shakespeare upends Ovid's male-based mythology.

> *Lucentio* ...for the time I study,
> Virtue and that part of Philosophy
> Will I apply, that treats of happiness,
> By virtue specially to be achieved. . . .
> *Tranio* To suck the sweets of sweet Philosophy.
> Only (good master) while we do admire
> This virtue, and this moral discipline,
> Let's be no Stoics, nor no stocks I pray,
> Or so devote to Aristotle's checks
> As Ovid; be an outcast quite abjured:
> Balk Logic with acquaintance that you have,
> And practice Rhetoric in your common talk,
> Music and Poesy use, to quicken you,
> The Mathematics, and the Metaphysics
> Fall to them as you find your stomach serves you:
> No profit grows, where is no pleasure tane:
> In brief sir, study what you most affect.
> **(The Taming of the Shrew 316-39)**

Instead, Tranio suggests casting out logic based in 'Mathematics' or 'Metaphysics' in favour of 'Music and Poesy'. Here in the early 1590s we see Shakespeare already aware he will be presenting his philosophy in the form of poetry to capture better his full appreciation of both language and art. Only by basing his philosophy around the female/male dynamic in nature can Shakespeare present a complete understanding.

> *Hector* Unlike young men, whom Aristotle thought
> Unfit to hear Moral Philosophy.
> The Reasons you allege, do more conduce
> To the hot passion of distempered blood,
> Than to make up a free determination
> 'Twixt right and wrong:
> **(Troilus and Cressida 1156-61)**

Shakespeare criticises Aristotle further in *Troilus and Cressida*. Before Hector equivocates after his perceptive analysis of the Trojan's dilemma, Shakespeare has him challenge Aristotle's prohibition on teaching moral philosophy to 'young men'.

<tro_1156-61> Shakespeare shows his disdain for Aristotle's prohibition when he organises a lengthy argument in his *Sonnets* to warn the youthful Master Mistress of the malconsequences of male-based idealism (Platonic or Aristotelian) to which youth is so susceptible – frequently with disastrous consequences.

Shakespeare reiterates his use of the female/male dynamic instead of Aristotelian metaphysics in *Twelfth Night*. Shakespeare has Toby wonder if their 'lives consist of the four Elements' and provides Andrew with an Epicurean rejoinder. <tn_705-11> However, neither Aristotle nor Epicurus are adequate before the natural logic of Shakespeare's sonnet set. And Feste repeats the rejection of Aristotle's elements later in the play. <tn_1269-70>

> Toby A false conclusion: I hate it as an unfill'd Can. To be up after midnight, and to go to bed then is early: so that to go to bed after midnight, is to go to bed betimes. Does not our lives consist of the four Elements?
> Andrew Faith so they say, but I think it rather consists of eating and drinking.   (Twelfth Night 705-11)

We also see evidence of Shakespeare's philosophic acumen when he routs the scepticism that debilitates doubting characters such as Hamlet and Macbeth that leads them

> Feste I might say Ele/ment, but the word is over-worn.
> (Twelfth Night 1269-70)

into increasing levels of tragedy. In his critique of both idealism and scepticism, Shakespeare anticipates the modern prejudice that, like Hamlet and Macbeth, we are not able to act in the world because our knowledge is insecure.

Instead, Shakespeare demonstrates in his comedies that, by basing his understanding in nature and accepting the mind develops from the body, characters can both resolve the quandaries foisted upon them by traditional apologetic beliefs and act decisively to bring about a sea change in the dynamic of their societies.

Shakespeare's plays within plays and the role-playing of characters such as Vincentio and Viola are part of his adroit performance as a playwright. Equally important are the passages of deliberate argument that demonstrate his forte as a unique and incisive philosopher. Both mock-plays and mock-arguments use female and male characters as argument places to point to the larger context of argument that is the whole play and even the whole Folio of plays.

Chapter 20: Thinking feelings and feeling thoughts

How often do the plays appeal to the audience's everyday sensory experiences? How pervasive is the sonnet understanding of truth as a continual dynamic of saying or even swearing? And what does Shakespeare have to say about the form of beauty he associates with sensations generated in the human mind? Is there also a similar correlation in the plays as in the sonnets between knowledge or judgment and the role of the eyes?

68: Entering the minds of Shakespeare's characters

The evidence suggests *Venus and Adonis* is Shakespeare's early attempt to present his nature-based philosophy in a long poem. Then, after writing *Love's Labour's Lost* as a purpose-made vehicle for the philosophy, we see him turning to a set of sonnets to avoid the dramatic limitations in presenting the philosophy on stage. The separation of dedicated argument evident in the sonnet set from his dramas on stage allows him to exploit the cathartic function of the plays more fully through the late 1590s and 1600s.

The more circumspect presentation by Shakespeare's characters of his philosophy in the plays enables an indirect appeal to the natural givens embedded behind male-based prejudices encultured in the theatregoer's forebrain. By writing parts for select characters that convey aspects of the philosophy, he incites the inborn natural philosophy in his audience's generic mind.

We have seen how Shakespeare's savvy female and male characters in the comedies act as go-betweens for his philosophy. Then there are many minor characters, particularly clowns or fools or even bastards, who drop telling bits of *Sonnet* logic into their conversations throughout their plays.

We have examined *F* for instances where characters or situations invoke nature, the female/male dynamic, increase and increase-to-poetry. We will now see how Shakespeare's preconditions from *Q* prepare the groundwork for his characterisation of beauty and truth and truth and beauty in the plays.

To look into Shakespeare's mind or to see more clearly his philosophic intent for his characters in *F* we follow the logical patterns he lays out in *Q*. He uses the generic characters of Mistress, Master Mistress and Poet to argue throughout the 154 sonnets for the natural logic of two types of sensations (both called beauty) and the dynamic of language (called truth).

In the plays, Shakespeare uses characters to clarify the philosophical relationship between sensations and language. Only characters who understand the logic of immediate sensations, the logic of saying and the logic of sensations the mind generates, can implement a social/political/religious constitution to replace divisive and murderous male-based hierarchies.

Shakespeare shows through his mature characters in the comedies that understanding base sensations and the dynamic of language leads to a deep understanding of the potentialities of emotions such as love and hate. Significantly, in the male-God and other godly excesses in the histories and tragedies, religious love and fear lead to an inversion of love and hate. By getting it right about the deepest sensations and feelings we experience, Shakespeare's mature characters show by example how to live and love effectively.

Just as Shakespeare articulates the dynamic of beauty/truth/beauty in his *Sonnets*, in *F* he explores an extensive catalogue of immature and mature love scenarios across his European theatre. In the comedies, mature love is the outcome for savvy characters. In contrast, in the histories and tragedies the misunderstandings and misrepresentations of truth and beauty lead to intellectual and emotional immaturity.

Shakespeare's philosophic aptitude is the encompassing sensibility from which all his plays contextualise the travesties of religion and state. His canny art spans the continent of his day because his wide-ranging insight drives his characterisation of the human mind. His thirty-six plays examine actor upon actor the relationship between the immediate senses, language as saying and the sensations peculiar to the mind sparked by the processes of thought.

In *Measure for Measure*, for instance, the Duke addresses not only the excesses of sensory indulgence in the sex-life of Vienna with its impact on language (especially that of Lucio). He also redresses the consequences of excessive idealism on the minds of Angelo and Isabella. Both violations lead to unwarrantable expectations and disastrous behaviour at odds with avowed ideals. Through his actions, Shakespeare's Duke demonstrates how to achieve mature love with a woman previously committed to the self-love of monastic life.

The Duke knows sworn vows are frequently foresworn or broken. This is because vows or oaths cannot fully represent the deeply felt sensations that remain inarticulate in the recesses of the mind. The play ends with the Duke administering justice based on natural philosophy. He assigns each of the offending characters a fate commensurate with their abuse of their sworn vows.

Shakespeare uses characters as argument places to critique God/nature and male/female illogicalities and restore the logic of increase to its priority over the erotic logic of mythologies. <1h4_23-31> While his nature-based rectification is intentionally dramatic and even mind shattering, harder to appreciate is the bone-shaking import of his brain surgery for the flow-on effect of those illogicalities into the ideas and ideals of generations of misinformed believers.

Henry IV **As far as to the Sepulcher of Christ,**
Whose Soldier now under whose blessed Cross
We are impressed and engag'd to fight...
To chase these Pagans in those holy Fields...
Which fourteen hundred years ago were nail'd
For our advantage on the bitter Cross.
(1 Henry IV 23-31)

When Shakespeare's characters give voice to the natural logic of truth and beauty in the plays they over-write the misconceptions engendered by millennia of skewed expectations. As we criss-cross the continent of old transfigurations, we witness Shakespeare's Herculean cleansing of the traditional volte-face.

69: Incoming sensations to the mind – beauty as seeing

To set up the philosophical consistency of the plays with dramatic authority Shakespeare deliberately activates every element in the Nature Template we derive in Part 1 from the layout of the 1609 *Sonnets*. Unlike apologists who seek psychological recourse by focusing primarily or exclusively on the mind half of the Template, Shakespeare rejoices in giving each and every element from the basic given of nature, to the body dynamic, to the deepest mind-based sensations unbridled influence on the stage. His dramatisation of the whole Template creates the depth and range of his insight into love and life.

By first laying down the nature-based foundation of the sexual/increase dynamic and the beauty/truth/beauty dynamic, Shakespeare is free to invent at will all the time conscious of the deeply emotional human love-reservoir. What the audience hears/sees in any one play contains an implied continuum of the basic givens that invoke them to fill out cathartically the rest of the verbal/visual spectrum. Shakespeare's imagery assists them to see the relevance of the words from their everyday lives in nature.

As part of the process, whether we experience the plays on stage or on the page, Shakespeare continually evokes incoming sensations to the mind. He steeps us in an earthy continent of sensory excitation. His characters move in a world of omnipresent sounds, tastes, sights, smells and touch and even poignant silence.

When Shakespeare surrounds us with the sights and sounds of everyday activities, he is ever conscious of the interrelationship between those immediate sensations and their journey further into the civilisation of the mind. By adhering to the Nature Template, he guarantees the

Demetrius **Yet do thy cheeks look red as Titan's face,**
Blushing to be encountred with a Cloud,
(Titus Andronicus 1104-5)
King **How bloodily the Sun begins to peer**
Above yon busky hill: the day looks pale
At his distemperature. **(1 Henry IV 2635-7)**
Othello **Nor scar that whiter skin of hers, than Snow,**
And smooth as Monumental Alabaster:
(Othello 3243-4)
Capulet **Out you green sickness carrion, out you baggage,**
You tallow face. **(Romeo and Juliet 2197-8)**
Helena **When wheat is green, when hawthorn buds appear,**
(A Midsummer Night's Dream 197)
Horatio **...I have heard**
The Cock that is the Trumpet to the day,
(Hamlet 148-9)
Lorenzo **When the sweet wind did gently kiss the trees,**
And they did make no noise,
(The Merchant of Venice 2406-7)
Falstaff **...and smell like Buckler's-berry in**
simple time **(The Merry Wives of Windsor 1415-6)**
Banquo **...that the Heaven's breath**
Smells wooingly here: **(Macbeth 439-40)**
Hamlet **...you**
Shall nose him as you go up the stairs into the Lobby.
(Hamlet 2697-8)
Angus **Now does he feel**
His secret Murders sticking on his hands,
(Macbeth 2194-5)
Florizell **...I take thy hand, this hand,**
As soft as Dove's-down, (The Winter's Tale 2185-6)
Friar **...The sweetest honey**
Is loathsome in his own deliciousness,
(Romeo and Juliet 1403-4)
Lysander **For as a surfeit of the sweetest things**
The deepest loathing to the stomach brings:
(A Midsummer Night's Dream 792-3)
The five senses

trajectory of sensory effects we experience is not gratuitous. We, from our deep subconscious, intuit he is playing with the precursors to every deliberated thought and imaginary ideal.

When we turn to Shakespeare's representation on the page and evocation on the stage of sights/sounds/smells/tastes/touches we find he engages all the senses. By bringing into play his characters' eyes, ears, noses, mouths and fingers, Shakespeare elicits responses from his audience's sensory experiences. <list_ fivesenses>

Across the European continent every dog, flower, corpse, bird, jewel, perfume, stone, flavour, or tune registers dark or light, black or white, foul or fair, sweet or tart. Shakespeare's apparent indiscriminateness in naming sensory experiences from the most fair to the most foul derives from his acceptance of the natural multiplicity of sensate nature. He does not put a governor on the range of sensory effects by preferential screening of incoming sensations to the mind.

Shakespeare relishes the sensations that arise from nature and particularly those that emanate from human nature. They all impinge on the human sensory organs to be delivered to the receptors in the brain to excite a myriad of unmediated responses in the mind. The audience in Shakespeare's Globe, from the galleries to the pits, experiences the immediacy of effects from every recited colour, <rj_971> stench, tone, velvet and iciness and from every acted expression, gesture or movement.

Romeo **How silver sweet, sound Lover's tongues by night,**
(Romeo and Juliet 971)

When music is heard or food is prepared or war is waged in the Roman, Windsor or Arden countrysides, the deliberateness of the deeds is always attended by sensory effects ranging from sweet vibrato to nauseous carnage. (jc_1501-3) Shakespeare recognises that all human activity is based in nature, that it centres on the female/male dynamic and that it would not play right if he ignores or disparages our animal capacity to absorb countless sensory inputs, fair and foul.

Antony **Cry Havoc, and let slip the Dogs of War,**
That this foul deed, shall smell above the earth
With Carrion men, groaning for Burial.
(Julius Caesar 1501-3)

Suffused with sensory data, Shakespeare's works celebrate nature. Without nature, a white-sound heaven would rule. As Milton demonstrates, hell is a necessary precursor to heaven. With religious blindness he sequels a grossly sensate *Paradise Lost* with an anodyne *Paradise Regained*.

The first issue the Mind half of the Nature Template addresses is the incoming sensations Shakespeare calls beauty. This form of beauty incorporates all incoming sensations, good or bad, sweet or rank. He uses the word beauty deliberately because all sensations evoke singular effects in the human mind. The impinging sensations are unmediated by language so are all indiscriminately beauteous.

Shakespeare recovers the Greek meaning of aesthetics or beauty as singular effects unmediated by thought. He argues against the prejudice that arises when fair is divorced from foul. In his natural world foul can be as fair as any fair overvalued

All witches **...fair is foul, and foul is fair,**
...
Macbeth **So foul and fair a day I have not seen.**
(Macbeth 12 & 137)

for idealistic advantage. <mac_12&137>

Shakespeare's Mistress evokes in the Poet the logic of sensory effects in *127* to *137* before instructing him in the logic of truth or saying in *138* to *152*. Shakespeare's clarity about the relationship between beauty and truth sharpens our minds as he moves us about the European theatre with its sensate cast of nature-orienteering characters. Once clear about sensory beauty, we can begin to comprehend Shakespeare's treatment of language in the plays.

70: Language as the relation of ideas in the mind – truth as saying

Shakespeare's recording of sensory experiences from the continent of dirt, animals and plants, though, is nothing compared to his creation of walking, talking dictionaries cum encyclopaedias whose musings reverberate throughout the palaces, streets, houses, forests and fields of their European environs.

Shakespeare shows in his *Sonnets* that the logical upshot of female-on-male intercourse for beings incited by sensations to a Babel of ideas leads to a never-ending stream of verbal interplay. Because we humans rarely stop talking or thinking on the way to the next generation, Shakespeare constructs his dramas principally of words, words, words – as Hamlet suspects.

We have seen how the female/male dynamic, which perpetuates the evolution of females and males, interlocks with the true/false dynamic of language. The grammar of words on words simulates the sexual dynamic for an increasing depth of understanding. Specifically, in the Prologue we see how Shakespeare's natural philosophy makes the connection between the abrogation of natural logic and the most blatant or 'direct' form of lying – believing without 'if'' in a male God.

It is through talking that we negotiate the 'endless jar between right and wrong', as Ulysses calls the give and take of verbal debate in *Troilus and Cressida*. <tro_575-7> And we have seen Hector criticise Aristotle for not teaching young men that truth is a 'free determination 'twixt right and wrong'. (tro_1156-61)

> *Ulysses* **Force should be right, or rather, right and wrong,**
> **(Between whose endless jar, Justice resides)**
> **Should lose her names, and so should Justice too.**
> **(Troilus and Cressida 575-7)**

> *Hector* **Unlike young men, whom Aristotle thought**
> **Unfit to hear Moral Philosophy.**
> **The Reasons you allege, do more conduce**
> **To the hot passion of distempered blood,**
> **Than to make up a free determination**
> **'Twixt right and wrong:**
> **(Troilus and Cressida 1156-61)**

Moreover, it is *Troilus and Cressida* – the opening tragedy with all the appearances of a prologue for the remaining tragedies – that seems supercharged with lessons on truth as saying. Shakespeare identifies the idealistic/romantic confusion over the logic of truth in its relation to beauty as the principal cause of humanly avoidable tragedy.

In her play, Cressida is the first to define the logic of truth or language. After a lively interchange with Pandarus over the meaning of words – whether Hector is

Pandarus **Faith to say truth, brown and not brown.**
Cressida **To say the truth, true and not true.**
   (Troilus and Cressida 252-3)

Troilus or Troilus is Hector – Cressida skewers the truth dynamic to Pandarus' gossipy tongue. <tro_252-3>

Next, we hear Ulysses argue that 'degree' is 'vizarded' and 'power' becomes 'appetite' when the use of 'force' fails to adjudicate between both 'right and wrong'. If right and wrong lose their names, justice is voided. Shakespeare examines the consequences when a fractious belief in a singular right is pursued religiously. He shows how an absolute right engenders the worst wrong forcing justice to restore the natural balance – often violently and seemingly inexplicably to those ignorant of the natural logic of language.

Hector   **...these Moral Laws**
Of Nature, and of Nation, speak aloud
To have her back returned. Thus to persist
In doing wrong, extenuates not wrong,
But makes it much more heavy. Hector's opinion
Is in this way of truth: yet ne'er the less,
My spritely brethren, I propend to you
In resolution to keep Helen still;
For 'tis a cause that hath no mean dependence,
Upon our joint and several dignities.
   (Troilus and Cressida 1174-83)

If Cressida understands the logic of truth as language and so deservedly survives her play, Shakespeare shows the fault of her Trojan compeers is not that they remain completely unaware of the truth dynamic in nature but that they decide to ignore it for short-term glory. We have seen how Hector analyses correctly the justice of the Greek cause but then decides he will bend 'truth' to the service of warmongering 'honour'. (tro_1174-83)

Troilus **and what truth can speak truest, not truer than**
Troilus.   **(Troilus and Cressida 1727-8)**
Troilus **I am as true, as truth's simplicity**
And simpler than the infancy of truth.
   (Troilus and Cressida 1801-2)
Troilus **O virtuous fight,**
When right with right wars who shall be most right:
   (Troilus and Cressida 1804-5)
Troilus **Yet after all comparisons of truth,**
(As truth's authentic author to be cited)
As true as Troilus, shall crown up the Verse,
And sanctify the numbers.
   (Troilus and Cressida 1813-6)
Troilus **Who I? alas it is my vice, my fault:**
While other fish with craft for great opinion,
I, with great truth, catch mere simplicity;
   (Troilus and Cressida 2494-6)

If Hector is mature enough to enunciate the truth dynamic but dies for forgoing his insight, Troilus survives his tragedy because immature Master Mistress-like he thinks dumbly that truth is a singular effect. Throughout his play, Troilus bleats out his adolescent idealistic conception of truth. Twice Shakespeare has him self-identify with simplistic truth, so misconstruing truth for beauty, a fault 66 dismisses so decisively. <tro_1727-8to2494-6)

In Shakespeare's script, the difference in maturity between Cressida and Troilus provides a sample of the rationale behind the interminable conflict of the Trojan War. Shakespeare depicts Troilus as a romantic/idealistic youth who simplifies the logic of truth, so destroying his love-match with the more mature Cressida. Like his brothers in arms, Troilus gets the logic of truth wrong because his culture inverts the natural priority of female to male. Troilus' fault is Troy's fault writ small. It is the blind fault behind the purposelessness of the Trojan War.

Moreover, it is to Cressida that Shakespeare gives the role of demonstrating the logical consequences of mistaking beauty for truth. Because Troilus distorts the logic of truth so completely by self-identifying with 'truth' as 'simplicity', Cressida has nowhere to go on the scale from true to false but to self-identify as 'false'. Effectively, the Aegean martial culture renders womanhood false by excluding women from power. Hence, Cressida willingly calls herself 'false' to show the natural logic of language behind the sexual and mental injustices done to women in a male-skewed world. <tro_1818to2362-3>

Cressida If I be false, or swerve a hair from truth,
(Troilus and Cressida 1818)
Cressida From false to false, amongst false Maids in love,
Upbraid my falsehood, when they've said as false,
(Troilus and Cressida 1824-5)
Cressida Yea, let them say, to stick the heart of falsehood
As false as Cressid.   (Troilus and Cressida 1829-30)
Pandarus ...   let all constant men be Troilusses, all
false women Cressids,   (Troilus and Cressida 1836-7)
Cressida Make Cressid's name the very crown of falsehood!
If ever she leave Troilus: (Troilus and Cressida 2362-3)

*Troilus...*O false Cressid! false, false, false:
Let all untruths stand by thy stained name,
(Troilus and Cressida 3175-6)

Troilus' condemnation of Cressida, which rings unjustly down history, is nothing but an involuntary confession of his corruption of natural understanding. With knowing but terrible irony, Cressida chances her reputation against a male-driven warrior culture – and the incorrect verdict of many is that she lost. <tro_3175-6>

A measure of the false expectations imposed on language by maladjusted males is the frequency with which Shakespeare uses forms of the words vow, swear and oath in *Troilus and Cressida* – thirty-four times at least. From the initial 'vow' in The Prologue made by the Greeks to exact revenge on Troy, <tro_7-11> to the vows made between Troilus and Cressida, <tro_1714-7&3136-9>

...from th'Athenian bay
Put forth toward Phrygia, and their vow is made
To ransack Troy, within whose strong emures
The ravish'd Helen, Menelaus' Queen,
With wanton Paris sleeps, and that's the Quarrel.
(Troilus and Cressida Prologue 7-11)

the fanatical weight given such logically forswearable pacts is at the heart of the tragedy of Troilus and Troy.

The misplaced faith a male dominant culture imposes on vows and oaths reflects the difference between the responses of females and males to the tenure guaranteed by swearing and forswearing. Throughout the play, Cressida and Troilus are at odds over the value of swearing – as are Hector and Cassandra. Cassandra

Cressida They say all Lovers swear more performance than they are able, and yet reserve an ability that they never perform: vowing more than the perfection of ten; and discharging less than the tenth part of one.
(Troilus and Cressida 1714-7)
Troilus If souls guide vows; if vows are sanctimony;
If sanctimony be the gods' delight:
If there be rule in unity it self,
This is not she: (Troilus and Cressida 3136-9)

challenges the 'polluted' status of vows made absolute to 'gods'. <tro_3214-6&3222-3>

As Shakespeare argues in his 154 sonnets, the miscalling of beauty as truth leads to

Hector Begone I say: the gods have heard me swear.
Cassandra The gods are deaf to hot and peevish vows;
They are polluted offerings, (Troilus and Cressida 3214-6)
Cassandra It is the purpose that makes strong the vow;
But vows to every purpose must not hold:
(Troilus and Cressida 3222-3)

contrary or tragic outcomes because the logic of language is treated as if it has the immediacy and undeniability of a sensation, whether the sensation is incited externally or internally.

Cressida is very clear about the connection between women's lack of rights and Troilus' inability to offer her mature love. Shakespeare compares Troilus' problems with Troy's problems to demonstrate the connection between sexual abuse and the abuse of language.

Feste   ...A sentence is but a chev'rel glove to a good wit, how quickly the wrong side may be turned outward.
Viola Nay that's certain: they that dally nicely with words, may quickly find them wanton.
Feste I would therefore my sister had no name Sir.
Viola Why man?
Feste Why sir, her name's a word, and to dally with that word, might make my sister wanton: But indeed, words are very Rascals, since bonds disgrac'd them.
Viola Thy reason man?
Feste Troth sir, I can yield you none without words, and words are grown so false, I am loath to prove reason with them.   (Twelfth Night 1224-37)

In *Twelfth Night, or, What you will*, Shakespeare illustrates the conjunction between the logic of language and the sexual dynamic in the interchange between Viola and Feste. He stages the exchange outside a church, whose apologetic theology misconstrues the logic of language so rendering truth and beauty inconsistent – as *101* complains. In an image both erotic and precise, Shakespeare characterises the logic of a sentence as capable of being a 'chev'rel' glove turned inside out. <tn_1224-37> It is precisely the grounding of the logic of the sentence in the sexual dynamic that ensures its meaningfulness as demonstrated by the highly erotic language of intercourse bandied about by the two caring and cunning wits.

When Viola contrasts Feste's banter with that of the 'Wise-men' of the Church, who through their turgid arguments show their folly, she acknowledges his grasp on the fundaments of language and hence on truth. In Feste, Viola recognises a fellow wit who has reconciled his masculine and feminine personae. Together they give come-uppance to the illogical prioritising of the male over the female by the Church. The Church's error lies in making too much of the Epiphany in Shakespeare's title *Twelfth Night* and not enough of the democracy of *What you will*.

Typically, confusion occurs between two uses of the word truth. In Q Shakespeare distinguishes between 'simple truth' and 'truth miscalled simplicity' (66). The first is the dynamic of language or saying and the second is the type of singular sensation experienced within the mind. For Shakespeare, Truth miscalled simplicity is elicited when the grammar of language is short-circuited within the mind through the agency of puns, poetry, and other devices to stimulate intuitions and other affective experiences.

The singularity of mind-based sensations and the unceasing interplay of the beauty/truth/beauty dynamic that continuously interrelates incoming sensations, language and sensations in the mind fosters the illusion the truth dynamic in language delivers singular or absolute truths. Like the Greeks who define aesthetics as perceptions unmediated by thought, Shakespeare understands that sensations whatever their origin are never more than sensations requiring the mediation of language to transform them from the sensed to the intelligible.

Effectively, truth or ethics is sandwiched between beauty or aesthetics as seeing and beauty or aesthetics as sensations in the mind. We have already considered beauty archetypally as seeing in the previous section and will examine the logic of mind-based sensations in the next.

Kate **Where did you study all this goodly speech?**
Petruchio **It is extempore, from my mother's wit.**
...
For I am he am born to tame you Kate,
    (The Taming of the Shrew 1141-56)

A survey reveals Shakespeare's plays and poems mention the word truth 323 times – plus the 25 instances in the 154 sonnets. Once we are clear about Shakespeare's use of the truth dynamic in terms of propositional language we can better understand how Shakespeare's poems and plays with their plethora of old and new coinages are the literary embodiment of the truth dynamic or the endless debate that is ethics.

Shakespeare's most dramatic demonstration of the truth dynamic is in *The Taming of the Shrew* where Katherine learns the interplay of true and false from Petruchio and applies it with verve in the final scene to avow apparent subservience

Petruchio **I say it is the Moon.**
Kate **I know it is the Moon.**
Petruchio **Nay then you lie: it is the blessed Sun.**
Kate **Then God be blest, it is the blessed sun,**
But sun it is not, when you say it is not.
And the Moon changes even as your mind:
What you will have it named, even that it is,
And so it shall be so for Katherine.
    (The Taming of the Shrew 2312-9)

to him. <shr_1141-56> <shr_2312-9> Her ironic tone shows she has now mastered language after he restores her connection to nature allowing her to reject the excessive male-based pride induced by her father's patriarchal strictures.

Orsino   **...how doest thou my good fellow**
Feste **Truly sir, the better for my foes, and the worse**
for my friends.
Orsino **Just the contrary: the better for thy friends.**
Feste **No sir, the worse.**
Orsino **How can that be?**
Feste **Marry sir, they praise me, and make an ass of me,**
now my foes tell me plainly, I am an Ass: so that by my
foes sir, I profit in the knowledge of my self, and by my
friends I am abused: so that conclusions to be as kisses, if
your four negatives make you two affirmatives, why
then the worse for my friends, and the better for my foes.
Orsino **Why this is excellent.   (Twelfth Night 2164-76)**

In plays like *Twelfth Night, or, What you will*, Orsino and Olivia are kept from the real potential of loving by their continued imprisonment within the conventions of male-skewed language (the *Twelfth Night* part of the title). It takes the linguistic cunning of Viola, who is cross-dressed in part to mock the idealised love expectations of the music-plagued Orsino and morose Olivia, to restore him by play's end

to a natural balance (the *What you will* part of the title). <tn_2164-76>

In Shakespeare's plays, the solution to an excessive dependence on sensation and emotion is achieved through dialogue (as in *Twelfth Night* and *The Taming of the Shrew*). Or, it fails to be achieved because of the inability to establish dialogue (as in *King Lear* and *Romeo and Juliet*). Or, it fails by the diversion of dialogue into apologetic cul-de-sacs of ethical compromise (as in the history plays).

Shakespeare knows that truth, as any form of saying, is the dynamic of ethics. His plays are ethical because more than any other dramas they achieve reconciliation through words (as in the verbal jousting of *Much Ado About Nothing*), or they examine the impasses when characters despair of doing so (as in the verbal constipation of *Hamlet*). Shakespeare knows words are basic to truth or ethics. The phrase 'the Word was God' is inimical to truth because it is a singular effect or a sensation unmediated by thought that is effectively stranded in the unlanguaged interstices of the human mind.

Shakespeare's proverbial wordiness, his willingness to invent words to accommodate nuances of meaning arises from his appreciation of the logical relationship between truth and beauty. In the plays, his ability to use words meaningfully is guaranteed by an appreciation of the basis of sensations and ideas in the dynamic of nature. Shakespeare never forgets the sexual dynamic and increase are the logical preconditions for any conscious process.

In *Twelfth Night, Measure for Measure, Love's Labour's Lost, The Taming of the Shrew, The Merchant of Venice*, to name a few plays, we see Viola, Vincentio, Berowne, Petruchio, Portia, and others, using language to effect a resolution of the psychological dysfunction with which the plays begin. Contrarily, in *Macbeth* and *Othello* we see Lady Macbeth and Iago using language to further their evil intent because the other characters – idealistic Othello and Desdemona and vacillating Macbeth – do not appreciate the logic of truth or saying.

Iago particularly uses language to confound those like Othello and Desdemona who, while they have an acute awareness of their emotional commitment to each other, are not prepared for the capacity of language to both represent and misrepresent a person's intentions. Although Desdemona is aware of the logic of

Desdemona For if he be not one, that truly loves you,
That errs in Ignorance, and not in Cunning,
I have no judgment in an honest face.
                                    (Othello 1643-5)

increase, her love for Othello unguards her when it comes to assessing Iago's archly verbalised plot – until it is too late. <oth_1643-5>

Sonnet *138* has the Mistress speak for the first time and swear she is made of truth. Then in *152*, the last of the Mistress sonnets devoted specifically to the truth dynamic, the words vow, swear, oath and forswear all occur as well as truth twice. Such a concentration of words referring to the most determined form of saying – the taking of vows or the making of oaths – suggests Shakespeare was acutely conscious of the implication of the logic of truth as saying.

When we examine *F* for the frequency of the words like swear, we find they occur across all the plays over 650 times in the various forms of vow, vows, swear, swears, swearing, forswear, oath, oaths. <kj_1210-20> Swear/ swears/swearing are in every play, vow/vows are missing only from *Much Ado About Nothing, 2 Henry IV* and *Macbeth* with oath/oaths absent from *Macbeth* alone.

Pandulph It is religion that doth make vows kept,
But thou hast sworn against religion:
By what thou swear'st against the thing thou swear'st,
And mak'st an oath the surety for thy truth,
Against an oath the truth, thou art unsure
To swear, swears only not to be forsworn,
Else what a mockery should it be to swear?
But thou dost swear, only to be forsworn,
And most forsworn, to keep what thou dost swear,
Therefore thy later vows, against thy first,
Is in thy self rebellion to thy self:
                                    (King John 1210-20)

Such frequent use of the language of avowal suggests Shakespeare understands the significance of cementing words into pacts and conventions. From amidst the unmediated sensations that enter the mind from the world about and the sensations generated exclusively in the recesses of the mind there arise passages of verbal contract that provide stability because of the conventional logic of language.

However, as *152* also explains, vows and oaths are equally capable of being

Dumaine Do not call it sin in me
That I am forsworn for thee.
    (Love's Labour's Lost 1452-3)

forsworn accompanied by a return to the sea of sensations and then a reformulation of words for a renewed pact of understanding. <lll_1452-3>

Shakespeare was able to hold the dynamic in mind because he bases his appreciation of the logic of language in nature and the sexual dynamic, which similarly resolves and dissolves. His plays have veracity unmatched by those who defend traditional conventions regardless of their demographic unsuitability across the European divides.

In many plays, the offending construct is the male-based hierarchy of Church and State. All the history plays are studies in the anomalies and injustices perpetuated by the ruling male-based theology and monarchy.

The birth of Elizabeth at the end of *Henry VIII*, and attempts by commentators to blunt its anti-patriarchal content, confirms Shakespeare wrote the play to pillory unbridled Church/State collusion. The divine right of kings is at the heart of *Henry VIII* as Henry rejects the Church of Rome to establish a Tudor sect. In the Church of England, Henry as King is second only to God. The murder-borne irony

Cranmer This Royal Infant, Heaven still move about her;
Though in her Cradle; yet now promises
Upon this Land a thousand thousand Blessings,
Which Time shall bring to ripeness: She shall be,
(But few now living can behold that goodness)
A Pattern to all Princes living with her,
And all that shall succeed: **(Henry VIII 3387-93)**

is that Henry is succeeded soon after by his daughter Elizabeth. <h8_3387-93>

The excesses of male-based belief also drive the tragedies of *Romeo and Juliet*, *Macbeth*, *Othello* and *King Lear* and others. This is particularly the case in *King Lear* where a delusionally idealistic Lear demands complete fealty from his daugh-

Lear That thou hast sought to make us break our vows,
Which we durst never yet; and with strain'd pride,
To come betwixt our sentences, and our power,
Which, nor our nature, nor our place can bear;
    (King Lear 182-5)

ters. <lr_182-5> After trenchant nature brings Lear into alignment with natural philosophy on the moors, he achieves limited insight into his male-based preju-

dices but still dies along with his victim/daughter Cordelia. Similarly, Gloucester dies when his bastard Edmund seeks justice for his enforced subservience to Gloucester's wedlock off-

Gloucester His breeding Sir, hath been at my charge. I have
so often blushed to acknowledge him, that now I am
brazed to't.   **(King Lear 12-14)**

spring Edgar. <lr_12-14> In *Cymbeline*, the twist in the tragedy is that Cymbeline's Queen is driven to masculine excesses to get ranking for her unprincely son, Cloten.

Shakespeare's freedom from the vicissitudes of taste – ultimately even the institution of the male God against nature is a quirk of taste – makes his works a universal recourse for those wanting democracy of choice. Even those constrained by conventions recognise in his works a panacea for their imbibed illogicality even if they will not forgo their beliefs.

Shakespeare's understanding of the logic of language, his freedom with words and hence with both incoming and internal sensations, gives his plays and poems their unequivocal surety. In all thirty-six plays, Shakespeare creates the drama and forges a resolution either by the play's end in the comedies or by catharsis in the mind of the audience in the tragedies after the curtain falls. He reminds us that while the excesses of sexual license in any culture can be debilitating they rarely lead to violence on the scale of male-based religious idealistic excesses that corrupt the natural logic of language.

To marvel at Shakespeare's precise and evocative word-power is to acknowledge, if only unintentionally, his consistent application of the natural logic of language he articulates in his 154 sonnets. Only when the logic of language is regained does love flourish in Shakespeare's plays.

71: Sensations generated within the mind – beauty as intuition and the sublime

If Shakespeare cast his mind's eye across the monuments of greater Europe and beyond, he could visualise such pinnacles of human achievement as Cheops' Pyramid in Egypt, Chartres Cathedral in France, Westminster Abbey in England, Hagia Sophia in Constantinople, Saint Peter's Basilica in Rome and even Elsinore Castle in Denmark. They all stand as expressions of ideas generated originally in the imaginary soul. He might consider, though, their portentous elevation at never more than one hundred and fifty meters or so above the earth's crust – which rises in many places to thousands of metres – a more than sufficient celebration of imaginary ideals born in the mind.

Such monuments and their ruins feature a number of times in the *Sonnets*. They are concrete manifestations of the human capacity to give expression to the beauty Shakespeare calls 'simplicity' (66) or expressions of the aesthetic ideals formed in the mind. He calls them simplicity because, like the singular beauty of incoming sensations or seeing, the monuments make concrete the apprehension of singular affects that surface from deep inside the human desire mechanism.

As expressions of ideas generated in the mind from sensations experienced deep in cranial space, such intense but low-lying God concentrations graph the relationship of the human imagination to the vastness of nature. No wonder 55 celebrates the 'contents' of the Poet's verse. It recognises the priority of nature over God-talk or any human expression/construction of internalised feelings and intuitions.

The plays are full of evocations of deep-mind sensations in the name of God – or any of the goddesses and gods from the many cultures across the European theatre. Europe is fly-spotted with monuments to those high-minded sensations.

Take away the monuments, take away human civilisation then God disappears altogether leaving a natural landscape untouched by the props of religiosity. Take away the commandments and dogmas, the priesthoods and monasticism and the God syndrome collapses like a Wonderland deck of cards that can only be reshuffled and restacked if the human hand has a mind to do so.

Cities such as Rome, Alexandria, Vienna, Venice and London, as celebrated centres of God devotion, belie the mountain, forest and plain distance between

Cleopatra You Lie up to the hearing of the Gods:
But if there be, nor ever were there one such
It's past the size of dreaming: Nature wants stuff
To vie strange forms with fancy, yet t'imagine
An Anthony were Nature's piece, 'gainst Fancy,
Condemning shadows quite.
(Antony and Cleopatra 3315-20)
Lear And take upon's the mystery of things,
As if we were Gods' spies:
(King Lear 2956-7)
Titus By nature made for murders and rapes.
Marcus O why should nature build so foul a den,
Unless the Gods delight in tragedies.
(Titus Andronicus 1602-4)
Cominius ...He is their God, he leads them like a thing
Made by some other Deity than Nature,
That shapes man Better:
(Coriolanus 3006-8)
Rosalind   ...be out of love with your
nativity, and almost chide God for making you that
countenance you are;
(As You Like It 1950-2)
Antipholus S The folded meaning of your words' deceit:
Against my soul's pure truth, why labour you,
To make it wander in an unknown field?
Are you a god? would you create me new?
(The Comedy of Errors 823-6)

God versus nature

them. In Shakespeare's day, pilgrimage routes forged out of human mileage provide devotional connectivity that would otherwise evaporate into nature.

Shakespeare's attitude to the diorama of European architecture equates to his evaluation of the role of the idealising imagination in human affairs. The imaginary God is an efflorescence on the natural dynamic mapped in the *Sonnets*. Unlike those who institute God-fearing religions by inverting the natural dynamic, Shakespeare is clearheaded about the products of the imagination. They are fundamental to human experience but their orbits are in perpetual transit before nature. <list_godversusnature>

Because the 'imaginary soul' (*27*) is the least understood and most abused faculty of the human mind, Shakespeare explores its manifestations and provides ways to rectify its misrepresentations. Each play examines a circumstance that takes the idealising capacity of the mind to excess. The worst excess is the illogical prioritisation of the male God over the priority status of the female. Each play examines the problem and either develops a workable solution or shows its fatal consequences.

When Shakespeare mentions God in his plays, he is conscious of its status as a mind-based sensation. By referencing the idea of God/s (whether Pagan or Christian) so freely throughout his works, he engages with the audience's capacity to receive and respond to deep sensations in the mind. The doctrinaire conversion of Shakespeare's works to Christianity – because parts sound Christian to some ears – is an ironic consequence of his ability to appreciate the logic of God talk without succumbing to the illogicality of believing an internal sensation of the mind creates nature.

Shakespeare's understanding of the truth dynamic of language and its synonym ethics means word for word, phrase for phrase, sentence for sentence, his ethics is engaged continuously in substantive debates because he is clear about its differentiation between incoming sensations and internal sensations referred to as God. We talk to God but God cannot talk except as we facilitate it. Hence, we hear our own expectations reflected back if we pray for God to intercede – as Richard III found to his cost. **<list_prayerperverted>**

Evoking sensations in the mind involves a non-propositional use of words. Puns, poetry or simple repetition translates words into sensations, even the deeper sensations of the imaginary soul. <mnd_1804-9&1814-8> The repetitive chant of prayer, for instance, signals its non-propositional purpose of inciting sensations in the mind. At best, its effect is to incite good feelings. At worst, it creates the illusion of a private communication with an unrepresentable affectation.

Bishop of Winchester **The Battles of the Lord of Hosts he fought:**
The Churches' Prayers made him so prosperous....
Gloucester **Name not Religion, for thou lovest the Flesh,**
And nere throughout the year to Church thou go'st,
Except it be to pray against thy foes.
                                     (1 Henry VI 39-40 & 50-2)
Queen Margaret **Cancel his bond of life, dear God I pray,**
That I may live and say, The Dog is dead.
                                     (Richard III 2848-9)
Quickly **...his worst fault is, that he is given to prayer; he is**
something peevish that way: but no body but has his
fault: **(The Merry Wives of Windsor 410-2)**

                     Prayer perverted

Theseus **The Poet's eye in a fine frenzy rolling, doth glance**
From heaven to earth, from earth to heaven.
And as imagination bodies forth the forms of things
Unknown; the Poet's pen turns them to shapes,
And gives to air nothing, a local habitation,
And a name...
Hippolita **But all the story of the night told over,**
And all their minds transfigured so together,
More witnesseth than fancies images,
And grows to something of great constancy;
But howsoever, strange, and admirable.
        (A Midsummer Night's Dream 1804-9 & 1814-8)

The opposite occurs with nature. We do not ask nature for anything because nature is the provider of everything we have and know. <aww_223-30> We do not say by nature, O nature, or pray to nature. We act toward nature as Shakespeare does. Only he, though, seems fully grounded in a globe-encompassing contentedness, whereas most of us are still green at sea.

Throughout his sonnets, poems and plays, Shakespeare brings us face-to-face with readily observable nature. In contrast, once believers make an act of faith in God they rarely precondition their God-talk with verifiable evidence of his existence.

Helena **Our remedies oft in ourselves do lie,**
Which we ascribe to heaven: the fated sky
Gives us free scope, only doth backward pull
Our slow designs, when we ourselves are dull.
What power is it, which mounts my love so high,
That makes me see, and cannot feed mine eye?
The mightiest space in fortune, Nature brings
To join like, likes; and kiss like native things.
        (Alls Well That Ends Well 223-30)

In the comedies, the females in charge (and the three gender balanced males in their plays) do not seek God-like recompense – as does the King in *Love's Labour's Lost*. Instead, Shakespeare has them act confident in their understanding of the logical relationship between language and the imagination. What in their male stage counterparts in the histories and tragedies is an idealising sensation run amok, in the savvy females (and three males) it is a reassuring faculty of intuition that guides their well-reasoned acts.

In their eleven comedies, females balance rationality and intuition by accessing their originary relationship to nature. In their comedies, the three mature males have gender-balanced their male-biased prejudices. Prospero, particularly, takes time out to inform Miranda of the change he wrought in his previously compromised attitude to the female/male dynamic.

When Harold Bloom drum-rolls Hamlet's contribution to the invention of the human, he merely highlights Hamlet's unsuccessful attempt to change from an adolescent ideologue to a judicious citizen. Because Bloom does not appreciate the *Sonnet* logic and the significance of the roles of Petruchio, Vincentio, and Prospero, he has no idea of the mature goal Shakespeare has Hamlet tragically fail to achieve. Even worse, Bloom includes Falstaff in his duet of heroes, again mistaking the inkling of invention for the full ocean of resolution achieved by the women of the comedies and the three male co-authors of their own destinies.

What marks out the kings of the histories and the leading males of the tragedies to a man is their devotion to illogically excessive ideals that insensitise them to saner intuitions. Instead, Shakespeare takes bitter pleasure showing that characters such as Iago in *Othello* and Edmund in *King Lear* and Macbeth in *Macbeth* do have an active intuition but their alienated circumstances drive them to use it for revenge rather than reconciliation.

In *King Lear* particularly, with its tragic double plot of two single-minded male-based ideologues, first Lear alienates his youngest daughter Cordelia. Then, Gloucester blindly rejects his natural-born son Edmund. Shakespeare's constant recourse is to take his characters back to nature to forge a recovery of their mind-based illogicalities. This is none truer than in *King Lear* where both belorded miscreants are subject to ego cleansing on the wind-swept heaths of Ancient Britain.

We have seen Shakespeare correct the youthful idealism of the Master Mistress in the *Sonnets* by revivifying his natural relationship with the Mistress. Similarly, he addresses the immaturity of Hal and Falstaff, of Bertram, Ferdinand, Troilus, Hamlet, Benedick, Orsino and Olivia,

> *Benedick*   ... Shall quips
> and sentences, and these paper bullets of the brain awe
> a man from the career of his humour? No, the world
> must be peopled. When I said I would die a bachelor, I
> did not think I should live till I were married, here comes
> Beatrice: by this day, she's a fair Lady, I do spy some
> marks of love in her.   (Much Ado About Nothing 1061-7)

and other psychologically mal-adjusted characters. <ado_1061-7> He redirects their fascination with mind-based prowess back into a sustaining relationship with the source of their mental powers and moral sense – the Mistress in nature.

By resorting to nature, Shakespeare demonstrates that the only answer to the unhealthy prioritisation of mind-based sensations is to tip the God priority on its head to re-establish the natural dynamic. He shows how the confusion of singular mind-based sensations with nature's singularity leads to many of the avoidable problems and disasters in the male God-fearing countries from Denmark to Libya and from Spain to Austria. His nature-based philosophy shows the way from God-induced hate to mature love.

Shakespeare appreciates that the dynamic of truth or saying in language has a moderating role between incoming sensations impinging on the body's sensors from the world about and the sensations generated in the mind through the use of language to create poetic or other singular effects. The perceptual to conceptual dynamic, from incoming beauty to debatable truth to intuitional beauty, is ever-present to the conscious human mind.

Both Q and F show how to represent the interrelationship without prejudice. Shakespeare's additions and transformations to source material from other authors changes, with only a few telling redirections, their idealising illogicality to nature-based logicality.

Shakespeare founds his challenging veracity on his mastery of the individual components in the natural template he structures into his 154 sonnets. His clarity about the logic of external sensations, language and internal sensations is critical to his ability to represent the world as it is.

Understanding the logic of mind-based sensations serves Shakespeare in other ways besides nailing unhealthy idealists to the cross of their misappropriated beauty. He crafts his poetry and music using the same understanding that gives him such devastating insight into his characters' imaginary souls.

Shakespeare attunes his drama and verse to the dynamic of the Nature Template. His unerring ear excites in the minds of his audience a visualisation of their own fallible reality. Shakespeare uses poetry, song, puns or other forms of pre-verbal and dramatic lan-

Troilus My Will enkindled by mine eyes and ears,
Two traded Pilots 'twixt the dangerous shores
Of Will, and Judgment.
            (Troilus and Cressida 1048-50)
Ulysses There's a language in her eye, her cheek, her lip:
Nay, her foot speaks, her wanton spirits look out
At every joint, and motive of her body:
            (Troilus and Cressida 2612-4)
Cressida Troilus farewell; one eye yet looks on thee;
But with my heart, the other eye, doth see.
Ah poor our sex; this fault in us I find:
The error of our eye, directs our mind.
What error leads must err: O then conclude,
Minds swayed by eyes, are full of turpitude.
            (Troilus and Cressida 3099-104)
Volumnia Action is eloquence, and the eyes of th'ignorant
More learned than the ears,   (Coriolanus 2177-8)
Cymbeline Mine eyes
Were not in fault, for she was beautiful:
Mine ears that hear her flattery, nor my heart,
That thought her like her seeming.
            (Cymbeline 3324-7)
                    Eyes

guage to connect the limits of intelligible speech with the effects generated in the aesthetic wonderland of intuitions, which he calls the mind's eye.

72: Eye to eye – the natural interface

In total, the words eye and eyes occur more than 1100 times across the Shakespearean canon and appear in every work a considerable number of times. He uses them more frequently and more consistently than the words God and Gods. Whereas the God(s) in the poems and plays refer to the many religious entities that populate the human imagination, the eyes in nearly all cases refer to the eyes of the human body and mind. Occasionally, by metaphorical extension, they refer to the sun.

Whereas many of the uses of the word God are clipped, as in involuntary exclamations or curses, the majority of the eye words are used with fulsome intent. In the plays, there is a persistent symbolic use of the eyes either as organs of sexual intercourse as or portals for human communication. <lll_79-96> Shakespeare affirms the relation between sexuality and mentality in the erotic structure of the 154 sonnets.

The pervasive appearance of eyes throughout the human experience that is Shakespeare's Europe perplexes many of his readers. <list_eyes> Louis Zukofsky in *Bottom: On Shakespeare* [note 5] mused on the eyeball-to-eyeball interface in the plays but could not explain the phenomenon.

Editors emend words such as 'their' in the *Sonnets* because

Berowne As painfully to pore upon a Book,
To seek the light of truth, while truth the while
Doth falsely blind the eye-sight of his look:
Light seeking light, doth light of light beguile:
So ere you find where light in darkness lies,
Your light grows dark by losing of your eyes.
Study me how to please the eye indeed,
By fixing it upon a fairer eye,
Who dazzling so, that eye shall be his heed,
And give him light that it was blinded by.
Study is like the heaven's glorious Sun,
That will not be deep search'd with saucy looks:
Small have continual plodders ever won,
Save base authority from other's Books.
These earthly Godfathers of heaven's lights,
That give a name to every fixed Star,
Have no more profit of their shining nights,
Than those that walk and wot not what they are.
(Love's Labour's Lost 79-96)

of a misinterpretation of its relationship to the two eyes of human intercourse. Some of the notorious 'their' to 'thy' changes occur because the role of both eyes

Berowne From women's eyes this doctrine I derive.
They sparkle still the right Promethean fire,
They are the Books, the Arts, the Academes,
That show, contain, and nourish all the world.
Else none at all in aught proves excellent.
Then fools you were these women to forswear:
(Love's Labour's Lost 1701-6)

is not appreciated. No wonder, then, Shakespeare's frequent recourse to the eye(s) in the plays causes a flutter amongst his critics.

In *14*, Shakespeare dismisses all forms of star or heaven gazing as the way to gauge the worth of the Master

Mistress. Instead, he announces truth and beauty is evaluated through the eyes.

The insight, expressed in *14* and published in Q around twenty years after Shakespeare starts writing his plays, appears early on in Berowne's paraphrase of *14* in *Love's Labour's Lost*. <lll_1701-6> Shakespeare arrays his continent of plays with discriminating eyeballs that blindside the multitude of goddesses or gods peopling the human imagination. <mv_1409-15>

Song Tell me where is fancy bred,
Or in the heart, or in the head:
How begot, how nourished.
It is engendered in the eyes,
With gazing fed, and Fancy dies,
In the cradle where it lies:
Let us all ring Fancies knell.
(The Merchant of Venice 1409-15)

Dolphin ... and in her eye I find
A wonder, or a wondrous miracle,
The shadow of my self formed in her eye,
Which being but the shadow of your son,
Becomes a son and makes your son a shadow:
I do protest I never loved my self,
Till now, infixed I beheld my self,
Drawn in the flattering table of her eye....
Philip Drawn in the flattering table of her eye,
Hanged in the frowning wrinkle of her brow,
And quartered in her heart, he doth espy
Himself love's traitor,   (King John 812-24)

Shakespeare underscores the predominance of eyes at the heart of human intercourse over heavenly bodies by the occasional characterisation of the sun as an eye or even heaven's eye. By humanising the sun with the properties of the human eye, he highlights the theological conceit of creation by an extra-stellar anthropomorphic God. <kj_812-24>

Sonnet *104* encapsulates the person-to-person function of the eyes with its 'your eye I eyed'. The looking into the eye of another involves seeing through the eye into the mind and heart or the mind's eye. As in 24, it is a two-way exchange.

> *Boy* Negligent student, learn her by heart.
> *Braggart* By heart, and in heart Boy.
> *Boy* And out of heart Master: all those three I will prove.
> *Braggart* What wilt thou prove?
> *Boy* A man, if I live (and this) by, in, and without, upon the instant: by heart you love her, because your heart cannot come by her: in heart you love her, because your heart is in love with her: and out of heart you love her, being out of heart that you cannot enjoy her.
> (Love's Labour's Lost 804-13)

In all the plays, Shakespeare reiterates the interconnectedness between the seeing eye and the mind's eye with its penetration to the bleeding heart and imaginary soul. He has the Braggart and Boy explain the relationship in *Love's Labour's Lost*. <lll_804-13>

Shakespeare also accounts for those whose eyes resist a free flow of communication because they neglect natural philosophy. Most common are those with overly teary eyes. Their tears erect a watery barrier to the give and take of human intercourse.

In *Twelfth Night*, Olivia is so self-involved in mourning for her brother she is awash with eyeish brine. While Viola manages to free Orsino from Olivia's lachrymose stranglehold, Olivia marries Viola's twin brother Sebastian, who confesses to being uncontrollably teary-eyed.   <list_eyestears>

> *Valentine* And water once a day her Chamber round
> With eye-offending brine: (Twelfth Night 35-6)
> *Helena* How came her eyes so bright? Not with salt tears.
> If so, my eyes are oftener washed than hers.
>   (A Midsummer Night's Dream 747-8)
> *Richard* Those eyes of thine, from mine have drawn salt Tears;
> Shamed their Aspects with store of childish drops:
>   (Richard III 344-5)
>   Eyes and tears

Viola's stage entry on the crest of a wave is mature and circumspect. In contrast, Sebastian represents males or overly masculinised females unable to mature beyond the sea salt of mother's amniotic fluid. Unlike Viola, Sebastian fails to achieve a mature relation of male/masculine to female/feminine.

Shakespeare mocks King Ferdinand in *Love's Labour's Lost* when he has him write a sonnet full of whimpering self-pity. The King, who is responsible for proposing a period of monastic seclusion from females, imagines the Princess of France will benefit from seeing herself reflected in the tears dribbling down his face. <lll_1362-9> Disingenuously, he insists she should not 'love thy self'. Yet, deluded by his own eloquence, he imagines himself

> *King* Nor shines the silver Moon one half so bright,
> Through the transparent bosom of the deep,
> As doth thy face through tears of mine give light:
> Thou shin'st in every tear that I do weep,
> No drop, but as a Coach doth carry thee:
> So ridest thou triumphing in my woe.
> Do but behold the tears that swell in me,
> And they thy glory through my grief will show:
>   (Love's Labour's Lost 1362-9)

gripped by immortal inspiration.

In Shakespeare's earthy continent, teary eyes call to mind not immortality beyond the stars but the pearly tears of sexual intercourse. Sonnet 34 provides a remedy for 'base clouds' that threaten to ruin a 'beauteous day'. It says 'those tears are pearl which thy love sheeds, and they are rich, and ransom all ill deeds'.

Shakespeare enlivens both eyes in their cheeky surrounds. <tro_2611-5>

In *A Midsummer Night's Dream*, the drops of potion into the eyes of the sleeping couples leads to a confusion of lovers that replicates the natural variability in sexual outcomes through increase. When Gloucester has his eyes removed in *King Lear*, he pays the price for his unnatural abuse of his sexual eye. His crime is to alienate his natural lust son Edmund in favour of his marriage bed son Edgar. <lr_3133-4> Similarly, Iago makes no bones about the connection between Desdemona's bedroom eye and her mind's eye. He will use one to confound the other. <oth_1129-40>

We saw *17* identify the logic of sensations or beauty with seeing and the logic of language or truth with the tongue. By recovering the natural logic of the face/groin dynamic, Shakespeare is able to pass from the eyes to the tongue and back to the eyes. He holds the face and the organs of reproduction together in a wordy fertility unmatched by others who doubt or deny their common logic. A number of plays relate the eyes and tongue specifically. <list_eyesandtongues>

Ulysses ...Fie, Fie, upon her:
There's a language in her eye, her cheek, her lip:
Nay, her foot speaks, her wanton spirits look out
At every joint, and motive of her body:
Oh these encounters so glib of tongue,
(Troilus and Cressida 2611-5)

Edgar The dark and vicious place where thee he got,
Cost him his eyes.   (King Lear 3133-4)

Iago ...she is sport for Jove.
Cassio She's a most exquisite Lady.
Iago And I'll warrant her, full of Game.
Cassio Indeed she's a most fresh and delicate creature.
Iago What an eye she has?
Methinks it sounds a parley to provocation.
Cassio An intuiting eye:
And yet me thinks right modest.
Iago And when she speaks,
Is it not an Alarum to Love?
Cassio She is indeed perfection.
Iago Well: happiness to their Sheets.
(Othello 1129-40)

Oliver If that an eye may profit by a tongue,
(As You Like It 2233)
Viola ... me thought her eyes had lost her tongue,
(Twelfth Night 676)
Scroope So may you by my dull and heavy Eye:
My Tongue hath but a heavier Tale to say:
(Richard II 1555-6)
Second Officer ...but he hath so planted his
Honours in their Eyes, and his actions in their Hearts, that
for their Tongues to be silent, and not confess so much,
(Coriolanus 1231-3)
Macduff O I could play the woman with mine eyes
And Braggart with my tongue.   (Macbeth 2080-1)
Cordelia A still soliciting eye, and such a tongue,
(King Lear 253)
Eyes and tongues

The richness of Shakespeare's language derives from the natural philosophy of the *Sonnets* put into practice across his European theatre. No wonder commentators such as Johnson, Coleridge and Eliot baulk at Shakespeare's fulsome evocation of life and art. They divorce their bodies from their minds and are forever adrift on a sea of sorrows.

Shakespeare's awareness of the logical relationship between incoming sensations, the dynamic of language and the sensations peculiar to the human mind gives his works a force and credibility not found elsewhere. By focusing on the role of the eyes, he engages fully the connectivity between nature and the sexual dynamic of female and male and the functions of the mind.

Chapter 21: From the sexual dynamic of life to myths of dying

Why does Shakespeare's natural alignment of the sexual body and the erotic mind prove so troublesome for so many? From where does he garner such a clear but rich interpenetration of body and mind so when his characters discuss life and death both are deeply realised on stage?

73: From the sexual body to the erotic mind

In the philosophy Shakespeare presents in Q, the differentiation between female and male in nature renews itself through increase. Consequently, the sexual dynamic and increase, along with the feminine and masculine relationships, find their natural home in Shakespeare's plays. Human sexual and gender characteristics drive the mythic depth of Shakespeare's dramas. When he gives expression to the erotic logic of language, he is conscious the most revealing example of language's erotic logic is in myths of origin.

Shakespeare's appreciation that language is fundamentally erotic allows him to access the full resources of human communication. His legendary inventiveness with language, which injects thousands of neologisms into modern speech, derives from his realisation articulated in the *Sonnets* that the erotic logic of language is rooted in the sexual dynamic of female and male in nature.

> Mercutio **This is the hag, when Maids lie on their backs,**
> **That presses them, and learns them first to bear,**
> **Making them women of good carriage:**
> **This is she.**
> Romeo ...**Thou talk'st of nothing.**
> Mercutio **True, I talk of dreams:**
> **Which are the children of an idle brain,**
> **Begot of nothing, but vain fantasy,**
> **(Romeo and Juliet 541-9)**

Shakespeare understands that sexual symbolism, erotic allusions, innuendo and puns <rj_541-9> <lll_109-15> are vehicles for accessing the heart of human content. His use of such literary devices is never gratuitous. The richness and believability of Shakespeare's language is due in large part to his adherence to the logic of the sexual dynamic as the source of truth and beauty – as he states in *14*.

> Ferdinand **Berowne is like and envious sneaping Frost,**
> **That bites the first borne infants of the Spring.**
> Berowne **Well, say I am, why should proud Summer boast,**
> **Before the Birds have any cause to sing?**
> **Why should I joy in any abortive birth?**
> **At Christmas I no more desire a Rose,**
> **Than wish a Snow in May's new fangled shows:**
> **(Love's Labour's Lost 109-15)**

The irony is that commentators' timidity leads them to call his deeply realised eroticism bawdy. They divert Shakespeare's serious intent by suggesting he titillates his writing to appeal to the bad taste of his audience. On the contrary, Shakespeare's appreciation of the logic of the erotic as the basis of myth makes him fearless in his use of the same deeply rooted language resource to convey his fully realised content.

The term bawdy does a double injustice to Shakespeare's critique of mythic erotics. It attempts to disarm his criticism and it reduces his profound intent to one of soft porn. Rather, biblical myth locks up eroticism in forbidding commandments leaving believers with little more than rude jokes to regale the faithful at Church galas. Shakespeare's characters do not fall back on jokes because they live out the rich eroticism of language.

Shakespeare liberates language from its imprisonment in traditional male-based mythologies. His female and male characters are equally at ease using language to its erotic limit. Secondary characters, particularly, use sexual innuendo freely to point up the conceit of their superiors.

There are a number of passages in *F* that show Shakespeare's easy awareness of the relationship between goddesses, gods and eroticism. Boyet in *Love's Labour's Lost* has his account of the sexual/verbal dynamic of 'eye' and 'tongue' seconded by the Ladies of France in mythical terms. <lll_755-61> Similarly, the Lord who stage-manages Christopher Sly's conversion to 'Lord' with a 'Lady' in the induction to *The Taming of the Shrew* sets the scene for Petruchio's recovery of Katherine's native ability with language. He recalls the moment when Io is surprised by the 'lively' counterfeit of art. <shr_206-8> In *Hamlet*, Ophelia calls on Jesus ('gis') and God ('Cock') as she recounts how Hamlet 'tumbled' her on the pretext of marriage. <ham_2796-803>

> *Boyet* But to speak that in words, which his eye hath disclosed.
> I only have made a mouth of his eye,
> By adding a tongue, which I know will not lie.
> *Rosaline* Thou art an old Love-monger and speakest skilfully.
> *Maria* He is Cupid's Grandfather and learns news of him.
> (Love's Labour's Lost 755-61)

> *Lord* We'll show thee Io, as she was a Maid,
> And how she was beguiled and surprised,
> As lively painted, as the deed was done.
> (The Taming of the Shrew 206-8)

Shakespeare has his female and male characters give expression to seemingly innocuous phrases that enter the minds of his audience whether or not they grasp the deep parody they imbibe. He penetrates their minds by feeding them snippets of their religious prejudices disguised in ellipses, puns or other verbal stunts. Words and phrases such as incony Jew, maculate and incardinate slip past the guard of the theatregoer to stir up their mythological language-basket.

> *Ophelia* By gis and by Saint Charity,
> Alack, and fie for shame:
> Young men will do't, if they come to't,
> By Cock they are to blame.
> Quoth she before you tumbled me,
> You promised me to Wed:
> So would I ha' done by yonder Sun,
> And thou hadst not come to my bed.
> (Hamlet 2796-803)

The 154 sonnets, with their recovery of the natural order with its priority of nature and the female, prepare us for the critique Shakespeare makes of male-based Gods. Further, the distinction between the fourteen comedies and the twenty-two histories and tragedies in *F* sets the scene for a two-way challenge to the illogicalities of male-based pride prolific throughout the Europe of Shakespeare's day. <kj_22-3>

> *Chattylion* The proud control of fierce and bloody war,
> To enforce these rights, so forcibly with-held.
> (King John 22-3)

Because the leading characters in the histories and tragedies exhibit sensibilities divorced from the sexual/erotic dynamic, their language is largely prosaic and perfunctory compared to the florid naturalism and gaminess in the speech of the minor characters. Most of Shakespeare's lovemaking and risk-taking rogues are irresistibly appealing because they use language rooted in nature – artlessly but evocatively, humorously but poignantly. <h5_856-60>

Boy A said once, the Devil would have him about / Women.
Hostess A did in some sort (indeed) handle Women:
but then he was rheumatic, and talked of the Whore of / Babylon.
(Henry V 856-60)

Conversely, there are minor characters like Malvolio whose verse or prose lacks the erotic frisson of their fellows, as if Shakespeare anticipates the prudery of his future detractors. <tn_2040-1> Shakespeare goes a step further and has some characters talk crudely as if to further aggravate the peevishness of future bookish malcontents. <mm_103-5>

Malvolio I think nobly of the soul, and no way approve
his opinion.   **(Twelfth Night 2040-1)**

When commentators treat such passages as bawdy, they miss the way Shakespeare's characters use language to the limit of its erotic resources. <ado_546-50> The same syndrome is at play when literature is reprieved from censorship despite its erotic intensity. For instance, in James Joyce's *Ulysses* and D. H. Lawrence's *Lady Chatterley's Lover*, both authors use the erotic resources of language mindful of its biological underpinning. Joyce and Lawrence deploy eroticism proto-mythically in the arena where Shakespeare is the mythic master.

Lucio Thou concludest like the Sanctimonious Pirate,
that went to sea with the Ten Commandments, but
scraped one out of the Table.
(Measure for Measure 103-5)

Beatrice   ...and the commendation is
not in his wit, but in his villany...
...I am sure he is in the Fleet, I would he had
boarded me. **(Much Ado About Nothing 546-50)**

Shakespeare also develops characters who, alienated from the physical world of the sexual, resort to the conceptual world of the erotic. In *Hamlet*, Hamlet and Ophelia are at first carefree lovers. However, as the sexual haste of his mother's marriage to fratricide Claudius dawns on Hamlet, he rages against Ophelia. As an expression of his alienation, he consigns her to the erotic confines of a nunnery, which Shakespeare dramatises as death by drowning.

Measure for Measure endorses the opposing trajectory. Isabella avoids erotic cloistering in a monastery, where she is a novice in nunnery. Instead, she achieves liberation in a sexual/erotic relationship with her philosophic compeer, Duke Vincentio. Isabella graduates from adolescent erotic vulnerability to mature mind-games in the dynamic of real life as Vincentio reengages her full linguistic capabilities.

74: Life and death in the European theatre

Every poem and play in the Shakespeare canon uses the words life and live, and death and dead. He also uses lives, dies, died and similar words extensively throughout his works. <**mm_1208-9&1246-7**>

In the natural economy of the *Sonnets*, nature and life are synonymous.

Duke **Be absolute for death: either death or life**
Shall thereby be the sweeter.
Claudio **To sue to live, I find I seek to die,**
And seeking death, find life:
(Measure for Measure 1208-9 & 1246-7)

Death is an event within the panorama of life. The true antonym to death is not life but birth. The phrase 'life and death' ignores the increase dynamic – as the first fourteen sonnets argue.

Occurring more than 750 times each, life and death outstrip the appearances of the biblical God. As we have seen, God occurs in only half the plays because he shares the limelight with the many other goddesses and gods that come and go in the European imagination. <**wt_3207-8**>

Instead, Shakespeare contextualises death within life across the European theatre. The ubiquity of death-within-life in the plays and poems is a measure of Shakespeare appreciation that in the day-to-day life of his towns and cities death is a mirage on the sea of increase. <**r3_3081-3**> The lifelikeness

Paulina **To see the Life as lively mocked, as ever**
Still Sleep mocked Death:
(The Winter's Tale 3207-8)

of Shakespeare's characters arises from his appreciation that life and death coalesce in the continuum of nature.

Richard **If I have killed the issue of your womb,**
To quicken your increase, I will beget
Mine issue of your blood, upon your Daughter:
(Richard III 3081-3)

In many of the comedies, Shakespeare's leads his characters out of death sentences imposed by mind-based prejudice. Consequently, the word life occurs more often – and usually by a considerable margin – over the word death. The exception is *Much Ado About Nothing*, yet no one dies on or off stage during the what-to-do about women's nothings.

Only two characters die after appearing on stage during a comedy. In *The Winter's Tale*, the boy Mamillius dies as his father Leontes loses the plot. Then a bear chases and kills Antigonus as he reluctantly abandons Leontes' 'bastard' baby on a beach. The head of Ragozine, a pirate who dies of fever off-stage in *Measure for Measure*, makes a very brief appearance as a substitute for Claudio's.

All's Well That Ends Well deals with the sickness of a King so mentions death and life a number of times. Life, though, still appears near twice as many times as death. *The Winter's Tale* follows Leontes' horrific attempts to do away with his wife and baby daughter. Yet life still dominates death by two to one.

The play that memorably confronts the deadly consequences of male-based idealism is *Measure for Measure*. Duke Vincentio, when talking to Claudio, gives Shakespeare's most stirring advocacy for his natural philosophy of life – and death within life.

To the Duke's philosophic clarity about life and death, Shakespeare complements the recalcitrance of the murderer Barnardine. Barnardine has no fear of death because he is perpetually drunk. <**mm_2010-1**> Shakespeare plays on the irony that Barnardine's nine disconsolate years on death row induces the same understanding of death-in-life the Duke arrives at after years of civic responsibility and reflection. If nunnery and debauchery are death sentences for those who ignore nature, simple Barnardine and the knowing Duke show that the only life after death is through life before death.

Provost (of Barnardine) ...insensible of mortality, and desperately mortal. (Measure for Measure 2010-1)

The Duke acknowledges the irony of a murderer reconciling himself to life by pardoning him at the play's end. He increases the irony by handing Barnardine over to the Friar for advice – the same Friar who assists the Duke in monkish deception up to the moment in the play when he doffs his Godly guise. <mm_2879-85>

Shakespeare's exposé of the relationship between life and death means *Measure for Measure* mentions death and life over ninety times. By comparison, the tragedy of *Romeo and Juliet* mentions them around ninety-four times. However, a history play, *The Life and Death of Richard the Third*, has the most mentions of death and life at 100. As we have seen, Shakespeare's account of King Richard's bloody reign of life and death also features the most Gods and seven Christians.

Duke Sirha, thou art said to have a stubborn soul
That apprehends no further than this world,
And squarest thy life according: Thou'rt condemn'd,
But for those earthly faults, I quit them all,
And pray thee take this mercy to provide
For better times to come: Friar advise him,
I leave him to your hand.
(Measure for Measure 2879-85)

Whereas death is rare in the comedies, in the histories it is an intricate part of the web of self-deceit and misguided loyalty. Many characters avow they would rather die than live if their death would further the cause of either the reigning monarch or a pretender to the throne. Throughout the histories, death seems to be an ever-present possibility in the shifting nests of loyalties and retributions governed by England's male God monarchs. <r3_239-40> The terrible irony Shakespeare exposes in his ten histories is that encultured in the God-based monarchies is a penchant to divide and murder at whim. <r3_1232-3>

Significantly, the history least covered in blood and gore is *Henry VIII*. Despite Henry's misogynistic reign, its twenty-six mentions of life outweigh its ten mentions of death. This is because Shakespeare celebrates Elizabeth's long and relatively peaceful reign after Henry's murderous divorces.

In the twelve tragedies,

Anne O God! which this Blood mad'st, revenge his death: O Earth! which this Blood drink'st, revenge his death. (Richard III 239-40)

there are frequent deaths including the deaths of title characters in ten. *Romeo and Juliet* and *Hamlet* have the greatest concentrations of death and life with death dominating both. When life breaks through, it often does so in comedic passages. Yet, even the comic turns fail to avert the tragic consequences of male-based mayhem.

King My Brother killed no man, his fault was Thought, And yet his punishment was bitter death.
(Richard III 1232-3)

In *Timon of Athens*, Timon dies voluntarily at the play's end amidst the 'embossed froth' of the sea. <tim_2587> Mother Nature audits the disaster of his male/masculine intransigence. It is as if Shakespeare sets the entire play within the Master Mistress sequence. Only at the end is Timon's male/masculine heaven-turned-hell lapped by the healing 'Sea' of the Mistress sequence.

Characters also reflect involuntarily on life and death and its relationship to increase. We hear Talbot worrying about his son in *1 Henry VI*. <1h6_2209&2231> Lear recovers his genealogical connectivity when reunited with Cordelia. <lr_2624-5> In *Coriolanus*, in a disingenuous avowal of loyalty, Cominius says he loves his country more than his 'own life', his 'wife' or 'womb's increase'. <cor_2397-401> And, none more so than when Henry VIII attempts to justify his conscience while his loins are inflamed by his insistence on a male heir. <h8_1197-9>

> *Messenger* Entomb'd upon the very hem o'th'Sea,
> (Timon of Athens 2587)

> *Talbot* In thee thy Mother dies, our Household's Name,
> ...Where is my other Life   (1 Henry VI 2209 & 2231)

> *Lear* When we are born, we cry that we are come
> To this great stage of Fools.   (King Lear 2624-5)

As we have seen, in only three plays is a baby born during the action. In *Titus Andronicus* Aaron argues his newborn son is as much a brother to Tamora's sons as they are to each other. In *The Winter's Tale*, Perdita is born offstage and only appears sixteen years later. In *Henry VIII* Elizabeth is baptised near the play's end.

> *Cominius*   ...I do love
> My Country's good, with a respect more tender,
> More holy, and profound, than mine own life,
> My dear Wife's estimate, her womb's increase,
> And the treasure of my Loins:
> (Coriolanus 2397-401)

In each case Shakespeare's argument is that despite beliefs contrary to natural philosophy, increase reasserts its inevitability. The eroticism in myth – or Shakespeare's dramas – is a consequence of increase not in spite of it.

> *King* Would it not grieve an able man to leave
> So sweet a Bedfellow? But Conscience, Conscience;
> O 'tis a tender place, and I must leave her.
> (Henry VIII 1197-9)

With these births, however, we witness the most enduring form of immortality on offer to humankind. Only half of Shakespeare's plays mention the word immortal and only a couple mention it three times. In Q, the Poet reminds the Master Mistress of the vanity of using verse as a memorial. Similarly, throughout the plays Shakespeare aligns claims to immortality with the self-deception afflicting the leading characters.

In *27*, the capacity for self-aggrandisement is a symptom of the 'soul's imaginary sight'. In the plays, soul or souls occurs in every play with the greatest concentrations in the histories where Church and Crown offer heavenly compensation for earthly loyalty.

While *The Merchant of Venice*, *Twelfth Night* and *Much Ado About Nothing* mention soul a number of times, they are outdone by *Hamlet* and *Othello*. Yet other tragedies like *Macbeth*, *Anthony and Cleopatra*, and *King Lear* have only a few mentions. The immortal soul is not a constant in Shakespeare's plays in keeping with his nature-based philosophy.

Richard III, though, has nearly twice as many mentions as its nearest rival in the histories, *Richard II*. King Richard III emerges more and more as the player who most toys with Christian transcendence. As a demi-God, he represents the capacity of the soul's imaginary sight for diverting the significance of increase as the norm for human perpetuation into the false hope of an immortal heaven.

Shakespeare's use of souls and immortality in the plays addresses the issue of life and death interdependency. He identifies character types most inclined to accept the male God promise of immortal life beyond the physical and psychological dangers of their day-to-day afflictions. Characters such as Richard III, Iago and Macbeth exploit the vulnerability to immortality to gain immediate advantage over uncritical believers.

It is a measure of Shakespeare's mythic awareness that his plays not only make real the relationship between mortality and immortality. In *Measure for Measure*, Vincentio and Barnardine show it takes no great intellectual wizardry or no wizardry at all to resolve the relationship between life and death. While myth provides sustenance for the upper reaches of the human mind, it provides no abiding content or contentedness if its eroticism of unearthy desires is disconnected from the sexual dynamic in nature.

Shakespeare's sustained naturalness, commented on by many, arises because he knows the difference between the sexual and the erotic and how they are connected. He is not susceptible to confusing the body and the mind as philosophers do who focus excessively on one or the other. His freedom carries over into his understanding of life and death where, because the mind is part of the body, death is part of life.

Chapter 22: Shakespearean irony

What is the distance between Shakespeare and the characters in his plays? How faithfully do the characters represent those unable to access their own natural philosophy? Is Shakespeare's intense irony dismissive of others or is it an unavoidable state of mind when thinking deeply about the relationship of humankind to nature?

75: Parody, sarcasm or irony – understanding Shakespeare

A complete account of Shakespeare's works needs to explain his pervasive irony. Our investigation suggests Shakespearean irony reveals the illogicalities propping up Church and Crown while revelling in the natural logic of life. Deeper than parody, deeper than sarcasm, Shakespearean irony exposes the roots of our susceptibility to male-based systems of power and thought.

We have seen Shakespeare source his plots from literature, chronicles, or histories that present a male-biased account of continental life. As none of Shakespeare's dialogue or the reportage in the chronicles is verbatim, then who can tell if the continental chroniclers were selective or even manipulative in choosing what to report? The bias of the chroniclers – or Shakespeare's ulterior purpose – affects the text the characters give voice to.

In the process, Shakespeare corrects the illogicalities bedevilling those texts by allowing his characters to be living representatives of the views he critiques. Hence, the kings, lords, bishops, or generals, by speaking their minds – prejudices and all – from their thrones, pulpits or battlefields, enable Shakespeare to show more completely the inconsistencies in their thoughts and deeds.

Included in his examination, and central to his critique, is the presentation of the dogmas and strictures of biblical faiths – primarily Catholic and Protestant but also Jewish and Muslim. In *Richard III*, *Henry VIII*, *Othello* and *The Merchant of Venice* each character beholden to a male God voices their faith in the relevant God/god and acts in the world in the light of their beliefs.

By allowing free expression of such beliefs generated in the imaginary soul, Shakespeare contextualises their expectations within his encompassing nature-based philosophy. <1h6_274-80> The double irony is evident in characters such as Viola, Vincentio, Prospero, Paulina, the Princess or the Abbess, who most closely align themselves with natural philosophy. They act more wisely than characters such as Olivia, Angelo, Antonio, Leontes, Ferdinand, or Egeon, who in varying degrees are vehicles for male-based prejudices.

> *Joan* ...I am by birth a Shepherd's Daughter,
> My wit untrained in any kind of Art:
> Heaven and our Lady gracious hath it pleased
> To shine upon my contemptible estate.
> Lo, whilst I waited on my tender Lambs,
> ...God's Mother deigned to appear to me,
> (1 Henry VI 274-80)

A further irony kicks in when religious commentators are caught in the act of amending or disparaging aspects of Shakespeare's works at odds with Judeo/Christian beliefs. Commentators are drawn initially to the apparent avowal of biblical beliefs emanating from characters sympathetic to their male-based views. However, they cannot abide the natural philosophy articulated by characters who do have Shakespeare's confidence. Neither can they countenance the natural logic of the resolution or catharsis at the play's end.

Because Shakespeare allows his characters to speak their desires and ambitions uncensored, <3h6_3157-9> then we should not be surprised kings and queens as much as their subjects are caught committing indiscretions and devising schemas, as we saw

> *Richard* **And this word [Love] which Gray-beards call Divine,**
> **Be resident in men like one another,**
> **But not in me: I am my self alone.**   (3 Henry VI 3157-9)

when Henry VIII lets his prick rule his conscience. By allowing the male-based syndrome full voice in his plays and by contextualising it within the natural dynamic of Q, Shakespeare generates the most intense irony possible.

Love's Labour's Lost captures the disjunction between male-based ambitions and natural outcomes. The play is an exacting example of Shakespeare's use of irony as a philosophic and dramatic tool.

Besides the devastating irony evident in the structure of every play, Shakespeare also allows lesser characters the scope to pillory the pretensions of their superiors through parody or sarcasm. First are the fools or jokers who revel in the freedom to poke fun at the prejudices of their masters. Typical is the fool in *King Lear*. More pointed is Shakespeare's use of characters to parody conventional religious, academic and civic attitudes, such as the gaff-making Curate, Pedant and Gallant in *Love's Labour's Lost*. <lll_1068-71>

> *Armado* **Thus doth thou hear the Nemean Lion roar,**
> **Gainst thee thou Lamb, that standest as his prey:**
> **Submissive fall his princely feet before,**
> **And he from forage will incline to play.**
>   **(Love's Labour's Lost 1068-71)**

A deeper mock shows itself in *As You Like It*. Shakespeare has melancholy Jaques play the part of a down-and-out poet whose seven ages of man speech is said by some to reflect Shakespeare's own droll sentiment. Instead, contrary to such hopes, the speech is a formulaic ditty, clever but too routine for the sprightly mind of Shakespeare. <ayl_901> Jaques expostulation

> *Jaques* **I can suck melancholy out of a song,**
> **(As You Like It 901)**

'all the world's a stage' falls short of Shakespeare's deeper insights into human nature in nature.

The instances of deep irony at the heart of every play are responses to the prevalence of male-based religions and their mal-consequences. The dramatic irony plus the localised parodying and sarcasm suggests Shakespeare's plays are not beholden to King and Church as claimed by some commentators.

76: Shakespeare – scapegoat for prejudice

Shakespeare's European theatre is a natural expanse within which human thoughts and feelings find purpose and resolution. The civilisation of female and male that holds the word Europe together increases out of nature.

Shakespeare's plays and poems are at one with the natural world. However, more than any other thinker/artist, Shakespeare not only extracts his meaning from nature, he explains precisely how he does so. It is because of – rather than in spite of – his unique level of reflexivity that he incorporates the most abstract machinations of humankind into his dramatic wordplay.

Unless this is the Shakespeare loved and understood by his commentators, then his works will appear disordered, problematic, harsh and addled with errors. Unfortunately, over the last 400 years, the majority of his admirers have been his worst advocates. They do not match their attraction to his work with an ability to leave aside their traditional prejudices that would enable them to recognise and accept his nature-based logic.

Because commentators insist Shakespeare was devoted to the Monarchy and Church, they attribute to others passages seen as offensive to the person of the Queen or King. Pope, Dryden, Tate, Johnson, Eliot, Wells, and many others, act in the interests of Church or Monarchy or both. Some even allege Shakespeare was distracted by the undue influence of a mistress or male lover.

In keeping with the evidence, though, Shakespeare's overview of the European scene means every word is part of his greater purpose of bringing all to audit before nature. There is no need to denigrate, excise, emend or otherwise excuse the plays as assembled in *F* by Shakespeare's colleagues Heminge and Condell.

Not only do Heminge and Condell rectify the shoddy publishing history of the plays from the 1590s and early 1600s, they seem to predict the unconscionable treatment the plays will receive in the hands of prejudiced commentators and editors in the future. Even better, at the end of their preface to *F*, they offer advice to those who 'do not like' the plays as they have assembled them as 'Truly set forth, according to their first ORIGINAL (their capitals)'.

Very bluntly, they say that those who have any form of difficulty with Shakespeare's work should read writers more sympathetic to their beliefs. In Shakespeare's day such writers might be Donne, Dante, Ovid, Chaucer, Jonson, Marlowe, Sidney, and many others who Heminge and Condell call his 'Friends', and for our purposes just about every writer since. <preface_hemingecondell>

And if then you do not like him, surely you are in some form of manifest danger, not to understand him. And so we leave you to other of his Friends, whom if you need, can be your guides: if you need them not, you can lead your selves, and others. And such Readers we wish him. (Preface – Heminge/Condell)

The history of interference in the plays ranks as the greatest offence ever perpetrated against a major literary figure. The forced conversion fosters a climate in which Shakespeare is made to perform the role of England's State and religious poet/playwright. In effect, Shakespeare becomes a fool to the natural philosophy of his own works.

If it is the case that the contents of the *Sonnets* are available from Q without wilful alteration and the same holds for *F*, then it is reasonable to presume Shakespeare prepared the *Sonnets* for publication and his colleagues managed to compile as accurate a presentation of his plays as possible. Certainly, Heminge and Condell claim as much a number of times in the prefatory material of *F*.

The male-based prejudices that drive those who would wish Bacon, De Vere, or Marlowe had written the plays, also motivates the majority of the textual reworking. The textual analysis used to justify changing the meanings of words, for altering parts spoken by characters and for adding or removing chunks of text gets its veneer of respectability from the support it provides for a Shakespeare converted to England's poet of State and Throne.

As levels at which to approach Shakespeare's works, the biographical doubters are the lowest, but they are not far below those who use textual analysis to determine what Shakespeare wrote or whether his editors/compositors are competent. Such literal approaches to Shakespeare, which do not take account of the mythic depth of his content grounded in the life and loves of the European environs, are bound to lead to ever deepening doubt.

When Caroline Spurgeon in *Shakespeare's Imagery* approaches Shakespeare in terms of his imagery, she expresses concern about the ravages perpetrated on the works. For instance, her analysis of imagery demonstrates Shakespeare's authorship of *Henry VIII*, of which the commentators give half to Fletcher. [**note 6**]

And some commentators do acknowledge Shakespeare's challenge to the illogicality of male God mythologies, Ted Hughes recovers the primacy of the female in his *Shakespeare and the Goddess of Complete Being*. [**note 7**] By focusing on the mythical dimensions apparent in Shakespeare's works, he at least avoids the pitfalls of textual prejudice. Unfortunately, in so doing he reverts to the period of Greek mythology prior to the Christian. Consequently, he discusses only fourteen of the plays – mainly the tragedies – and dismisses the increase sonnets as the persuasion of hired labour and sees *116* and *129* as the key sonnets.

As Samuel Johnson says so succinctly of his own uninspired guesswork, he expected his emendations would be overturned by others. In his own words: 'I was forced to censure those whom I admired, and could not but reflect, while I was dispossessing their emendations, how soon the same fate might happen to my own'. [**note 8**]

The commentators inevitably reveal the groundlessness of their alterations and the prejudices behind their interference. Gary Taylor's recent attempt to reconstruct a supposed lost play of Shakespeare by writing as if he was Shakespeare reveals the depths of self-deceit current commentary harbours.

77: What is a philosophy based in nature

In Part 1, we show Shakespeare has a nature-based philosophy, which he articulates in his *Sonnets* of 1609. In Part 2, we examine how he uses the plots of his plays and longer poems to case study the philosophy. Just what sort of philosophy is it that bases itself in nature and the sexual dynamic?

There are frequent references in *Q* and *F* that demonstrate Shakespeare is familiar with the rules of traditional rhetoric and aware of traditional philosophers. He parodies traditional apologetics in plays like *The Two Gentlemen of Verona*, and uses words like philosophy, argument, reason, will and syllogism. He mentions

Aristotle and appears critical of Platonic conceits. Moreover, there is evidence he was aware of his French contemporary Montaigne.

How does Shakespeare give his works their deeply philosophic or even logical sensibility? Why does he bewilder academic philosophers of whatever ilk leaving them searching for answers in traditional philosophy? The answer to both questions lies in the overarching role of myth in a culture.

Traditional philosophic topics such as causation (first cause), the relation of God and nature, the mind-body problem, the relationship between good and evil and the identity of the self, all presume on a mythology where a God creates the world. Consequently, a professor who can argue against the existence of God yet believes mathematics is true in all possible worlds still does not understand the logic of myth.

What does a philosophy look like then that refutes the illogicalities of myth-based dogmas. While philosophers like Spinoza, Nietzsche, Bergson and even Wittgenstein explore the relationship of God and nature, each remains beholden to the biblical myth. In what way does Shakespeare break free of traditional myth – supported by apologetic philosophy – to lay down the logic for all myths?

We have seen how Shakespeare treats the female and male characters in his plays as premises in a philosophic argument. The female and male dynamic conveys his philosophic content. He inverts biblical myth by acknowledging as givens nature and the female/male sexual priorities. On that basis, he argues for increase and the sensory and intellectual attributes of the mind. Using this sound logic, he gives expression to human relationships in nature at the mythic level while creating believable characters.

In the plays, Shakespeare engages with the representatives of Church and State to challenge the mythic presumptions they hold sacred. He surrounds them with characters whose sensibilities are more aligned with the female/male dynamic in nature.

Shakespeare's intent is not to chronicle the histories of England's kings, nor merely to modernise the many plots he borrows from other authors. His deeper purpose is to critique the illogical presumptions of traditional beliefs at the level of female/male interrelationship in nature and institute a coherent philosophy for humankind within nature. Once we accept this is his intent, then contrary commentary is revealed as an apologetic ploy to divert attention from Shakespeare's consistent purpose.

Shakespeare's works overturn the expectations of apologists and threaten their politico-religious compromises. This will not sound odd because Shakespeare addresses such crimes in his plays. Characters like Claudius, Iago, King Ferdinand, Angelo, Capulet and Montague, Lear, Leontes, Coriolanus, Timon and others act for their immediate advantage only to be shown the consequences either comically or tragically. The histories, as reconstructions of the machinations of England's kings, comment on the divorce of Church and State from natural philosophy.

Shakespeare's philosophy – as odd and new as it may seem – lays down the logical conditions for human existence in nature. It accounts for the logic of human increase and the deepest mythic expression of human thoughts and feelings. No other philosopher achieves Shakespeare's natural consistency combined with mythic expression.

78: Contents and contentedness – meaning and fulfilment

In Q, the words content and contentedness are a measure of Shakespeare's philosophy of reason and love. In F, the word content appears in every play. The level of content and contentedness each occurrence evokes has echoes in the degree to which various characters are aware of their nature-based roots.

We have seen how Shakespeare's plays examine specific outbreaks of religious warfare and persecution across the European theatre. He analyses the religious illogicality behind the violence in the English histories and the European tragedies. In his comedies, he offers an antidote to its worst consequences.

Each comedy shows how to find contentedness by giving expression to the content inherent in the logic of nature. In Q, we saw the sonnets 'contain' the 'contents' for deeply realised 'contentedness'. While no play is as systematic as the 154 sonnets in articulating the conditions for its contents, each play speaks to the audience's natural capacity to resolve human discontent.

In the histories and tragedies, the contents/contentedness resolution is largely implied. In contrast, the comedies provide case studies of their natural resolution. Shakespeare's combination of critique and resolution explains the abiding interest in his works. They refuse to offer heavenly distractions.

By redressing the biblical God/nature priority and the male/female priority in every play, Shakespeare removes a major impediment to human contentedness. As he says in *The Rape of Lucrece*, while we cannot prevent natural disasters we can proscribe religious illogicality to gain intellectual and emotional maturity.

Shakespeare aligns the female/male with the feminine/masculine so his contents accommodate all dispositions and all sexual/gender orientations. This is evident in his ability to create hundreds of believable characters across the thirty-six plays in F.

Shakespeare's lack of prejudice arises from his nature-based philosophy. In adhering to its natural logic, he avoids the exigencies of taste – as he claims in *32* and *80*. Hence, the appeal of his works to a universal constituency over the last 400 years unmatched by other authors, who fall victim to period tastes. His plays do not suffer if performed out of genre or period.

Characters as diverse as Olivia and Portia in the comedies, and Macbeth and Iago in the tragedies represent differing human types in nature. Because Shakespeare draws them all from nature, they exhibit facets of the variety of human sexual types and inner personae. The contents of each play works because Shakespeare creates no disjunction between the variety in the world about and our complex minds.

The deep irony evident throughout Shakespeare's works underwrites his uniquely reflexive philosophy of life and love. In an enforced culture of illogical male-based prejudices, he recognises the givens of nature, the sexual dynamic of female and male, the increase dynamic as the basis for truth and beauty, or language and art. The natural relationship between contents and contentedness in Shakespeare's plays arises from the philosophic clarity behind his literary insights.

Chapter 23: Immature and mature love in the plays

How does the love Shakespeare identifies in the Sonnets as beyond rhyme or style fit with the love opportunities given the characters in the plays? How differently do the tragedies and comedies in particular consider the natural love Shakespeare celebrates?

79: Immature love in the tragedies

Shakespeare unites love and understanding in the 154 sonnets like no one before him – or since. He links a full understanding of the logic of human relationships in nature with the deepest experience and expression of mature human ideas, emotions and art.

Throughout the thirty-six plays in *F*, Shakespeare applies the criteria of maturity without prejudice. When leading characters accept their birthright, nature-based philosophy they enter into relationships of emotional maturity, as in the comedies. Contrarily, if the lead characters fail to achieve a unity of thoughts and feelings they leave the stage disaffected or dead, as in the histories and tragedies.

If nothing else, Shakespeare's plays demonstrate how to achieve mature love or they present the malconsequences of failing to do so. In this section, a synopsis of a number of the tragedies will show how Shakespeare treats the love life of his characters in the light of our discoveries. The sketches should identify the underlying cause of the love/hate dynamic Shakespeare explores in the context of the *Sonnet* philosophy.

In *F*, *The Tragedy of Troilus and Cressida*, to give the play its full title, is the only tragedy to begin with a prologue. According to The Prologue, the pretext for the 'cruel war' or 'quarrel' is the 'ravished Helen, Menelaus' Queen' with whom the 'wanton Paris sleeps'. Although Paris and Helen's Trojan war backdrops the play, we want to understand why Shakespeare focuses on Pandarus' failed love match between Troilus and Cressida.

Early in *Troilus and Cressida*, in an aside to the audience, Cressida reveals her genuine love for Troilus but also admits her reservations about his ability to be a mature life partner. Potentially, Troilus can lead Cressida to her 'heart's Contents', as the *Sonnets* promise. However, she anticipates his Master Mistress mind-set will incite him to assume 'command' over her. <tro_440-53> Her fears play out in the context of the

> Cressida Words, vows, gifts, tears, & loves full sacrifice,
> He offers in another's enterprise:
> But more in Troilus thousand fold I see,
> Than in the glass of Pandar's praise may be;
> Yet I hold off. Women are Angels wooing,
> Things won are done, joy's soul lies in the doing;
> That she beloved, knows nought, that knows not this;
> Men prize the thing ungained, more than it is.
> That she was never yet, that ever knew
> Love got so sweet, as when desire did sue:
> Therefore this maxim out of love I teach;
> 'Achievement, is command; ungained, beseech.
> That though my heart's Contents firm love doth bear,
> Nothing of that shall from mine eyes appear.
> **(Troilus and Cressida 440-53)**

blood fest now in its seventh year as both Greeks and Trojans shore up patriarchal domination over females.

Shakespeare reinforces Cressida's judgment about understanding and love when Ulysses discusses the political abrogation of truth in the following scene. Cressida and Ulysses are on the same page about the logic of truth or justice – as the endless jar between right and wrong. Cressida is acutely conscious of its significance for mature love.

Cressida's appreciation of the natural dynamic initially makes her cautious in the face of Troilus' intellectual and emotional immaturity. When, half way through the play, Cressida admits her depth of love to Troilus, she identifies 'men's priviledge' in the ruling patriarchy as the cause of both her reticence and her apparent lying. <tro_1748-60>

Cressida **Hard to seem won: but I was won my Lord**
With the first glance; that ever pardon me,
If I confess much you will play the tyrant:
...
But though I lov'd you well, I wooed you not,
And yet good faith I wisht my self a man;
Or that we women had men's priviledge
Of speaking first.   (Troilus and Cressida 1748-60)

Shakespeare makes it clear that the falseness Cressida takes upon herself is a logical result of Troilus identifying himself with 'truth's simplicity'. <tro_1727-8&1801-2>

Troilus **and what truth can speak truest, not truer than**
Troilus.   (Troilus and Cressida 1727-8)
Troilus **I am as true, as truth's simplicity**
And simpler than the infancy of truth.
**   (Troilus and Cressida 1801-2)**

Acting on her declaration of love, Cressida spends a night with Troilus and emerges besotted. On hearing she is to be sent to the Greek camp in exchange for a Trojan commander, she is at first distraught. However, Troilus blunts her genuine emotion when, in a jealous fit, he blurts he does not trust her. <tro_2445-73> Troilus' behaviour confirms Cressida's premonition about his adolescent mind-set. His immaturity sets her free despite recently avowing and consummating her love.

Troilus **Hear me my love: be thou but true of heart.**
Cressida **I true? how now? what wicked deem is this?**
...
Troilus **But yet be true.**
Cressida **O heavens: be true again?**
...
Troilus **Alas, a kind of godly jealousy;**
Which I beseech you call a virtuous sin:
Makes me afraid.
Cressida **O heavens, you love me not!**
**   (Troilus and Cressida 2445-73)**

Vindicated, Cressida is free to join the Greeks. She revels in their company, with only a token memory of Troilus. When Troilus acts out his jealousy and spies on her conversing with Diomed, her new gained freedom incites him to ever-increasing levels of rage.

Troilus **Beshrew the witch! with venomous wights she stays**
As hideously as hell; but flies the grasps of love,
**   (Troilus and Cressida 2272-3)**
Ulysses   **...but he, in heat of action,**
Is more vindicative than jealous love.
**   (Troilus and Cressida 2668-9)**

Shakespeare has Ulysses note the vindictiveness of Troilus' 'jealous love' already apparent when Troilus accuses Cressida of being a 'witch'. <tro_2272-3&2668-9>   As in *Macbeth*, witches are creations of the disturbed male/masculine mind. They represent males at odds with female priority and their own feminine personae.

The depth of Troilus' alienation from his natural philosophy – and hence from a balanced relationship with the woman he loves – is evident in his flip from idealistic/romantic 'love' to full-blown 'hate'. <tro_3164-5&3563> His hate of Diomed is in proportion to his lack of insight into the toxic male-dominant futility of the Trojan War. Shakespeare shows in *Troilus and Cressida* the consequences of the love/hate flip/flop – a syndrome he escapes from under the tutelage of Anne Hathaway (as his Poet recounts in *145*).

Troilus ...as much as I do Cressida love;
So much by weight, hate I her Diomed,
(Troilus and Cressida 3164-5)
Troilus No space of Earth shall sunder our two hates,
(Troilus and Cressida 3563)

Troilus and Cressida do not die in their play because their failed love-match is a symptom rather than a cause of the intellectual and emotional malaise afflicting both sides of the Aegean. Instead, Hector dies in part because he fails to act on his acceptance that Helen's wrongful abduction by Paris starts the war. Hector has the 'power' to right a wrong but sides with those who, like immature Troilus, put their male-based 'honour' first.

Diomed He like a puling Cuckold, would drink up
The lees and dregs of a flat tamed piece:
You like a lecher, out of whorish loins,
Are pleased to breed out your inheritors:
Both merits poised, each weighs no less nor more,
But he as he, which heavier for a whore.
(Troilus and Cressida 2237-42)

Troilus and Cressida gets its emotional intensity from Shakespeare running side-by-side the opposing responses of Helen and Cressida to male immaturity. He has Diomed cast Helen in the role of a 'bawdy'

whore. Diomed both confirms her reputation as the worst whore in the *Folio* and labels her husband and lover as equally culpable for the male-based Greek/Trojan conflict. <tro_2237-42> Whatever Helen's

Helen 'Twill make us proud to be his servant Paris:
Yea what he shall receive of us in duty,
Gives us more palm in beauty than we have:
Yea overshines our self.
Sweet above thought I love thee.
(Troilus and Cressida 1627-31)

emotional relationship was to Menelaus and however deep her 'love' for Paris, <tro_1627-31> Diomed leaves no doubt about her mindless opportunism. <tro_2245-50>

Diomed For every false drop in her baudy veins,
A Grecian's life hath sunk: for every scruple
Of her contaminated carrion weight,
A Trojan hath been slain. Since she could speak,
She hath not given so many good words breath,
As for her, Greeks and Trojans suffred death.
(Troilus and Cressida 2245-50)

Shakespeare's Cressida, like Viola, demands maturity from her partners. By calling herself 'false', she mocks Troilus' claim to be the fountain of 'truth'. More pointedly, she refuses jealousy dressed as 'love' as she knows it is but 'hate'.

The male-dominance of Helen by Menelaus and Paris, and her effective acquiescence, results in male/masculine violence of the ten-year war. In contrast, because Cressida refuses to comply with male-based strictures, she is free to side with either Trojans or Greeks as both are wrong. By embracing falseness, she defuses male prejudice. In Shakespeare's play, her application of natural logic begins the end of the war – as Troilus realises.

Shakespeare dramatises the intellectual and emotional divide between immature and mature love in *Troilus and Cressida* to explore conflict resolution. The play's partial avoidance of tragedy makes it a fitting prologue for the remaining tragedies. The tragedy in the following plays is not that named characters die but that they die unnecessarily because they misconstrue their relationship to nature and the female and hence their capacity to feel, think, and act naturally.

The best known of Shakespeare's tragic love plays is *Romeo and Juliet*. What makes Romeo and Juliet's fateful romance in Verona so poignant? More than in any other play, *Romeo and Juliet* contrasts the intransigence of male-based dominance and control with freely sworn oaths between two young lovers who display genuine emotional reciprocity. Their guileless faith and trust in the Church seals their fate.

Shakespeare shows up the hypocrisy in male-based systems of power and influence. He has Capulet, Juliet's father, first give her freedom to accept or reject Paris' hand in marriage. Then the accommodating father turns despot when his daughter prefers a love-match with the hated enemy Montague. <rj_263-6&2202-4> The play's subtext is an unsubtle analogy between the interpersonal male-driven enmity and the warfare between male-based sects in the Reformation.

Capulet But woo her gentle Paris, get her heart,
My will to her consent, is but a part,
And she agree, within her scope of choice,
Lies my consent,
...
Capulet Hang thee young baggage, disobedient wretch,
I tell thee what, get thee to Church a Thursday,
Or never after look me in the face.
(Romeo and Juliet 263-6 & 2202-4)

The tragedy of Romeo and Juliet is that their fathers' truculence cuts short their freely avowed love. Shakespeare appeals to the nature-based and female-based givens in the audience's mind to elicit sympathy for two lovers subjected to the murderous ultimatums of patriarchy. As the play argues, <rj_3165-9> there is no justification for male-based impositions that lead to fatal outcomes for innocent lovers.

Prince Where be these Enemies? Capulet, Montague,
See what a scourge is laid upon your hate,
That Heaven finds means to kill your joys with Love;
And I, for winking at your discords too,
Have lost a brace of Kinsmen: All are punish'd.
(Romeo and Juliet 3165-9)

From the double suicide of Romeo and Juliet, we shift to the similarly fated love match between Anthony and Cleopatra. However, in contrast to the love of like minds in *Romeo and Juliet*, Cleopatra's meeting with Anthony is a love mismatch of contrary minds. Cleopatra shows in her first few lines that she has a natural sensibility while Anthony's is twisted by patriarchy. <ant_21-5> Cleopatra's sound understanding of the dynamic of love is a blind spot for the more romantic/idealistic Anthony who, as Cleopatra accuses, does not even love his Roman wife Fulvia. <ant_52-3>

Cleopatra If it be Love indeed, tell me how much.
Anthony There's beggary in the love that can be reckoned.
Cleopatra I'll set a bourn how far to be belov'd.
Anthony Then must thou needs find out new Heaven, new Earth.   (Anthony and Cleopatra 21-5)

Furthermore, the Roman connection sets the tragic scene for Anthony and Cleopatra's deaths. Shakespeare subplots the triumvirate of Roman generals Anthony, Caesar and Lepidus with a mock of the male-based trinity of a later Rome governed by warmongering males – the popes and bishops of Christian darkness.

Cleopatra's defeat by the Romans

Cleopatra Excellent falsehood:
Why did he marry Fulvia, and not love her?
(Anthony and Cleopatra 52-3)

Othello **My Soul hath her content so absolute**
That not another comfort like to this,
Succeeds in unknown Fate.
Desdemona **The Heavens forbid**
But that our Loves
And Comforts should increase
Even as our days do grow!
Othello **Amen to that (sweet Powers)**
I cannot speak enough of this content,
It stops me here: it is too much of joy.
And this, and this the greatest discords be
That e'er our hearts shall make.
(Othello 969-80)

heralds the subservience of women to the religious dogmas of the male God. With her suicide, the Queen of Egypt signals the demise of mature love in the civilised world and the institution of a reign of adolescent self-love under Augustus Caesar that becomes the model for millennia of religiously justified monarchies.

Like young Romeo and Juliet, the worldlier Othello and Desdemona seem to enjoy a genuine love-match. <oth_969-80>

Yet, because they have not matured their understanding of the logic of language to match their emotional suitability, Othello and Desdemona still meet an untimely fate.

We saw Desdemona confront her father with the logic of increase stating that she (like Cordelia) owes half her love to him and half to Othello. <oth_526-36> However, Othello does not respond to her insight because patriarchal prejudice still clouds his judgment.

Brabantio **Where most you owe obedience?**
...
Desdemona **I do perceive here a divided duty.**
To you I am bound for life, and education:
My life and education both do learn me,
How to respect you. You are the Lord of duty,
I am hitherto your Daughter. But here's my Husband;
And so much duty, as my Mother showed
To you, preferring you before her Father:
So much I challenge, that I may profess
Due to the Moor my Lord.   **(Othello 526-36)**

In contrast, and to Othello and Desdemona's undoing, Othello's ensign Iago does grasp the capacity of language to represent and misrepresent. He uses it to manipulate their blind idealism. <oth_745-8> Iago's insight into the logic of language is rancid because, like biblical dogma, it distorts natural logic. Compared to the joyous couple, his jealousy sets him against the freely avowed love Othello and Desdemona declare.

Iago **The Moor is of a free, and open Nature,**
That thinks men honest, that but seem to be so,
And will be as tenderly be led by'th'Nose
As Asses are: **(Othello 745-8)**

Shakespeare's *Othello* is not primarily about race, nor jealousy or betrayal. It tracks the consequences when two lovers do not have a full understanding of what the sonnets call truth. The play is a lesson in the mature use of language. Without that insight, the hell and demon in the two lovers' names surfaces to blind them to unsound argument.

In his tragedy, Hamlet is unable to cultivate his soul-mate love for Ophelia. He becomes fatally distracted by the verbal and emotional deceit that beguiles his mother into marrying the uncle who murders his father.

The tragedy of *Hamlet* is that Claudius inserts himself in the line of male dominance using the familiar tools of male usurpation – murder and duplicity. In the first few lines, Shakespeare has Claudius pervert the increase argument to baffle the guileless Hamlet. <ham_268-74>

Both Hamlet's birthright love through increase for his mother and his natural affection for Ophelia are estranged by his mother's blindness to Claudius' Iago-like mimicking of female wisdom. Then, to compound the male-based syndrome,

Claudius 'Tis sweet and commendable
In your Nature Hamlet,
To give these mourning duties to your Father:
But you must know, your Father lost a Father,
That Father lost, lost his, and the Survivor bound
In filial Obligation, for some term
To do obsequious Sorrow.   (Hamlet 268-74)

dead King Hamlet abets the impending tragedy by advising Hamlet in a vision to use 'conceit' on his 'weak' mother. <ham_2490-4>

By not insisting his mother reveal what she suspects of his father's death and by not confronting Claudius when he was praying (albeit insincerely), Hamlet's religious sensibility misses an opportunity to forestall Claudius' plans to have Laertes kill him. The result, male-domination style, is the death of them all. <ham_2350-5>

Ghost Do not forget: this Visitation
Is but to whet thy almost blunted purpose.
But look, Amazement on thy Mother sits;
O step between her, and her fighting Soul,
Conceit in weakest bodies, strongest works.
          (Hamlet 2490-4)

Shakespeare has Hamlet experience the consequences of love shafted on every conceivable front. There is murderous love, no love through increase, no love through conscious understanding and no love through the heightened emotions of the inner sensations of the mind.

Hamlet Now might I do it pat, now he is praying,
And now I'll do it, and so he goes to Heaven,
And so am I reveng'd: that would be scann'd,
A Villain kills my Father, and for that
I his sole Son, do this same Villain send
To heaven.   (Hamlet 2350-5)

As the play heats up, Hamlet is bereft of the lines of increase and poetry that could add 'words, words, words' to his inborn natural philosophy. No wonder nature-alienated Hamlet bemoans the elevation of dusty 'Man' and, as a mere afterthought, 'Woman'. <ham_1350-6>

In the three previous tragedies, the protagonists get their maladjusted natural philosophy readjusted by other characters in the plot. In *Macbeth*, Macbeth and Lady Macbeth do the fatal damage to themselves. The deeper desolation of *Macbeth*, or the more perverse calamity, flows from the natural love Macbeth and his wife once share that turns rancid under the influence of male-based power. That power is epitomised by the idealistic warmonger, King Duncan. <mac_445-9>

Hamlet ...What a piece of work is a man! how Noble in Reason? how infinite in faculty? in form and moving how express and admirable? in Action, how like an Angel? in apprehension, how like a God? the beauty of the world, the Paragon of Animals; and yet to me, what is this Quintessence of Dust? Man delights not me; no, nor Woman neither;   (Hamlet 1350-6)

Shakespeare again examines how naturally avowed love without an understanding of the dynamic of truth and beauty is twisted by power to murder mindlessly. When Macbeth's Queen dies, he itemises the effect of his entrapment in a purely mind-based syndrome. <mac_2338-49> If he mortgages all his tomorrows against the present life to the 'last Syllable of Recorded time', then at the final audit Nature reveals that the 'Tale' he tells himself signifies 'nothing'. Like Hamlet, Macbeth is a victim of love bereft of a mature understanding of the logic of words – or even syllables.

Duncan See, see our honour'd Hostess:
The Love that follows us, sometime is our trouble,
Which still we thank as Love. Herein I teach you,
How you shall bid God-'ild us for your pains,
And thank us for your trouble.   (Macbeth 445-9)

Macbeth She should have died hereafter;
There would have been a time for such a word:
To morrow, and to morrow, and to morrow,
Creeps in this petty pace from day to day,
To the last Syllable of Recorded time:
And all our yesterdays, have lighted Fools
The way to dusty death. Out, out, brief Candle,
Life's but a walking Shadow, a poor Player,
That struts and frets his hour upon the Stage,
And then is heard no more. It is a Tale
Told by an Idiot, full of sound and fury
Signifying nothing.   (Macbeth 2338-49)

In *Macbeth*, Shakespeare documents the male-based inversion of love and hate. He pillories the misogynistic representation of women as witches in the masculinising imagination – only Macbeth and Banquo see the witches. To counter the biblical-like eroticism of the Macbeth's denial of nature, he deploys Macduff – who was untimely ripped from his mother's womb. Unloving Macduff cuts short the male-based evil by using a dosage of the same evil to remedy the male/masculine godhead that is *Macbeth*.

There is no love in a masculine/masculine world except self-love (as argued in the increase sonnets). The institution of self-love enforces an unconstitutional denial of nature and the female/male dynamic. By rejecting their feminine personae, Macbeth and Lady Macbeth murder their own lives and loves – as *9* predicts.

Only Malcolm, in his lengthy exchange with Macduff, sounds as if he has a mature grasp of the logic of truth. He applies knowingly the involuntary lesson in immature language gained on the knee of his father's self-serving idealism to expose Macduff's cupidity and then stage-manage his bewilderment. <mac_1956-60>

Malcolm At no time broke my Faith, would not betray
The Devil to his Fellow and delight
No less in truth than life. My first false speaking
Was this upon myself. What I am truly
Is thine, and my poor Country's to command:
        (Macbeth 1956-60)

In *Coriolanus*, Caius Martius and his mother Volumnia attempt to reconcile their natural love (guaranteed by increase) with the adolescent martial virtues her son visits upon all by way of murderous prowess. <cor_3456-8> Symptomatic of Coriolanus' lack of emotional growth (represented by the son/mother vulnerability) is Virgilia, Coriolanus' wife. She should be his mature partner in love

Volumnia Making the Mother, wife, and Child to see,
The Son, the Husband, and the Father tearing
His Country's Bowels out;   (Coriolanus 3456-8)

but is no more than a backdrop to Shakespeare's examination of Coriolanus' failure to achieve maturation beyond the breast.

The tragedy of Coriolanus lies in his inability to relinquish his martial emotions in a climate of male-based prejudice. <cor_179-85> How can he mature his love and understanding when the democracy of the senate still accepts the militaristic mind-set of Roman Italy? When male-based power usurps female/male partnership it sets in motion a blood-fest out of which there seems no escape but further bloodletting.

For his part, King Lear suffers the consequences of loving himself more than his three daughters. Lear alienates mature love when he demands absolute love from each of them. In the subplot, Gloucester

Coriolanus   ...What would you have, you Curs,
That like nor Peace, nor War? The one affrights you,
The other makes you proud. He that trusts to you,
Where he should find you Lions, finds you Hares:
Where Foxes, Geese you are: No surer, no,
Than is the coal of fire upon the Ice,
Or Hailstone in the Sun.   (Coriolanus 179-85)

alienates his bastard son Edmund when he fails to love both sons equally.

Cordelia   ...I love your Majesty
According to my bond, no more nor less...
You have begot me, bred me, loved me.
I return those duties back as are right fit,
Obey you, Love you, and most Honour you.
Why have my Sisters Husbands, if they say
They love you all? Happily when I shall wed,
That Lord, whose hand must take my plight, shall carry
Half my love with him, half my Care, and Duty,
Sure I shall never marry like my Sisters.
                        (King Lear 98-110)

When Cordelia avows half her love to Lear based on increase, she identifies the path to mature love. <lr_98-110> But for Shakespeare's purpose, she escapes to France as her headstrong father undergoes nature's audit on the heath.

Meanwhile   Edmund, Cordelia's natural counterpart, enacts dark justice. He visits on his profligate father Gloucester the blindness of putting convention before birthright. <lr_3133-4> However, Gloucester's awakening, like Lear's partial recovery of nature-based insight, is too little too late.

Edgar The dark and vicious place where thee he got,
Cost him his eyes.   (King Lear 3133-4)

Edmund's clear perception of the problem early in the play requires a bloody resolution as the only remedy to the entrenched male-based intransigence of Lear and Gloucester. Neither Lear nor Gloucester gains a mature understanding of the logic of swearing and forswearing to reconcile content and contentedness. In *King Lear* Shakespeare's tragic double plot

Lear   ...unaccommodated man, is no more but such a poor, bare, forked A-
nimal as thou art.   (King Lear 1887-9)

accentuates the consequences when head-strong despots act out their immaturity of thought and feeling. <lr_1887-9>

Lear is an exemplary case study for all the subsequent Kings of England. Shakespeare shows how to reject the male-skewed world of biblical divisiveness and regain a natural interrelationship with the female in a world of democratic sensibility.

In the eight out of twelve tragedies considered, there is a strong relationship between the lack of mature love in the leading characters and their appreciation of the logic of life Shakespeare articulates in Q. *Titus Andronicus, Cymbeline, Timon of Athens* and *Julius Caesar* also illustrate aspects of the disjunction between love and understanding in male-based ideation and emotion.

If Shakespeare challenges the usurpation of the originary status of the female in nature by male-based systems of belief, then his tragedies follow the 154 sonnets in making the case against the abrogation of natural thoughts and feelings.

Turning briefly to the histories, we can apply the same investigative process as in the tragedies. By the standards of Shakespeare's natural philosophy, the largely loveless unions of the Kings of England paint portraits of emotions and expectations sacrificed for political and frequently murderous advantage. Typically, in *Henry V* the gratuitous battlefield glory Henry attains in revenge-soaked Europe compromises his marriage to Katherine of France. As Shakespeare anticipates in the Epilogue, Europe's male-based troubles resurface when the life of their son, Henry VI, is cut short.

80: Maturing love in the comedies

We turn from the tragedies (and histories) to the comedies. Our study of the comedies in the previous sections suggests Shakespeare applies his nature-based philosophy to bring leading characters to intellectual and emotional maturity.

Shakespeare as playwright directs the action in all the comedies but, in a few, he allows proto-playwrights (including three males) to make calls based on their achieved maturity of mind and heart. Crucially, no male in the tragedies is mature enough to resolve the psychological predicament in their plays.

Shakespeare's successful application of the *Sonnet* philosophy in the fourteen comedies precedes the abrogation of natural logic in the twenty-two histories and tragedies in *F*. However, our analysis of the relation between immature and mature love considers the tragedies first to feel the full effect of their inadequacies before exploring the conditions for mature love in the comedies.

To assess the relationship between the comedies and tragedies, we focus first on the last comedy, *The Winter's Tale*. Its position in the *Folio* suggests it might have something to say about the syndrome of immature love that blights the tragedies to come.

We found correspondences between the geographic orientations of the two early poems of 1593 and 1594 and *The Tempest* to indicate Shakespeare intends Prospero's play to be the first comedy in *F*. Are there substantive reasons why *The Winter's Tale* concludes the comedies?

Shakespeare divides *The Winter's Tale* into two mirrored parts with Time's 'Chorus' introducing act four. Acts one to three record the near-tragic events in wintery Sicily, act four celebrates spring regrowth in Bohemia sixteen years later with act five revelling in the mirrorical return to a summery Sicily.

Significantly, Sicilian Lord Camillo has a pivotal role in both halves. Early on, he helps Polixenes flee to Bohemia and later he assists Perdita and Florizel escape back to Sicily. While not as prescient as Paulina when she fronts for Hermione throughout the play, Shakespeare recognises Camillo's canny insights when he marries the cunning Paulina at the play's end.

Moreover, Shakespeare has Camillo give the rationale for the position of the play in *F* in the first scene. In the first few lines, Camillo describes to Bohemian Archidamus the adolescent Master Mistress or Adonis type mindset of both kings. Camillo observes that instead of maturing their childhood 'affection', both 'Sicilia' and 'Bohemia' have become so ensconced in royal conventions and formalities that their 'Loves' persist only in the disembodied 'Heavens'. <wt_24-34> As in *As You Like It*, courtly life has so denatured the two men that Camillo predicts their loves 'cannot choose but branch now'.

Camillo Sicilia cannot show himself over-kind to Bohemia: They were train'd together in their Child-hoods; and there rooted betwixt them then such an affection, which cannot choose but branch now. Since their more mature Dignities, and Royal Necessities, made separate-on of their Society, their Encounters (though not Personal) hath been Royally attornyed with inter-change of Gifts, Letters, loving Embassies, that they have seemed to be together, though absent: shook hands, as over a Vast; and embraced as it were from the ends of opposed Winds. The Heavens continue their Loves.

(The Winter's Tale 24-34)

The first to experience the emotional disconnectedness of heavenly love is Leontes when in a fit of jealous rage he orders his wife and baby put to death. <wt_1012-7> However, Hermione and Perdita escape Leontes' murderous God-driven revenge through the actions of Paulina and her husband Antigonus. <wt_1260-9>

> *Leontes* A Callat
> Of boundless tongue, who late hath beat her Husband
> And now baits me: This Brat is none of mine,
> It is the issue of Polixenes.
> Hence with it, and together with the Dam,
> Commit them to the fire.
>   (The Winter's Tale 1012-7)

In the toxic winter of the first half, while Hermione and Perdita avoid Leontes' heavens-bent meltdown, Mamillius dies of distress, a bear kills Antigonus on the coast of Bohemia and the crew of his ship drowns at sea. *The Winter's Tale* takes us as close as any comedy to the tragic outcomes of the histories and tragedies that follow.

> *Leontes* Your Actions are my Dreams.
> You had a Bastard by Polixenes,
> And I but dream'd it:.........so thou
> Shalt feel our Justice; in whose easiest passage,
> Look for no less than death.
>   (The Winter's Tale 1260-9)

Shakespeare, though, drags the action away from full-blown tragedy in the spring-like resolution in the second half. The final comedy in *F* is an object lesson in how to avoid the tragic consequences of immature heaven-cloistered love that blights the following twenty-two plays. To accentuate the primary cause of the near miss, Shakespeare folds the play back on itself.

Not only do all estranged characters return to Sicily from Bohemia in Act 5, in Act 4 the previously untested Polixenes flips into a murderous rage when he discovers his princely son Florizel and Perdita (adopted as a shepherd's daughter) have sworn lifelong betrothal without recourse to his heaven-sanctioned patriarchal authority. <wt_2269-85>

Polixenes determines to kill Perdita and adds the telling signs of male/masculine emotional adolescence by frequently calling her a

> *Polixenes* I'll have thy beauty scratch'd with briers, and made
> More homely than thy state. ....If ever henceforth, thou
> These rural Latches to his entrance open,
> Or hope his body more with thy embraces,
> I will devise a death, as cruel for thee
> As thou art tender to't.   (The Winter's Tale 2269-85)

witch. <wt_2265-7> Earlier Leontes similarly calls Paulina a Callat, a Dam and a gross hag who he would have burnt.

> *Polixenes*   ...And thou, fresh piece
> Of excellent Witchcraft, who of force must know
> The royal Fool thou copest with.
>   (The Winter's Tale 2265-7)

Back in Sicily, it takes the mock death of Hermione and the mock miracle of her reappearance to shock her husband Leontes into mature love, free of jealously. <wt_1429-35> Shakespeare shows that immature love does not have the insight to either trust intuitively or enquire intelligently about love's fidelities. Leontes' close friendship with Polixenes from boyhood leads to a denatured male-based culture that is vulnerable to jealousy and revenge. Both men lack the feminine wiles to evaluate Hermione's or any female's trustworthiness.

Appropriately, from mock monastic asylum nearby, Hermione and her

> *Leontes*   ...(unto
> Our shame Perpetual) once a day, I'll visit
> The Chapel where they lie, and tears shed there
> Shall be my recreation. So long as Nature
> Will bear up with this exercise, so long
> I daily vow to use it. Come, and lead me
> To these sorrows. (The Winter's Tale 1429-35)

friend Paulina stage-manage Leontes' sixteen years of punishment. The interval allows his daughter Perdita, whom Leontes as good as murders by consigning her to a deserted seashore, to ripen into a teen shepherdess in Bohemia. Shakespeare deepens the irony when Perdita falls in love with Florizel the son of his hated doppelganger Polixenes. <wt_1915-6&1929-30>

Perdita **This youth should say 'twer well: and only therefore Desire to breed by me....**
That wear upon your Virgin-branches yet
Your Maiden heads growing:
(The Winter's Tale 1915-6 & 1929-30)

Even with the deaths of the lesser characters Mamillius, Antigonus and the sailors at sea in the first half, *The Winter's Tale* falls short of qualifying as a full tragedy. However, by adding Paulina's mock announcement of Hermione's death from grief, Shakespeare's first three acts mimic the tragedies that follow. Then, in the final two acts of this transitional comedy, he shows how to avoid the murderous adolescent mind-based male-based syndrome of the adjacent tragedies (and histories).

In summary, the final comedy in *F* examines the onset of tragic consequences where innocent characters fall victim to the jealous love of immature males. The first half goes more viral than any previous comedy until mature love reasserts itself in the second half. The play ends with Hermione's spoof miracle that mocks the adolescent fantasy world epitomised by 'Leontes and Polixenes' immature heaven-marooned friendship.

Amelia has a similar though less dramatic role in *The Comedy of Errors* when she re-emerges from an abbey door in the last scene. However, her less dramatic disappearance at sea during a storm before curtain call reinforces the semi-tragic significance of Hermione's feigned death at the heart of the pseudo-tragic first half of *The Winter's Tale*.

Shakespeare's nature-based challenge to the presumption of male-based heaven-conferred right and rank runs as a lightning arc through *The Winter's Tale* to show mature love flourishes only in the natural democracy of female/male partnership. Unlike the hapless males in the following tragedies, Leontes and Polixenes learn a double lesson from Hermione, Paulina and Perdita in how to mature their emotions and hence their understanding.

Turning to the earlier comedies, in *The Taming of the Shrew*, Shakespeare demonstrates mature love cannot flourish without a firmly bedded understanding of the natural logic of language. As we have seen, Shakespeare sets up a 'history' lesson. The Induction characterises idealistic/romantic love as a dream-like illusion for Christopher Sly (as a hoodwinked 'Lord') and his male Lady (as 'our Lady'). Then, when the recently arrived actors begin their play, Shakespeare leaves the traditional expectations of love behind as Petruchio shows Kate how to attain mature love.

On a visit to Padua from Verona, well-heeled Petruchio <shr_623-4> rescues disaffected Kate from her male-induced truculence. The outcome of the play suggests Kate's problem is the consequence of a patriarchal mind-set that alienates her

Petruchio **Crowns in my purse I have, and goods at home,**
And so am come abroad to see the world.
(The Taming of the Shrew 623-4)

when young from the natural logic of language. Her father Baptista's refusal to let younger sister Bianca be wooed until Kate agrees to marry speaks of a male mired in the language of male dominance. <shr_350-3>

> *Baptista* Gentlemen, importune me no farther,
> For now I am firmly resolved d'you know:
> That is, not to bestow my youngest daughter,
> Before I have a husband for the elder:
> (The Taming of the Shrew 350-3)

Petruchio's challenge is to turn language strangulated by misogynist beliefs into a tool for communicating love and understanding. The treatment the feminine/masculine-adjusted Petruchio administers to Kate when he takes her home to Verona matches the crime. <shr_1141-56> By teaching Kate to appreciate that language can both swear something is the case and forswear it is not, he frees her from bondage in a masculinised lexicon. She recovers her natural wit enabling her to love and understand without prejudice. <shr_2011>

> *Kate* Where did you study all this goodly speech?
> *Petruchio* It is extempore, from my mother's wit.
> ...
> For I am he am born to tame you Kate,
> (The Taming of the Shrew 1141-56)

When Petruchio challenges the wives at the play's end to avow their love for their husbands, Kate can say tongue-in-cheek she is an obedient wife. She appreciates the irony that the other wives, including her sister Bianca, swear obedience but do not act on their avowals.

> *Kate* Thou feed'st me with the very name of meat.
> (The Taming of the Shrew 2011)

Kate's love for Petruchio is given freely both intellectually and emotionally and so is the mature love Shakespeare makes palpable in the *Sonnets*. <shr_2738-9>

> *Petruchio* Why there's a wench: Come on, and kiss me Kate.
> (The Taming of the Shrew 2738-9)

As with *The Taming of the Shrew*, in *Much Ado About Nothing* Shakespeare orchestrates the verbal banter between Beatrice and Benedick to overcome male/masculine-bred self-regard. <ado_231-8> Yet, where the maturer Petruchio 'tames' the intemperate Kate, *Much Ado About Nothing* provides two studies in what might have happened had Romeo and Juliet been allowed to mature their compatibility.

> *Benedick* That a woman conceived me, I thank her: that she brought me up, I likewise give her most humble thanks:...... I will live a Bachelor.
> *Don Pedro* Well, if ever thou doest fall from this faith, thou wilt prove a notable argument.
> (Much Ado About Nothing 231-8)

Shakespeare contrasts Hero and Claudio's convention-bound romance with the sharp-witted love match between Beatrice and Benedick. Hero is an outwardly compliant female with a wily humour. For his part, Claudio's overly romantic temperament predisposes him to outbreaks of jealousy. The feigned death of Hero after Claudio's false accusations mimics his need to die to himself to achieve feminine/masculine maturity. <ado_1760-8>

> *Claudio* O Hero! What a Hero hadst thou been
> If half thy outward graces had been placed
> About the thoughts and counsels of thy heart?
> But fare thee well, most foul, most fair, farewell
> Thou pure impiety, and impious purity,
> For thee I'll lock up all the gates of Love,
> And on my eye-lids shall Conjecture hang,
> To turn all beauty into thoughts of harm,
> And never shall it be more gracious.
> (Much Ado About Nothing 1760-8)

With Beatrice and Benedick,

we see something of the Mistress and Master Mistress from the *Sonnets*. At first Benedick avows his preference for perpetual bachelorhood (with martial values included). His immaturity means Beatrice will not enter a relationship until he matures sufficiently to accept the natural equality her sex deserves. She critiques the biblical version of creation <**ado_469-74&489-90**> on the way to establishing a marriage based in the logic of language and mature love. As with the Poet and Mistress in *138*, their avowal of strongly rooted affection does not dim their love of verbal jousting.

Beatrice **Not till God make men of some other metal than earth, would it not grieve a woman to be over-mastered with a piece of valiant dust....**
Adam's sons are my brethren, and truly I hold it a sin to match in my kindred....
I have a good eye uncle, I can see a Church by daylight.
     (Much Ado About Nothing 469-74 & 489-90)

If it takes the mock death of Hermione and the mock miracle of her return to shock her husband Leontes into mature love, free of jealously in *The Winter's Tale*, it takes the mock disguise of a monk to rectify both sacred and profane love in *Measure for Measure*. In the play, which Shakespeare has Vincentio mastermind artfully, the disguised Duke elevates the near-nunnish Isabella into mature love where she becomes fluent in both language and emotions.

Meantime, Claudio and Juliet are subject to a perversion of natural justice <**mm_158-64**>. Under the arch-idealist Angelo, their consummation of love (which results in Juliet's pregnancy) leads to the death penalty for him and banishment for her.

To rectify the situation, Shakespeare stage-manages Vin-

Bawd   **...I saw him arrested: saw him carried away: and which is more, within these three days his head to be chopp'd off....**
I am too sure of it: and it is for getting Madam Julietta with child.   (Measure for Measure 158-64)

centio into the role of the Poet of the *Sonnets* to 'cure' by 'ill' (*118/119*) the emotional malaise that is Vienna. In his monkish disguise, Vincentio leads Isabella from her Master Mistress-like self regard into a Mistress-like command of the erotic logic of language. <**mm_2325-33**>

Isabella **To speak so indirectly I am loath,**
I would say the truth, but to accuse him so
That is your part, yet I am advised to do it,
He says, to veil full purpose....
Besides he tells me, that if peradventure
he speaks against me on the adverse side,
I should not think it strange, for 'tis a physic
That's bitter, to sweet end.
     (Measure for Measure 2325-33)

Shakespeare demonstrates, through a judicious use of his self-defrocking monk, that excessive idealism can be used against itself to cure either monastic or whorehouse perversions of natural love. By the final scene, the Duke realigns the love expectations of his varied cast of characters toward maturity.

All's Well That Ends Well examines a similar love dynamic to that which Beatrice and Benedick negotiate in *Much Ado About Nothing*. Rather than Beatrice playing out the natural implications of courting, this time Helena controls the action from within her marriage to Bertram. Helena spends less time using tricky circumlocutions to challenge Bertram's Master Mistress mentality. Instead, she holds Bertram to his word after deceiving him with a bed-trick where in one cunning act she gets his child and ring.

Shakespeare matures the love/hate dynamic of his two protagonists by giv-

Helen That such sweet use make of what they hate,
When saucy trusting of the cozened thoughts
Defiles the pitchy night, so lust doth play
With what it loathes,
     (All's Well That Ends Well 2464-7)

ing them a firm grounding in the logic of language. <aww_2464-7> Learning language both as a dynamic of swearing and forswearing and a vehicle for punning repartee, leads Bertram to see Helena is more than worthy of his love. That he denied Helena her conjugal rights because of her lower rank as an orphaned child adopted by his mother is an offence against nature. Once repudiated, though, the offender can love maturely. Hence, Bertram's seemingly rapid change of mind at the play's end. <aww_3053-4>

Bertram If she my Liege can make me know this clearly,
I'll love her dearly, ever, ever dearly.
     (All's Well that Ends Well 3053-4)

That worthy love is a consequence of understanding the logic of language is also the theme of *Twelfth Night, or, What you will*. Viola has the role of the Poet of the *Sonnets* when she seeks to cure Orsino of his overly romantic disposition. <tn_13-19> With the assistance of Feste, who is her verbal counterpart, she trains Orsino in the give and take of dialogue, so freeing him from his soulful melancholy. <tn_1004-7> At the play's end he recognises her as his 'Master's Mistress' so acknowledging her role as the Mistress who matures his boyish foibles.

Orsino O Spirit of Love, how quick and fresh art thou,
That notwithstanding thy capacity,
Receiveth as the Sea. Nought enters there,
Of what validity, and pitch so ere,
But falls into abatement, and low price
Even in a minute; so full of shapes is fancy,
That it alone, is high fantastical.
     (Twelfth Night 13-19)

Viola   ...Was not this love indeed?
We men may say more, swear more, but indeed
Our shows are more than will: for still we prove
Much in our vows, but little in our love.
     (Twelfth Night 1004-7)

In the sub plot, Viola's overly emotive twin brother Sebastian is married off to the similarly disposed Olivia. Shakespeare's other characters exhibit a mix of verbal fun and consternation. They provide a lively context in which his judicious application of the Twelfth Night God of religious Epiphany (alias Viola/Cesario) is appropriate to correct the disorientating pretensions of all – except academic Malvolio.

The play with the greatest range of love scenarios is *Love's Labour's Lost*. Shakespeare has four women from France cross the border into Spanish Navarre to correct the idealistic love expectations of four love-estranged men. The monastic retreat, touted by the King of Navarre as the source of divine love, proves to be no more than a flight of fancy when the four savvy females rout the four witless males. <lll_1011-5>

Shakespeare seems to take particular delight in displaying his skill at depicting four levels of love in the inferior sonnets penned by each of the love-struck males. *Love's Labour's Lost* follows the sonnet logic closely. It aligns nature, then women, then men and then language and then the

Boyet Do not curst wives hold that self-sovereignty
Only for praise sake, when they strive to be
Lords o'er their Lords?
Princess Only for praise, and praise we may afford,
To any Lady that subdues a Lord.
     (Love's Labour's Lost 1011-5)

deeper sensations of the mind to show the way to mature love.

In the seven other comedies, a similar drama plays out. They reveal a ripening of love under Shakespeare's mature pen.

Mrs Ford and Mrs Page tumble the love expectations of basket case Falstaff in *The Merry Wives of Windsor*. Hermia in *A Midsummer Night's Dream* challenges her father's right to choose her love partner under threat of nunnery and death. While Portia magisterially runs the main plot toward mature love, Jessica leaps out her father's window to pursue true love in *The Merchant of Venice*.

With feminine guile, Rosalind cross-dresses as Ganymede to entice Orlando out of his poetic reverie in *As You Like It*. Julia in male guise provokes Protheus into love in *The Two Gentlemen of Verona*. Egeon reconnects with the mature love of his wife after witnessing the duplicity of male-on-male behaviour in *The Comedy of Errors*. And, Prospero in *The Tempest* ensures Miranda and Ferdinand avow their love genuinely before they get married more formally under the auspices of Greek goddesses.

We can draw a diagram, as we did for the sonnets, to reveal the erotic shape of Shakespeare's arrangement of the plays in *F*. <diagram_folio-template> The rounded comedies act as an indictment of the

| 14 Female-based Comedies | 10 Male-based Histories | 12 Male-based Tragedies |

1623 Folio template

shafting that occurs throughout the histories and tragedies. Mature love respects the natural dynamic.

In his comedies, Shakespeare explores mature love to provide a lesson in forgoing male-based excesses. In contrast, the tragedies (and histories) spotlight the inability of males – and females – to achieve mature love in a male-based culture of homicidal prejudice.

Concluding the examination of the Comedies, Histories and Tragedies

In Part 1 we analysed the 154 sonnets in Q for evidence of intent or structure. We were able to show there is considerable organisation in the 154-sonnet set. By taking account of the various levels of structuring, it seems Shakespeare uses the sonnet form in a set of sonnets to present a consistent and comprehensive nature-based philosophy.

In Part 2 we examine F for evidence the nature-based philosophy Shakespeare publishes in Q is the philosophy behind all his plays and longer poems. It does seem the plays and poems answer at every stage to the sonnet logic.

Crucial is the analysis of the layout of F. The division of F by Shakespeare's colleagues into fourteen comedies, ten histories and twelve tragedies has correspondences with the structuring of the sonnets. It seems the 1623 arrangement acknowledges the originary status of female over male.

In the comedies, eleven females and three mature males forge nature-based resolutions of male/masculine driven conflict. The comedies act as case studies in the utility of the sonnet philosophy. In contrast, the ten histories examine the illogical and murderous consequences when male-based religion and monarchy usurps power absolutely. The tragedies then present twelve worst-case scenarios of male prejudice and abuse through 2000 years of mind-driven mayhem and killing.

The sonnet philosophy also explains incidental aspects of F. It shows why *The Tempest* is first play, why *The Winter's Tale* is the last comedy and why *Troilus and Cressida* acts as a prologue for the other tragedies. It also clarifies why *The Taming of the Shrew* begins with an 'Induction' and why the tragedies end with the death of not Cymbeline but his Queen.

F's arrangement reinforces the nature-based insights Shakespeare lays out in the *Sonnets* where he restores the female to her prior status and critiques male-based mind-driven excesses. Commentators who do not understand the sonnet philosophy inevitably emend, reattribute, or otherwise quibble over details.

Nature is ubiquitous, singular and occasionally thunderous throughout the plays. Shakespeare's female and male characters are the biological/logical argument places for his nature-based philosophy. The multitude of goddesses, gods and other figments of the human imagination are but pop-up manifestations of the soul's imaginary sight (27) on the European stage.

Consequently, the increase argument with its dramatic implications for patrimony and bastards is a recurring theme. Shakespeare invokes primary sensory experiences and then demonstrates the logic of language with swearing and forswearing of oaths and witty dialogue in every play. Importantly, for his depth of dramatic catharsis, he generates a mythic level of expression in all the plays and in some plays corrects mythological presumptions with deliberate cross-dressing.

Shakespeare's frequent focus on love in the plays and longer poems accords with the argument for mature love throughout Q. In the comedies, love is the epitome of human emotive contentedness that follows the realisation of the philosophic contents from within nature. Shakespeare contrasts the reformative value and wellbeing of love in the comedies to the fate of overly idealistic love in the male-based histories and tragedies.

We have looked to the works of Shakespeare for evidence and accepted only findings that repeatedly assert themselves. It seems Shakespeare's works confront us with a philosophy without parallel in human history. *Venus and Adonis*, *The Rape of Lucrece*, *The Phoenix and the Turtle*, the 1609 *Sonnets* and the 1623 *Folio* appear to come from the same philosophic mind.

When Shakespeare lifts plots from the chronicles or literature, his aim is not to reproduce history accurately. Historical analysis or interpretation of his work is unavailing because he holds his characters to the standard of human nature within nature. Only Shakespeare's philosophy presented in Q provides the required depth of understanding.

In Part 3, we will examine the implications of our findings for global awareness. As no one has previously appreciated Shakespeare's 154-sonnet philosophy, nor its basis for his longer poems and *Folio* of plays, we can begin to re-evaluate his status as a poet and playwright in the light of the current global interest in his works.

Part 3

The wooden Globe

taking the plays to the world

Preliminary to a realignment at the Globe

When exploring the 154 sonnets from Q in Part 1, and then case-studying the thirty-six plays from F in Part 2, we contrast the process of revealing their nature-based philosophy with Columbus' lost-at-sea search for Asia.

As wayward as the metaphor might be for portraying the history of Shakespearean scholarship, it is inexplicable that commentators have spent oceans of ink misunderstanding Shakespeare. Not one ventures into the nature-based logic of the 154 sonnets in Q much less determines its relevance for the thirty-six plays in F.

Columbus' miscalculations, fanned by beliefs at odds with nature, deflate his globe-conquering ambitions. In contrast, Shakespeare's nature-based philosophy and natural wit align his plays and poems as vehicles for global adventuring.

Unlike the commentators, whose preconceptions override contrary indications, in Part 1 we follow the evidence. Then, in Part 2, we use the philosophy revealed in the sonnets to demonstrate how closely F conforms to Q.

With the arguments in Parts 1 and 2 in mind, we now ask in Part 3 how conscious Shakespeare is of the global implications for his nature-based philosophy. Did he formulate a prescription for global consciousness to counter the mind-based disorders raging in the European theatre?

We penetrate the cylindrical arena where Shakespeare presents many of his plays to examine the current worldwide interest in Shakespeare's works. With the recent trend to produce all his plays in one year, in what way does Shakespeare's global sensibility anticipate the overthrow of the prejudices and injustices in force around his 'Wooden O'?

Chapter 24: A devious debut and fiery finale

Where is Shakespeare in 1599 when his colleagues move The Theatre from Shoreditch to Bankside and rename it the Globe Theatre? What part did he play in naming the relocated theatre with globe-balancing Hercules posing over the entrance? Do his plays acknowledge the conjunction?

81: A new investigative procedure

Our examination in Part 1 of the structuring and contents of the 1609 *Sonnets* proceeded somewhat inductively. Our investigation shows Shakespeare gives considerable thought to the layout and numbering of the 154 sonnets in Q. Because their arrangement is so profound and deeply emotive, we presume Shakespeare is responsible.

Then, in Part 2, we turn our attention to the plays in *F*. To demonstrate the relationship between the sonnets and plays, we follow a complementary procedure, that of arguing by deduction. Our deductive approach, using the natural logic of Q, seems to confirm Shakespeare wrote the plays from the vantage of the 154-sonnet philosophy. This suggests Shakespeare publishes Q in 1609, twenty years after he starts writing the plays, to present the philosophy behind all his plays and longer poems.

In turn, Part 3 will argue neither by induction to search for unknown structure nor by deduction to show conformity to an existing structure. Instead, it will develop a case by analogy. We will consider the circumstances at the Globe Theatre to highlight significant connections between the Bankside Globe 400 years ago and Shakespeare's status as a global phenomenon. How aware is Shakespeare that he is writing not just for the European demographic he examines in *F* but for a world four centuries later with a firmly bedded global consciousness?

If Shakespeare publishes Q to present the philosophy behind all his plays and poems, then what are the implications of revealing such a significant philosophy to the global intellect and its emotional resources? We will follow the philosophy as it moves beyond traditional male-based religions, apologetics and scepticism to institute a natural philosophy in sympathy with global expectations for life and love.

82: Moving the Theatre to the Globe – Shakespeare's part

In Part 1 we map the nature-based philosophy Shakespeare embeds in generic Q. Then in Part 2, we use the philosophy from the unnamed and undated sonnets to penetrate the European plays in *F*. From our insights into *F*, we illuminate the social, political and religious conventions at the heart of greater Europe. We find them based illogically yet ironically in the male-driven usurpation of mythological eroticism.

The nature-based perspective of Shakespeare's *Sonnets*, *Folio* and four longer poems meet in the theatre called the Globe on the south bank of the Thames. In what way does the Globe Theatre serve both as the symbolic centre of Shakespeare's imaginary world and, by analogy, as a symbol for the larger implications of his works on the world stage?

In *Henry V*, from around 1599, Shakespeare has Henry refer to the Globe Theatre as 'this Wooden O'. <h5_13-15> Shakespeare nails in one quip both the full-moon symbolism of the twenty-eight Mistress sonnets and the eroticism basic to all expression.

Prologue   ... Or may we cram
Within this Wooden O, the very Casques
That did affright the Air at Agincourt?
          (Henry V 13-15)

The female/feminine compass of the Globe, with its jostling actors and audience, revisits the symbolic thrust of the *Sonnets* and plays and poems. Nature and the sexual dynamic are the preconditions for the erotic drama occurring within its circular walls. As the staging point for life's theatrics, the multi-sided timber structure is playfully erotic.

From 1599 on, the principal venue for the presentation of Shakespeare's plays is the Globe Theatre. However, the polygonal structure located on the South Bank of the Thames stood originally as The Theatre at Shoreditch in North West London from 1576 to 1598. In 1598, the Burbage brothers and their colleagues (including Shakespeare?) move its timbers across the Thames, and a reconstruction opens as the Globe Theatre on its new site in 1599.

The Theatre-cum-Globe Shakespeare knows from his early days as a playwright burns down accidentally in 1613 during a performance of *Henry VIII*. Rebuilt in 1614 it remains in use until closed by the Puritans in 1642 and pulled down in 1644.

An unsubstantiated account asserts that shortly after the transition from Shoreditch to Bankside, the owners decide to fly a flag featuring Hercules shouldering a globe to announce the first performance of *Julius Caesar* in the new theatre. Similarly, history has it that a permanent crest over the main entrance – also depicting Hercules and a globe – carries the classical motto 'Totus mundus agit histrionem' or 'the whole world is a playhouse'.

Jaques **All the world's a stage,**
And all the men and women, merely Players;
          (As You Like It 1118-9)

However reliable the accounts are, the motto recurs modified when Jaque's proclaims 'all the world's a stage' <ayl_1118-9> in *As You Like It*, which was also performed at the Globe. Antonio in *The Merchant of Venice* concurs with Jaques sentiment when he suggests the state of the 'world' reflects a character's mental disposition. <mv_85-7>

Antonio **I hold the world but as the world Gratiano,**
A stage, where every man must play a part,
And mine a sad one.   (The Merchant of Venice 85-7)

The combination of the Wooden O from *Henry V* and 'all the world's a stage' from *As You Like It*, with the echo in *The Merchant of Venice*, suggests Shakespeare participates in naming the Bankside venue the Globe. The circular theatre on the bank of the Thames extends the impact of his European-based plays from the. generic logic of the *Sonnets* to the circumnavigatable planet Earth.

To what degree is Shakespeare conscious he writes for all the inhabitants on a recently mapped Earth as he addresses himself through female and male parts to the Globe's yard and galleries? Why did Shakespeare and his colleagues rename The Theatre the Globe Theatre? Why did they choose the word Globe and not words like Nature, Earth or World?

Even though Shakespeare uses the word nature over 300 times in the plays, to call the playhouse the Nature sounds odd because in everyday use the word nature does not accept articles such as the, a, or an. Moreover, in the English lexicon – and in Shakespeare's works – generic nature is always singular. Plural natures refers only to the variety of human natures within nature.

The word Earth also appears around 300 times in F. It refers to the blue/green planet in its trajectory through the starry heavens. Unlike the word nature whose oneness is generic, the word Earth can occur in the plural. For instance, in all probability there are other Earths in the universe. Whichever way, the word Earth refers to a verifiable planet, so the name does not evoke the range of reality and myth at play on Shakespeare's stage.

When we examine instances of the word world throughout F, we find it occurs as both singular and plural. It refers to any constituency circumscribed by human activity or imagination. Not only a geographic domain, it conjures up the known universe as well as imaginary worlds with their ever-changing pantheons of goddesses and gods. Unlike singular nature, we can talk of one world or many worlds. The word world relates less to the physical planet as a whole and more to conceptualised constructs demarked by demographic or imaginary interests.

Shakespeare makes a clear distinction between nature and world/s in *As You Like It*. He has melancholy Jaques intone 'all the world's a stage' as he launches into his formulaic seven ages speech. Whereas Duke Senior embraces nature, Jaques' melancholy comes from his cliché-ridden world-weariness, a syndrome confirmed when he decides to pursue a religious life at the play's end.

Contrary to most interpretations, Jaques' world-view is not Shakespeare's. Whereas Shakespeare bases his understanding in nature, Jaques' circumscribed musings reinforce the obvious. No world created on the Globe's stage can replicate nature. Nature is rampant and indefinable compared to the circumscribed strutting by players either within the Wooden O or on a geographically bounded stage like the European. Maybe Shakespeare appreciates the irony that when his plays are performed on the jutting stage at the Wooden O, the actors play out a European drama within the context of the theatre as an encompassing Globe.

Hamlet   ...O God, O God!
How weary, stale, flat, and unprofitable
Seems to me all the uses of this world?
(Hamlet 316-8)

Logically, nature at large cannot be a stage because it contextualises the very possibility of staging. Hence, we get a clearer understanding of Hamlet's groan – 'O God! God! How weary, stale, flat and unprofitable, seem to me all the uses of this world!' <ham_316-8> Shakespeare's critique of Hamlet's God-based frustration is that Hamlet (along with all Shakespeare's tragic males) is bemired in a circumscribed world-view. Like Jaques, Hamlet struggles to understand a world that rejects the efficacy of nature and the female-to-male sexual dynamic as the means to comprehend the logic of all world-views within nature.

In contrast to alternative names, the Globe draws an imaginary network of spherical lines about the Earth in keeping with its role of incorporating all the possible world-views humans create. The name Globe also marks the conceptual boundary between human global ambitions and/or fantasies and the illimitable dynamic of nature.

It is entirely appropriate, then, that the Shoreditch Theatre is renamed the Globe rather than the Nature, the Earth or the World. Even the other words in the plays that refer to planetary presences such as ball, sphere and orb do not make the connection between consciousness and the planet as does the Globe.

We regard nature involuntarily as the continuous dynamic out of which the imagination evolves. Hence, nature contextualises the function of the theatre and is the groundedness within which the idea of a theatre locates its meaning. At the beginning of the third millennium, we now talk freely of a global consciousness as the epitome of inclusiveness and apprehension for humans in nature. Shakespeare and his colleagues neatly finger the possibility when they call the re-built theatre at Bankside the Globe.

83: Hercules' globe

Notwithstanding the hearsay accounts of Hercules blazoned over the Globe entrance in 1599, Shakespeare does mention Hercules forty times throughout his plays (five using the alternate name Alcides).

There is an oddity, though, in that Shakespeare and his colleagues choose Hercules over Atlas, the usual bearer of the globe. In Greek myth, Hercules shoulders the globe very briefly. He needs Atlas to retrieve the golden apples from the Hesperides, Atlas' daughters, so he offers to hold the globe while Atlas is away. <lll_1691-2> Relieved of the globe, on his return Atlas tries to trick Hercules into holding it permanently. However, Hercules plays his own trick to return the globe to Atlas.

Berowne **For Valour, is not Love a Hercules?**
Still climbing trees in the Hesperides.
(Love's Labour's Lost 1691-2)

We also need to know whether Hercules' globe is celestial or Earthy. Although classical statuary depicts Atlas' globe as a celestial sphere, it does seem the globe Hercules and Atlas exchange in the Shakespearean context is the earthy globe or 'load' as Rosencrantz calls it in *Hamlet*.

The eleven mentions of 'globe' in Shakespeare's plays refer to the spherical Earth or to spherical body parts such as breasts or head (see quotes below). The usage accords with period depictions of Atlas or Hercules holding a terrestrial globe rather than the celestial sphere. In the sixteenth century the word 'atlas' had come to describe a mapped sphere of the Earth or a collection of maps.

In contrast to Shakespeare's frequent mentions of Hercules, Atlas appears only twice in the plays. On one occasion Cleopatra associates Anthony's globe conquering ambitions with Atlas' burden. <ant_550> Instead, Shakespeare's focus on Hercules' labours,

Cleopatra **The demy Atlas of this Earth,**
(Anthony and Cleopatra 550)

and his 'load', suggests an interest in a male who relieves himself of a weighty burden, through trickery if necessary.

If Atlas is a strongman weighed down with the nature/female symbolism of the earthy (or celestial) globe, then what does the brief intervention of Hercules achieve? The Garden of the Hesperides, from which Hercules retrieves the golden apples with Atlas' assistance, is at the western extreme of the Mediterranean. In Greek, Hesperia is the 'Western Land' beyond which is the limitless ocean.

Atlas represents the male-dominated world of classical mythology. He both symbolises the male delusion that the female globe needs his support and has daughters confined to the furthermost end of terra cognito. So, in effect, Hercules recovers the female/feminine in the form of apples from the edge of the unbounded female/feminine ocean. His gender correcting experiences are similar to those of Odysseus, who spends twenty years at sea shedding his male-based martial pride to enter a mature relationship with Penelope.

Unlike Atlas, who fails to relinquish the load of the female globe, Hercules escapes playfully with the golden apples. The symbolism suggests he now freely inter-relates his masculine and feminine personae. If the anecdotes are correct, Shakespeare's gender-correcting plays occur under the banner of Hercules' recovery of feminine/masculine cunning. <cor_3017-8>

Menenius As Hercules did shake down Mellow Fruit: You have made fair work.   (Coriolanus 3017-8)

Moreover, Shakespearean drama is acted out on the masculine thrust stage (remembering the columns on either side of the stage evoke the Pillars of Hercules) within the encompassing feminine Globe Theatre. At the Globe, Shakespeare's plays re-enact the natural interrelationship between female and male under the aegis of Hercules' gender rectifying trickery.

Departing theatregoers either leave the Globe liberated like Hercules or remain like Atlas forever bearing the weight of female ostracism. If they misconstrue the poignancy of Hercules' rectification of male-based conceits, they remain oppressed by the burdensome delusion of female unfathomableness.

Most references to Hercules in Shakespeare's plays are to his various labours rather than specifically to the Atlas incident. All twelve labours aim to correct the male rage in which he kills his children. There is one moment, though, where Shakespeare seems to draw a clear connection between Hercules' trickery in avoiding the load of the globe and the trickery that playgoers should be wise to if they are to leave the Globe Theatre unencumbered with the burden of believing the wrong import of Shakespeare's works.

Immediately before the most famous play within a play, where Shakespeare has Hamlet trick Claudius into admitting the burden of his guilt, Rosencrantz invokes the lesson of Hercules' close encounter. (ham_1408> In Hamlet's rejoinder, Shakespeare indicates just what is required to avoid leaving a performance

Rosencrantz **Ay that they do, my Lord, Hercules and his load too.**
(Hamlet 1408)

with a great load. Hamlet is sufficiently wise to conceive Atlas-like of a trick to reveal what is not 'Natural' in Claudius' actions. Hamlet, though, is not wise enough to Hercules-like use 'Philosophy' to avoid the same fate for himself within his own play. <ham_1409-14>

It seems Shakespeare's lesson for playgoers to his Globe Theatre is not to be tricked into accepting an unnatural burden, which his nature-based philosophy provides the antidote to – if like Hercules they are wary enough. The inability of playgoers for 400 years to appreciate Shakespeare's philosophy means the modern enthusiasts who reconstruct the Globe Theatre are like Atlas lumbered with the load Hercules adroitly avoids.

> *Hamlet* It is not strange: for mine Uncle is King of Denmark, and those that would make mows at him while my father lived; give twenty, forty, an hundred Ducats a piece, for his picture in Little. There is something in this more than Natural, if Philosophy could find it out.   (Hamlet 1409-14)

If Hercules did hoist a globe on his shoulders over the doorway of the relocated theatre, his is not so much a show of strength as a statement of what it means to sustain two heads on high. His own head is a thinking, breathing, emoting cranium. In contrast, Hercules' globe, as a spherical pseudo-head, is a mock of its bony neighbour. It is a down-sized mother earth with its mapped-on continents mimicking the many mental constructs played out in the Globe's amphitheatre.

Hercules' feat is not that he has the physical strength to balance a sphere of earth, water, fire and air on his shoulders. Rather, in holding a global construct above his head, he admits his god-bred powers are

> *Hamlet* Oh all you host of Heaven! Oh Earth; what else? And shall I couple Hell? Oh fie: hold my heart; And you my sinews, grow not instant Old; But bear me stiffly up: Remember thee? I, thou poor Ghost, while memory holds a seat In this distracted Globe: (Hamlet 777-82)

fabrications of the human mind. The two spheres, cranium and pseudo-cranium, mismatched on a crouching muscle man, speak to Hercules' erotic brain muscle. <ham_777-82>

If Shakespeare conspires with his colleagues to erect an image of Hercules over the Globe's entrance, can we presume his motivation is to represent a genuflecting

> *Oberon* Then my Queen in silence sad, Trip we after the night's shade; We the Globe can compass soon, Swifter than the wandering Moon.
>   (A Midsummer Night's Dream 1613-6)

muscle man who speaks to the logical relationship between the sexual body and erotic mind played out in his works? <mnd_1613-6> The Globe is a globe where Shakespeare's mythic mind-games are recycled to assuage the desire mechanism of the human spirit. <tit_2334-5>

> *Titus* And then I'll come and be thy Waggoner, And whirl along with thee about the Globes.
>   (Titus Andronicus 2334-5)

With the Globe as a simulated human skull, Hercules provides a powerful reminder that anything is possible as long as the divide between the sexual dynamic of the human body and the erotic logic that supports the double illusion in conceptual theatrics is held high for all to see.

Not only does the Globe mimic the planet-cum-skull, its multifaceted structure says something about the mind's capacity for a multiplicity of

> *Margaret*   ...Let me hear from thee: For wheresoever thou art in this world's Globe, I'll have an Iris that shall find thee out.
>   (2 Henry VI 2122-4)

mental constructs. While nature remains singular and constant, the multitude of goddesses and gods and their mythological words, words, words proliferate in the polygonal Bankside playhouse. <2h6_2122-4>

84: The Earth and the Globe

Unlike human skulls, of which there are many, there is just the one Earth, and we refer to the Earth as a globe in the singular. Different from the

Richard Discomfortable Cousin, knowest thou not,
That when the searching Eye of Heaven is hid
Behind the Globe, that lights the lower World,
(Richard II 1392-4)

existence of many world-views on Earth (just about as many as there are human skulls within which to dream them up), and similar to the sun and the moon being called globes, <r2_1392-4> the Earth as globe is a conceptual whole.

Dromio of Syracuse No longer from head to foot, than from hip to hip: she is spherical, like a globe: I could find out Countries in her.   (The Comedy of Errors 904-6)

Shakespeare also refers to parts of the human body as globes. The description of Nell's

rotund midriff in *The Comedy of Errors* <err_904-6> and Lucrece's ivory breasts in her poem are two compelling images. <rl_407-8>

In the exchange between Dromio and Antipholus of Ephesus, Shakespeare plays word-games with Nell's body parts, as if her anatomy comes from countries

Her breasts, like Ivory globes circled with blue,
A pair of maiden worlds unconquered,
(The Rape of Lucrece 407-8)

around the globe. He derives a belly laugh from the national characteristics of Germany, Spain, England, Scotland, France, America, Indies and the Netherlands. Moreover, his wit points to the globe as a construct imposed over the suggestivity of a plump body or a rounded breast.

So the threat to the permanency of the earthy globe in Ulysses' famous speech

Ulysses   ...The bounded Waters,
Should lift their bosoms higher than the Shores,
And make a sop of all this solid Globe:
(Troilus and Cressida 570-2)

in *Troilus and Cressida* <tro_570-2> is not so much a threat to the solidity of the Earth but a comment on the fragility of mental constructs

that impose a globular form over the natural shapes of bodies and breasts. More significant is the caution not to take too literally the scenarios Shakespeare presents at the Bankside Globe. Within their entrancing form is a critique of the mind-based attitudes they re-enact.

Prospero characterises the syndrome toward the end of *The Tempest*. While deconstructing the magical island he conjures in the minds of his colleagues, Pros-

pero anticipates the dissolution of the 'great globe'. <tmp_1823-7> As Shakespeare argues in the *Sonnets*, nature persists over and above the structures

Prospero The Cloud-capped Towers, the gorgeous Palaces,
The solemn Temples, the great Globe it self,
Yea, all which it inherit, shall dissolve,
And like this insubstantial Pageant faded
Leave not a rack behind: (Tempest 1823-7)

built by humankind. This means it also persists over the imaginary capacity of the humankind to elicit from shapes in the round an image as ubiquitous as the globe.

It is left to Othello to draw the distinction between the Earth as a solid planet, orbiting in concert with the sun and moon, and the emotive constructs generated in the imaginary soul of humankind.

Othello **Me thinks, it should be now a huge Eclipse**
Of Sun, and Moon; and that th'affrighted Globe
Did yawn at Alteration.   (Othello 3362-4)

In his distracted state, as he plays out his final murderous act on the Globe's wooden stage, his concern for an 'affrighted globe' conflates the globe as a construct with the natural world of Earth, Sun and Moon. <oth_3362-4>

Anecdotal evidence provides a strong link between Shakespeare's nature-based philosophy and the global consciousness heralded at the newly named Globe. The inclusion of references to the Globe in his plays suggests he is aware of the global implications of writing for a European sensibility in the throes of colonising the planet.

Chapter 25: Re-discovering nature's globe

How unique are Shakespeare's works with their nature-based philosophy, their analysis of the European sensibility and their anticipation of global consciousness? Where can we look in the history of thought to measure his breadth and depth of achievement?

85: Global blind spots

The absence of proper names in Q provides a clue that Shakespeare presents his nature-based philosophy in the 154 sonnets. Moreover, the organisation of the fourteen comedies, and twenty-two histories and tragedies in F could be a cue from Shakespeare's colleagues, or even Anne Hathaway, about his intentions. The plays as arranged in F present contrasting case studies of the distance between our inherent natural philosophy and the male-based paradigms in force across Europe.

If, in turn, the Globe Theatre symbolises Shakespeare's ambition for his works on the world stage, then why has no one aligned the *Sonnets*, the *Folio* and the Globe so a flood of illumination issues from them.

In the light of our discoveries, 400 years ago Shakespeare arrives at an understanding whose consistency and comprehensiveness is well ahead of his time and is still in many respects ahead of ours. Why has no one previously extracted Shakespeare's nature-based philosophy to bring his critical program into play for the modern global consciousness? What keeps us from appreciating the natural philosophy behind his universally acclaimed poetry and drama?

We have seen Shakespeare demonstrate the malconsequences of illogical paradigms in the histories and tragedies. Like his Poet in *126*, he audits the errors of adolescently obsessive male-based idealists and overly masculinised females. In this light, the greatness commentators attribute to Shakespeare's tragedies is no triumph of the human imagination. Rather, we see Shakespeare attack the tenacious grip on the human imagination of male/masculine-based enclaves of nature alienation and mind-driven conflict.

We have followed Shakespeare in the comedies as he reduces male/masculine dominance and aggression to achieve a natural partnership between female and male, feminine and masculine. Can we emulate Shakespeare and throw hate away from love – as he recounts in *145*. Can we escape from male-driven biblical guilt to recover our natural sensibility, as Duke Senior puts it eloquently in *As You Like It*?

<ayl_607-11>

Duke Senior **Now my Co-mates, and brothers in exile:**
Hath not old custom made this life more sweet
Than that of painted pomp? Are not these woods
More free from peril than the envious Court?
Here feel we not the penalty of Adam,

(As You Like It 607-11)

To get a measure of Shakespeare's achievement, we will track briefly through crucial developments in the history of ideas. We take particular interest in thinkers who go some way toward reconciling female and male in nature for a global appreciation of the dynamic of truth and beauty, as Shakespeare calls ethics (morals) and aesthetics (art).

86: Playing around with myth

If our reading is true to the intent of Shakespeare's works, then the nature-based philosophy he articulates in Q and F presents the default criteria for human flowering in the global village. More than that, because the philosophy is basic to human nature, it should also be the philosophy applicable to earlier times when there are but tribal villages.

We should be able to track on the one hand attempts over the last few centuries to institute and enforce male-God mythologies that were developed in proto-urban cultures a few thousand years ago. On the other hand, we should find evidence of natural philosophy's tendency to reassert its common sense priorities.

In Shakespeare's comedies, the recovery of natural philosophy brings a cessation of violence and murder resulting from patriarchal prejudice exacerbated by blind belief in one or other male God/gods. In contrast, the denial of natural philosophy due to ecclesiastical/monarchical collusion, as dramatised in the histories and tragedies, leads to gratuitous murder and mayhem. If the unilateral imposition of male-based commandments or doctrines throughout a culture overrides natural justice, what is the fire-talk before prophets source God's Word from above and carve it in stone?

Archaeologists and cultural anthropologists find evidence in ancient civilisations 30,000 or so years before the invention of writing that the human female gets her due as the precursor for the male. In keeping with a balanced female/male dynamic, the male plays out his natural role of partnership. [note 1]

Artefacts from Hittite, Minoan and other prehistoric societies show esteem for the female or goddess with the female form predominant in statuettes or in carved female attributes such as the vulva. The objects are often found in rooms or niches possibly set aside for veneration of the natural order.

However, a dramatic change occurs around 4000 years ago. This is the period when writing first appears in cultures throughout the Middle East. Warrior male and scribal male culture takes ascendancy and writes females into a subsidiary role.

Previously, in oral cultures the word of the speaker is liable to change at every outing. Now the written word gives greater permanence and enforceability to customary beliefs. Male scribes take advantage of their superior muscle to invert natural philosophy for demographic gain and legitimise the inversion in texts such as Genesis and the Pentateuch.

The nailing of Christ to the cross a couple of thousand years later registers only point one on the Richter scale compared to the earlier level nine rift in human sensibility and understanding. We continue to hear the indelible echo of that moment in history when twenty-first century fundamentalists claim that page by page their holy books convey the infallible words of a male God.

Then, around BC/AD, the Son of God – capitalising on his Father's passion for imaginary love – invokes neighbourly love in the context of male-God worship. However, by not addressing male/female illogicality, he creates new channels of misogynist opportunity for institutional Christianity.

Ironically, when evangelists construe Christ out of the man Jesus they eroticise his birth and death. Because mythic eroticism is conditional on nature and the sexual dynamic, the Gospel writers unwittingly acknowledge the derivative status of their founding myth.

At a profound level, the eroticism in myth satisfies vicariously the desire in the human mind to account for origins and ends. It was only necessary for the prophets or evangelists to inscribe a ready-made male-based program to attract the susceptible into the fold and persecute the rest.

However, the patent illogicality of enforcing the priority of a male God over nature leads to the questioning of scribal authority. The challenges range from the philosophical to the violent as splinter religious movements form and reform under modified doctrines.

The standard response to schisms is to outlaw the dissenters as heretics. The possibility of heresy is of some interest as Shakespeare mentions *Heretic* in *124* and a further ten times in the plays. In *The Winter's Tale*, Shakespeare points up the grim irony of male-based heresy when he has Paulina identify wife-and-child murderer Leontes as the real heretic. <wt_1040-3>

> *Leontes* **I'll ha'thee burnt.**
> *Paulina* **I care not:**
> **It is an Heretic that makes the fire,**
> **Not she which burns in't.**
> **(The Winter's Tale 1040-3)**

Yet, when considering the deeply philosophical challenge of Shakespeare's works to male-based presumption, the philosophic responses of apology and scepticism are of greater interest. In defence of male-God illogicalities, apologetic thinkers such as Augustine, Thomas Aquinas, Rene Descartes and Baruch Spinoza attempt to justify the inverted mythic conventions of the patriarchal/misogynistic churchmen.

In opposition, sceptical thinkers such as John Locke, David Hume and Friedrich Nietzsche demonstrate the inconsistencies in the idea of a creator God. However, even the sceptics fail to analyse the erotic logic of myth. They overlook the inverted logic of male/female ascendancy. Their oversight forestalls insights into why biblical myth appeals to the nature-alienated mind.

87: The apologetic/sceptical impasse

For 4000 years, political sanction of male-based beliefs leads to the erection of many imposing edifices across greater Europe. In concert with the architectural thrust skyward, there is a rich vein of art, music and poetry from the ever-changing demography of religious denominations. A timeline illustrates the part they play at periods in history but also shows that when the stylistic impetus no longer flourishes they decline rapidly.

Over the centuries, the architectural and artistic highpoints are undermined not so much by physical degradation but through neglect following mind-based schisms. The poorly constructed doctrines and dogmas on which the bricks and mortar are laid produce continual heresies.

Yet, amidst the conceptual undermining, we can locate attempts to formulate a consistent philosophy based in nature. Aquinas and Spinoza, particularly, felt the need to re-relate God to nature.

Around 1270 Thomas Aquinas (1225-74), originally a student at the University of Naples but now teaching at the University of Paris, sought to accommodate Aristotle's understanding of nature to Saint Augustine's City of God. His attempt to reconcile nature with God is at first considered heresy by the Church. However, as the Church soon discovers, there is equivocation room enough in the Aristotle/Augustine/Aquinas triumvirate to justify its male God salvation business.

Two centuries later in the Netherlands, Baruch Spinoza (1632-77) argues nature and God are one and the same. By 1670, Spinoza rejects Rene Descartes' mind/body dichotomy in which the body is cast as a bit of machinery and the mind thinks everything of itself. Instead, he argues for a unitary interrelationship of a natural body and spiritual mind. Nevertheless, his claim that nature and God are one and the same glibly confuses the grammar of the two words nature and God. As we have seen, nature is always singular and ever-present whereas God (who is still a male for Baruch) is never present and as an imaginary entity is readily divisible into other goddesses and gods.

A century on, in the 1730s, David Hume (1711-76) leaves his hometown Edinburgh and lives in France where he writes a lengthy work he later publishes in condensed form as *A Treatise of Human Nature*. Unlike Aquinas and Spinoza who try to accommodate the idea of God to nature, Hume argues against knowing anything beyond immediate sense experience. Religion for Hume is merely a response of primitive 'man' (sic) to the incomprehensible forces of nature.

Hume sees religion misrepresenting nature and he holds religion, like a science, accountable to empirical investigation. However, Hume takes little account of the mind's capacity to imagine mythic stories of goddesses and gods. He does not investigate the philosophic implications of configuring the relationship between mind and nature in literary forms. This is despite presenting his arguments against religion as a literary dialogue. By conflating the two distinct functions of the mind – reason and art – into one, Hume could only be sceptical about the human capacity for understanding the world and hence for being at one with nature.

The attempts to reconcile God with nature by uncompromising apologists as Aquinas and to equate God and nature by quibbling apologists as Spinoza, plus the scepticism resulting from Hume's deletion of the God notion from the human mind are trumped by a constitutional response.

In the 1790s, Thomas Jefferson (1743-1826) contextualises the unsatisfactory compromises with a complete separation of an intercessionary God of the Churches from a State based in the 'Laws of Nature'. 'Nature's God' plays no part in his own creation. Jefferson as a Deist accepts a logical schism between an almighty God and the world he creates. Jefferson, though, does not challenge the male-based status of God.

When, in 1882, Friedrich Nietzsche (1844-1900) proclaims the 'death of God' in *The Gay Science*, he deletes the concept God from the dictionary. God exits in all forms, but mainly in his biblical guise as creator of the world. Unlike Hume who argues against the existence of God, Nietzsche realises God is a mind based phenomenon who only needs a conceptual death certificate to end his reign.

However, Nietzsche, appreciating that the name of God is tacked onto human morals, goes where Hume would not. He develops an understanding of good and evil appropriate to a proposed breed of super-humans. However, since Nietzsche fails to understand the body to mind dynamic in nature, he creates a morality of privilege – just like the Ten Commandments. Not surprising then, when Nietzsche tries to understand Shakespeare, he falls for the biographical trivia that Francis Bacon wrote Shakespeare.

The next step in the recovery of natural philosophy, on the way to redressing the illogical prioritising of the male over the female by apologists, begins with the stargazing of Galileo Galilei. We then move to planet Earth with the evolutionary biology of Charles Darwin. Following that, we examine the workings of the human mind in the ordinary language philosophy of Ludwig Wittgenstein. Then we explore the depths of the human imagination in the mythic art of Marcel Duchamp.

88: Galileo telescopes the heavens – Darwin restores the mind to the body

Galileo Galilei (1564-1642) was born the same year as Shakespeare. In 1609, the year Shakespeare publishes Q, Galileo also forges a date with history when he demonstrates his homemade telescope. He views phenomena he is not supposed to see if the Ptolemaic geocentric universe helps God the Creator hold sway.

Galileo observes the Moon is spherical, which implies the Earth is also a sphere. Furthermore, he discovers moons orbiting Jupiter. This suggests the planets of the solar system likewise circle the Sun. Galileo's newfound evidence for heliocentricity proves the Earth is not the centre of the universe. The God who creates man and adds woman as an afterthought does not look as kindly on the Earth as his Bible claims.

Although Galileo remains a Catholic, his astronomical observations of Jupiter's moons published in 1610 show that hitching understanding to the Commandments of an absentee God exposes them as male-prejudiced conventions. Unintentionally, maybe, Galileo's findings exemplify how the natural philosophy of the global consciousness reasserts itself despite the edicts of those who usurp power in the name of a male God.

The Churches of the time show their displeasure at Galileo's discoveries by confining him to house arrest for the remainder of his life. Even more petulantly, the Church authorities turn to the theories of Galileo's fellow astronomer, Tyco Brahe. Because Brahe cannot accept the implications of his own meticulous observations, he devises a compromise for the Holy Church.

If Galileo finds evidence for a natural understanding of planetary motions that lays the foundation for a coherent understanding of the universe, two centuries later in Down south-east of London, Charles Darwin (1809-82) produces evidence in *The Origin of Species* to demonstrate humankind is an evolved species on a planet many hundreds of millions of years old.

What Galileo does for our understanding of the Earth in space, Darwin does for our understanding of the biosphere. Both sets of findings are contrary to biblical dogmas God delivers from beyond the universe. It seems God needs a lesson or two about his universe and about his favourite creature, man. Or else man's imagination is self-destructing and his abuse of language is unravelling.

Darwin does not stop at showing humankind evolves on a planet for millions of years. In *The Descent of Man and Selection in Relation to Sex*, he argues, in the light of accumulated evidence, that the full spectrum of mental powers and moral sense evolve from the capabilities and sympathies of species preceding humans in evolution. For Darwin, human love is an evolved emotion at least as important for human survival as natural selection.

As David Loye points out, Darwin mentions survival of the fittest only twice in *The Descent of Man*. [note 2] In contrast, he mentions love and morality over ninety times each. Darwin argues that love originates with the development of sexual organisms hundreds of millions of years ago and flourishes in the interpersonal relationships of Homo sapiens.

Unfortunately, as Loye maintains, Neo-Darwinians' fascination with genes prevents a mature assessment of Darwin's focus on love in *The Descent of Man*. DNA-atheists such as Richard Dawkins forestall the full application of Darwin's challenge to the prejudices of religious dogma.

The eventual acceptance – albeit equivocal – of Galileo's findings by the Church, and the more recent acceptance of Darwin's evidence, sees a peeling back of unnatural and misogynistic doctrines. However, if the example of the Neo-Darwinists is a measure of progress, there is not yet a full understanding of the natural logic of language. Even more critically, there is no appreciation of the natural logic of mythic expression, especially as it affects religious fundamentalists who cling to their anti-nature beliefs.

To understand better the power of language to create an imaginary reality we now turn to the philosopher Ludwig Wittgenstein. After early mistakes in formulating the logic of language, Wittgenstein bases his mature philosophy on the undeniable givens of 'nature' and 'parents'. Then we will consider the artist Marcel Duchamp. In his *Large Glass*, Duchamp encapsulates the erotic logic of myth to recover the originary status of the female for an inclusive mythic expression.

89: Wittgenstein's natural language – Duchamp's mythic art

The first thinker to develop a philosophy that rejects apologetics or unsound metaphysics is Viennese-born and Cambridge-based Ludwig Wittgenstein (1889-1951). He replaces the syndrome of justification with a process of investigation. Wittgenstein avoids the illogicalities of metaphysics by describing the logical relationship between the facts of the world and language's capacity to represent the world.

Wittgenstein's first attempt to escape from philosophic methods that imprison understanding in scribal enclaves of imaginary beings leans on the findings of atomic physics. Wittgenstein thinks he can show the basic constituents of thought are logically atomic (or 'simple') and molecular (or 'complex'). He publishes his *Tractatus Logico-Philosophicus* in 1921 with claims to a final solution to the problems of philosophy.

To Wittgenstein's embarrassment, he realises the atomic/molecular model does not account for the way humans use language in practice. Wittgenstein now accepts that neither the heavenly metaphysics of imaginary goddesses and gods of traditional philosophy nor the earthly metaphysics of atomic particles have the correct multiplicity to represent the logic of language.

Wittgenstein turns his attention to the way humans learn and apply ordinary language. He begins to describe the way languages use agreed rules or conventions based on publicly determined criteria. He calls the logic of communication language games because languages are constructed using rules and no one rule accounts for all the possibilities of language in practice.

Significantly, the mature Wittgenstein, around the time of World War II, realises the undeniable facts of nature and parents provide the grounds for all language games. Although different cultures have different conventions according to their needs, nature is a given for any language game as are the facts of parents or forebears. While language games require agreed on axioms, commandments, conventions, rules or laws to function at all, every culture on the globe treats nature and the role of parents as beyond question.

While Wittgenstein accepts that nature (including the fact of parents) provides the unquestioned grounds for all languages, he does not ask how the undeniable givens characterise the deepest expression in a culture, the language of myth. We turn to the French artist, Marcel Duchamp (1887-1968), to discover how Wittgenstein's insights apply to the most reflexive language game, the mythic.

Duchamp, sidelined by his artistic peers in Paris (including his two brothers), spends a few months of 1912 in Munich. While in Munich he conceives his major work *The Bride Stripped Bare by Her Bachelors, Even* (1923: aka *The Large Glass*). Its penetrating depiction of the logic of myth makes it the seminal work of both his career and twentieth century art. As the Mexican poet and diplomat Octavio Paz puts it, Duchamp's *Large Glass* provides effectively a criticism of myth and formulates the myth of criticism. [**note 3**]

The iconography of *The Large Glass* depicts the female and male dynamic as central to myths of origins. All goddesses and gods are born non-biologically through virgins, legs, heads, spilt blood, etc. Critically, Duchamp's female and male entities interact erotically and never sexually.

This means the eroticism at the heart of all myths shows they derive logically from the sexual dynamic in nature. The implication is that the dynamic of female and male in nature is basic to all languages and that all languages are logically erotic.

Duchamp looks to myth because it gives artistic expression to the most basic relationships between humankind and nature. He realises that eroticism in myths indicates they are but stories – deeply significant stories but still stories.

As a form of art that evokes unknowable beginnings, myth cannot be scientifically accurate. Consequently, myth is not literally believable. When myths that prioritise male-based beliefs over the female are enforced literally for power and dominance the consequences are always diabolical.

In his *Large Glass*, Duchamp corrects the most basic inversion in traditional myth. Because the human female is biologically the precursor for the male, Duchamp gives the female natural ascendency over the male. This one move makes the mythic dynamic of *The Large Glass* fully representative of reality while still acknowledging that myths as works of art are logically erotic.

As Paz intuits, there is no disjunction between the mythic dynamic of Duchamp's *Large Glass* and reality. If believed in literally, it can do no harm. At the same time, Duchamp criticises all previous myth-based religions that invert the female/male dynamic in nature.

Modern global consciousness makes it possible for Wittgenstein and Duchamp to gain an overview of the logic of language and art. Our investigation, though, suggests 300 years earlier Shakespeare arrives at a more complete formulation of the logic of language and mythic art just when the world is on the cusp of global awareness. Furthermore, Shakespeare encapsulates the new sensibility at the aptly named Globe.

90: The woman in Shakespeare

Shakespeare's works anchor the originary status of the female to the heart of his nature-based philosophy. The 154-sonnet set with its two sequences represents the natural relationship between the encompassing female and subsidiary male who returns to the female for perpetuation. From the evidence, it seems the plays and longer poems conform to the natural prescription in Q.

Shakespeare emphasises the dual dynamic of female/male sexual differentiation and feminine/masculine gender dispositions. Although the female/feminine is the precursor biologically, the male/masculine defines and extends human potentiality in cultural, political, religious and social spheres.

The uniqueness of Shakespeare's nature-based philosophy in Q, and his expression of that understanding in poetry and drama on the European stage at the London Globe, brings us to the comtemporary debate on the female/male dynamic. We turn to the work of two women to highlight advances toward natural justice. But we also ask why even female commentators do not appreciate Shakespeare's works for their female-based natural philosophy.

One of the more visible advocates for women's issues over the last forty years is Germaine Greer (1939-). By courting controversy and even contradiction, Greer focuses attention where discrimination affects women. Her books *The Female Eunuch* (1970) and *Sex and Destiny* (1984) challenge prejudices toward women and provide a platform for her advocacy of women's rights.

Greer also has a reputation as a Shakespearean scholar. A recent publication, *Shakespeare's Wife* (2007), argues that Anne Hathaway was a self-determined woman in a mature and enduring relationship with Shakespeare. *Shakespeare's Wife* also makes a case for Anne's influence on the 1623 *Folio*.

Yet when Greer writes a commentary on *King Lear* in her *Shakespeare* (1986), [**note 4**] she presents Lear as Christian saint assailed by dark nature. This is despite knowing Shakespeare shifts the source play, *King Leir*, away from its original Christian psychology. Greer reads into *King Lear* a male-based Christian religiosity foreign to Shakespeare's works.

Why Greer endorses the male-biased re-conversion of *King Lear* is a puzzle. Or, it would be a puzzle if not for her ignorance of the nature-based logic of Q. She misreads Shakespeare's profound understanding of the mythic logic of art that underscores his reworked *King Leir*. Like many commentators who struggle to understand *King Lear*, Greer resorts to Christian mythology as the only way she knows to characterise its mythic profundity.

Not as controversial in her advocacy for women's rights as Greer is cultural anthropologist and partnership rights advocate Riane Eisler (1937-). Eisler is a more consistent and deeper thinker than Greer. In books like *The Chalice and the Blade* (1987) and *Sacred Pleasure, Spirituality and the Politics of the Body* (1996) Eisler argues that the human female is the biological precursor for the male. She also has a clear understanding of the difference between the sexual and the erotic.

Eisler insists the natural inter-relationship of female and male means not dominance by one or the other but natural partnership intended in nature to be of benefit to both. In keeping with her insight, she establishes the Partnership Way, and makes a significant contribution to human rights for women and men.

Unfortunately, like Greer, Eisler's incomplete understanding of the mythic logic of art leads her to accept a reading of *The Taming of the Shrew* that reckons Shakespeare was anti-female. Her misreading of Shakespeare's intent occurs despite many commentators acknowledging the irony in Katherine's avowal of subjection to her husband Petruchio at the play's end.

Even though both women make significant contributions to the cause of women's rights, they are unaware of Shakespeare's nature-based philosophy that recovers the originary status of female to male. The consequences are apparent when Eisler's husband David Loye expresses uncritical admiration for the overly romanticised biopic *Shakespeare in Love* in his book *Darwin in Love*. [**note 5**]

There is a significant history of women's liberation from the tyranny of male-based dogmas and doctrines. Yet the advance toward women's rights as a constitutional issue is still fraught by enclaves of religious misogyny. Across the globe, the acceptance of a genuine partnership between female and male is still sporadic. That the generic term human rights does not automatically confer on women an equality in partnership is symptomatic of the deliberate skewing of values over the last 4000 or so years.

Many voices challenge the corruption of human partnership values at the heart of male-based religions. Male-God institutions such as Vatican City and Buckingham Palace are now ring fenced impotent ritual-bound enclaves. The European Constitution may follow the American Constitution in finding against the admissibility of the word God.

It is not sufficient for women to assert their rights and gain equality before the law. While there is exemplary justice in women recovering their natural rights, there is also poignancy when men not only admit past injustices but bring to the table an expression of nature-based creativity.

A quick trip through the history of ideas before or since Shakespeare's day reveals no thinker or artist matches his depth and range of understanding. The most we can say is some individuals in their particular disciplines edge toward aspects of Shakespeare's philosophy.

Chapter 26: Global strategies

What is Shakespeare's strategy as he accommodates those in his day not able to comprehend fully the extent and incisiveness of his nature-based philosophy? What preparations does he make for the assimilation of his ideas over the following centuries?

91: Shakespeare's first editions as default texts

The evidence suggests the 1609 *Sonnets* articulate Shakespeare's nature-based philosophy, the 1623 *Folio* presents his solution to social, political and religious prejudices, and the Globe Theatre anticipates a global demographic. We argue that Q and F are authorial and Shakespeare participates in naming the Globe.

Doubts cast on the authenticity of Q and on the authorship of F over the last 400 years result from blindness to Shakespeare's nature-based philosophy. Now, at the beginning of the twenty-first century, there are frequent calls for a return to Q and F.

Commentators are reassessing Q and theatre companies are basing their productions on F (and the earlier quartos) either verbatim or in part to regain something of Shakespeare's meaning. Moreover, the Globe Theatre is standing again at South Bank with replicas appearing in the USA, Japan and Europe. The trend towards the originals rebuffs attempts to dissociate Shakespeare from his works, rework the plays or write whole plays in his name.

The list of deliberate detractors is nearly as long as the catalogue of Shakespearean literature in the British Library. However, this is not the place to pillory the history of dubious intentions or out-right bad faith. The evidence presented here shows how to bring into focus the 1609 and 1623 editions without harm either to Shakespeare or our consciences.

A return to the original editions, though, is not enough in itself. When Ted Hughes writes *Shakespeare and the Goddess of Complete Being* in 1992, he recognises that Shakespeare recovers the priority of the female over the male. Unfortunately, rather than appreciate the mythic logic behind Shakespeare's critique, Hughes backtracks to ancient times to reconfigure the plays – and the *Sonnets* – in terms of Greek goddesses and gods. [**note 6**]

Hughes' return to Greek myths has parallels with the psychiatric analysis of Shakespeare's works by Sigmund Freud. Freud brings ancient myths to bear on Hamlet's woes by treating his family ructions as a psychological malaise afflicting Shakespeare without appreciating Shakespeare's logical critique of male-based mythologies.

Similarly, Freud's one-time friend Carl Jung looks to Shakespeare's works for examples of arcane symbolism from various mythologies. Unlike Duchamp and Shakespeare, he fails to extract the logic of mythic expression. Together, the pairing of Freud and Jung perpetuates the illogicality of male-based myth instead of accepting the female/male dynamic in nature as the basis for all thought and emotions.

92: Natural cunning

How did Shakespeare feel writing in an age unprepared for his nature-based insights? Was he content at the prospect of being misinterpreted well beyond his lifetime? Moreover, what would have been his fate if Crown or Church had understood his philosophy? The cryptic organisation of aspects of Q could speak to his awareness of its revolutionary contents.

To get a measure of Shakespeare's attitude to his mythic insights and the inability of his contemporaries to understand him, we can compare Darwin's concern about the impact of his scientific findings on a bible-bred public not prepared for the evolutionary revelations of *The Descent of Man*.

Likewise, Wittgenstein could not bring himself to publish the manuscript of *Philosophical Investigations* before he died in 1951. In an academic culture that trivialises deep thought, he wonders if even one person would understand him by the end of the century.

Similarly, Duchamp fabricates a room-size diorama *Etant donnes* in complete secrecy for twenty years and plans for its installment and opening after his death in 1968. No artist, including Duchamp's Surrealist friend Andre Breton, knows of the new work, and no one since is as rigorous as Duchamp in exposing the mythic logic of art.

Shakespeare's appreciation that nature and the sexual dynamic are givens for the possibility of truth and beauty means he places no overwrought value on the constructs of the mind. For Shakespeare, the contents and contentedness available in his works are more important than their form, rhyme or style. His nature-based understanding is mortgage free compared to the prudential attitude toward life and death in biblical beliefs.

We have seen how Shakespeare publishes the longer poems in 1593 and 1594 as early essays in nature-based contents. Then he prepares Q for publication in the years before 1609 to present the definitive expression of his philosophy. By comparison, each play, with its premium on entertainment, provides a partial slice through the full contents in Q.

It would seem Shakespeare avoids charges of heresy or treason because his philosophic contents are contiguous with the expression of love in his sonnets. Similarly, the dramatic function of the plays obscures their basis in the nature-based philosophy of the *Sonnets*. Moreover, only half the plays are published in Shakespeare's lifetime and even then very haphazardly. They were not viewed together in the more revealing organisation of the *Folio* until seven years after his death.

Yet most of what we uncover in this volume is available free to view in the *Sonnets*, the *Folio* and the longer poems. Because most artists and writers do not operate at the mythic level, they fail to comprehend the significance of Shakespeare's mythic realignment for a global sensibility. His cunning insight is that he can present his ideas blatantly and even blasphemously because most viewers cannot penetrate what they mistake for conventional window dressing.

Instead, commentators mishear the works and reduce them to the religious, social or artistic constructs with which they are familiar. Many are attracted to Shakespeare's works but then alter and emend them according to their imbibed prejudices.

Shakespeare has it both ways. His native cunning allows him to get away with what others in his day are censored or even persecuted for. Then the same cunning guarantees him a European and now a worldwide audience of minds attracted like moths to his works. The limitations imposed on their understanding of the logic of life draws them to the mythic erotics glowing in Q and F.

93: Predicting the future

Using Shakespeare's nature and female-based philosophy evident in Q and F, we can now assess his predictions for a global demography. What are his prognostications from his European and proto-global vantage during the Elizabethan and Jacobean reigns?

In his ten histories, he foresees the demise of the monarchies synonymous with his age. Over the next 400 years, European monarchies either dissolve completely or remain as rudimentary appendages. Their once frequent warmongering is reduced to ceremonial guard manoeuvres.

Shakespeare's critique of male-based illogicalities also anticipates the removal of the Churches from the halls of power into cloisters to minister the psychological needs of the adolescent mind. Shakespeare's political/social/religious reordering anticipates Jefferson's complete separation of Church and State in the American Constitution. In liberal democracies, the once powerful Churches as the principal fomenters of Godly excesses have no direct influence on the State.

Associated with the undemocratic power of the Churches and their compliant monarchies is the violence meted out to individuals and groups simply because their beliefs are at odds with ruling dogmas. By arguing against the iniquities of mind-based division and persecution, Shakespeare's works predict a global age when gratuitous mind-driven violence is reduced considerably and in some nations is absent for decades if not centuries.

The arrangement of the plays in F reflects the implications of ignoring the natural female-driven logic of life. In the comedies, the females lead the males (or feminine/masculine balanced males correct overly masculinised females) toward reconciliation and self-realisation. In the histories and tragedies, headstrong males or their hapless male/female victims lead their casts into increasing levels of gratuitous violence and mayhem across the European theatre.

Every one of Shakespeare's histories and tragedies provides examples. Julius Caesar and Coriolanus bring summary justice on themselves for profiting from victorious carnage. In *Henry V*, Williams reminds Henry of the murderousness and pointlessness of war. <h5_1982-94> A trite symbolic disagreement causes the War of the Roses. Offended pride exacerbated by illogical beliefs drives the blood fest in *Richard III*.

In all the plays, Shakespeare shows that perceived rather than real injustices

Williams **But if the Cause be not good, the King himself hath a heavy Reckoning to make, when all those Legs, and Arms, and Heads, chopped off in a Battle, shall join together at the latter day, ... for how can they charitably dispose of any thing, when Blood is their argument? Now, if these men do not die well, it will be a black matter for the King, that led them to it; who to disobey, were against all / pro portion of subjection.   (Henry V 1982-94)**

incite the acts or threats of violence and murder. The mind-driven iniquities he addresses are resolved in his plays and poems through a judicious use of words. He disarms the perversion of words that male-based beliefs use to justify violence.

The recovery of natural philosophy after millennia of male-based usurpation has been unstoppable as the world becomes more and more of a global marketplace with fewer places for institutional illogicalities and prejudices to hide. Leading the way from his self-designed residence Monticello, Jefferson not only circumscribes the power of the Churches in the Constitution, he designs Virginia University with its library at the centre instead of the traditional chapel.

The stain-glass windows shining Gothic light on the faithful are meant to be radiating symbols of religious unity. Instead, they quickly become bastions of male-based prejudice. They echo a time when tribal isolation harboured cultural practices unsanctioned by global approbation. Some nations still operate under covenants bunkered by neo-tribal fear.

The relegation of Churches to their own back pews is only the immediate consequence of the revolution in political rights anticipated by Shakespeare and implemented in part following the French and American Revolutions. Gradually, in keeping with Shakespeare's dramatisation of the originary female to male in *F* and *Q* and longer poems, the global dynamic of female/male partnership is moving centre stage.

Shakespeare's women fascinate generations of commentators because no other playwright has females so resolutely in charge. No other artist, except maybe for female artists ignored in the scramble for male-artistic immortality, exacts full accountability for the excesses of male/masculine domination. No one appreciates the philosophy in *Q* to achieve personal content through aligning the forces of nature for a global sensibility.

While Shakespeare's primary focus is on female/male human rights, in two plays he humanises the iniquities of racial prejudice. In *Titus Andronicus*, Aaron the Moor, despite his dubious association with Tamora, argues their part-black son is equal to her other sons. Because Shakespeare bases his understanding in the natural dynamic of female and male with its consequences in increase, then racial and religious prejudices (Aaron is Muslim) favouring male-based dominance have no standing in the Shakespearean theatre.

In *Othello, the Moor of Venice*, Shakespeare creates a Moor who has feelings not unlike any other suitor to Desdemona. Othello is as liable to misjudgement as any man when faced with the determined lies of his best friend. As a Muslim, Othello is beset like Aaron with male-based idealistic expectations. Shakespeare's play cuts to the heart of all prejudice by detailing the fate of a male – and female – who are not reconciled fully to the female/male dynamic in nature.

Shakespeare also predicts an age when the mythic logic of language and art is better understood. The distorting effects of biblical and other myths that prioritise mind over body and male over female are untenable for a global sensibility. Like Duchamp, who shines a headlight into the prevailing darkness of twentieth century art, Shakespeare's vision is removing the clouds of millennial darkness to liberate the practice and understanding of art.

Duchamp is the first artist since Shakespeare to make a series of art works that intentionally sublimate both the female/male and feminine/masculine dynamics into its iconography. Because Duchamp's achievement is not yet understood, then we can appreciate why Shakespeare's more comprehensive understanding is only gradually making itself felt in the global culture.

94: The Wooden O as a Trojan horse

Shakespeare knows the plays he writes for the global stage do no more than re-enact the relationship between humankind and nature. Like Darwin, who extrapolates from artificial selection to theorise about the natural world, and like Duchamp, whose pervasive irony acknowledges the gap between the sexual and the erotic, Shakespeare knew his mythic works are but wooden replicas of the natural world – hence the 'Wooden O'.

Shakespeare reiterates in Q that art can do no more than imitate life. At its most poignant, art reflects the capacity of the mind to evoke deep feelings of connectivity with the whole of life as nature. Shakespeare knows his plays and poetry are but an erotic outcome of the sexual dynamic driving humankind within nature. The cylindrical theatre, populated by the comings and goings of actors and audience, is never more than a staging point in the dynamic of life and love.

The male God is a re-creator dependent on nature and the sexual dynamic for traction. Hence, the religious mind-based feeling called God struggles to make headway against the stream of biological givens. Only by syllogising notions such as first cause, self, or immortality can God-belief command attention.

Shakespeare understands both syndromes and appreciates their hold on the human imagination. When he constructs his Wooden O, he knows the actors within the Globe literarily imbibe and regurgitate his contents wholesale to the mythic-receptive audience. When actors perform Shakespeare's works, the contents entrance the mind's eye because he produces a fair replica of the mind on the stage.

For 400 years, unbeknown to his audience, Shakespeare infiltrates their minds at every outing with his natural philosophy. Moreover, with the reconstruction of the Globe Theatre in London in the late twentieth century, modern enthusiasts re-enact on Shakespeare's behalf the moment of the Trojan horse's entry into the citadel of Priam and sons.

The rebuilding of the Bankside Globe in 1997, near where it pronounced Shakespeare's dramatic message 400 years ago, recalls the Trojan moment. The Greeks, up-anchoring for Ithaca, give the impression their ten-year siege is over. However, stowed within the bowels of the wooden horse are Greek warriors ready to surprise the female-nabbing Trojans.

Similarly, the enthusiastic neo-Trojans of 1997 carry into the re-created Bankside roundhouse the contents of Shakespeare's works. The breach in the stonewall of traditional apologetics, which distorts the intellectual space inside the Globe for centuries, opens the door for Shakespeare's nature-based philosophy.

Hector Paris and Troilus...
If Helen then be wife to Sparta's King
(As it is known she is) these Moral Laws
Of Nature, and of Nation, speak aloud
To have her back returned. Thus to persist
In doing wrong, extenuates not wrong,
But makes it much more heavy. Hector's opinion
Is in this way of truth: yet ne'er the less,
My spritely brethren, I propend to you
In resolution to keep Helen still;
For 'tis a cause that hath no mean dependence,
Upon our joint and several dignities.
      (Troilus and Cressida 1153-83)

Ironically, Shakespeare explores the infiltration of his female-based contents into the soul of male-based conflict in one of his tragedies. *Troilus and Cressida* plays with the implications of infiltration. From behind the Trojan walls, after the duplicity of fighting a prolonged war over a raped hostage, <tro_1153-83> emerges a Cressida willing to escape from Troilus' blighted attitude to women. Puncturing the male-based high-handedness, she gives heart to the Greek camp with her ready wit and feisty temperament.

Shakespeare likewise sends a book of sonnets, a volume of plays and two long poems into the world with wit and liveliness to begin the process of invigorating the cause of natural justice.

Cressida, whom the slow-witted Pandarus pillories as the woman who will bear the curse of womankind, <tro_1818-30> slips in and out of the martial cultures to effect the release of womanhood

Cressida If I be false, or swerve a hair from truth,
When time is old and hath forgot it self:...
From false to false, amongst false Maids in love,
Upbraid my falsehood, when they've said as false,...
Yea, let them say, to stick the heart of falsehood
As false as Cressid.   (Troilus and Cressida 1818-30)

from the mindless wars of male pride and misogyny. That equivocating Hector is the one who dies in Shakespeare's play, rather than Troilus or Cressida, suggests the tragedy resides not in courage on the battlefield but in the.inability of those who have the power and insight to act according to natural justice.

Shakespeare's publication of Q shows he knew how to position his philosophy so his plays retain their currency. He patiently prepares the sonnet set and writes the plays in F to give dramatic voice to his contents. His drama and poetry continues to beguile a world not yet ready for his global foresight.

Chapter 27: Beyond the Wooden O

How can we better prepare our minds to comprehend Shakespeare's philosophy? How can we best look into the works that look back at us looking?

95: Starry navigating

Columbus' inability to calculate his precise latitude when navigating the globe anticipates the difficulties Shakespeare's admirers have when they struggle to orientate themselves to the natural philosophy of the *Sonnets*. Similarly, they experience difficulties aligning the *Folio* of thirty-six European-based plays with the Globe's earthy resonances.

The cognitive shortcomings multiply if Shakespeare's interpreters believe Church steeples point to a heaven light-years higher than the Alps. Such heady expectations lead many to religiously melo-dramatise Shakespeare's global vision. Giuseppe Verdi dumbs down *Othello* and *The Merry Wives of Windsor* into the misnamed *Otello* and *Falstaff*.

When, in 1997, Shakespeare enthusiasts resurrect the Globe Theatre near its original site at South Bank, they assist Shakespeare's interior purpose of reanimating the role of humanity within encompassing nature. Ironically, ignorant of the sonnet philosophy, their enthusiasm is a victory for nature-bound Earth, which Shakespeare's 1599 Globe celebrates.

The analogy between nature and the Globe is instructive. Shakespeare knows the Wooden O is a construct not unlike the constellations of the Zodiac. Overweening belief in either causes conceptual flights of fancy to become unearthed. Rather, nature provides the context within which the artefacts of civilisation come and go.

The common problem Columbus and Shakespeare's idealising and romanticising admirers share is in putting too much faith in navigating by the starry heavens. The Poet advises in *14* against stargazing. Moreover, Shakespeare demonstrates in his plays how to stop fruitful analogy ballooning into outright fantasy.

To measure where Shakespeare's natural philosophy sits in relation to traditional metaphysics, and hence what makes his philosophy opaque to so many, we turn to the Christian poet William Blake. Blake serves our purpose because he glories in star-bound metaphysics at a time when scientific advances are consigning God's heaven ever further away from planet Earth.

Blake captures the contrary mood succinctly with his aphorism: Born in Stars, we live on Earth as Poets. [**note 7**] At first glance, Blake's stars/Earth/poets trajectory seems to accord with natural science. The planet Earth is born from interstellar matter and thence we as poets live on Earth amongst the stars.

However, Blake's claim to be born in stars conflates biology and cosmology. In Blake's starry imagination, he reduces to a literary instant what evolution takes billions of years to accomplish. Blake's unbounded imagination reckons that as poets we are born in the stars with Earth at best an inert catalyst.

Similarly, in male-based Genesis, nature forms the unredeemable backdrop for original sin with the female exposed to a litany of literary abuse. Effectively, such idealising minds side-step Mother Earth to find solace in the starlight of Father-driven hopes.

Other males, or masculine orientated females, regard nature negatively. Carl Jung is apprehensive about dark nature, [note 8] while Camille Paglia talks of 'the untransformed energy of nature, sheer sex and violence' and 'nature's terrible amorality'. [note 9]

Thinkers of a rational disposition respond piquantly to the excommunication of evolutionary Earth. They validate the Earth part of the aphorism by accepting the evidence for human evolution and reject the starry metaphysics of indulgent poetics.

Yet, rationalists over-correct the metaphysicians' snub of planet Earth. Instead of accommodating intuitive poets, the rationalist imagines a gene-driven brain in a gene-determined world. Ironically, many rationalists who ignore the poets have no difficulty believing in an apocalyptic Big Bang. By not accounting for the logic of myth, believers in the Big Bang recapitulate the male-based eroticism of biblical myth.

Unfortunately, these mirror-image religious and scientific scenarios currently define the battlefield in the classrooms and lecture theatres of modern life. They are antagonistic and irreconcilable in their refusal to naturalise each other's blind spots in science and art respectively. Such irreconcilability, though, is anathema to the global village.

A few thinkers disentangle the two prejudices. Darwin dedicates two-thirds of *The Descent of Man and Selection in Relation to Sex* to the erotic. He explores at an elementary level the aesthetics of secondary sexual characteristics.

In his *Tractatus*, Wittgenstein circumscribes metaphysical expression and places it beyond the capacity of scientific language. In his later work, summarised in *Philosophical Investigations*, he moves tentatively toward a natural philosophy embracing a variety of expressive worlds or 'forms of life'. He realises all forms of language are based in the givens of nature and parents.

Duchamp connects the role of mythic poets with an earthy realism and a critique of the metaphysics of stellar flight. Duchamp's configuration of the female/male dynamic in his *Large Glass* rectifies the illogicality of imposing male-based dominance in biblical and other myths.

If biologically the human female is the precursor for male, then why is God male? In Blake's original trajectory from 'Stars', by way of 'Earth', to 'Poets' we see in one sense it accords with evolution. The formation of the male gives the female increased evolutionary potential. However, as the male is an appendage of the female, and no male of any mammalian species is capable of increase without recourse to the female, then the female/male dynamic is the basis for our evolutionary advance.

We turn to Shakespeare, then, for a philosopher/poet who best combines all three aspects of the Blakean aphorism. He successfully navigates the trajectory from 'Poets' to 'Stars' for humans on 'Earth'. When Shakespeare's emenders and reattributers miss his overarching connection of poets, Earth and stars they cut and paste his works to try to make sense of them from belief systems that destroy his global interplay.

96: The chink in the wall

The star-born poets and Earth-born rationalists hit a brick wall when they get too close to Shakespeare's consistency and comprehensiveness. They also struggle with Duchamp's artistic integrity. Both are stymied by their inbred dispositions. Because they favour one or other of the truncated trajectories they cannot see how Shakespeare provides a way through to a seamless poets/Earth/stars interrelationship.

The 154 sonnets present an impenetrable wall to distracted minds, or worse an inviting surface with impenetrable depths. Yet, throughout Shakespeare's 154 sonnets, thirty-six plays and four poems, he provides hundreds of eyes through which to view his picture of humanity – as 24 celebrates.

Symptomatic of the blindness is the sonnet emenders' inability to hear Shakespeare give voice to his mind's eye. They change the plural their to the singular thy a number of times where the their is plural because it refers to both eyes.

To get a twentieth century analogy we need only turn to Duchamp. He watches as admirers misrepresent his achievement. After thirty years of incomprehension by even his closest friends and colleagues, Duchamp creates a major work in secret. From 1946 to 1966, he assembles the components for a room-sized diorama Etant donnes, which is unveiled only after his death in 1968.

At the Philadelphia Art Gallery, Duchamp's diorama is behind a wooden door with two eye-level peepholes. Visible through the peepholes is a jagged hole in a brick wall. Beyond the hole is a recumbent nude female form made of pig's skin. She is lying legs apart with her sex toward the viewer on a bed of twigs with her head concealed. In her raised left hand she holds a gas lamp against a naturalistic backdrop of waterfall, trees and sky. The whole effect is lit artificially.

In Etant donnes, Duchamp gives expression to the same mythic content he presents in the earlier Large Glass. However, after thirty years of misunderstanding, he constructs a final work of realism within an enclosed room to present the viewer with a metaphor for both understanding and misunderstanding. Duchamp simultaneously mimics the inability to penetrate the brick wall by believers and sceptics, and creates an entry point for those willing to move beyond either theism or atheism.

By eyeing the peepholes in the rustic wooden door, viewers look into a reconstruction of their mythic minds. The dead and buried Duchamp returns the viewer's gaze by looking directly into their eyes through his artifice Etant donnes. Duchamp enables the viewer to make the conceptual effort to penetrate the wall of their incomprehension.

Shakespeare's experience is similar when he publishes Q to barely a mention in the literature of the day. His more popular plays are hits because he writes them as vehicles to disseminate his philosophy.

In *A Midsummer Night's Dream*, Shakespeare provides a mocking instance of a wall with a crannied hole through which lovers see each other eye to eye. However, Shakespeare's mechanicals, who merely spy each other without seeing into their own minds, mock the audience who cannot see themselves in Shakespeare's looking at them.

97: Global architecture

In Shakespeare's plays, and reputedly over the door of the Globe Theatre, there are reminders of the double relationship between Hercules' head and body and the globe he supports as a duplicate head. Moreover, as we have seen, Hercules shows how to escape adroitly from the burdensome load or conceit that weighs Atlas down.

The templates we generate earlier for the erotic shape of the sonnets and the relationship of female/feminine comedies and male/masculine histories and tragedies, both reveal a tension between the circular shape of the female dynamic and the rectangular shape of the male dynamic.

When Hercules briefly relieves Atlas of the globe, he demonstrates how to reconcile the female and male dynamic to recover his natural philosophy. Through the Hercules' metaphor, Shakespeare seems to celebrate the eroticism of the Wooden O's feminine compass and the male projection of the Globe's jutting stage.

We can form a template to represent the drama enacted between Atlas and Hercules. <diagram_atlasherculestemplate> Shakespeare seems to be saying that only those who appreciate the trickery Hercules employs against Atlas can leave the globe contented – as 72 promises. Atlas' stolid acceptance of the female as a burden, except for the brief moment when he travels West to see his daughters, persists today in the scant recognition of the female as precursor.

Hercules performs his labours to mature his understanding of nature and reconcile himself to the female. Put to his labours by the Goddess Hera for murdering his own children, Hercules (Heracles or Hera-famed in the Greek) solves the problem of female/male dysfunction through hard-earned realisations.

The Hercules' template il-lustrates the engagement between female and male, that resolves the

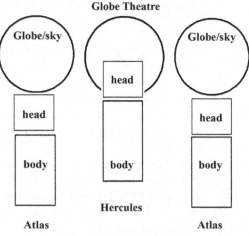

Atlas & Hercules template

standoff between male and female Shakespeare highlights in the *Q* and *F* templates. **<diagram_herculestemplate>**

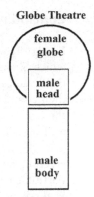

Globe Theatre

female globe

male head

male body

Hercules

Hercules template

Unlike Shakespeare, modern Atlases do not question the structural inequality at the heart of religious, political and social injustices. The implication is that only those alert to the natural dynamic of female to male escape the illusion of female oppression to recover their natural partnership of feminine and masculine personae in nature.

Whether in his 154-sonnet set, his *Folio* of plays, his four longer poems or on stage at the Globe Theatre, Shakespeare reiterates the logic of the sexual dynamic in nature as constitutional of human language and art.

Everywhere throughout Shakespeare's works and working environment there are clues and reminders of the means to access the philosophy within us. Only our language-based conventions keep us from viewing the givens that power our seeing.

Concluding the realignment at the Globe

In Part 1, we survey the *Sonnets* of 1609 to discover a highly structured set in which Shakespeare presents his philosophy of love and life. Then in Part 2, using the findings of Part 1, we reveal considerable coherence between the main sonnet themes and the major themes in the plays and poems. The quality and quantity of the crossover is such that the balance of judgment favours a sonnet-based source for the philosophy behind all the plays and poems.

Now, in Part 3, we speculate on Shakespeare's involvement in the transport, erection and renaming of the original Theatre as the Globe at South Bank. Fortuitous or not, the shift from The Theatre to the Globe Theatre corresponds to Shakespeare's nature-based philosophy.

It is hard to avoid the conclusion Shakespeare intends an unbroken connection between the generic sonnets in Q, his European continent of poems and plays and the Globe playhouse. The 154-sonnet set in Q has logical correspondences with the thirty-six plays in F and the four long poems from 1593 to 1609 and the Globe of 1599.

Shakespeare, who adapts to his advantage scripts from other writers, appears alert to any circumstance to broadcast his nature-based philosophy with its critique of male-based prejudice. He uses cryptic numerology in the *Sonnets*, toys with drop-down and pop-up imaginary goddesses and gods in the plays, and rides the symbolism of Hercules and his shouldered globe. Shakespeare appropriates such devices either outright if they echo his nature-based content, or with devastating irony if they are associated with theocratic/monarchic injustices.

Shakespeare's mature expression goes public at the Globe. It is the symbolic staging point for his nature-based philosophy. Shakespeare's plays when staged at the Globe carry an extra charge of subtle by-play not available when produced in an outdoor amphitheatre or other natural settings.

The consistent and comprehensive nature-based philosophy in the *Sonnets* anticipates the more circumscribed deliberations of Darwin, Wittgenstein and Duchamp. Shakespeare is a contemporary of Galileo at a time when the globe is set free from Ptolemaic geocentricity. He is a precursor to Jefferson who institutes the social revolution in human rights that is secular democracy.

These thinkers and others attempt to formulate an understanding for an increasingly global sensibility. It is Shakespeare, though, who provides the most coherent philosophy for the global demographic.

Moreover, Shakespeare appreciates that mature human love revels in the full trajectory from nature to the most deliberate constructs of the human mind. The Globe brings together the dramatic conditions for a memorable catharsis, both intellectual and emotional.

By bringing his nature-based plays onto the world stage at the Globe, and by aligning the trajectory of his poems and sonnets with the same care, Shakespeare's audience is caught in the healing catharsis of their invisible attractivity.

For our part, Shakespeare presents the evidence and lets us draw conclusions as we need for our global sensibility. For Shakespeare's part, by getting it right at the Globe, he gets it right for the planet.

Chapter 28: Mr. Shakespeare...

Is the evidence in Parts 1 to 3 sufficient to demonstrate Shakespeare organises his sonnets to articulate a nature-based philosophy as the philosophy behind all his plays and poems for a global constituency? Has justice been done to Shakespeare's works while accounting for both his intellectual and emotional artistry?

98: Reviewing the conclusions from Parts 1 to 3

We began assessing the evidence for a substantive philosophy in Shakespeare's works by examining the organisation of the 154 sonnets. Then we noted the correspondences between the sonnets and the plays and longer poems. We concluded by musing on the significance of the Globe Theatre.

To recap, in Part 1 we investigate the 1609 edition of *Shake-speares Sonnets* with its 154-sonnet set and companion *A Lover's Complaint*. We discover a degree of intentionality that makes it hard to deny they contain a philosophy of unprecedented intellectual integrity and emotional maturity. Shakespeare's sonnet set is different from every other comparable sequence. It contains major structural features with numerous subsidiary elements. Its uniqueness and coherence lead us to say Shakespeare publishes Q in 1609 to present his nature-based philosophy.

From the 154-sonnet set, we turn in Part 2 to the thirty-six plays in the *Folio* of 1623. Armed with the evidence of a systematic philosophy in Q, it is not difficult to show the plays make most sense when viewed in the light of the sonnet philosophy. The correspondences between the plays and longer poems and the organisation of the plays in F echo the nature/female/male dynamic of Q with its implications for increase, poetry, argument and love. In short, it seems all or most of the problems associated traditionally with Shakespeare's plays dissolve with the application of the sonnet logic.

Consequently, we no longer give top billing to the great tragedies. Instead, we accept the comedies as the primary vehicles for his philosophy. This contrasts with commentators who consign the comedies (and histories) to minor roles and mine the sonnets fruitlessly for biographical or historical data.

Having advanced from the generic sonnets to a European theatre of plays, we then examine their connection to the Globe playhouse. If Shakespeare is conscious of the connection between the Bankside Globe and the world at large, it is difficult to avoid the conclusion the 154 sonnets and thirty-six plays and four longer poems are written with global implications in mind.

How aware, then, is Shakespeare of the unique and all-embracing philosophy we unearth from his works. How conscious is he of the sonnet philosophy as he writes the plays? Did he think of the sonnet set as a satellite to the extensive European continent of plays and outlying poems? How aware is he of the plays' global significance as he writes of European life, loves and times?

As we follow Shakespeare, we highlight the deliberate argument apparent in the organisation of the 154 sonnets, in the arrangement of the plays and in the syllogistic passages issuing from the mouths of canny characters. Although, in Part 1, we experiment with the process of induction, and then, in Part 2, take advantage of the logic of deduction until, in Part 3, we resort to analogy, these argumentative techniques are nothing compared to the overarching philosophy on which Shakespeare bases his works.

Shakespeare's philosophy is comprehensive in that it takes account of the complete dynamic all the way from nature to ideals generated in the mind. It is also logically consistent in that he places every component in the complete dynamic correctly to build a flawless picture of human life and love within nature.

It is difficult to avoid the conclusion Shakespeare's plays and poems have such integrity because he bases his philosophy in nature. Consequently, when we read the plays or see them performed on stage we are the beneficiaries of the natural dynamic he grounds in the comedies and then takes to its logical edge in the human strivings and excesses played out in the histories and tragedies.

Crucial to Shakespeare's consistency of characterisation and dramatics is his regard for the natural originary status of female to male. The arrangement of the 154 sonnets, the ordering of the thirty-six plays, the thematics of the four long poems and the shape of the Globe Theatre all configure the relationship of female to male essential for logical and emotional depth. Because Shakespeare respects the natural dynamic of human female and male, he is not susceptible to the illogicality of instituting a male God over all else.

Shakespeare's works bear witness to the simplicity and depth of his clarity about sensations and language. This is only possible because he adheres to natural philosophy. By respecting the logical distinction between incoming sensations (beauty), language (truth) and internal sensations (beauty), his works provide a coherent expression of human understanding and emotions.

We have seen how Wittgenstein eventually realises nature and parents provide the unmediated givens basic to all language games. By recognising the connection between nature as the overall dynamic of life and language games as forms of life within nature, Wittgenstein identifies the logical grounds for all human intelligence.

When we hear Shakespeare grounding his sonnets in nature for a sound philosophy, we can see why he identifies the givens more precisely and more exhaustively than does Wittgenstein. Shakespeare shows us how to move effortlessly from the vastness of nature to the inner resources of mind.

From the start, Shakespeare recognises nature as the basic given behind all the conventions of language. Nature has a resiliency that half-life imaginary goddesses and gods do not share. Rather than talk just of parents, Shakespeare recognises the female is the originary entity for the male. He avoids the inconsistencies in prioritising a male God. Then he acknowledges the logic of increase.

By accepting nature, with its sexual dynamic and requirement for increase, Shakespeare is able to account logically for human sensory, cognitive and intuitive activity. He first recognises that sensory input enters awareness unmediated by thought and undimmed by language. Next, the swearing and forswearing of language builds on the vocalisation of incoming sensations. Finally, for a complete understanding of the human sensibility, are the sensations arising from within the mind. They arise unbidden from sublimated thoughts – or from words and images created in poetry or art.

The givens all the way from nature to the sensations the mind generates internally constitute the natural logic of Shakespeare's philosophy. Respecting the givens enables Shakespeare to act and write with consistency and inventiveness free of cant or hyperbole. From the sonnets to the plays and poems and on to the Globe, we hear a maturity in thought and love because his basic philosophy is sound.

Why, then, do some compare Shakespeare's works to the Bible? As we have seen, his philosophy has all the elements of mythic expression, including the logical relationship of the sexual and the erotic. However, his nature-based philosophy allows his mythic expression to be more profound than that of the Bible. Furthermore, his refusal to nourish false hopes means his works are not subject to religious veneration.

We have uncovered a coherent philosophy with no precedent. Shakespeare's philosophy is more comprehensive than the tentative forays into the same territory by modern thinkers such as Darwin, Wittgenstein and Duchamp. The flow on effects of its explanatory power for modern philosophical issues around the status of nature and mind has only been touched on in these pages. How, then, can we better understand Shakespeare's philosophy of human life and love?

99: Impenetrable and unfathomable

Can we begin to explain the absence from the literature on Shakespeare of these insights into the philosophy of his sonnets, plays and poems? What does it mean to bring together the work of Darwin, Duchamp and Wittgenstein to understand Shakespeare and move beyond the remaining vestiges of male dominance of the last 4000 years?

Unfortunately, Tertiary, which is responsible for upholding the old beliefs, now focuses largely on vocational learning. It is no longer capable of providing an all-encompassing basis for understanding.

The evidence shows the inadequate Tertiary paradigm afflicts most approaches to Shakespeare's works. Under the guise of scholarship, textual analysis over the last few decades justifies 300 years of unnecessary emendations and reattributions to the sonnets and plays. Academics disguise their ignorance of Shakespeare's contents when they alter words and reallocate plays. They reveal their lack of insight when they attribute Shakespeare's plays to his contemporaries, none of whom is capable of formulating a sound philosophy.

We have drawn a comparison between the reception history of Shakespeare's works and those of Marcel Duchamp. Symptomatic of the difficulty is the dismissal of Duchamp's *readymades* as throwaway jokes. [note 10] Most commentators have little idea of the significance of the *Large Glass*, so misunderstand the role of the *readymades*.

If, in two hundred years time, commentators are still unable to understand

Duchamp's *Large Glass* and other works, a textual academic of the day would begin to attribute portions to various artists of the period. They would assign the cubist imagery to Picasso, the mechanical imagery to Picabia, the puns to Jarry, an image of breasts to Delvaux, etc.

However, such a reattribution process ignores the evidence that Duchamp intentionally incorporates the styles of other artists into his overarching content. He does so both to assert his critical overview of other art styles and as part of his achievement of laying down the logical conditions for any mythic expression – in his *Large Glass* and *Etant donnes*.

Shakespeare, like Duchamp but at a much deeper level, both critiques other authors and lays out the logical conditions for any mythic expression in his *Sonnets* as the basis for all of his poems and plays. There is, then, no need for the depredations of emendation and reattribution. Whatever indications academics find for other authors in Shakespeare's works, they are far more likely evidence of his inclusiveness rather than one to one collaboration with his contemporaries.

The thirty-six plays in *F* make perfect sense once the philosophy Shakespeare embeds in *Q* is understood. As with a full understanding of Duchamp, there is no need to separate out acceptable parts from those considered offensive and search for a rationale to enjoy or dismiss them.

On offer is an unprecedented opportunity to understand how artists as unique as Shakespeare and Duchamp think and feel. It should then be possible to curtail the unfortunate experiments of academics and initiate an advanced level of Quaternary learning and investigation.

100: Intelligent loving and loving intelligence

The expression of Shakespearean love in his philosophical sonnets is both deeply profound and fully representative of human experience in nature – including the ideals generated in the mind. Little wonder, then, if Shakespeare publishes the 154 sonnets to present the philosophy behind all his poems and plays, his dramatic works exercise such a deep but barely understood hold both on everyday thought and on the profoundest imaginings of the human mind.

Lytton Strachey predicts in 1905 that 'for its solution (the mystery of the *Sonnets*) seem to offer hopes of a prize of extraordinary value – nothing less than a true insight into the most secret recesses of the thoughts and feelings of perhaps the greatest man who ever lived'. **[note 11]** This brief volume shows Shakespeare did reveal his profoundest thoughts in his 154 sonnets. Better than that, on the wealth of evidence presented here, Shakespeare manages to convey his deepest emotions and, because of the universality of his nature-based philosophy, they are the mature emotions basic to continued human well-being.

This book points the way to the prospect of entertaining a combination of Shakespeare's thoughts and feelings for the first time in 400 years. When we download and embed in thought and action the sonnet philosophy of 1609 – along with a mature experience of love – Shakespeare's sonnets dissolve to reveal the living contents of his ideas and emotions.

At this moment of increased global awareness, many are turning to Shakespeare's works with the expectation they offer, as Strachey intimates 100 years ago, a 'prize of extraordinary value' – the deepest of human 'thoughts and feelings'. Understanding Shakespeare's common sense philosophy is the key to accessing a mature experience of love brought to life by a poet, dramatist and philosopher with profound global insight.

Shakespeare's publication of his philosophy in the 154 sonnets of 1609 benefits from years of refining their contents in his plays and poems in the context of the Globe. Every play and poem Shakespeare writes enriches our appreciation of our inherent philosophy.

101: Room for doubt

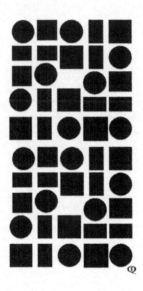

Notes

Part 1:

Note 1:   Alistair Fowler, *Triumphal Forms, Structural Patterns in Elizabethan Poetry*, Cambridge, CUP, 1970.

Note 2:   T. S. Eliot, Introduction, G Wilson Knight, *The Wheel of Fire*, London, Methuen, 1965.

Part 2:

Note 1:   Germaine Greer, *Shakespeare's Wife*, London, Bloomsbury, 2007

Note 2:   Harold Bloom, *The Invention of the Human*, London, Fourth Estate, 1999

Note 3:   www.rscshakespeare.co.uk, *RSC Blog*, June 13, 2008

Note 4:   Harold Bloom, op cit.

Note 5:   Louis Zukofsky, *Bottom: On Shakespeare*, Austin, Texas, Ark Press, 1963

Note 6:   Caroline Spurgeon, *Shakespeare's Imagery*, Cambridge University Press, 1971.

Note 7:   Ted Hughes, *Shakespeare and the Goddess of Complete Being*, Faber and Faber, 1991.

Note 8:   Samuel Johnson, *The Lives of the Poets*, P531

Part 3:

Note 1:   Riane Eisler, *The Chalice and the Blade*, San Francisco, Harper Row, 1987; Riane Eisler, *Sacred Pleasure, Spirituality and the Politics of the Body*, Harper San Francisco, 1996

Note 2:   David Loye, *Darwin's Lost Theory of Love*, Lincoln, toExcel, 2000.

Note 3:   Octavio Paz, *Marcel Duchamp or The Castle of Purity*, Trans. Donald Gardner, London, Cape Goliard, 1970

Note 4:   Germaine Greer, *Shakespeare*, Oxford, Oxford University Press, 1886

Note 5:   David Loye, *Darwin's Lost Theory of Love*, Lincoln, toExcel, 2000.

Note 6:   Ted Hughes, *Shakespeare and the Goddess of Complete Being,* London, Faber &Faber, 1992

Note 7:   Quote from: Ecke Bonk, *Monte Carlo Method*, Vienna, Schirmer/Mosel, 2007.

Note 8:   Carl Jung, *Man and His Symbols*, London, Anchor, 1964.

Note 9:   Camille Paglia, *Sexual Personae: Art and Decadence from Nefertiti to Emily Dickinson*, London, Penguin, 1991.

Note 10:   Denis Dutton, *The Art Instinct*, Oxford, Oxford University Press, 2009

Note 11:   From: Peter Jones, *Shakespeare Casebook,* London, Macmillan, 1977.

Facsimile of the 1609 Sonnets

SHAKE-SPEARES

SONNETS

Neuer before Imprinted.

———————————————————

———————————————————

AT LONDON
By *G. Eld* for *T. T.* and are
to be folde by *William Aſpley.*
1609.

TO.THE.ONLIE.BEGETTER.OF.
THESE.INSVING.SONNETS.
M^r.W.H. ALL.HAPPINESSE.
AND.THAT.ETERNITIE.
PROMISED.

BY.

OVR.EVER-LIVING.POET.

WISHETH.

THE.WELL-WISHING.
ADVENTVRER.IN.
SETTING.
FORTH.

T.T.

SHAKE-SPEARES,
SONNETS.

FRom faireſt creatures we deſire increaſe,
  That thereby beauties *Roſe* might neuer die,
But as the riper ſhould by time deceaſe,
His tender heire might beare his memory:
But thou contracted to thine owne bright eyes,
Feed'ſt thy lights flame with ſelfe ſubſtantiall ſewell,
Making a famine where aboundance lies,
Thy ſelfe thy foe,to thy ſweet ſelfe too cruell:
Thou that art now the worlds freſh ornament,
And only herauld to the gaudy ſpring,
Within thine owne bud burieſt thy content,
And tender chorle makſt waſt in niggarding:
    Pitty the world,or elſe this glutton be,
    To eate the worlds due,by the graue and thee.

2

VVHen fortie Winters ſhall beſeige thy brow,
  And digge deep trenches in thy beauties field,
Thy youthes proud liuery ſo gaz'd on now,
Wil be a totter'd weed of ſmal worth held:
Then being askt,where all thy beautie lies,
Where all the treaſure of thy luſty daies;
To ſay within thine owne deepe ſunken eyes,
Were an all-eating ſhame,and thriftleſſe praiſe.
How much more praiſe deſeru'd thy beauties vſe,
If thou couldſt anſwere this faire child of mine
Shall ſum my count,and make my old excuſe
Proouing his beautie by ſucceſſion thine.

B   This

SHAKE-SPEARES

This were to be new made when thou art ould,
And see thy blood warme when thou feel'st it could,

3

LOoke in thy glasse and tell the face thou vewest,
Now is the time that face should forme an other,
Whose fresh repaire if now thou not renewest,
Thou doo'st beguile the world, vnblesse some mother.
For where is she so faire whose vn-eard wombe
Disdaines the tillage of thy husbandry?
Or who is he so fond will be the tombe,
Of his selfe loue to stop posterity?
Thou art thy mothers glasse and she in thee
Calls backe the louely Aprill of her prime,
So thou through windowes of thine age shalt see,
Dispight of wrinkles this thy goulden time.
  But if thou liue remembred not to be,
  Die single and thine Image dies with thee.

4

VNthrifty louelinesse why dost thou spend,
Vpon thy selfe thy beauties legacy?
Natures bequest giues nothing but doth lend,
And being franck she lends to those are free:
Then beautious nigard why doost thou abuse,
The bountious largesse giuen thee to giue?
Profitles vserer why doost thou vse
So great a summe of summes yet can'st not liue?
For hauing traffike with thy selfe alone,
Thou of thy selfe thy sweet selfe dost deceaue,
Then how when nature calls thee to be gone,
What acceptable *Audit* can'st thou leaue?
  Thy vnus'd beauty must be tomb'd with thee,
  Which vsed liues th'executor to be.

5

THose howers that with gentle worke did frame,
The louely gaze where euery eye doth dwell
Will play the tirants to the very same,

                                          And

SONNETS.

And that vnfaire which fairely doth excell:
For neuer resting time leads Summer on,
To hidious winter and confounds him there,
Sap checkt with frost and lustie leau's quite gon.
Beauty ore-snow'd and barenes euery where,
Then were not summers distillation left
A liquid prisoner pent in walls of glasse,
Beauties effect with beauty were bereft,
Nor it nor noe remembrance what it was.
   But flowers distil'd though they with winter meete,
   Leese but their show,their substance still liues sweet.

6

THen let not winters wragged hand deface,
  In thee thy summer ere thou be distil'd:
Make sweet some viall;treasure thou some place,
With beautits treasure ere it be selfe kil'd:
That vse is not forbidden vsery,
Which happies those that pay the willing lone;
That's for thy selfe to breed an other thee,
Or ten times happier be it ten for one,
Ten times thy selfe were happier then thou art,
If ten of thine ten times refigur'd thee,
Then what could death doe if thou should'st depart,
Leauing thee liuing in posterity?
   Be not selfe-wild for thou art much too faire,
   To be deaths conquest and make wormes thine heire.

7

LOe in the Orient when the gracious light,
  Lifts vp his burning head,each vnder eye
Doth homage to his new appearing sight,
Seruing with lookes his sacred maiesty,
And hauing climb'd the steepe vp heauenly hill,
Resembling strong youth in his middle age,
Yet mortall lookes adore his beauty still,
Attending on his goulden pilgrimage:
But when from high-most pich with wery car,

         B 2   Like

SHAKE-SPEARES

Like feeble age he reeleth from the day,
The eyes(fore dutious)now conuerted are
From his low tract and looke an other way:
    So thou,thy selfe out-going in thy noon:
    Vnlok'd on diest vnlesse thou get a sonne.

8

MVsick to heare,why hear'st thou musick sadly,
Sweets with sweets warre not , ioy delights in ioy:
Why lou'st thou that which thou receaust not gladly,
Or else receau'st with pleasure thine annoy ?
If the true concord of well tuned sounds,
By vnions married do offend thine eare,
They do but sweetly chide thee, who confounds
In singlenesse the parts that thou should'st beare:
Marke how one string sweet husband to an other,
Strikes each in each by mutuall ordering;
Resembling fier,and child, and happy mother,
Who all in one,one pleasing note do sing:
    Whose speechlesse song being many,seeming one,
    Sings this to thee thou single wilt proue none.

9.

IS it for feare to wet a widdowes eye,
That thou consum'st thy selfe in single life?
Ah;if thou issulesse shalt hap to die,
The world will waile thee like a makelesse wife,
The world wilbe thy widdow and still weepe,
That thou no forme of thee hast left behind,
When euery priuat widdow well may keepe,
By childrens eyes,her husbands shape in minde:
Looke what an vnthrift in the world doth spend
Shifts but his place,for still the world inioyes it
But beauties waste; hath in the world an end,
And kept vnvsde the vser so destroyes it:
    No loue toward others in that bosome sits
    That on himselfe such murdrous shame commits.

10.

SONNETS.

10

FOr shame deny that thou bear'ft loue to any
Who for thy felfe art fo vnprouident
Graunt if thou wilt,thou art belou'd of many,
But that thou none lou ft is moft euident:
For thou art fo poffeft with murdrous hate,
That gainft thy felfe thou ftickft not to confpire,
Seeking that beautious roofe to ruinate
Which to repaire fhould be thy chiefe defire :
O change thy thought,that I may change my minde,
Shall hate be fairer log'd then gentle loue?
Be as thy prefence is gracious and kind,
Or to thy felfe at leaft kind harted proue,
    Make thee an other felfe for loue of me,
    That beauty ftill may liue in thine or thee.

11

AS faft as thou fhalt wane fo faft thou grow'ft,
In one of thine,from that which thou departeft,
And that frefh bloud which yongly thou beftow'ft,
Thou maift call thine,when thou from youth conuerteft,
Herein liues wifdome,beauty,and increafe,
Without this follie,age,and could decay,
If all were minded fo,the times fhould ceafe,
And threefcoore yeare would make the world away:
Let thofe whom nature hath not made for ftore,
Harfh,featurelefle,and rude , barrenly perrifh,
Looke whom flie beft indow'd,fhe gaue the more;
Which bountious guift thou fhouldft in bounty cherrifh,
    She caru'd thee for her feale,and ment therby,
    Thou fhouldft print more,not let that coppy die.

12

VVHen I doe count the clock that tels the time,
And fee the braue day funck in hidious night,
When I behold the violet paft prime,
And fable curls or filuer'd ore with white :
When lofty trees I fee barren of leaues,
Which erft from heat did canopie the herd

B 3   And

SHAKE-SPEARES

And Sommers greene all girded vp in sheaues
Borne on the beare with white and bristly beard:
Then of thy beauty do I question make
That thou among the wastes of time must goe,
Since sweets and beauties do them-selues forsake,
  And die as fast as they see others grow,
    And nothing gainst Times sieth can make defence
    Saue breed to braue him,when he takes thee hence.

13

O That you were your selfe,but loue you are
  No longer yours,then you your selfe here liue,
Against this cumming end you should prepare,
And your sweet semblance to some other giue.
So should that beauty which you hold in lease
Find no determination,then you were
You selfe again after your selfes decease,
When your sweet issue your sweet forme should beare.
Who lets so faire a house fall to decay,
Which husbandry in honour might vphold,
Against the stormy gusts of winters day
And barren rage of deaths eternall cold?
  O none but vnthrifts,deare my loue you know,
  You had a Father,let your Son say so.

14

NOt fro n the stars do I my iudgement plucke,
  And yet me thinkes I haue Astronomy,
But not to tell of good,or euil lucke,
Of plagues,of dearths,or seasons quallity
Nor can I fortune to breefe mynuits tell;
Pointing to each his thunder, raine and winde,
Or say with Princes if it shal go wel
By oft predict that I in heauen finde,
But from thine eies my knowledge I deriue,
And constant stars in them I read such art
As truth and beautie shal together thriue
If from thy selfe,to store thou wouldst conuert:

                                          Or

SONNETS.

Or elfe of thee this I prognofticate,
Thy end is Truthes and Beauties doome and date.

15

WHen I confider euery thing that growes
　Holds in perfection but a little moment.
That this huge ftage prefenteth nought but fhowes
Whereon the Stars in fecret influence comment.
When I perceiue that men as plants increafe,
Cheared and checkt euen by the felfe-fame skie:
Vaunt in their youthfull fap, at height decreafe,
And were their braue ftate out of memory.
Then the conceit of this inconftant ftay,
Sets you moft rich in youth before my fight,
Where waftfull time debateth with decay
To change your day of youth to fullied night,
　And all in war with Time for loue of you
　As he takes from you, I ingraft you new.

16

BVt wherefore do not you a mightier waie
　Make warre vppon this bloudie tirant time?
And fortifie your felfe in your decay
With meanes more bleffed then my barren rime?
Now ftand you on the top of happie houres,
And many maiden gardens yet vnfet,
With vertuous wifh would beare your liuing flowers,
Much liker then your painted counterfeit:
So fhould the lines of life that life repaire
Which this (Times penfel or my pupill pen)
Neither in inward worth nor outward faire
Can make you liue your felfe in eies of men,
　To giue away your felfe, keeps your felfe ftill,
　And you muft liue drawne by your owne fweet skill,

17

VVHo will beleeue my verfe in time to come
　If it were fild with your moft high deferts?

B 4　　　　　　　Though

SHAKE-SPEARES

Though yet heauen knowes it is but as a tombe
Which hides your life , and shewes not halfe your parts:
If I could write the beauty of your eyes,
And in fresh numbers number all your graces,
The age to come would say this Poet lies,
Such heauenly touches nere toucht earthly faces.
So should my papers (yellowed with their age)
Be scorn'd,like old men of lesse truth then tongue,
And your true rights be termd a Poets rage,
And stretched miter of an Antique song.
    But were some childe of yours aliue that time,
    You should liue twise in it,and in my rime.

18.

SHall I compare thee to a Summers day?
Thou art more louely and more temperate:
Rough windes do shake the darling buds of Maie,
And Sommers leafe hath all too short a date:
Sometime too hot the eye of heauen shines,
And often is his gold complexion dimm'd,
And euery faire from faire some-time declines,
By chance,or natures changing course vntrim'd:
But thy eternall Sommer shall not fade,
Nor loose possession of that faire thou ow'st,
Nor shall death brag thou wandr'st in his shade,
When in eternall lines to time thou grow'st,
    So long as men can breath or eyes can see,
    So long liues this,and this giues life to thee,

19

DEuouring time blunt thou the Lyons pawes,
And make the earth deuoure her owne sweet brood,
Plucke the keene teeth from the fierce Tygers yawes,
And burne the long liu'd Phænix in her blood,
Make glad and sorry seasons as thou fleet'st,
And do what ere thou wilt swift-footed time
To the wide world and all her fading sweets:
But I forbid thee one most hainous crime,

O

SONNETS.

O carue not with thy howers my loues faire brow,
Nor draw noe lines there with thine antique pen,
Him in thy courfe vntainted doe allow,
For beauties patterne to fucceding men.
 Yet doe thy worft ould Time difpight thy wrong,
 My loue fhall in my verfe euer liue young.

20

A Womans face with natures owne hand painted,
 Hafte thou the Mafter Miftris of my paffion,
A womans gentle hart but not acquainted
With fhifting change as is falfe womens fafhion,
An eye more bright then theirs,leffe falfe in rowling:
Gilding the obiect where-vpon it gazeth,
A man in hew all *Hews* in his controwling,
Which fteales mens eyes and womens foules amafeth.
And for a woman wert thou firft created,
Till nature as fhe wrought thee fell a dotinge,
And by addition me of thee defeated,
By adding one thing to my purpofe nothing.
 But fince fhe prickt thee out for womens pleafure,
 Mine be thy loue and thy loues vfe their treafure.

21

SO is it not with me as with that Mufe,
 Stird by a painted beauty to his verfe,
Who heauen it felfe for ornament doth vfe,
And euery faire with his faire doth reherfe,
Making a coopelment of proud compare
With Sunne and Moone,with earth and feas rich gems:
With Aprills firft borne flowers and all things rare,
That heauens ayre in this huge rondure hems,
O let me true in loue but truly write,
And then beleeue me,my loue is as faire,
As any mothers childe,though not fo bright
As thofe gould candells fixt in heauens ayer.
 Let them fay more that like of heare-fay well,
 I will not prayfe that purpofe not to fell.
    C

SHAKE-SPEARES

22

MY glasse shall not perswade me I am ould,
So long as youth and thou are of one date,
But when in thee times forrwes I behould,
Then look I death my daies should expiate.
For all that beauty that doth couer thee,
Is but the seemely rayment of my heart,
Which in thy brest doth liue,as thine in me,
How can I then be elder then thou art?
O therefore loue be of thy selfe so wary,
As I not for my selfe,but for thee will,
Bearing thy heart which I will keepe so chary
As tender nurse her babe from faring ill,
    Presume not on thy heart when mine is slaine,
    Thou gau'st me thine not to giue backe againe.

23

AS an vnperfect actor on the stage,
Who with his feare is put besides his part,
Or some fierce thing repleat with too much rage,
Whose strengths abondance weakens his owne heart;
So I for feare of truft,forget to say,
The perfect ceremony of loues right,
And in mine owne loues strength seeme to decay,
Ore-charg'd with burthen of mine owne loues might:
O let my books be then the eloquence,
And domb presagers of my speaking brest,
Who pleade for loue,and look for recompence,
More then that tonge that more hath more exprest.
    O learne to read what silent loue hath writ,
    To heare wit eies belongs to loues fine wiht.

24

MIne eye hath play'd the painter and hath steeld,
thy beauties forme in table of my heart,
My body is the frame wherein ti's held,
And perspectiue it is best Painters art.
For through the Painter must you see his skill,

To

SONNETS.

To finde where your true Image pictur'd lies,
Which in my bosomes shop is hanging stil,
That hath his windowes glazed with thine eves:
Now see what good-turnes eyes for eies haue done,
Mine eyes haue drawne thy shape,and thine for me
Are windowes to my brest, where-through the Sun
Delights to peepe,to gaze therein on thee
   Yet eyes this cunning want to grace their art
   They draw but what they see,know not the hart.

25

Let those who are in fauor with their stars,
Of publike honour and proud titles bost,
Whilst I whome fortune of such tryumph bars
Vnlookt for ioy in that I honour most;
Great Princes fauorites their faire leaues spread,
But as the Marygold at the suns eye,
And in them-selues their pride lies buried,
For at a frowne they in their glory die.
The painefull warrier famosed for worth,
After a thousand victories once foild,
Is from the booke of honour rased quite,
And all the rest forgot for which he toild:
   Then happy I that loue and am beloued
   Where I may not remoue nor be remoued.

26

Lord of my loue,to whome in vassalage
Thy merrit hath my dutie strongly knit;
To thee I send this written ambassage
To witnesse duty, not to shew my wit.
Duty so great,which wit so poore as mine
May make seeme bare,in wanting words to shew it;
But that I hope some good conceipt of thine
In thy soules thought(all naked) will bestow it:
Til whatsoeuer star that guides my mouing,
Points on me gratiously with faire aspect,
And puts apparrell on my tottered louing,

C 2   To

SHAKE-SPEARES,

To fhow me worthy of their fweet refpect,
   Then may I dare to boaft how I doe loue thee,
   Til then,not fhow my head where thou maift proue me

27

WEary with toyle,I haft me to my bed,
   The deare repofe for lims with trauaill tired,
But then begins a iourny in my head
To worke my mind,when boddies work's expired.
For then my thoughts(from far where I abide)
Intend a zelous pilgrimage to thee,
And keepe my drooping eye-lids open wide,
Looking on darknes which the blind doe fee.
Saue that my foules imaginary fight
Prefents their fhaddoe to my fightles view,
Which like a iewell(hunge in gaftly night)
Makes blacke night beautious,and her old face new.
   Loe thus by day my lims,by night my mind,
   For thee,and for my felfe,noe quiet finde.

28

HOw can I then recurne in happy plight
   That am debard the benifit of ret ?
When daies oppreffion is not eazd by night,
But day by night and night by day oprett.
And each(though enimes to ethers raigne)
Doe in confent fhake hands to torture me,
The one by toyle,the other to complaine
How far I toyle,ftill farther off from thee.
I tell the Day to pleafe him thou art bright,
And do'ft him grace when clouds doe blot the heauen:
So flatter I the fwart complexiond night,
When fparkling ftars twire not thou guil'ft th' eauen.
   But day doth daily draw my forrowes longer,(ftronger
   And night doth nightly make greefes length feeme

29

VVHen in difgrace with Fortune and mens eyes,
   I all alone beweepe my out-caft ftate,

                    And

SONNETS.

And trouble deafe heauen with my bootlesse cries,
And looke vpon my selfe and curse my fate,.
Wishing me like to one more rich in hope,
Featur'd like him,like him with friends possest,
Desiring this mans art,and that mans skope,
With what I most inioy contented least,
Yet in these thoughts my selfe almost despising,
Haplye I thinke on thee, and then my state,
(Like to the Larke at breake of daye arising)
From sullen earth sings himns at Heauens gate,
　For thy sweet loue remembred such welth brings,
　That then I skorne to change my state with Kings.

30

WHen to the Sessions of sweet silent thought,
　I sommon vp remembrance of things past,
I sigh the lacke of many a thing I sought,
And with old woes new waile my deare times waste:
Then can I drowne an eye(vn-vs'd to flow)
For precious friends hid in deaths dateles night,
And weepe a fresh loues long since canceld woe,
And mone th'expence of many a vannisht sight.
Then can I greeue at greeuances fore-gon,
And heauily from woe to woe tell ore
The sad account of fore-bemoned mone,
Which I new pay as if not payd before.
　But if the while I thinke on thee (deare friend)
　All losses are restord,and sorrowes end.

31

Thy bosome is indeared with all hearts,
　Which I by lacking haue supposed dead,
And there raignes Loue and all Loues louing parts,
And all those friends which I thought buried.
How many a holy and obsequious teare
Hath deare religious loue stolne from mine eye,
As interest of the dead,which now appeare,
But things remou'd that hidden in there lie,

C 3　　　　　　　　To

SHAKE-SPEARES

Thou art the graue where buried loue doth liue,
Hung with the tropheis of my louers gon,
Who all their parts of me to thee did giue,
That due of many,now is thine alone.
   Their images I lou'd, I view in thee,
   And thou(all they)haſt all the all of me.

32

IF thou ſuruiue my well contented daie,
  When that churle death my bones with duſt ſhall couer
And ſhalt by fortune once more re-ſuruay:
Theſe poore rude lines of thy deceaſed Louer:
Compare them with the bett'ring of the time,
And though they be out-ſtript by euery pen,
Reſerue them for my loue, not for their rime,
Exceeded by the hight of happier men.
Oh then voutſafe me but this louing thought,
Had my friends Muſe growne with this growing age,
A dearer birth then this his loue had brought
To march in ranckes of better equipage:
   But ſince he died and Poets better proue,
   Theirs for their ſtile ile read,his for his loue.

33

FVll many a glorious morning haue I ſeene,
  Flatter the mountaine tops with ſoueraine eie,
Kiſſing with golden face the meddowes greene;
Guilding pale ſtreames with heauenly alcumy:
Anon permit the baſeſt cloudes to ride,
With ougly rack on his celeſtiall face,
And from the for-lorne world his viſage hide
Stealing vnſeene to weſt with this diſgrace:
Euen ſo my Sunne one early morne did ſhine,
With all triumphant ſplendor on my brow,
But out alack,he was but one houre mine,
The region cloude hath mask'd him from me now.
   Yet him for this,my loue no whit diſdaineth,
   Suns of the world may ſtaine,whē heauens sun ſtainteh.

34

SONNETS.

34

VVHy didft thou promife fuch a beautious day,
And make me trauaile forth without my cloake,
To let bace cloudes ore-take me in my way,
Hiding thy brau'ry in their rotten fmoke.
Tis not enough that through the cloude thou breake,
To dry the raine on my ftorme-beaten face,
For no man well of fuch a falue can fpeake,
That heales the wound, and cures not the difgrace:
Nor can thy fhame giue phificke to my griefe,
Though thou repent , yet I haue ftill the loffe,
Th'offenders forrow lends but weake reliefe
To him that beares the ftrong offenfes loffe.
    Ah but thofe teares are pearle which thy loue fheeds,
    And they are ritch, and ranfome all ill deeds.

35

NO more bee greeu'd at that which thou haft done,
Rofes haue thornes, and filuer fountaines mud,
Cloudes and eclipfes ftaine both Moone and Sunne,
And loathfome canker liues in fweeteft bud.
All men make faults, and euen I in this,
Authorizing thy trefpas with compare,
My felfe corrupting faluing thy amiffe,
Excufing their fins more then their fins are:
For to thy fenfuall fault I bring in fence,
Thy aduerfe party is thy Aduocate,
And gainft my felfe a lawfull plea commence,
Such ciuill war is in my loue and hate,
    That I an acceffary needs muft be,
    To that fweet theefe which fourely robs from me,

36

LEt me confeffe that we two muft be twaine,
Although our vndeuided loues are one:
So fhall thofe blots that do with me remaine,
Without thy helpe, by me be borne alone.
In our two loues there is but one refpect,

                                        Though

SHAKE-SPEARES

Though in our liues a seperable spight,
Which though it alter not loues sole effect,
Yet doth it steale sweet houres from loues delight,
I may not euer-more acknowledge thee,
Least my bewailed guilt should do thee shame,
Nor thou with publike kindnesse honour me,
Vnlesse thou take that honour from thy name:
    But doe not so, I loue thee in such sort,
    As thou being mine, mine is thy good report.

37

AS a decrepit father takes delight,
  To see his actiue childe do deeds of youth,
So I, made lame by Fortunes dearest spight
Take all my comfort of thy worth and truth.
For whether beauty, birth, or wealth, or wit,
Or any of these all, or all, or more
Intitled in their parts, do crowned sit,
I make my loue ingrafted to this store:
So then I am not lame, poore, nor dispis'd,
Whilst that this shadow doth such substance giue,
That I in thy abundance am suffic'd,
And by a part of all thy glory liue:
    Looke what is best, that best I wish in thee,
    This wish I haue, then ten times happy me.

38

HOw can my Muse want subiect to inuent
  While thou dost breath that poor'st into my verse,
Thine owne sweet argument, to excellent,
For euery vulgar paper to rehearse:
Oh giue thy selfe the thankes if ought in me,
Worthy perusal stand against thy sight,
For who's so dumbe that cannot write to thee,
When thou thy selfe dost giue inuention light?
Be thou the tenth Muse, ten times more in worth
Then those old nine which rimers inuocate,
And he that calls on thee, let him bring forth

                        Eternall

SONNETS.

Eternal numbers to out-liue long date.
   If my flight Muſe doe pleaſe theſe curious daies,
   The paine be mine,but thine ſhal be the praiſe.

39

OH how thy worth with manners may I ſinge,
   When thou art all the better part of me?
What can mine owne praiſe to mine owne ſelfe bring;
And what is't but mine owne when I praiſe thee,
Euen for this,let vs deuided liue,
And our deare loue looſe name of ſingle one,
That by this ſeperation I may giue:
That due to thee which thou deſeru'ſt alone:
Oh abſence what a torment wouldſt thou proue,
Were it not thy ſoure leiſure gaue ſweet leaue,
To entertaine the time with thoughts of loue,
VVhich time and thoughts ſo ſweetly doſt deceiue,
   And that thou teacheſt how to make one twaine,
   By praiſing him here who doth hence remaine.

40

TAke all my loues,my loue,yea take them all,
   What haſt thou then more then thou hadſt before?
No loue,my loue,that thou maiſt true loue call,
All mine was thine,before thou hadſt this more:
Then if for my loue,thou my loue receiueſt,
I cannot blame thee,for my loue thou vſeſt,
But yet be blam'd,if thou this ſelfe deceaueſt
By wilfull taſte of what thy ſelfe refuſeſt.
I doe forgiue thy robb'rie gentle theeſe
Although thou ſteale thee all my pouerty:
And yet loue knowes it is a greater griefe
   /beare loues wrong,then hates knowne iniury.
   Laſciuious grace,in whom all il wel ſhowes,
   Kill me with ſpights yet we muſt not be foes.

41

THoſe pretty wrongs that liberty commits,
   When I am ſome-time abſent from thy heart,

        D   Thy

SHAKE-SPEARES.

Thy beautie,and thy yeares full well befits,
For still temptacion followes where thou art.
Gentle thou art,and therefore to be wonne,
Beautious thou art,therefore to be assailed.
And when a woman woes,what womans sonne,
Will sourely leaue her till he haue preuailed.
Aye me,but yet thou mighst my seate forbeare,
And chide thy beauty,and thy straying youth,
Who lead thee in their ryot euen there
Where thou art forst to breake a two-fold truth:
　　Hers by thy beauty tempting her to thee,
　　Thine by thy beautie beeing false to me.

42

THat thou hast her it is not all my griefe,
　　And yet it may be said I lou'd her deerely,
That she hath thee is of my wayling cheefe,
A losse in loue that touches me more neerely.
Louing offendors thus I will excuse yee,
Thou doost loue her,because thou knowst I loue her,
And for my sake euen so doth she abuse me,
Suffring my friend for my sake to approoue her,
If I loose thee,my losse is my loues gaine,
And loosing her,my friend hath found that losse,
Both finde each other,and I loose both twaine,
And both for my sake lay on me this crosse,
　　But here's the ioy,my friend and I are one,
　　Sweete flattery,then she loues but me alone.

43

WHen most I winke then doe mine eyes best see,
　　For all the day they view things vnrespected,
But when I sleepe,in dreames they looke on thee,
And darkely bright,are bright in darke directed.
Then thou whose shaddow shaddowes doth make bright,
How would thy shadowes forme,forme happy show,
To the cleere day with thy much cleerer light,
When to vn-seeing eyes thy shade shines so?

How

SONNETS.

How would (I say)mine eyes be bleſſed made,
By looking on thee in the liuing day?
When in dead night their faire imperfect ſhade,
Through heauy ſleepe on ſightleſſe eyes doth ſtay?
    All dayes are nights to ſee till I ſee thee,
    And nights bright daies when dreams do ſhew thee me,

44

IF the dull ſubſtance of my fleſh were thought,
Iniurious diſtance ſhould not ſtop my way,
For then diſpight of ſpace I would be brought,
From limits farre remote,where thou dooſt ſtay,
No matter then although my foote did ſtand
Vpon the fartheſt earth remoou'd from thee,
For nimble thought can iumpe both ſea and land,
As ſoone as thinke the place where he would be.
But ah,thought kills me that I am not thought
To leape large lengths of miles when thou art gone,
But that ſo much of earth and water wrought,
I muſt attend,times leaſure with my mone.
    Receiuing naughts by elements ſo ſloe,
    But heauie teares,badges of eithers woe.

45

THe other two,ſlight ayre,and purging fire,
Are both with thee,where euer I abide,
The firſt my thought,the other my deſire,
Theſe preſent abſent with ſwift motion ſlide.
For when theſe quicker Elements are gone
In tender Embaſſie of loue to thee,
My life being made of foure,with two alone,
Sinkes downe to death,oppreſt with melancholie.
Vntill liues compoſition be recuied,
By thoſe ſwift meſſengers return'd from thee,
Who euen but now come back againe aſſured,
Of their faire health,recounting it to me.
    This told,I ioy,but then no longer glad,
    I ſend them back againe and ſtraight grow ſad.

D 2   Mine

SHAKE-SPEARES.

46

MIne eye and heart are at a mortall warre,
How to deuide the conqueft of thy fight,
Mine eye,my heart their pictures fight would barre,
My heart,mine eye the freeedome of that right,
My heart doth plead that thou in him dooftlye,
(A clofet neuer pearft with chriftall eyes)
But the defendant doth that plea deny,
And fayes in him their faire appearance lyes.
To fide this title is impannelled
A queft of thoughts,all tennants to the heart,
And by their verdict is determined
The cleere eyes moyitie,and the deare hearts part.
    As thus,mine eyes due is their outward part,
    And my hearts right,their inward loue of heart.

47

BEtwixt mine eye and heart a league is tooke,
And each doth good turnes now vnto the other,
When that mine eye is famifht for a looke,
Or heart in loue with fighes himfelfe doth fmother;
With my loues picture then my eye doth feaft,
And to the painted banquet bids my heart:
An other time mine eye is my hearts gueft,
And in his thoughts of loue doth fhare a part.
So either by thy picture or my loue,
Thy feife away,are prefent ftill with me,
For thou nor farther then my thoughts canft moue,
And I am ftill with them,and they with thee.
    Or if they fleepe, thy picture in my fight
    Awakes my heart,to hearts and eyes delight.

48

HOw carefull was I when I tooke my way,
Each trifle vnder trueft barres to thruft,
That to my vfe it might vn-vfed ftay
From hands of falfehood,in fure wards of truft ?
But thou,to whom my iewels trifles are,

                                        Moft

SONNETS.

Moſt worthy comfort,now my greateſt griefe,
Thou beſt of decieſt,and mine onely care,
Art left the prey of euery vulgar theeſe.
Thee haue I not lockt vp in any cheſt,
Saue where thou art not,though I feele thou art,
Within the gentle cloſure of my breſt,
From whence at pleaſure thou maiſt come and part,
   And euen thence thou wilt be ſtolne I feare,
   For truth prooues theeuiſh for a prize ſo deare.

49

AGainſt that time (if euer that time come)
When I ſhall ſee thee frowne on my defects,
When as thy loue hath caſt his vtmoſt ſumme,
Cauld to that audite by aduiſ'd reſpects,
Againſt that time when thou ſhalt ſtrangely paſſe,
And ſcarcely greete me with that ſunne thine eye,
When loue conuerted from the thing it was
Shall reaſons finde of ſetled grauitie.
Againſt that time do I inſconce me here
Within the knowledge of mine owne deſart,
And this my hand,againſt my ſelfe vpreare,
To guard the lawfull reaſons on thy part,
   To leaue poore me,thou haſt the ſtrength of lawes,
   Since why to loue,I can alledge no cauſe.

50

HOw heauie doe I iourney on the way,
When what I ſeeke (my wearie trauels end)
Doth teach that eaſe and that repoſe to ſay
Thus farre the miles are meaſurde from thy friend.
The beaſt that beares me,tired with my woe,
Plods duly on,to beare that waight in me,
As if by ſome inſtinct the wretch did know
His rider lou'd not ſpeed being made from thee:
The bloody ſpurre cannot prouoke him on,
That ſome-times anger thruſts Into his hide,
Which heauily he anſwers with a grone,

D 3   More

SHAKE-SPEARES.

More fharpe to me then fpurring to his fide,
   For that fame grone doth put this in my mind,
   My greefe lies onward and my ioy behind.

51

THus can my loue excufe the flow offence,
   Of my dull bearer, when from thee I fpeed,
From where thou art, why fhoulld I haft me thence,
Till I returne of pofting is noe need.
O what excufe will my poore beaft then find,
When fwift extremity can feeme but flow,
Then fhould I fpurre though mounted on the wind,
In winged fpeed no motion fhall I know,
Then can no horfe with my defire keepe pace,
Therefore defire (of perfects loue being made)
Shall naigh noe dull flefh in his fiery race,
But loue, for loue, thus fhall excufe my iade,
   Since from thee going he went wilfull flow,
   Towards thee ile run, and giue him leaue to goe.

52

SO am I as the rich whofe bleffed key,
   Can bring him to his fweet vp-locked treafure,
The which he will not eu'ry hower furuay,
For blunting the fine point of feldome pleafure.
Therefore are feafts fo follemne and fo rare,
Since fildom comming in the long yeare fet,
Like ftones of worth they thinly placed are,
Or captaine Iewells in the carconet.
So is the time that keepes you as my cheft,
Or as the ward-robe which the robe doth hide,
To make fome fpeciall inftant fpeciall bleft,
By new vnfoulding his imprifon'd pride.
   Bleffed are you whofe worthineffe giues skope,
   Being had to tryumph, being lackt to hope.

53

VVHat is your fubftance, whereof are you made,
   That millions of ftrange fhaddowes on you tend?
                         Since

SONNETS.

Since euery one,hath euery one,one shade,
And you but one,can euery shaddow lend:
Describe *Adonis* and the counterfet,
Is poorely immitated after you,
On *Hellens* cheeke all art of beautie set;
And you in *Grecian* tires are painted new:
Speake of the spring,and foyzon of the yeare,
The one doth shaddow of your beautie show,
The other as your bountie doth appeare,
And you in euery blessed shape we know.
  In all externall grace you haue some part,
  But you like none,none you for constant heart,

54

OH how much more doth beautie beautious seeme,
  By that sweet ornament which truth doth giue,
The Rose lookes faire, but fairer we it deeme
For that sweet odor,which doth in it liue:
The Canker bloomes haue full as deepe a die,
As the perfumed tincture of the Roses,
Hang on such thornes,and play as wantonly,
When sommers breath their masked buds disclofes;
But for their virtue only is their show,
They liue vnwoo'd, and vnrespected fade,
Die to themselues . Sweet Roses doe not so,
Of their sweet deathes, are sweetest odors made:
  And so of you,beautious and louely youth,
  When that shall vade,by verse distils your truth.

55

NOt marble, nor the guilded monument,
  Of Princes shall out-liue this powrefull rime;
But you shall shine more bright in these contents
Then vnswept stone, besmeer'd with sluttish time.
When wastefull warre shall *Statues* ouer-turne,
And broiles roote out the worke of mafonry,
Nor *Mars* his sword, nor warres quick fire shall burne:
The liuing record of your memory.

                           Gainst

SHAKE-SPEARES.

Gainſt death, and all obliuious emnity
Shall you pace forth, your praiſe ſhall ſtil finde roome,
Euen in the eyes of all poſterity
That weare this world out to the ending doome.
  So til the iudgement that your ſelfe ariſe,
  You liue in this, and dwell in louers eies.

56

S weet loue renew thy force, be it not ſaid
  Thy edge ſhould blunter be then apetite,
Which but too daie by feeding is alaied,
To morrow ſharpned in his former might.
So loue be thou, although too daie thou fill
Thy hungrie eies, euen till they winck with fulneſſe,
Too morrow ſee againe, and doe not kill
The ſpirit of Loue, with a perpetual dulneſſe:
Let this ſad *Intrim* like the Ocean be
Which parts the ſhore, where two contracted new,
Come daily to the banckes, that when they ſee.
Returne of loue, more bleſt may be the view.
  As cal it Winter, which being ful of care,
  Makes Sômers welcome, thrice more wiſh'd, more rare :

57

B Eing your ſlaue what ſhould I doe but tend,
  Vpon the houres, and times of your deſire?
I haue no precious time at al to ſpend;
Nor ſeruices to doe til you require.
Nor dare I chide the world without end houre,
Whilſt I (my ſoueraine) watch the clock for you,
Nor thinke the bitterneſſe of abſence ſowre,
VVhen you haue bid your ſeruant once adieue.
Nor dare I queſtion with my ieallous thought,
VVhere you may be, or your affaires ſuppoſe,
But like a ſad ſlaue ſtay and thinke of nought
Saue where you are, how happy you make thoſe.
  So true a foole is loue, that in your Will,
  (Though you doe any thing) he thinkes no ill.

58

SONNETS.

58

THat God forbid,that made me firſt your ſlaue,
  I ſhould in thought controule your times of pleaſure,
Or at your hand th' account of houres to craue,
Being your vaſſail bound to ſtaie your leiſure.
Oh let me ſuffer(being at your beck)
Th' impriſon'd abſence of your libertie,
And patience tame,to ſufferance bide each check,.
Without accuſing you of iniury.
Be where you liſt,your charter is ſo ſtrong,
That you your ſelfe may priuiledge your time
To what you will,to you it doth belong,
Your ſelfe to pardon of ſelfe-doing crime.
    I am to waite,though waiting ſo be hell,
    Not blame your pleaſure be it ill or well.

59

IF their bee nothing new,but that which is,
  Hath beene before , how are our braines beguild,
Which laboring for inuention beare amiſſe
The ſecond burthen of a former child ?
Oh that record could with a back-ward looke,
Euen of fiue hundreth courſes of the Sunne,
Show me your image in ſome antique booke,
Since minde at firſt in carrecter was done.
That I might ſee what the old world could ſay,
To this compoſed wonder of your frame,
Whether we are mended,or where better they,
Or whether reuolution be the ſame.
    Oh ſure I am the wits of former daies,
    To ſubiects worſe haue giuen admiring praiſe.

60

LIke as the waues make towards the pibled ſhore,
  So do our minuites haſten to their end,
Each changing place with that which goes before,
In ſequent toile all forwards do contend.
Natiuity once in the maine of light,

E   Crawls

Crawles to maturity,wherewith being crown'd,
Crooked eclipſes gainſt his glory fight,
And time that gaue,doth now his gift confound.
Time doth tranſſixe the ſloriſh ſet on youth,
And delues the paralels in beauties brow,
Feedes on the rarities of natures truth,
And nothing ſtands but for his ſieth to mow.
    And yet to times in hope,my verſe ſhall ſtand
    Praiſing thy worth,diſpight his cruell hand.

61

IS it thy wil,thy Image ſhould keepe open
My heauy eie ids to the weary night?
Doſt thou deſire my ſlumbers ſhould be broken,
While ſhadowes like to thee do mocke my ſight?
Is it thy ſpirit that thou ſend'ſt from thee
So farre from home into my deeds to prye,
To find out ſhames and idle houres in me,
The skope and tenure of thy Ielouſie?
O no,thy loue though much,is not ſo great,
It is my loue that keepes mine eie awake,
Mine owne true loue that doth my reſt defeat,
To plaie the watch-man euer for thy ſake.
    For thee watch I,whilſt thou doſt wake elſewhere,
    From me farre of , with others all to neere.

62

SInne of ſelfe-loue poſſeſſeth al mine eie,
And all my ſoule,and al my euery part;
And for this ſinne there is no remedie,
It is ſo grounded inward in my heart.
Me thinkes no face ſo gratious is as mine,
No ſhape ſo true,no truth of ſuch account,
And for my ſelfe mine owne worth do define,
As I all other in all worths ſurmount.
But when my glaſſe ſhewes me my ſelfe indeed
Beated and chopt with tand antiquitie,
Mine owne ſelfe loue quite contrary I read

Selfe

SONNETS.

Selfe, so selfe louing were iniquity,
  T'is thee(my selfe)that for my selfe I praise,
  Painting my age with beauty of thy daies,

63

A Gainst my loue shall be as I am now
  With times iniurious hand chrusht and ore-worne,
When houres haue dreind his blood and fild his brow
With lines and wrincles,when his youthfull morne
Hath trauaild on to Ages steepie night,
And all those beauties whereof now he's King
Are vanishing,or vanisht out of sight,
Stealing away the treasure of his Spring.
For such a time do I now fortifie
Against confounding Ages cruell knife,
That he shall neuer cut from memory
My sweet loues beauty,though my louers life.
    His beautie shall in these blacke lines be seene,
    And they shall liue , and he in them still greene.

64

VV Hen I haue seene by times fell hand defaced
  The rich proud cost of outworne buried age,
When sometime loftie towers I see downe rased,
And brasse eternall slaue to mortall rage.
When I haue seene the hungry Ocean gaine
Aduantage on the Kingdome of the shoare,
And the firme soile win of the watry maine,
Increasing store with losse,and losse with store.
When I haue seene such interchange of state,
Or state it selfe confounded, to decay,
Ruine hath taught me thus to ruminate
That Time will come and take my loue away.
    This thought is as a death which cannot choose
    But weepe to haue,that which it feares to loose.

65

S Ince brasse,nor stone,nor earth,nor boundlesse sea,
  But sad mortallity ore-swaies their power,

How

How with this rage shall beautie hold a plea,
Whose action is no stronger then a flower?
O how shall summers hunny breath hold out,
Against the wrackfull siedge of battring dayes,
When rocks impregnable are not so stoute ,
Nor gates of steele so strong but time decayes?
O fearefull meditation, where alack,
Shall times best Iewell from times chest lie hid?
Or what strong hand can hold his swift foote back,
Or who his spoile or beautie can forbid?
   O none,vnlesse this miracle haue might,
   That in black inck my loue may still shine bright.

66

TYr'd with all these for restfull death I cry,
  As to behold desert a begger borne,
And needie Nothing trimd in iollitie,
And purest faith vnhappily forsworne,
And gilded honor shamefully misplast,
And maiden vertue rudely strumpeted,
And right perfection wrongfully disgrac'd,
And strength by limping sway disabled ,
And arte made tung-tide by authoritie,
And Folly (Doctor-like) controuling skill,
And simple-Truth miscalde Simplicitie,
And captiue-good attending Captaine ill.
   Tyr'd with all these,from these would I be gone,
   Saue that to dye,I leaue my loue alone.

67

AH wherefore with infection should he liue,
  And with his presence grace impietie,
That sinne by him aduantage should atchiue,
And lace it selfe with his societie ?
Why should false painting immitate his cheeke,
And steale dead seeing of his liuing hew?
Why should poore beautie indirectly seeke,
Roses of shaddow,since his Rose is true?

                            Why

SONNETS.

Why fhould he liue,now nature banckrout is,
Beggerd of blood to blufh through liuely vaines,
For fhe hath no exchecker now but his,
And proud of many,liues vpon his gaines?
   O him fhe ftores,to fhow what welth fhe had,
   In daies long fince,before thefe laft fo bad.

68

THus is his cheeke the map of daies out-worne,
   When beauty liu'd and dy'ed as flowers do now,
Before thefe baftard fignes of faire were borne,
Or durft inhabit on a liuing brow?
Before the goulden treffes of the dead,
The right of fepulchers,were fhorne away,
To liue a fcond life on fecond head,
Ere beauties dead fleece made another gay:
In him thofe holy antique howers are feene,
Without all ornament,it felfe and true,
Making no fummer of an others greene,
Robbing no ould to dreffe his beauty new,
   And him as for a map doth Nature ftore,
   To fhew faulfe Art what beauty was of yore.

69

THofe parts of thee that the worlds eye doth view,
   Want nothing that the thought of hearts can mend:
All toungs(the voice of foules)giue thee that end,
Vttring bare truth,euen fo as foes Commend.
Their outward thus with outward praife is crownd,
But thofe fame toungs that giue thee fo thine owne,
In other accents doe this praife confound
By feeing farther then the eye hath fhowne.
They looke into the beauty of thy mind,
And that in gueffe they meafure by thy deeds,
Then churls their thoughts(although their eies were kind)
To thy faire flower ad the rancke fmell of weeds,
   But why thy odor matcheth not thy fhow,
   The folye is this,that thou doeft common grow.

E 3

That

SHAKE-SPEARES

70

THat thou are blam'd fhall not be thy defe&,
For flanders marke was euer yet the faire,
The ornament of beauty is fufpe&,
A Crow that flies in heauens fweeteft ayre.
So thou be good,flander doth but approue,
Their worth the greater beeing woo'd of time,
For Canker vice the fweeteft buds doth loue,
And thou prefent'ft a pure vnftayined prime.
Thou haft paft by the ambufh of young daies,
Either not affayld,or victor beeing charg'd,
Yet this thy praife cannot be foe thy praife,
To tye vp enuy,euermore inlarged,
    If fome fufpect of ill maskt not thy fhow,
    Then thou alone kingdomes of hearts fhouldft owe.

71

NOe Longer mourne for me when I am dead,
Then you fhall heare the furly fullen bell
Giue warning to the world that I am fled
From this vile world with vildeft wormes to dwell:
Nay if you read this line,remember not,
The hand that writ it,for I loue you fo,
That I in your fweet thoughts would be forgot,
If thinking on me then fhould make you woe.
O if(I fay)you looke vpon this verfe,
When I (perhaps) compounded am with clay,
Do not fo much as my poore name reherfe;
But let your loue euen with my life decay.
    Leaft the wife world fhould looke into your mone,
    And mocke you with me after I am gon.

72

O Leaft the world fhould taske you to recite,
What merit liu'd in me that you fhould loue
After my death(deare loue)forget me quite,
For you in me can nothing worthy proue.
Vnleffe you would deuife fome vertuous lye,

To

SONNETS.

To doe more for me then mine owne defert,
And hang more praife vpon deceafed I,
Then nigard truth would willingly impart:
O leaft your true loue may feeme falce in this,
That you for loue fpeake well of me vntrue,
My name be buried where my body is,
And liue no more to fhame nor me,nor you.
   For I am fhamd by that which I bring forth,
   And fo fhould you,to loue things nothing worth.

73

THat time of yeeare thou maift in me behold,
  When yellow leaues,or none,or few doe hange
Vpon thofe boughes which fhake againft the could,
Bare rn'wd quiers, where late the fweet birds fang.
In me thou feeft the twi-light of fuch day,
As after Sun-fet fadeth in the Weft,
Which by and by blacke night doth take away,
Deaths fecond felfe that feals vp all in reft.
In me thou feeft the glowing of fuch fire,
That on the afhes of his youth doth lye,
As the death bed,whereon it muft expire,
Confum'd with that which it was nurrifht by.
   This thou perceu'ft,which makes thy loue more ftrong,
   To loue that well,which thou muft leaue ere long.

74

BVt be contented when that fell areft,
  With out all bayle fhall carry me away,
My life hath in this line fome intereft,
Which for memoriall ftill with thee fhall ftay.
When thou reueweft this,thou doeft reuew,
The very part was confecrate to thee,
The earth can haue but earth,which is his due,
My fpirit is thine the better part of me,
So then thou haft but loft the dregs of life,
The pray of wormes,my body being dead,
The coward conqueft of a wretches knife,

To

SHAKE-SPEARES

To bafe of thee to be remembred,
    The worth of that,is that which it containes,
    And that is this, and this with thee remaines.

75

SO are you to my thoughts as food to life,
    Or as fweet feafon'd fhewers are to the ground;
And for the peace of you I hold fuch ftrife,
As twixt a mifer and his wealth is found.
Now proud as an inioyer,and anon
Doubting the filching age will fteale his treafure,
Now counting beft to be with you alone,
Then betterd that the world may fee my pleafure,
Some-time all ful with feafting on your fight,
And by and by cleane ftarued for a looke,
Poffeffing or purfuing no delight
Saue what is had,or muft from you be tooke.
    Thus do I pine and furfet day by day,
    Or gluttoning on all,or all away,

76

VVHy is my verfe fo barren of new pride?
    So far from variation or quicke change?
Why with the time do I not glance afide
To new found methods,and to compounds ftrange?
Why write I ftill all one,euer the fame,
And keepe inuention in a noted weed,
That euery word doth almoft fel my name,
Shewing their birth,and where they did proceed?
O know fweet loue I alwaies write of you,
And you and loue are ftill my argument:
So all my beft is dreffing old words new,
Spending againe what is already fpent:
    For as the Sun is daily new and old,
    So is my loue ftill telling what is told,

77

THy glaffe will fhew thee how thy beauties were,
    Thy dyall how thy pretious mynuits wafte,

The

SONNETS.

The vacant leaues thy mindes imprint will beare,
And of this booke, this learning maift thou tafte.
The wrinckles which thy glaffe will truly fhow,
Of mouthed graues will giue thee memorie,
Thou by thy dyals fhady ftealth maift know,
Times theeuifh progreffe to eternitie.
Looke what thy memorie cannot containe,
Commit to thefe wafte blacks, and thou fhalt finde
Thofe children nurft, deliuerd from thy braine,
To take a new acquaintance of thy minde.
  Thefe offices, fo oft as thou wiltlooke,
  Shall profit thee and much inrich thy booke.

78

SO oft haue I inuok'd thee for my Mufe,
  And found fuch faire affiftance in my verfe,
As euery *Alien* pen hath got my vfe,
And vnder thee their poefie difperfe.
Thine eyes, that taught the dumbe on high to fing,
And heauie ignorance aloft to flie,
Haue added fethers to the learneds wing,
And giuen grace a double Maieftie.
Yet be moft proud of that which I compile,
Whofe influence is thine, and borne of thee.
In others workes thou dooft but mend the ftile,
And Arts with thy fweete graces graced be.
  But thou art all my art, and dooft aduance
  As high as learning, my rude ignorance.

79

WHilft I alone did call vpon thy ayde,
  My verfe alone had all thy gentle grace,
But now my gracious numbers are decayde,
And my fick Mufe doth giue an other place.
I grant (fweet loue)thy louely argument
Deferues the trauaile of a worthier pen,
Yet what of thee thy Poet doth inuent,
He robs thee of, and payes it thee againe,

F

He

SHAKE-SPEARES

He lends thee vertue,and he ftole that word,
From thy behauiour,beautie doth he giue
And found it in thy cheeke: he can affoord
No praife to thee,but what in thee doth liue.
  Then thanke him not for that which he doth fay,
  Since what he owes thee,thou thy felfe dooft pay.

80

O How I faint when I of you do write,
  Knowing a better fpirit doth vfe your name,
And in the praife thereof fpends all his might,
To make me toung-tide fpeaking of your fame.
But fince your worth(wide as the Ocean is)
The humble as the proudeft faile doth beare,
My fawfie barke (inferior farre to his)
On your broad maine doth wilfully appeare.
Your fhalloweft helpe will hold me vp a floate,
Whilft he vpon your foundleffe deepe doth ride,
Or (being wrackt) I am a worthleffe bote,
He of tall building,and of goodly pride.
  Then If he thriue and I be caft away,
  The worft was this,my loue was my decay.

81

OR I fhall liue your Epitaph to make,
  Or you furuiue when I in earth am rotten,
From hence your memory death cannot take,
Although in me each part will be forgotten.
Your name from hence immortall life fhall haue,
Though I (once gone) to all the world muft dye,
The earth can yeeld me but a common graue,
When you intombed in mens eyes fhall lye,
Your monument fhall be my gentle verfe,
Which eyes not yet created fhall ore-read,
And toungs to be, your beeing fhall rehearfe,
When all the breathers of this world are dead,
  You ftill fhall liue (fuch vertue hath my Pen)
  Where breath moft breaths,euen in the mouths of men.

I grant

SONNETS.

82

I Grant thou wert not married to my Mufe,
And therefore maieſt without attaint ore-looke
The dedicated words which writers vſe
Of their faire ſubieƈt,bleſſing euery booke.
Thou art as faire in knowledge as in hew,
Finding thy worth a limmit paſt my praiſe,
And therefore art inforc'd to ſeeke anew,
Some freſher ſtampe of the time bettering dayes.
And do ſo loue,yet when they haue deuiſde,
What ſtrained touches Rhethorick can lend,
Thou truly faire,wert truly ſimpathizde,
In true plaine words ,by thy true telling friend.
　　And their groſſe painting might be better vſ'd,
　　Where cheekes need blood,in thee it is abuſ'd.

83

I Neuer ſaw that you did painting need,
And therefore to your faire no painting ſet,
I found (or thought I found) you did exceed,
The barren tender of a Poets debt :
And therefore haue I ſlept in your report,
That you your ſelfe being extant well might ſhow,
How farre a moderne quill doth come to ſhort,
Speaking of worth,what worth in you doth grow,
This ſilence for my ſinne you did impute,
Which ſhall be moſt my glory being dombe.
For I impaire not beautie being mute,
When others would giue life,and bring a tombe.
　　There liues more life in one of your faire eyes,
　　Then both your Poets can in praiſe deuiſe.

84

W Ho is it that ſayes moſt,which can ſay more,
　　Then this rich praiſe,that you alone,are you,
In whoſe confine immured is the ſtore,
Which ſhould example where your equall grew.
Leane penurie within that Pen doth dwell,

F 2　　　　　　　　　　　That

SHAKE-SPEARES

That to his ſubieƈt lends not ſome ſmall glory,
But he that writes of you,if he can tell,
That you are you,ſo dignifies his ſtory.
Let him but coppy what in you is writ,
Not making worſe what nature made ſo cleere,
And ſuch a counter-part ſhall fame his wit,
Making his ſtile admired euery where.
    You to your beautious bleſſings adde a curſe,
    Being fond on praiſe,which makes your praiſes worſe.

85

MY toung-tide Muſe in manners holds her ſtill,
  While comments of your praiſe richly compil'd,
Reſerue their Charaƈter with goulden quill,
And precious phraſe by all the Muſes fil'd.
I thinke good thoughts,whilſt other write good wordes,
And like vnlettered clarke ſtill crie Amen,
To euery Himne that able ſpirit affords,
In poliſht forme of well refined pen.
Hearing you praiſd,I ſay 'tis ſo, 'tis true,
And to the moſt of praiſe adde ſome-thing more,
But that is in my thought,whoſe loue to you
  Though words come hind-moſt)holds his ranke before,
    Then others,for the breath of words reſpeƈt,
    Me for my dombe thoughts,ſpeaking in effeƈt.

86

VVAs it the proud full ſaile of his great verſe,
    Bound for the prize of (all to precious) you,
That did my ripe thoughts in my braine inhearce,
Making their tombe the wombe wherein they grew?
Was it his ſpirit,by ſpirits taught to write,
Aboue a mortall pitch,that ſtruck me dead?
No,neither he,nor his compiers by night
Giuing him ayde,my verſe aſtoniſhed.
He nor that affable familiar ghoſt
Which nightly gulls him with intelligence,
As viƈtors of my ſilence cannot boaſt,

                                                    I was

Sonnets.

I was not sick of any feare from thence.
    But when your countinance fild vp his line,
    Then lackt I matter,that infeebled mine.

87

FArewell thou art too deare for my possessing,
    A, d like enough thou knowst thy estimate,
The Cha ter of thy worth giues thee releasing:
My bonds in thee are all determinate.
For how do I hold thee but by thy granting,
And for that ritches where is my deseruing?
The cause of this faire guift in me is wanting,
And so my pattent back againe is sweruing.
Thy selfe thou gau'st,thy owne worth then not knowing,
Or mee to whom thou gau'st it,else mistaking,
So thy great guift vpon misprision growing,
Comes home againe,on better iudgement making.
    Thus haue I had thee as a dreame doth flatter,
    In sleepe a King,but waking no such matter.

88

VVHen thou shalt be dispode to set me light,
    And place my merrit in the eie of skorne,
Vpon thy side,against my selfe ile fight,
And proue thee virtuous,though thou art forsworne:
With mine owne weakenesse being best acquainted,
Vpon thy part I can set downe a story
Of faults conceald,wherein I am attainted :
That thou in loosing me,shall win much glory:
And I by this wil be a gainer too,
For bending all my louing thoughts on thee,
The iniuries that to my selfe I doe,
Doing thee vantage,duble vantage me.
    Such is my loue,to thee I so belong,
    That for thy right,my selfe will beare all wrong.

89

SAy that thou didst forsake mee for some falt,
    And I will comment vpon that offence,

        The

SHAKE-SPEARES

Speake of my lamenesse, and I straight will halt:
Against thy reasons making no defence.
Thou canst not(loue)disgrace me halfe so ill,
To set a forme vpon desired change,
As ile my selfe disgrace,knowing thy wil,
I will acquaintance strangle and looke strange:
Be absent from thy walkes and in my tongue,
Thy sweet beloued name no more shall dwell,
Least I(too much prophane)should do it wronge:
And haplie of our old acquaintance t ell.
    For thee,against my selfe ile vow debate,
    For I must nere loue him whom thou dost hate.

90

THen hate me when thou wilt, if euer,now,
    Now while the world is bent my deeds to crosse,
Ioyne with the spight of fortune,make me bow,
And doe not drop in for an after losse:
Ah doe not,when my heart hath scapte this sorrow,
Come in the rereward of a conquerd woe,
Giue not a windy night a rainie morrow,
To linger out a purposd ouer-throw.
If thou wilt leaue me, do not leaue me last,
When other pettie griefes haue done their spight;
But in the onset come,so stall I taste
At first the very worst of fortunes might.
    And other straines of woe, which now seeme woe,
    Compar'd with losse of thee,will not seeme so.

91

SOme glory in their birth,some in their skill,
    Some in their wealth, some in their bodies force,
Some in their garments though new-fangled ill:
Some in their Hawkes and Hounds,some in their Horse.
And euery humor hath his adiunct pleasure,
Wherein it findes a ioy aboue the rest,
But these perticulers are not my measure,
All these I better in one generall best.

                                        Thy

SONNETS.

Thy loue is bitter then high birth to me,
Richer then wealth,prouder then garments coſt,
Of more delight then Hawkes or Horſes bee:
And hauing thee,of all mens pride I boaſt.
    Wretched in this alone,that thou maiſt take,
    All this away,and me moſt wretched make.

92

BVt doe thy worſt to ſteale thy ſelfe away,
For tearme of life thou art aſſured mine,
And life no longer then thy loue will ſtay,
For it depends vpon that loue of thine.
Then need I not to feare the worſt of wrongs,
When in the leaſt of them my life hath end,
I ſee,a better ſtate to me belongs
Then that,which on thy humor doth depend.
Thou canſt not vex me with inconſtant minde,
Since that my life on thy reuolt doth lie,
Oh what a happy title do I finde,
Happy to haue thy loue, happy to die!
    But whats ſo bleſſed faire that feares no blot,
    Thou maiſt be falce, and yet I know it not.

93

SO ſhall I liue,ſuppoſing thou art true,
Like a deceiued husband ſo loues face,
May ſtill ſeeme loue to me,though alter'd new:
Thy lookes with me,thy heart in other place.
For their can liue no hatred in thine eye,
Therefore in that I cannot know thy change,
In manies lookes,the falce hearts hiſtory
Is writ in moods and frounes and wrinckles ſtrange.
But heauen in thy creation did decree,
That in thy face ſweet loue ſhould euer dwell,
What ere thy thoughts, or thy hearts workings be,
Thy lookes ſhould nothing thence, but ſweetneſſe tell.
    How like *Eaues* apple doth thy beauty grow,
    If thy ſweet vertue anſwere not thy ſhow.

                                       94

SHAKE-SPEARES

94

THey that haue powre to hurt,and will doe none,
That doe not do the thing,they moſt do ſhowe,
Who mouing others,are themſelues as ſtone,
Vnmooued,could,and to temptation ſlow:
They rightly do inherrit heauens graces
And husband natures ritches from expence,
They are the Lords and owners of their faces,
Others,but ſtewards of their excellence:
The ſommers flowre is to the ſommer ſweet,
Though to it ſelfe,it onely liue and die,
But if that flowre with baſe infection meete,
The baſeſt weed out-braues his dignity:
   For ſweeteſt things turne ſowreſt by their deedes,
   Lillies that feſter, ſmell far worſe then weeds.

95

HOw ſweet and louely doſt thou make the ſhame,
Which like a canker in the fragrant Roſe,
Doth ſpot the beautie of thy budding name?
Oh in what ſweets doeſt thou thy ſinnes incloſe!
That tongue that tells the ſtory of thy daies,
(Making laſciuious comments on thy ſport)
Cannot diſpraiſe,but in a kinde of praiſe,
Naming thy name, bleſſes an ill report.
Oh what a manſion haue thoſe vices got,
Which for their habitation choſe out thee,
Where beauties vaile doth couer euery blot,
And all things turnes to faire,that eies can ſee!
   Take heed(deare heart)of this large priuiledge,
   The hardeſt knife ill vſ'd doth looſe his edge.

96

SOme ſay thy fault is youth,ſome wantoneſſe,
Some ſay thy grace is youth and gentle ſport,
Both grace and faults are lou'd of more and leſſe:
Thou makſt faults graces,that to thee reſort:
As on the finger of a throned Queene,

                          The

SONNETS.

The baseſt ıewell wil be well eſteem'd:
So are thoſe errors that in thee are ſeene,
To truths tranſlated,and for true things deem'd.
How many Lambs might the ſterne Wolſe betray,
If like a Lambe he could his lookes tranſlate,
How many gazers mighſt thou lead away,
If thou wouldſt vſe the ſtrength of all thy ſtate?
　But doe not ſo,I loue thee in ſuch ſort,
　As thou being mine,mine is thy good report,

97

HOw like a Winter hath my abſence beene
From thee,the pleaſure of the fleeting yeare?
　What freezings haue I felt,what darke daies ſeene?
What old Decembers bareneſſe euery where?
And yet this tıme remou'd was ſommers time,
The teeming Autumne big with ritch increaſe,
Bearing the wanton burthen of the prime,
Like widdowed wombes after their Lords deceaſe:
Yet this aboundant iſſue ſeem'd to me,
But hope of Orphans,and vn-fathered fruite,
For Sommer and his pleaſures waite on thee,
And thou away,the very birds are mute,
　Or if they ſing,tis with ſo dull a cheere,
　That leaues looke pale,dreading the Winters neere.

98

FRom you haue I beene abſent in the ſpring,
When proud pide Aprill (dreſt in all his trim)
Hath put a ſpirit of youth in euery thing:
That heauie *Saturne* laught and leapt with him,
Yet nor the laies of birds,nor the ſweet ſmell
Of different flowers in odor and in hew,
Could make me any ſummers ſtory tell:
Or from their proud lap pluck them where they grew:
Nor did I wonder at the Lillies white,
Nor praiſe the deepe vermillion in the Roſe,
They weare but ſweet,but figures of delight:

G　　　　　　　　　　Drawne

SHAKE-SPEARES.

Drawne after you, you patterne of all those.
  Yet seem'd it Winter still,and you away,
  As with your shaddow I with these did play.

99

THe forward violet thus did I chide,
  Sweet theefe whence didst thou steale thy sweet that
If not from my loues breath,the purple pride,   (smels.
Which on thy soft checke for complexion dwells?
In my loues veines thou hast too grosely died,
The Lillie I condemned for thy hand,
And buds of marierom had stolne thy haire,
The Roses fearefully on thornes did stand,
Our blushing shame,an other white dispaire:
A third nor red,nor white,had stolne of both,
And to his robbry had annext thy breath,
But for his theft in pride of all his growth
A vengfull canker eate him vp to death.
    More flowers I noted,yet I none could see,
    But sweet,or culler it had stolne from thee.

100

VVHere art thou Muse that thou forgetst so long,
    To speake of that which giues thee all thy might?
Spendst thou thy furie on some worthlesse songe,
Darkning thy powre to lend base subiects light.
Returne forgetfull Muse,and straight redeeme,
In gentle numbers time so idely spent,
Sing to the eare that doth thy laies esteeme,
And giues thy pen both skill and argument.
Rise resty Muse,my loues sweet face suruay,
If time haue any wrincle grauen there,
If any,be a Satire to decay,
And make times spoiles dispised euery where.
    Giue my loue fame faster then time wasts life,
    So thou preuenst his sieth,and crooked knife.

101

OH truant Muse what shalbe thy amends,

                                                    For

SONNETS.

For thy neglect of truth in beauty di'd?
Both truth and beauty on my loue depends:
So doft thou too,and therein dignifi'd:
Make anfwere Mufe,wilt thou not haply faie,
Truth needs no collour with his collour fixt,
Beautie no penfell,beauties truth to lay:
But beft is beft,if neuer intermixt.
Becaufe he needs no praife,wilt thou be dumb?
Excufe not filence fo,for't lies in thee,
To make him much out-liue a gilded tombe:
And to be praifd of ages yet to be.
  Then do thy office Mufe,I teach thee how,
  To make him feeme long hence,as he fhowes now.

102

MY loue is ftrengthned though more weake in fee-
     I loue not leffe,thogh leffe the fhow appeare, (ming
That loue is marchandiz'd,whofe ritch efteeming,
The owners tongue doth publifh euery where.
Our loue was new,and then but in the fpring,
When I was wont to greet it with my laies,
As *Philomell* in fummers front doth finge,
And ftop: his pipe in growth of riper daies:
Not that the fummer is leffe pleafant now
Then when her mournefull himns did hufh the night,
But that wild mufick burthens euery bow,
And fweets growne common loofe their deare deiight.
  Therefore like her,I fome-time hold my tongue:
  Becaufe I would not dull you with my fonge.

103

ALack what pouerty my Mufe brings forth,
     That hauing fuch a skope to fhow her pride,
The argument all bare is of more worth
Then when it hath my added praife befide.
Oh blame me not if I no more can write!
Looke in your glaffe and there appeares a face,
That ouer-goes my blunt inuention quite,
Dulling my lines,and doing me difgrace.

G 2   Were

SHAKE-SPEARES.

Were it not sinfull then striuing to mend,
To marre the subiect that before was well,
For to no other passe my verses tend,
Then of your graces and your gifts to tell.
    And more,much more then in my verse can sit,
    Your owne glasse showes you,when you looke in it.

104

TO me faire friend you neuer can be old,
    For as you were when first your eye I eyde,
Such seemes your beautie still:Three Winters colde,
Haue from the forrests shooke three summers pride,
Three beautious springs to yellow *Autumne* turn'd,
In processe of the seasons haue I seene,
Three Aprill perfumes in three hot Iunes burn'd,
Since first I saw you fresh which yet are greene.
Ah yet doth beauty like a Dyall hand,
Steale from his figure,and no pace perceiu'd,
So your sweete hew,which me thinkes still doth stanc:
Hath motion,and mine eye may be deceaued.
    For feare of which,heare this thou age vnbred,
    Ere you were borne was beauties summer dead.

105

LEt not my loue be cal'd Idolatrie,
    Nor my beloued as an Idoll show,
Since all alike my songs and praises be
To one,of one,still such,and euer so.
Kinde is my loue to day,to morrow kinde,
Still constant in a wondrous excellence,
Therefore my verse to constancie confin'de,
One thing expressing,leaues out difference.
Faire,kinde,and true,is all my argument,
Faire,kinde and true,varrying to other words,
And in this change is my inuention spent,
Three theams in one,which wondrous scope affords.
    Faire,kinde,and true,haue often liu'd alone.
    Which three till now,neuer kept seate in one.

When

SONNETS.

106

WHen in the Chronicle of wasted time,
  I see discriptions of the fairest wights,
And beautie making beautifull old rime,
In praise of Ladies dead,and louely Knights,
Then in the blazon of sweet beauties best,
Of hand,of foote,of lip,of eye,of brow,
I see their antique Pen would haue exprest,
Euen such a beauty as you maister now.
So all their praises are but prophesies
Of this our time,all you prefiguring,
And for they look'd but with deuining eyes,
They had not still enough your worth to sing :
    For we which now behold these present dayes,
    Haue eyes to wonder,but lack toungs to praise.

107

NOt mine owne feares,nor the prophetick soule,
  Of the wide world,dreaming on things to come,
Can yet the lease of my true loue controule,
Supposde as forfeit to a confin'd doome.
The mortall Moone hath her eclipse indur'de,
And the sad Augurs mock their owne presage,
Incertenties now crowne them-selues assur'de,
And peace proclaimes Oliues of endlesse age.
Now with the drops of this most balmie time,
My loue lookes fresh,and death to me subscribes,
Since spight of him Ile liue in this poore rime,
While he insults ore dull and speachlesse tribes.
    And thou in this shalt finde thy monument,
    When tyrants crests and tombs of brasse are spent.

108

VVHat's in the braine that Inck may character,
  Which hath not figur'd to thee my true spirit,
What's new to speake,what now to register,
That may expresse my loue,or thy deare merit ?
Nothing sweet boy,but yet like prayers diuine,
                G 3   I must

SHAKE-SPEARES.

I muft each day fay ore the very fame,
Counting no old thing old, thou mine, I thine,
Euen as when firft I hallowed thy faire name.
So that eternall loue in loues frefh cafe,
Waighes not the duft and iniury of age,
Nor giues to neceffary wrinckles place,
But makes antiquitie for aye his page,
  Finding the firft conceit of loue there bred,
  Where time and outward forme would fhew it dead,

109

O Neuer fay that I was falfe of heart,
  Though abfence feem'd my flame to quallifie,
As eafie might I from my felfe depart,
As from my foule which in thy breft doth lye:
That is my home of loue, if I haue rang'd,
Like him that trauels I returne againe,
Iuft to the time, not with the time exchang'd,
So that my felfe bring water for my ftaine,
Neuer beleeue though in my nature raign'd,
All frailties that befiege all kindes of blood,
That it could fo prepofterouflie be ftain'd,
To leaue for nothing all thy fumme of good:
  For nothing this wide Vniuerfe I call,
  Saue thou my Rofe, in it thou art my all.

110

A Las 'tis true, I haue gone here and there,
  And made my felfe a motley to the view,
Gor'd mine own thoughts, fold cheap what is moft deare,
Made old offences of affections new.
Moft true it is, that I haue lookt on truth
Afconce and ftrangely: But by all aboue,
Thefe blenches gaue my heart an other youth,
And worfe effaies prou'd theo my beft of loue,
Now all is done, haue what fhall haue no end,
Mine appetite I neuer more will grin'de
On newer proofe, to trie an older friend,
A God in loue, to whom I am confin'd.

                                        Then

SONNETS.

Then giue me welcome next my heauen the bef
Euen to thy pure and moſt moſt louing breſt.

111

O For my ſake doe you wiſh fortune chide,
  The guiltie goddeſſe of my harmfull deeds,
That did not better for my life prouide,
Then publick meanes which publick manners breeds.
Thence comes it that my name receiues a brand,
And almoſt thence my nature is ſubdu'd
To what it workes in,like the Dyers hand,
Pitty me then,and wiſh I were renu'de,
Whilſt like a willing pacient I will drinke,
Potions of Eyſell gainſt my ſtrong infection,
No bitterneſſe that I will bitter thinke,
Nor double pennance to correct correction.
    Pittie me then deare friend,and I aſſure yee,
    Euen that your pittie is enough to cure mee.

112

Y Our loue and pittie doth th'impreſſion fill,
  Which vulgar ſcandall ſtampt vpon my brow,
For what care I who calles me well or ill,
So you ore-greene my bad,my good alow?
You are my All the world,and I muſt ſtriue,
To know my ſhames and praiſes from your tounge,
None elſe to me,nor I to none aliue,
That my ſteel'd ſence or changes right or wrong,
In ſo profound *Abiſme* I throw all care
Of others voyces,that my Adders ſence,
To cryttick and to flatterer ſtopped are:
Marke how with my neglect I doe diſpence.
    You are ſo ſtrongly in my purpoſe bred,
    That all the world beſides me thinkes y'are dead.

113

S Ince I left you,mine eye is in my minde,
  And that which gouernes me to goe about,
Doth part his function,and is partly blind,

Seemes

SHAKE-SPEARES.

Seemes feeing,but effectually is out:
For it no forme deliuers to the heart
Of bird,of flowre,or fhape which it doth lack,
Of his quick obiects hath the minde no part,
Nor his owne vifion houlds what it doth catch:
For if it fee the rud'ft or gentleft fight,
The moft fweet-fauor or deformedft creature,
The mountaine,or the fea,the day,or night:
The Croe,or Doue,it fhapes them to your feature.
   Incapable of more repleat,with you,
   My moft true minde thus maketh mine vntrue.

114

OR whether doth my minde being crown'd with you
    Drinke vp the monarks plague this flattery ?
Or whether fhall I fay mine eie faith true,
And that your loue taught it this *Alcumie?*
To make of monfters,and things indigeft,
Such cherubines as your fweet felfe refemble,
Creating euery bad a perfect beft
As faft as obiects to his beames affemble:
Oh tis the firft,tis flatry in my feeing,
And my great minde moft kingly drinkes it vp,
Mine eie well knowes what with his guft is greeing,
And to his pallat doth prepare the cup.
   If it be poifon'd,tis the leffer finne,
   That mine eye loues it and doth firft beginne.

115

THofe lines that I before haue writ doe lie,
   Euen thofe that faid I could not loue you deerer,
Yet then my iudgement knew no reafon why,
My moft full flame fhould afterwards burne cleerer.
But reckening time,whofe milliond accidents
Creepe in twixt vowes,and change decrees of Kings,
Tan facred beautie,blunt the fharp'ft intents,
Diuert ftrong mindes to th' courfe of altring things:
Alas why fearing of times tiranie,

                        Might

SONNETS.

Might I not then fay now I loue you beft,
When I was certaine ore in-certainty,
Crowning the prefent,doubting of the reft:
   Loue is a Babe , then might I not fay fo
   To giue full growth to that which ftill doth grow.

119

L Et me not to the marriage of true mindes
   Admit impediments,loue is not loue
Which alters when it alteration findes,
Or bends with the remouer to remoue.
O no,it is an euer fixed marke
That lookes on tempefts and is neuer fhaken;
It is the ftar to euery wandring barke,
Whofe worths vnknowne,although his higth be taken
Lou's not Times foole,though rofie lips and cheeks
Within his bending fickles compaffe come,
Loue alters not with his breefe houres and weekes,
But beares it out euen to the edge of doome:
   If this be error and vpon me proued,
   I neuer writ,nor no man euer loued.

117

A Ccufe me thus,that I haue fcanted all,
   Wherein I fhould your great deferts repay,
Forgot vpon your deareft loue to call,
Whereto al bonds do tie me day by day,
That I haue frequent binne with vnknown mindes,
And giuen to time your owne deare purchaf'd right,
That I haue hoyfted faile to al the windes
Which fhould tranfport me fartheft from your fight.
Booke both my wilfulneffe and errors downe,
And on iuft proofe furmife,accumilate,
Bring me within the leuel of your frowne,
But fhoote not at me in your wakened hate:
   Since my appeale faies I did ftriue to prooue
   The conftancy and virtue of your loue

H   118

SHAKE-SPEARES
118

Like as to make our appetites more keene
With eager compounds we our pallat vrge,
As to preuent our malladies vnseene,
We sicken to shun sicknesse when we purge.
Euen so being full of your nere cloying sweetnesse,
To bitter sawces did I frame my feeding;
And sicke of wel-fare found a kind of meetnesse,
To be diseas'd ere that there was true needing.
Thus pollicie in loue t'anticipate
The ills that were,not grew to faults assured,
And brought to medicine a healthfull state
Which rancke of goodnesse would by ill be cured.
    But thence I learne and find the lesson true,
    Drugs poyson him that so fell sicke of you.

119

What potions haue I drunke of *Syren* teares
Distil'd from Lymbecks foule as hell within,
Applying feares to hopes,and hopes to feares,
Still loosing when I saw my selfe to win?
What wretched errors hath my heart committed,
Whilst it hath thought it selfe so blessed neuer?
How haue mine eies out of their Spheares bene fitted
In the distraction of this madding feuer?
O benefit of ill, now I find true
That better is, by euil still made better.
And ruin'd loue when it is built anew
Growes fairer then at first,more strong,far greater.
    So I returne rebukt to my content,
    And gaine by ills thrise more then I haue spent,

120

That you were once vnkind be-friends mee now,
And for that sorrow , which I then didde feele,
Needes must I vnder my transgression bow,
Vnlesse my Nerues were brasse or hammered steele,
For if you were by my vnkindnesse shaken

As

SONNETS.

As I by yours , y'haue paſt a hell of Time,
And I a tyrant haue no leaſure taken
To waigh how once I ſuffered in your crime.
O that our night of wo might haue remembred
My deepeſt ſence,how hard true ſorrow hits,
And ſoone to you,as you to me then tendred
The humble ſalue,which wounded boſomes fits!
   But that your treſpaſſe now becomes a fee,
   Mine ranſoms yours,and yours muſt ranſome mee.

121

TIS better to be vile then vile eſteemed,
  When not to be,receiues reproach of being,
And the iuſt pleaſure loſt,which is ſo deemed,
Not by our feeling,but by others ſeeing.
For why ſhould others falſe adulterat eyes
Giue ſalutation to my ſportiue blood?
Or on my frailties why are frailer ſpies;
Which in their wils count bad what I think good?
Noe,I am that I am,and they that leuell
At my abuſes,reckon vp their owne,
I may be ſtraight though they them-ſelues be beuel
By their rancke thoughtes,my deedes muſt not be ſhown
   Vnleſſe this generall euill they maintaine,
   All men are bad and in their badneſſe raigne.

122.

T Thy guift,,thy tables,are within my braine
  Full characterd with laſting memory,
Which ſhall aboue that idle rancke remaine
Beyond all date euen to eternity.
Or at the leaſt,ſo long as braine and heart
Haue facultie by nature to ſubſiſt,
Til each to raz'd obliuion yeeld his part
Of thee,thy record neuer can be miſt?
That poore retention could not ſo much hold,
Nor need I tallies thy deare loue to skore,
Therefore to giue them from me was I bold,

H 2

To

SHAKE-SPEARES

To truft thofe tables that receaue thee more,
  To keepe an adiunckt to remember thee,
  Were to import forgetfulneffe in mee.

123

NO! Time, thou fhalt not boft that I doe change,
  Thy pyramyds buylt vp with newer might
To me are nothing nouell,nothing ftrange,
They are but dreffings of a former fight:
Our dates are breefe,and therefor we admire,
What thou doft foyft vpon vs that is ould,
And rather make them borne to our defire,
Then thinke that we before haue heard them tould:
Thy regifters and thee I both defie,
Not wondring at the prefent,nor the paft,
For thy records,and what we fee doth lye,
Made more or les by thy continuall haft:
  This I doe vow and this fhall euer be,
  I will be true difpight thy fyeth and thee.

124

YF my deare loue were but the childe of ftate,
  It might for fortunes bafterd be vnfathered,
As fubiect to times loue,or to times hate,
Weeds among weeds,or flowers with flowers gatherd.
No it was buylded far from accident,
It fuffers not in fmilinge pomp,nor falls
Vnder the blow of thralled difcontent,
Whereto th'inuiting time our fafhion calls:
It feares not policy that *Heriticke*,
Which workes on leafes of fhort numbred howers,
But all alone ftands hugely pollitick,
That it nor growes with heat,nor drownes with fhowres.
  To this I witnes call the foles of time,
  Which die for goodnes,who haue liu'd for crime.

125

VVEr't ought to me I bore the canopy,
  With my extern the outward honoring,

Or

Sonnets.

Or layd great bafes for eternity,
Which proues more fhort then waft or ruining?
Haue I not feene dwellers on forme and fauor
Lofe all,and more by paying too much rent
For compound fweet;Forgoing fimple fauor,
Pittifull thriuors in their gazing fpent.
Noe,let me be obfequious in thy heart,
And take thou my oblacion,poore but free,
Which is not mixt with feconds,knows no art,
But mutuall render,onely me for thee.
   Hence,thou fubbornd*Informer*, a trew foule
   When moft impeacht,ftands leaft in thy controule.

126

O Thou my louely Boy who in thy power,
  Doeft hould times fickle glaffe,his fickle,hower;
Who haft by wayning growne,and therein fhou'ft,
Thy louers withering,as thy fweet felfe grow'ft.
If Nature(foueraine mifteres ouer wrack)
As thou goeft onwards ftill will plucke thee backe,
She keepes thee to this purpofe,that her skill.
May time difgrace,and wretched mynuit kill.
Yet feare her O thou minnion of her pleafure,
She may detaine,but not ftill keepe her trefure!
Her *Audite*(though delayd)anfwer'd muft be,
And her *Quietus* is to render thee.

(   )
(   )

127

I N the ould age blacke was not counted faire,
  Or if it weare it bore not beauties name:
But now is blacke beauties fucceffiue heire,
And Beautie flanderd with a baftard fhame,
For fince each hand hath put on Natures power,
Fairing the foule with Arts faulfe borrow'd face,
Sweet beauty hath no name no holy boure,
But is prophan'd, if not liues in difgrace.

H 3   Therefore

SHAKE-SPEARES

Therefore my Mistersse eyes are Rauen blacke,
Her eyes so suted, and they mourners seeme,
At such who not borne faire no beauty lack,
Slandring Creation with a false esteeme,
    Yet so they mourne becomming of their woe,
    That euery toung saies beauty should looke so.

128

HOw oft when thou my musike musike playst,
Vpon that blessed wood whose motion sounds
With thy sweet fingers when thou gently swayst,
The wiry concord that mine eare coufounds,
Do I enuie those Iackes that nimble leape,
To kisse the tender inward of thy hand,
Whilst my poore lips which should that haruest reape,
At the woods bouldnes by thee blushing stand.
To be so tikled they would change their state,
And situation with those dancing chips,
Ore whome their fingers walke with gentle gate,
Making dead wood more blest then liuing lips,
    Since sausie Iackes so happy are in this,
    Giue them their fingers, me thy lips to kisse.

129

TH'expence of Spirit in a waste of shame
Is lust in action, and till action , lust
Is periurd, murdrous, bloudy full of blame,
Sauage, extreame, rude, cruell, not to trust,
Inioyd no sooner but dispised straight,
Past reason hunted, and no sooner had
Past reason hated as a swollowed bayt,
On purpose layd to make the taker mad.
Made In pursut and in possession so,
Had, hauing, and in quest, to haue extreame,
A blisse in proofe and proud and very wo,
Before a ioy propos'd behind a dreame,
    All this the world well knowes yet none knowes well,
    To shun the heauen that leads men to this hell.

                                                                My

SONNETS.

130

MY Miſtres eyes are nothing like the Sunne,
Currall is farre more red,then her lips red,
If ſnow be white why then her breſts are dun:
If haires be wiers,black wiers grow on her head:
I haue ſeene Roſes damaskt,red and white,
But no ſuch Roſes ſee I in her cheekes,
And in ſome perfumes is there more delight,
Then in the breath that from my Miſtres reekes.
I loue to heare her ſpeake,yet well I know,
That Muſicke hath a farre more pleaſing ſound:
I graunt I neuer ſaw a goddeſſe goe,
My Miſtres when ſhee walkes treads on the ground.
     And yet by heauen I thinke my loue as rare,
     As any ſhe beli'd with falſe compare.

131

THou art as tiranous,ſo as thou art,
As thoſe whoſe beauties proudly make them cruell;
For well thou know'ſt to my deare doting hart
Thou art the faireſt and moſt precious Iewell.
Yet in good faith ſome ſay that thee behold,
Thy face hath not the power to make loue grone;
To ſay they erre,I dare not be ſo bold,
Although I ſweare it to my ſelfe alone.
And to be ſure that is not falſe I ſweare
A thouſand grones but thinking on thy face,
One on anothers necke do witneſſe beare
Thy blacke is faireſt in my iudgements place.
     In nothing art thou blacke ſaue in thy deeds,
     And thence this ſlaunder as I thinke proceeds.

132

THine eies I loue,and they as pittying me,
Knowing thy heart torment me with diſdaine,
Haue put on black,and louing mourners bee,
Looking with pretty ruth vpon my paine,

And

And truly not the morning Sun of Heauen
Better becomes the gray cheeks of th' Eaſt,
Nor that full Starre that vſhers in the Eauen
Doth halfe that glory to the ſober Weſt
As thoſe two morning eyes become thy face:
O let it then as well beſeeme thy heart
To mourne for me ſince mourning doth thee grace,
And ſute thy pitty like in euery part.
   Then will I ſweare beauty her ſelfe is blacke,
   And all they foule that thy complexion lacke.

133

BEſhrew that heart that makes my heart to groane
For that deepe wound it giues my friend and me;
I'ſt not ynough to torture me alone,
But ſlaue to ſlauery my ſweet'ſt friend muſt be.
Me from my ſelfe thy cruell eye hath taken,
And my next ſelfe thou harder haſt ingroſſed,
Of him,my ſelfe,and thee I am forſaken,
A torment thrice three-fold thus to be croſſed :
Priſon my heart in thy ſteele boſomes warde,
But then my friends heart let my poore heart bale,
Who ere keepes me,let my heart be his garde,
Thou canſt not then vſe rigor in my Iaile.
   And yet thou wilt,for I being pent in thee,
   Perforce am thine and all that is in me.

134

SO now I haue confeſt that he is thine,
   And I my ſelfe am morgag'd to thy will,
My ſelfe Ile forfeit,ſo that other mine,
Thou wilt reſtore to be my comfort ſtill:
But thou wilt not,nor he will not be free,
For thou art couetous,and he is kinde,
He learnd but ſuretie-like to write for me,
Vnder that bond that him as faſt doth binde.
The ſtatute of thy beauty thou wilt take,
Thou vſurer that put'ſt forth all to vſe,

                                        And

SONNETS.

And ſue a friend,came debter for my ſake,
So him I looſe through my vnkinde abuſe.
　Him haue I loſt, thou haſt both him and me,
　He paies the whole,and yet am I not free.

135

WHo euer hath her wiſh,thou haſt thy *Will*,
　　And *Will* too boote,and *Will* in ouer-plus,
More then enough am I that vexe thee ſtill,
To thy ſweet will making addition thus.
Wilt thou whoſe will is large and ſpatious,
Not once vouchſafe to hide my will in thine,
Shall will in others ſeeme right gracious,
And in my will no faire acceptance ſhine:
The ſea all water,yet receiues raine ſtill,
And in aboundance addeth to his ſtore,
So thou beeing rich in *Will* adde to thy *Will*,
One will of mine to make thy large *Will* more.
　Let no vnkinde,no faire beſeechers kill,
　Thinke all but one,and me in that one *Will*.

136

IF thy ſoule check thee that I come ſo neere,
　Sweare to thy blind ſoule that I was thy *Will*,
And will thy ſoule knowes is admitted there,
Thus farre for loue, my loue-ſute ſweet fullfill.
Will, will fulfill the treaſure of thy loue,
I fill it full with wils,and my will one,
In things of great receit with eaſe we prooue,
Among a number one is reckon'd none.
Then in the number let me paſſe vntold,
Though in thy ſtores account I one muſt be,
For nothing hold me ſo it pleaſe thee hold,
That nothing me,a ſome-thing ſweet to thee.
　Make but my name thy loue,and loue that ſtill,
　And then thou loueſt me for my name is *Will*.

137

THou blinde foole loue,what dooſt thou to mine eyes,
　　　　　　　I　　　　　　　　That

That they behold and fee not what they fee :
They know what beautie is,fee where it lyes,
Yet what the beft is,take the worft to be.
If eyes corrupt by ouer-partiall lookes,
Be anchord in the baye where all men ride,
Why of eyes falfehood haft thou forged hookes,
Whereto the iudgement of my heart is tide?
Why fhould my heart thinke that a feuerall plot,
Which my heart knowes the wide worlds common place?
Or mine eyes feeing this,fay this is not
To put faire truth vpon fo foule a face,
    In things right true my heart and eyes haue erred,
    And to this falfe plague are they now tranfferred.

138

*W*Hen my loue fweares that fhe is made of truth,
    I do beleeue her though I know fhe lyes,
That fhe might thinke me fome vntuterd youth,
Vnlearned in the worlds falfe fubtilties.
Thus vainely thinking that fhe thinkes me young,
Although fhe knowes my dayes are paft the beft,
Simply I credit her falfe fpeaking tongue,
On both fides thus is fimple truth fuppreft :
But wherefore fayes fhe not fhe is vniuft ?
And wherefore fay not I that I am old ?
O loues beft habit is in feeming truft,
And age in loue,loues not t'haue yeares told.
    Therefore I lye with her,and fhe with me,
    And in our faults by lyes we flattered be.

139

O Call not me to iuftifie the wrong,
    That thy vnkindneffe layes vpon my heart,
Wound me not with thine eye but with thy toung,
Vfe power with power,and flay me not by Art,
Tell me thou lou'ft elfe-where;but in my fight,
Deare heart forbeare to glance thine eye afide,
What needft thou wound with cunning when thy might

Is

SONNETS.

Is more then my ore-preſt defence can bide?
Let me excuſe thee ah my loue well knowes,
Her prettie lookes haue beene mine enemies,
And therefore from my face ſhe turnes my foes,
That they elſe-where might dart their iniuries :
    Yet do not ſo,but ſince I am neere ſlaine,
    Kill me out-right with lookes,and rid my paine.

140

BE wiſe as thou art cruell,do not preſſe
  My toung-tide patience with too much diſdaine :
Leaſt ſorrow lend me words and words expreſſe,
The manner of my pittie wanting paine.
If I might teach thee witte better it weare,
Though not to loue,yet loue to tell me ſo,
As teſtie ſick-men when their deaths be neere,
No newes but health from their Phiſitions know.
For if I ſhould diſpaire I ſhould grow madde,
And in my madneſſe might ſpeake ill of thee,
Now this ill wreſting world is growne ſo bad,
Madde ſlanderers by madde eares beleoued be.
    That I may not be ſo, nor thou be lyde,   (wide.
    Beare thine eyes ſtraight , though thy proud heart goe

141

IN faith I doe not loue thee with mine eyes,
  For they in thee a thouſand errors note,
But 'tis my heart that loues what they diſpiſe,
Who in diſpight of view is pleaſd to dote.
Nor are mine eares with thy toungs tune delighted,
Nor tender feeling to baſe touches prone,
Nor taſte, nor ſmell, deſire to be inuited
To any ſenſuall feaſt with thee alone :
But my fiue wits,nor my fiue ſences can
Diſwade one fooliſh heart from ſeruing thee,
Who leaues vnſwai'd the likeneſſe of a man,
Thy proud hearts ſlaue and vaſſall wretch to be :
    Onely my plague thus farre I count my gaine,
    That ſhe that makes me ſinne,awards me paine.

I 2   Loue

SHAKE-SPEARES

142

LOue is my sinne,and thy deare vertue hate,
Hate of my sinne,grounded on sinfull louing,
O but with mine, compare thou thine owne state,
And thou shalt finde it merrits not reprouuing,
Or if it do,not from those lips of thine,
That haue proplian'd their scarlet ornaments,
And seald false bonds of loue as oft as mine,
Robd others beds reuenues of their rents.
Be it lawfull I loue thee as thou lou'st those,
Whome thine eyes wooe as mine importune thee,
Roote pittie in thy heart that when it growes,
Thy pitty may deserue to pittied bee.
　　If thou doost seeke to haue what thou doost hide,
　　By selfe example mai'st thou be denide.

143

LOe as a carefull huswife runnes to catch,
One of her fethered creatures broake away,
Sets downe her babe and makes all swift dispatch
In pursuit of the thing she would haue stay:
Whilst her neglected child holds her in chace,
Cries to catch her whose busie care is bent,
To follow that which flies before her face:
Not prizing her poore infants discontent;
So runst thou after that which flies from thee,
Whilst I thy babe chace thee a farre behind,
But if thou catch thy hope turne back to me:
And play the mothers part kisse me,be kind.
　　So will I pray that thou maist haue thy *Will*,
　　If thou turne back and my loude crying still.

144

TWo loues I haue of comfort and dispaire,
Which like two spirits do sugiest me still,
The better angell is a man right faire:
The worser spirit a woman collour'd il.
To win me soone to hell my femall euill,

Tempteth

SONNETS.

Tempteth my better angel from my fight,
And would corrupt my faint to be a diuel:
Wooing his purity with her fowle pride.
And whether that my angel be turn'd finde,
Sufpect I may,yet not directly tell,
But being both from me both to each friend,
I geffe one angel in an others hel.
　　Yet this fhal I nere know but liue in doubt,
　　Till my bad angel fire my good one out.

145

THofe lips that Loues owne hand did make,
　　Breath'd forth the found that faid I hate,
To me that languifht for her fake:
But when fhe faw my wofull ftate,
Straight in her heart did mercie come,
Chiding that tongue that euer fweet,
Was vfde in giuing gentle dome:
And tought it thus a new to greete:
I hate fhe alterd with an end,
That follow'd it as gentle day,
Doth follow night who like a fiend
From heauen to hell is flowne away.
　　I hate,from hate away fhe threw,
　　And fau'd my life faying not you.

146

POore foule the center of my finfull earth,
　　My finfull earth thefe rebbell powres that thee array,
Why doft thou pine within and fuffer dearth
Painting thy outward walls fo coftlie gay?
Why fo large coft hauing fo fhort a leafe,
Doft thou vpon thy fading manfion fpend?
Shall wormes inheritors of this exceffe
Eate vp thy charge?is this thy bodies end?
Then foule liue thou vpon thy feruants loffe,
And let that pine to aggrauat thy ftore;
Buy tearmes diuine in felling houres of droffe:

13   Within

Within be fed, without be rich no more,
    So shalt thou feed on death,that feeds on men,
    And death once dead,ther's no more dying then.

147

MY loue is as a feauer longing still,
    For that which longer nurseth the disease,
Feeding on that which doth preserue the ill,
Th'vncertaine sicklie appetite to please:
My reason the Phisition to my loue,
Angry that his prescriptions are not kept
Hath left me,and I desperate now approoue,
Desire is death,which Phisick did except.
Past cure I am,now Reason is past care,
And frantick madde with euer-more vnrest,
My thoughts and my discourse as mad mens are,
At randon from the truth vainely exprest.
    For I haue sworne thee faire,and thought thee bright,
    Who art as black as hell,as darke as night.

148

O Me! what eyes hath loue put in my head,
    Which haue no correspondence with true sight,
Or if they haue,where is my iudgment fled,
That censures falsely what they see aright?
If that be faire whereon my false eyes dote,
What meanes the world to say it is not so?
If it be not,then loue doth well denote,
Loues eye is not so true as all mens:no,
How can it? O how can loues eye be true,
That is so vext with watching and with teares?
No maruaile then though I mistake my view,
The sunne it selfe sees not,till heauen cleeres.
    O cunning loue,with teares thou keepst me blinde,
    Least eyes well seeing thy foule faults should finde.

149

CAnst thou O cruell,say I loue thee not,
    When I against my selfe with thee pertake:

Doe

SONNETS.

Doe I not thinke on thee when I forgot
Am of my selfe, all tirant for thy sake?
Who hateth thee that I doe call my friend,
On whom froun'ft thou that I doe faune vpon,
Nay if thou lowrft on me doe I not spend
Reuenge vpon my selfe with present mone?
What merrit do I in my selfe respect,
That is so proude thy seruice to dispise,
When all my beft doth worfhip thy defect,
Commanded by the motion of thine eyes.
   But loue hate on for now I know thy minde,
   Thofe that can see thou lou'ft,and I am blind.

150

OH from what powre haft thou this powrefull might,
  VVith insufficiency my heart to sway,
To make me giue the lie to my true fight,
And fwere that brightneffe doth not grace the day?
Whence haft thou this becomming of things il,
That in the very refuse of thy deeds,
There is such ftrength and warrantife of skill,
That in my minde thy worft all beft exceeds?
Who taught thee how to make me loue thee more,
The more I heare and see iuft cause of hate,
Oh though I loue what others doe abhor,
VVith others thou fhouldft not abhor my ftate.
   If thy vnworthineffe raifd loue in me,
   More worthy I to be belou'd of thee.

151

LOue is too young to know what confcience is,
  Yet who knowes not confcience is borne of loue,
Then gentle cheater vrge not my amiffe,
Leaft guilty of my faults thy sweet selfe proue.
For thou betraying me, I doe betray
My nobler part to my grofe bodies treafon,
My foule doth tell my body that he may,
Triumph in loue,flefh ftaies no farther reafon,

                                              But

SHAKE-SPEARES

But ryfing at thy name doth point out thee,
As his triumphant prize,proud of this pride,
He is contented thy poore drudge to be
To ftand in thy affaires,fall by thy fide.
　　No want of confcience hold it that I call,
　　Her loue,for whofe deare loue I rife and fall.

152

IN louing thee thou know'ft I am forfworne,
But thou art twice forfworne to me loue fwearing,
In act thy bed-vow broake and new faith torne,
In vowing new hate after new loue bearing:
But why of two othes breach doe I accufe thee,
When I breake twenty:I am periur'd moft,
For all my vowes are othes but to mifufe thee:
And all my honeft faith in thee is loft.
For I haue fworne deepe othes of thy deepe kindneffe:
Othes of thy loue,thy truth,thy conftancie,
And to inlighten thee gaue eyes to blindneffe,
Or made them fwere againft the thing they fee.
　　For I haue fworne thee faire:more periurde eye,
　　To fwere againft the truth fo foule a lie.

153

CVpid laid by his brand and fell a fleepe,
A maide of *Dyans* this aduantage found,
And his loue-kindling fire did quickly fteepe
In a could vallie-fountaine of that ground:
Which borrowd from this holie fire of loue,
A dateleffe liuely heat ftill to indure,
And grew a feething bath which yet men proue,
Againft ftrang malladies a foueraigne cure:
But at my miftres eie loues brand new fired,
The boy for triall needes would touch my breft,
I fick withall the helpe of bath defired,
And thether hied a fad diftemperd gueft.
　　But found no cure,the bath for my helpe lies,
　　Where *Cupid* got new fire;my miftres eye.

SONNETS.

154

THe little Loue-God lying once a sleepe,
  Laid by his side his heart inflaming brand,
Whilst many Nymphes that vou'd chast life to keep,
Came tripping by, but in her maiden hand,
The fayrest votary tooke vp that fire,
Which many Legions of true hearts had warm'd,
And so the Generall of hot desire,
Was sleeping by a Virgin hand disarm'd.
This brand she quenched in a coole Well by,
Which from loues fire tooke heat perpetuall,
Growing a bath and healthfull remedy,
For men diseasd, but I my Mistriffe thrall,
    Came there for cure and this by that I proue,
    Loues fire heates water, water cooles not loue.

FINIS.

K   A

A Louers complaint.

BY

WILLIAM SHAKE-SPEARE.

FRom off a hill whofe concaue wombe reworded,
A plaintfull ftory from a fiftring vale
My fpirrits t'attend this doble voyce accorded,
And downe I laid to lift the fad tun'd tale,
Ere long efpied a fickle maid full pale
Tearing of papers breaking rings a twaine,
Storming her world with forrowes, wind and raine.

Vpon her head a plattid hiue of ftraw,
Which fortified her vifage from the Sunne,
Whereon the thought might thinke fometime it faw
The carkas of a beauty fpent and donne,
Time had not fithed all that youth begun,
Nor youth all quit, but fpight of heauens fell rage,
Some beauty peept, through lettice of feat'd age.

Oft did fhe heaue her Napkin to her eyne,
Which on it had conceited charecters:
Laundring the filken figures in the brine,
That feafoned woe had pelleted in teares,
And often reading what contents it beares:
As often fhriking vndiftinguifht wo,
In clamours of all fize both high and low.

Some-times her leueld eyes their carriage ride,
As they did battry to the fpheres intend:
Sometime diuerted their poore balls are tide,
To th'orbed earth ;fometimes they do extend,
Their view right on, anon their gafes lend,

To

COMPLAINT

To euery place at once and no where fixt,
The mind and fight diſtraɛtedly commxit.

Her haire nor looſe nor ti'd in formall plat,
Proclaimd in her a careleſſe hand of pride;
For ſome vntuck'd deſcended her ſheu'd hat,
Hanging her pale and pined cheeke beſide,
Some in her threeden fillet ſtill did bide,
And trew to bondage would not breake from thence,
Though ſlackly braided in looſe negligence.

A thouſand fauours from a maund ſhe drew,
Of amber chriſtall and of bedded Iet,
Which one by one ſhe in a riuer threw,
Vpon whoſe weeping margent ſhe was ſet,
Like vſery applying wet to wet,
Or Monarches hands that lets not bounty fall,
Where want cries ſome;but where exceſſe begs all.

Of folded ſchedulls had ſhe many a one,
Which ſhe peruſ d,ſighd,tore and gaue the flud,
Crackt many a ring of Poſied gold and bone,
Bidding them find their Sepulchers in mud,
Found yet mo letters ſadly pend in blood,
With ſleided ſilke,ſeate and affeɛtedly
Enſwath'd and ſeald to curious ſecrecy.

Theſe often bath'd ſhe in her fluxiue eies,
And often kiſt,and often gaue to teare,
Cried O falſe blood thou regiſter of lies,
What vnapproued witnes dooſt thou beare!
Inke would haue ſeem'd more blacke and damned heare!
This ſaid in top of rage the lines ſhe rents,
Big diſcontent,ſo breaking their contents.

A reuerend man that graz'd his cattell ny,
K 2   Some.

A LOVERS

Sometime a blusterer that the ruffle knew
Of Court of Cittie, and had let go by
The swiftest houres obserued as they flew,
Towards this afflicted fancy saftly drew:
And priuiledg'd by age desires to know
In breefe the grounds and motiues of her wo.

So slides he downe vppon his greyned bat;
And comely distant sits he by her side,
When hee againe desires her, being satte,
Her greeuance with his hearing to deuide:
If that from him there may be ought applied
Which may her suffering extasie asswage
Tis promist in the charitie of age.

Father she saies, though in mee you behold
The iniury of many a blasting houre;
Let it not tell your Iudgement I am old,
Not age, but sorrow, ouer me hath power;
I might as yet haue bene a spreading flower
Fresh to my selfe, if I had selfe applyed
Loue to my selfe, and to no Loue beside.

But wo is mee, too early I atttended
A youthfull suit it was to gaine my grace;
O one by natures outwards so commended,
That maidens eyes stucke ouer all his face,
Loue lackt a dwelling and made him her place.
And when in his faire parts shee didde abide,
Shee was new lodg'd and newly Deified.

His browny locks did hang in crooked curles,
And euery light occasion of the wind
Vpon his lippes their silken parcels hurles,
Whats sweet to do, to do wil aptly find,
Each eye that saw him did inchaunt the minde:

For

COMPLAINT.

For on his vifage was in little drawne,
What largeneffe thinkes in parradife was fawne.

Smal fhew of man was yet vpon his chinne,
His phenix downe began but to appeare
Like vnfhorne veluet,on that termleffe skin
Whofe bare out-brag'd the web it feem'd to were.
Yet fhewed his vifage by that coft more deare,
And nice affections wauering ftood in doubt
If beft were as it was,or beft without.

His qualities were beautious as his forme,
For maiden tongu'd he was and thereof free;
Yet if men mou'd him,was he fuch a ftorme
As oft twixt May and Aprill is to fee,
When windes breath fweet,vnruly though they bee.
His rudeneffe fo with his authoriz'd youth,
Did liuery falfeneffe in a pride of truth.

Wel could hee ride, and often men would fay
That horfe his mettell from his rider takes
Proud of fubiection,noble by the fwaie,   (makes
What rounds,what bounds,what courfe what ftop he
And controuerfie hence a queftion takes,
Whether the horfe by him became his deed,
Or he his mannad'g, by'th wel doing Steed.

But quickly on this fide the verdict went,
His reall habitude gaue life and grace
To appertainings and to ornament,
Accomplifht in him-felfe not in his cafe:
All ayds them-felues made fairer by their place,
Can for addicions,yet their purpof'd trimme
Peec'd not his grace but were al grac'd by him.

So on the tip of his fubduing tongue

K 3   All

A LOVERS

All kinde of arguments and question deepe
Al replication prompt, and reason strong
For his aduantage still did wake and sleep
To make the weeper laugh, the laugher weemet
He hadthe dialect and different skil,
Catching al passions in his craft of will.

That hee didde in the general bosome raigne
Of young, of old, and sexes both inchanted,
To dwel with him in thoughts, or to remaine
In personal duty, following where he haunted,
Consent's bewitcht, ere he desire haue granted,
And dialogu'd for him what he would say,
Askt their own wils and made their wils obey.

Many there were that did his picture gette
To serue their eies, and in it put their mind,
Like fooles that in th' imagination set
The goodly obiects which abroad they find
Of lands and mansions, theirs in thought assign'd,
And labouring in moe pleasures to bestow them,
Then the true gouty Land-lord which doth owe them.

So many haue that neuer toucht his hand
Sweetly suppos'd them mistresse of his heart:
My wofull selfe that did in freedome stand,
And was my owne fee simple (not in part)
What with his art in youth and youth in art
Threw my affections in his charmed power,
Reseru'd the stalke and gaue him al my flower.

Yet did I not as some my equals did
Demaund of him, nor being desired yeelded,
Finding my selfe in honour so forbidde,
With safest distance I mine honour sheelded,
Experience for me many bulwarkes builded

Of

COMPLAINT.

Of proofs new bleeding which remaind the foile
Of this falfe Iewell, and his amorous fpoile.

But ah who euer fhun'd by precedent,
The deftin'd ill fhe muft her felfe affay,
Or forc'd examples gainft her owne content
To put the by-paft perrils in her way?
Counfaile may ftop a while what will not ftay:
For when we rage, aduife is often feene
By blunting vs to make our wits more keene,

Nor giues it fatisfaction to our blood,
That wee muft curbe it vppon others proofe.
To be forbod the fweets that feemes fo good,
For feare of harmes that preach in our behoofe,
O appetite from iudgement ftand aloofe!
The one a pallate hath that needs will tafte,
Though reafon weepe and cry it is thy laft.

For further I could fay this mans virtrue,
And knew the patternes of his foule beguiling,
Heard where his plants in others Orchards grew,
Saw how deceits were guilded in his fmiling,
Knew vowes, wer e euer brokers to defiling,
Thought Characters and words meerly but art,
And baftards of his foule adulterat heart.

And long vpon thefe termes I held my Citty,
Till thus hee gan befiege me : Gentle maid
Haue of my fuffering youth fome feeling pitty
And be not of my holy vowes affraid,
Thats to ye fworne to none was euer faid,
For feafts of loue I haue bene call'd vnto
Till now did nere inuite nor neuer vovv.

All my offences that abroad you fee
K 4   Are

A Lovers

Are errors of the blood none of the mind:
Loue made them not,with acture they may be,
Where neither Party is nor trew nor kind,
They fought their fhame that fo their fhame did find,
And fo much leffe of fhame in me remaines,
By how much of me their reproch containes,

Among the many that mine eyes haue feene,
Not one whofe flame my hart fo much as warmed,
Or my affection put to th, fmalleft teene,
Or any of my leifures euer Charmed,
Harme haue I done to them but nere was harmed,
Kept hearts in liueries,but mine owne was free,
And raignd commaunding in his monarchy.

Looke heare what tributes wounded fancies fent me,
Of palyd pearles and rubies red as blood:
Figuring that they their paffions likewife lent me
Of greefe and blufhes, aptly vnderftood
In bloodleffe white,and the encrimfon'd mood,
Effects of terror and deare modefty,
Encampt in hearts but fighting outwardly.

And Lo behold thefe tallents of their heir,
With twifted mettle amoroufly empleacht
I haue receau'd from many a feueral faire,
Their kind acceptance, wepingly befeecht,
With th'annexions of faire gems inricht,
And deepe brain'd fonnets that did amplifie
Each ftones deare Nature,worth and quallity.

The Diamond?why twas beautifull and hard,
Whereto his inuif'd properties did tend,
The deepe greene Emrald in whofe frefh regard,
Weake fights their fickly radience do amend.
The heauen hewd Saphir and the Opall blend

                                        With

COMPLAINT.

With obiects manyfold; each feuerall ftone,
With wit well blazond fmil'd or made fome mone,

Lo all thefe trophies of affections hot,
Of penfiu'd and fubdew'd defires the tender,
Nature hath chargd me that I hoord them not,
But yeeld them vp where I my felfe muft render:
That is to you my origin and ender :
For thefe of force muft your oblations be,
Since I their Aulter, you enpatrone me.

Oh then aduance(of yours)that phrafeles hand,
Whofe white weighes downe the airy fcale of praife,
Take all thefe fimilies to your owne command,
Hollowed with fighes that burning lunges did raife:
What me your minifter for you obaies
Workes vnder you,and to your audit comes
Their diftract parcells,in combined fummes.

Lo this deuice was fent me from a Nun,
Or Sifter fanctified of holieft note,
Which late her noble fuit in court did fhun,
Whofe rareft hauings made the bloffoms dote,
For fhe was fought by fpirits of ritcheft cote,
But kept cold diftance,and did thence remoue,
To fpend her liuing in eternall loue.

But oh my fweet what labour ift to leaue,
The thing we haue not,maftring what not ftriues,
Playing the Place which did no forme receiue,
Playing patient fports in vnconftraind giues,
She that her fame fo to her felfe contriues,
The fcarres of battaile fcapeth by the flight,
And makes her abfence valiant,not her might.

Oh pardon me in that my boaft is true,
                    L   The

A Lovers

The accident which brought me to her eie,
Vpon the moment did her force subdewe,
And now she would the caged cloifter flies:
Religious loue put out religions eye:
Not to be tempted would she be enur'd,
And now to tempt all liberty procure.

How mightie then you are, Oh heare me tell,
The broken bofoms that to me belong,
Haue emptied all their fountaines in my well:
And mine I powre your Ocean all amonge:
I strong ore them and you ore me being strong,
Must for your victorie vs all congest,
As compound loue to phifick your cold brest.

My parts had powre to charme a facred Sunne,
Who difciplin'd I dieted in grace,
Beleeu'd her eies, when they t' affaile begun,
All vowes and confecrations giuing place:
O moft potentiall loue, vowe, bond, nor fpace
In thee hath neither fting, knot, nor confine
For thou art all and all things els are thine.

When thou impreffeft what are precepts worth
Of ftale example? when thou wilt inflame,
How coldly thofe impediments ftand forth
Of wealth of filliall feare, lawe, kindred fame,   (fhame
Loues armes are peace, gainft rule, gainft fence, gainft
And fweetens in the fuffring pangues it beares,
The *Alloes* of all forces, fhockes and feares.

Now all thefe hearts that doe on mine depend,
Feeling it breake, with bleeding groanes they pine,
And fupplicant their fighes to you extend
To leaue the battrie that you make gainft mine,
Lending fofe audience, to my fweet defigne,

                                                          And

COMPLAINT.

And credent foule,to that ftrong bonded oth,
That fhall preferre and vndertake my troth.

This faid,his watrie eies he did difmount,
Whofe fightes till then were leaueld on my face,
Each cheeke a riuer running from a fount,
With brynifh currant downe-ward flowed a pace:
Oh how the channell to the ftreame gaue grace!
Who glaz'd with Chriftall gate the glowing Rofes,
That flame through water which their hew inclofes,

Oh father,what a hell of witch-craft lies,
In the fmall orb of one perticular teare?
But with the invndation of the eies:
What rocky heart to water will not weare?
What breft fo cold that is not warmed heare,
Or cleft effect,cold modefty hot wrath:
Both fire from hence,and chill extincture hath.

For loe his paffion but an art of craft,
Euen there refolu'd my reafon into teares,
There my white ftole of chaftity I daft,
Shooke off my fober gardes,and ciuill feares,
Appeare to him as he to me appeares:
All melting,though our drops this diffrence bore,
His poifon'd me, and mine did him reftore.

In him a plenitude of fubtle matter,
Applied to Cautills,all ftraing formes receiues,
Of burning blufhes,or of weeping water,
Or founding palenefse: and he takes and leaues,
In eithers aptnefse as it beft deceiues:
To blufh at fpeeches ranck , to weepe at woes
Or to turne white and found at tragick fhowes.

That not a heart which in his leuell came,
L 2   Could

THE LOVERS

Could ſcape the haile of his all hurting ayme,
Shewing faire Nature is both kinde and tame :
And vaild in them did winne whom he would maime,
Againſt the thing he ſought,he would exclaime,
When he moſt burnt in hart-wiſht luxurie,
He preacht pure maide,and praiſd cold chaſtitie.

Thus meerely with the garment of a grace,
The naked and concealed feind he couerd,
That th'vnexperient gaue the tempter place,
Which like a Cherubin aboue them houerd,
Who young and ſimple would not be ſo louerd.
Aye me I fell,and yet do queſtion make,
What I ſhould doe againe for ſuch a ſake.

O that infected moyſture of his eye,
O that falſe fire which in his cheeke ſo glowd :
O that fore'd thunder from his heart did flye,
O that ſad breath his ſpungie lungs beſtowed,
O all that borrowed motion ſeeming owed,
Would yet againe betray the fore-betrayed,
And new peruert a reconciled Maide.

FINIS.

Index

Individual Shakespeare sonnets, poems, plays and characters appear under the relevant Shakespeare entry.

Entries in bold italics reference the many quotations and diagrams throughout the text.

166; Colatium, 106; Constantinople, 166;
Cyprus, 105; Dead Sea, 138; Denmark, 105,
126, 166, 169; Down, 219; Eastern Mediterranean, 105; Edinburgh, 218; Egypt, 105,
166; Elsinore Castle, 166; England, 105, 137,
151, 166, 178, 183, 184, 185, 213; Ephesus,
116; Europe, 119, 135, 138, 139; France, 105,
135, 137, 166, 195, 201, 213, 218; Germany,
213; Greece, 126; Hagia Sophia, 166; Iberian
Peninsula, 138; Illyria, 105, 146; Italy, 106,
119, 128, 194; Ithaca, 229; Libya, 169; London, 166, 229; Malta, 145; Mediterranean,
211; Milan, 106, 121, 146; Mount Blanc, 138;
Munich, 221; Naples, 106, 146, 218; Navarre,
201; Netherlands, 213, 218; Nile Delta,
105; Northern Britain, 105; North Sea, 138;
Padua, 198; Paphos, 128; Paris, 218, 221;
Red Sea, 138; Rome, 106, 166, 191; Saint
Peter's Basilica, 166; Scotland, 105, 151, 213;
Scottish Grampians, 105; Shoreditch, 208,
210; Sicily, 116, 196, 197; Spain, 105, 169,
213; Thames, 208; Troy, 111, 126, 160, 161;
Tunis, 107; Turkey, 105; Tyrrhenian coast,
106; Venice, 145, 166; Verona, 198; Vienna,
116, 120, 121, 146, 166, 200; Westminster
Abbey, 166; Windsor, 105, 158 — ; Greeks,
125, 161, 188, 189, 229; happy imitator of
Nature, 108; Heminge, John, 108, 183; Histories. *See* Histories; histories and tragedies,
131, 156, 168, 176, 197, 215, 216, 227, 234,
238; twenty-two, 131, 175, 196, 197, 215;
imaginary island, 106; imposters, 108; own
plays, 120; preface, 183; **preface_heminge-
condell**, 183; Prologue/prologue, 125, 126,
159, 161, 188, 190, 203; Roman, 158, 191,
194; stage-manage, 120, 121; thirty-six
plays, 105, 108, 110, 113, 119, 139, 145, 150,
152, 156, 165, 186, 188, 206, 231, 233, 236,
237, 240; three genres, 119; titles, 124, 126;
character, 125; generic, 124, 127; male, 127;
To the great Variety of Readers, 108; Tragedies. *See* Tragedies; Trojans, 125, 188, 229,
230; True Original Copies, 108; universality,
105
Shakespeare's Globe, 158, 213, 215, 225, 239;
1599, 208, 210; 1997, 229; Bankside, 210,
213, 229, 230, 237; Burbage brothers, 208;
consciousness, 206, 207, 210, 215; Globe
Theatre, 207, 211, 212, 215, 222, 225, 229,
230, 231, 234, 235, 236, 237, 238; Hercules,
208; implications, 206; intellect and emotion, 207; sensibility, 206; South Bank, 208,
231, 236; stage, 209; Thames, 208; theatrics,
208; The Theatre, 208, 236; Trojan horse,
229; Wooden O, 206, 208, 209, 229, 231, 234
Shakespeare's Plays, 74, 99, 102, 164, 165, 183,

186, 203, 206, 211, 222, 236, 237, 238, 239;
characters, 155; commendations, 108;
commentators, 184, 185; contents, 78, 226;
cross-dressing, 139; dialogue, 163; dramatic
ploys, 144; erotic banter, 147; eyes, 171, 172;
gender, 174; Globe, 208, 215; God, 167, 168;
goddesses and gods, 112; Hercules, 234;
injustices, 228; irony, 182; life and death,
176; nature, 110, 209, 229; nature template,
94, 157; philosophy, 103, 217; plays within
plays, 149; religion, 116; *Sonnets*, 207, 240;
truth, 162
Shakespeare's Plays - individual;
All's Well that Ends Well, 119, 132, 133, 134, 147,
177, 200; *aww_125-33*, 147; *aww_131-3*,
111; *aww_140-50*, 134; *aww_223-30*, 168;
aww_2464-7, 201; *aww_3053-4*, 133, 201
A Midsummer Night's Dream, 111, 119, 132,
136, 144, 173, 202, 234; *mnd_1613-6*, 212;
mnd_1804-9&1814-8, 168
Anthony and Cleopatra, 105, 123, 179; *ant_21-5*,
191; *ant_52-3*, 191; *ant_550*, 210
As You Like It, 1, 2, 111, 119, 132, 140, 182,
196, 202, 208, 209, 215; *ayl_607-11*, 1, 215;
ayl_901, 182; *ayl_1118-9*, 208; *ayl_1221-30*,
1; *ayl_2372-77*, 2; *ayl_2659-76*, 2
Coriolanus, 125, 179, 194; *cor_179-85*, 194;
cor_2397-401, 179; *cor_3017-8*, 211;
cor_3456-8, 194
Cymbeline, 114, 117, 123, 125, 140, 165,
195; *cym_522-4*, 123; *cym_3126-8*, 114;
cym_3288-90, 126
Hamlet, 110, 112, 114, 116, 119, 123, 127,
144, 145, 149, 163, 175, 176, 178, 179,
192, 210; *ham_268-74*, 192; *ham_316-
8*, 209; *ham_639-40*, 110; *ham_777-82*,
212; *ham_1350-6*, 193; *ham_1408*, 211;
ham_1409-14, 212; *ham_1444-8*, 119;
ham_1629-32, 144; *ham_1737-9*, 122;
ham_1970-4, 148; *ham_2350-5*, 193;
ham_2490-4, 193; *ham_2796-803*, 175;
ham_3313-20, 114
Henry IV Part 1, 122, 135, 152; *1h4_23-31*, 156
Henry IV Part 2, 152, 164; *2h4_1498-510*, 104
Henry V, 113, 123, 137, 195, 208, 227; *h5_13-15*,
208; *h5_852-5&tn_2344*, 134; *h5_856-60*,
176; *h5_1982-94*, 228; *h5_1990-4*, 123;
h5_3350-7, 137; *h5_3376-81*, 137
Henry VIII, 112, 114, 124, 127, 134, 148, 165,
178, 179, 181, 184, 208; *h8_1197-9*, 179;
h8_2294-7, 116; *h8_2369-71*, 115; *h8_2504-
5*, 116; *h8_2968-73*, 124, 148; *h8_3058-60*,
112; *h8_3356-7*, 116; *h8_3387-93*, 165
Henry VI Part 1, 123, 179; *1h4_13-15*,
111; *1h6_3*, 116; *1h6_274-80*, 181;
1h6_2209&2231, 179

continued over

CPSIA information can be obtained
at www.ICGtesting.com
Printed in the USA
BVOW06s2111140317
478532BV00017B/843/P